Mike Davis was born in 1946 in San Bernardino, California. For many years he was a local anti-war, then trade-union, activist in Southern California. He returned to school in the 1970s thanks to a scholarship from the Amalgamated Meatcutters Union. Aside from years spent as a meatcutter and heavy-duty truckdriver, he has more recently worked as an editor and teacher. He is a member of the editorial collective of the *New Left Review* as well as an editor of *The Year Left: an American Socialist Yearbook* (Verso).

THE HAYMARKET SERIES
General Editor, Michael Sprinker

The Haymarket Series is a new publishing initiative by Verso offering original studies of politics, history, and culture focused on North America. The series will present innovative but representative views from across the American left on a wide range of topics of current and continuing interest to socialists in North America and throughout the world. A century after the first May Day, the American left remains in the shadow of those martyrs which this series honors and commemorates. The studies in the Haymarket Series testify to the living legacy of activism and political commitment for which they gave up their lives.

THE YEAR LEFT
An American Socialist Yearbook, volume I — "Focus on the 1984
U.S. Elections," ed. Mike Davis, Fred Pfeil, and Michael Sprinker

PRISONERS OF THE AMERICAN DREAM
Politics and Economy in the History of the American
Working Class
by Mike Davis

MARXISM IN THE U.S.
by Paul Buhle (forthcoming in 1986)

THE YEAR LEFT
An American Socialist Yearbook, volume II — "Focus on
Race and Ethnicity," ed. Manning Marable, Fred Pfeil,
and Michael Sprinker (forthcoming in 1986)

THE CALIFORNIA MIRACLE
Capital's Fertile Land, ed. Dick Walker (forthcoming in 1987)

THE PARADOX OF AMERICAN SOCIAL
DEMOCRACY
by Robert Brenner (forthcoming in 1987)

Mike Davis

Prisoners of the American Dream

Politics and Economy
in the History of the US Working Class

Verso is the imprint of New Left Books

British Library
Cataloguing in Publication Data

Davis, Mike
    Prisoners of the American Dream: politics and economy in the history of the U.S.
    working class.
    1. Labor and laboring classes — United States —
    History
    I. Title
    305.5′62′0973   HD8066

First published 1986
© Mike Davis 1986

Second Impression 1987

Verso
15 Greek Street, London W1V 5LF

Typeset in Baskerville by
Leaper and Gard Ltd, Bristol

Printed in Great Britain by
Thetford Press Limited, Thetford, Norfolk

ISBN 0-86091-131-4
ISBN 0-86091-840-8 Pbk

Contents

This book is dedicated,
in the memory of Magdaleña Mora,
to the combatants of the FMLN

Foreword

These essays appear at a paradoxical moment in US history, on the centenary of the first May Day and fifty years after the great CIO sitdown strikes. Until very recently these anniversaries would have invited Panglossian reflections on the success of a peaceable institutionalization of the class struggle in the United States. After all, according to most textbook accounts, the Haymarket martyrs and the Flint strikers were, whatever their own visions of their activity, inadvertent heroes in the rise of a pluralist industrial order based on collective bargaining. For all of its early drama and violence, the trade-union movement — like the later Black liberation struggle — was supposedly settled into a placid tributary of liberal progress.

Such a view, however persistent in textbooks, is no longer tenable in reality. On every side, supposedly irreversible achievements of the New Deal or Great Society are, in fact, undergoing reversal. As organized labor enters its second century, it faces not the security of a 'mature' industrial relations system, but a decline of its membership and the threat of deunionization. Likewise the civil rights organizations, their forward momentum already checked in the early 1970s, fight losing rearguard battles against the Reagan administration's aggressive campaign to roll back affirmative action and other moderate reforms.

This accelerating rightward realignment of economic and political power demands a reconsideration of the main currents of modern American history. The smug liberal teleology of US history, with its happy endings in a perpetually self-reforming 'society of affluence', scarcely accords with the new politics of inequality and social revanchism that have become dominant since the late 1970s. Equally out of date, I shall argue, are the two main radical correlates of this teleology, the contrasting theories of a 'hegemonic' corporate liberalism or — alternatively — a 'surrogate socialist' Democratic Party.

For what is most striking about the United States in the 1980s is not the one dimensionality of consciousness (*per* popular Marcusean analyses of the 1960s) but the increasing one-sidedness of the class struggle. Nowhere in the advanced capitalist bloc, with the partial exception of Japan, has trade-union power collapsed so precipitously or under such brutal pressure. Nowhere, not even in Thatcher's Britain, has the New Right succeeded in mobilizing such a broad spectrum of propertied strata or effecting such a sweeping redistribution of national income to the benefit of the collective middle class. And nowhere has

capital enjoyed such unfettered freedom to experiment with new
accumulation strategies or to shift investment between sectors and
regions regardless of social cost. The result has been the emergence of a
new social and cultural landscape of intensifying class and racial polarizations: a 'late imperial' order that has diverted the modest streams of
reform to feed the insatiable appetites of a bloated 'have' coalition and
to extend the arms race into outer space.

To the extent that the rise of this post-reformist complex of interests
— which virtually ensures Reaganism an afterlife, even in the advent of
a Democratic succession — confounds liberal and populist historio-
graphies, it also poses old questions with a new urgency. The first of
these questions — addressed in Part One below — concerns the fate of
the working class in the most powerful capitalist society. Why has
American labor, for all of its cultural and organizational assets, been so
weak as a class force? The problem here is not only the classical
question of 'why is there no socialism in America?', but, more broadly,
of why labor in America has been so relatively unsuccessful in the political representation of its short- or long-term interests? The first two
chapters reconsider, in some detail, the conjunctural intersections
between trade-union militancy and the political system, proposing
elements of an explanation for the failure of independent labor politics
as well as for the persistent inability of labor-liberal forces to 'capture'
the Democratic Party. Further aspects of organized labor's 'unhappy
marriage' with the Democrats are taken up in later chapters as well,
particularly the AFL-CIO's impotence to prevent a displacement of
New Deal reformism by a fundamentally conservative 'neo-liberalism'.
Chapter three, meanwhile, re-examines the illusory 'social contract' at
the point of production and traces the origins of the current management offensive that is threatening unionism across the breadth of the
private sector.

The converse of labor's historical weakness, of course, is the unique
balance of power — under *democratic* conditions — that has favored
all the bourgeois classes in American society. In the first chapter I
argue that the ballast of capital's hegemony in American history has
been the repeated, autonomous mobilizations of the mass middle strata
in defense of petty accumulation and entrepreneurial opportunity. In
the second half of the book — which surveys the political and economic
terrain of Reaganism — I attempt to show that it was precisely these
forces, not labor or the welfare state, that constituted the principal
constraint on the direction of economic restructuring in the 1970s. The
result, which I sketch out in chapters five and six, is a logic of 'overconsumptionism' that attempts to sustain booming middle-class

affluence and corporate profitability through new levels of exploitation of the working poor as well as, increasingly, the traditional industrial working class.

The key to the temporary success of this strategy has been the recharged role of the federal government in ensuring the expanded reproduction of middle-strata claims to the national income. As I argue in Part Two, Democratic neo-liberalism as well as Reaganism asserts that the first function of the state is to provide welfare to the well-to-do and preserve a dynamic frontier of entrepreneurial, professional and rentier opportunity. The necessary cost of such a politics — especially given the growing reorientation of the economy from mass demand to an enlarged up-scale market — has been the abandonment of the reformist politics pioneered by the New Deal. Indeed, I try to show that the historic realignment that is occurring *within* the two parties, as much or more as *between* them, involves the relinquishment of any serious appeal to full employment politics or social equality. In chapter seven I analyse at length the contradictions immanent in the strategy of attempting to utilize a rightward moving Democratic Party as a vehicle for the historic demands of the labor or civil rights movement. I also consider how the de facto exclusion of Black demands from any serious representation in bourgeois politics opens the possibility, if nothing more, of future 'Rainbow' coalitions as a mass base for independent socialist politics.

Yet at the same time it is a central thesis of this book that the future of the Left in the United States is more than ever before bound up with its ability to organize solidarity with revolutionary struggles against American imperialism. Chapters five and six, in considering the new domestic configuration of US capitalism since 1980, also advance theses about the changing forms of American international domination. It is my contention that US hegemony is not so much 'declining', as commonly asserted, as being reshaped around a more unilateral practice of economic and military intervention. The age of 'democratic capitalism' characterized by the capacity of the capitalist world system progressively to extend the franchise of bourgeois democracy and the effective demand of mass consumption has been brought to a temporary terminus, which might yet prove permanent — partly because of the weakness of the left and the labor movement within the United States itself. Having precluded reformist solutions in most of the Third World — above all in the Western Hemisphere — the American ruling classes are left with the fantastically dangerous illusion that US nuclear-strategy superiority can somehow be used to police an increasingly turbulent world economy.

It will, I am sure, be clear to the reader that this book is, first and foremost, an intervention in recent debates about the direction of the US Left. Its overall design, therefore, has been dictated by strategic questions rather than by more conventional contours of historiography or economic analysis. To introduce a personal note, my own political biography (at forty) is fairly typical of the cohort of the 1960s New Left: first, immersion in the mass civil rights movement (CORE), followed by anti-war work (SDS and the Communist Party), then by a considerable stint within the trade-union opposition (Southern California Teamsters). The essays in the first half of the book constitute, for better or worse, my attempt to work out the central dilemma that confronts anyone who tries to work as a socialist within the American labor movement: the paradoxical disparities between economic militancy and political passivity, individual awareness and collective lack of confidence. The second part of the book, developing the critique of labor and the Democrats commenced in Chapter Two, is in part a polemic against the illusion that the Left must ally with the 'left wing of the possible' through the Democratic Party. It also critically engages with those viewpoints that have analysed the rise of the Right since 1978 as an essentially supra-economic, 'ideological' or 'cultural' phenomenon; arguing instead for the priority of a materially-determined field of political forces. Finally I try to identify elements of an alternative strategy. Although it would be shameless, almost comical, to pretend to assert 'what is to be done' at this confusing and transitional point in time, it is nonetheless possible, and necessary, to signal those real historical forces which do exist to sustain the project — and the responsibility — of an internationalist Left in the United States.

Acknowledgements

A partisan contribution of this kind must first of all acknowledge its partisans. Although none of the following individuals could be taxed with responsibility for eccentric views of mine, each has long sustained me with the example of their commitment and tenacity: Nancy Blaustein, Jan Breidenbach, Johanna Brenner, Lauri Goldsmith, Samira Haj, Dorothy Healey, Levi Kingston, Warren Montag, Brian Moore, Roberto Naduris, Bob Novick, Judy Perez, Ron Schneck, Carole and Jim Stone, Eduardo Torres, Gene Warren, Suzie Weissman, and Milt and Edith Zaslow. Since the days when we were the smallest (and shortest) political tendency in the world, Seymour Kramer has kept me supplied with patience and irony. In Belfast, Michele and Martin Clarke more than once took me in from the rain, nourishing me with friendship and irrepressible wit.

At various points in their history, individual essays have had the benefit of keen comments from Jon Amsden, Anthony Barnett, Robert Brenner, John Laslett, Charles Post, Alexander Saxton, and Richard Walker. I have also received invaluable encouragement and inspiration from Adolfo Gilly, Fred Halliday, Lene Koch, Alain Lipietz, Lars Mjøset, Kim Moody, Göran Therborn and Kees van der Pilj. Without Wallace Douglas's newspaper clippings and political gossip from the Midwest this book would have been far more difficult. Most of all I have enjoyed the good fortune of having had the support and stimulus of my comrades at the New Left Review and New Left Books (Verso). Despite my various misdemeanors and delays, Neil Belton — the editor of Verso in London — has had almost irrational faith in the completion of this enterprise, while Mike Sprinker — the editor of the Haymarket Series — has pulled me over the bad humps while tirelessly improving my Mid-Atlantic prose. Perry Anderson has been critically engaged with this project from the first draft, with advice and commentary. Finally I owe thanks of another, special kind to Brigid Loughran: the image of our daughter Roísín dances through these pages, memories of an unforgettable summer in Oregon.

Part One:
Labor and American Politics

1

Why the US Working Class is Different

In 1828 — as Karl Marx once reminded his readers — a group of Philadelphia artisans organized the first 'Labor Party' in world history. One hundred and fifty years later, a television news camera depicted a group of modern Philadelphia workers arguing in their local tavern over the candidates in the 1980 presidential election. Against a background of irreverent catcalls and hisses, one worker tepidly defended Carter as the 'lesser evil', while another, with even less ardour, tried to float the idea of a 'protest' vote for Reagan. Finally, with the nodding assent of most of the crowd, a rather definitive voice spelled out the name of the popular choice in the campaign: N-O-T-A, ('none of the above'). He underlined his point with the declaration that he intended to occupy a barstool rather than a polling booth on election day.

In no other capitalist country is mass political abstentionism as fully developed as in the United States, where a 'silent majority' of the working class has sat out more than half the elections of the last century.[1] Arguably, this mute, atomized protest is the historical correlative of the striking absence of an independent political party of the proletariat in the country that once invented both the labor party and May Day.

Perhaps no other dimension of American history is simultaneously as salient and as difficult for Marxist theory as the complex evolution of the economic class struggle in relation to a political system that has managed to repulse every attempt to create an alternative class politics. A signal absence of working-class self-organization and consciousness comparable in scope to that represented in every other capitalist country by the prevalence of laborist, social-democratic, or Communist parties is the specter that has long haunted American Marxism. As a first approach to the problem it may be useful briefly to review the

---

[1] 'The United States has consistently had the highest abstention rate to be found in any Western political system during the past fifty years'. Walter Dean Burnham, 'The United States: The Politics of Heterogeneity', in Richard Rose, (ed.), *Electoral Behaviour: a Comparative Handbook*, New York and London 1974, p. 697.

perspective that classical revolutionary theory has offered on 'American exceptionalism'.

At one time or another, Marx, Engels, Kautsky, Lenin, and Trotsky all become fascinated with the prospects for the development of a revolutionary movement in the United States. Although each emphasized different aspects of contemporary social dynamics, they shared the optimistic belief that 'in the long run' the differences between European and American levels of class consciousness and political organization would be evened out by objective laws of historical development. In their view, the American working class was a more or less 'immature' version of a European proletariat. Its development had been retarded or deflected by various conjunctural and, therefore, *transient* conditions: the 'frontier', continuous immigration, the attraction of agrarian-democratic ideologies bound up with petty-bourgeois property, the international hegemony of American capital, and so on. Once these temporary conditions began to be eroded — through the closing of the frontier, the restriction of European immigration, the triumph of monopoly over small capital, the decline of US capital's lead in world industrial productivity — then more profound and permanent historical determinants arising out of the very structure of the capitalist mode of production would become decisive. In this shared scenario, a systemic economic crisis of American society would unleash class struggles on a titanic scale. Furthermore the very breadth and violence of this economic class struggle would provoke escalating conflicts with state power. In such a crisis the bourgeois-democratic institutions of American society — previously an obstacle to class coalescence — would provide a springboard for independent political action and the formation of a mass labor or socialist party. Stages of development that had taken the European proletariat generations to traverse would be 'compressed' in America by an accelerated process of 'combined and uneven development'.

Thus Engels, writing in 1886, had little doubt that the dramatic growth of the Knights of Labor, together with the massive vote for Henry George in New York City's mayoralty election, signalled the birth of mass labor politics in America. (Engels, in fact, exhorted the 'backward' English labor movement to take these more 'advanced' American events as their model.) A similar conclusion was drawn by Lenin with regard to the apparent giant strides of the Socialist Party in the elections of 1912, and by Trotsky when, in the aftermath of the great sit-down strikes of 1936-37, a labour party again seemed likely to emerge.[2]

Unfortunately, all these hopes for a qualitative political transformation of the class struggle in the United States have remained stillborn. The premonitory signs of a political break in the middle eighties turned out to be spurious, as renewed ethnic and racial divisions undermined the embryonic unification of Eastern industrial workers. Fledgling 'labor parties' collapsed, as workers were successfully reabsorbed into a capitalist two-party system that brilliantly manipulated and accentuated cultural schisms in the working class. The six per cent of the presidential vote that Gene Debs won in 1912 — internationally acclaimed as the beginning of the Socialist Party's ascent to majority representation of the American proletariat — turned out to be its high-water mark, followed by bitter conflict and fragmentation. The socialist fratricide was, in turn, a manifestation and symptom of the profound antagonisms within the early twentieth-century labor movement between organized 'native' craftsmen and unorganized masses of immigrant labourers.

The Great Depression furnished the most ironic experience of all. Despite a cataclysmic collapse of the productive system and the economic class war that the crisis unleashed, the political battlements of American capitalism held firm. Indeed, it can be argued that the hegemony of the political system was reinforced and extended during this period. The same workers who defied the machine guns of the National Guard at Flint or chased the deputies off the streets during the semi-insurrectionary Minneapolis General Strike were also the cornerstone of electoral support for Roosevelt. The millions of young workers aroused by the struggle for industrial unionism were simultaneously mobilized as the shock troops of a pseudo-aristocratic politician whose avowed ambition was 'the salvation of American capitalism'. To the extent that so-called 'labor' or 'farmer-labor' parties emerged in industrial areas of the midwest or north-east, they remained scarcely more than advance detachments and satellites of the New Deal.

Thus, in spite of the periodic intensity of the economic class struggle and the episodic appearance of 'new lefts' in every generation since the

[2] Cf. Karl Marx and Friedrich Engels, *Letters to Americans, 1848–1895*, New York 1953, pp. 149–150, 239, 243–244, and 258; V.I. Lenin , 'In America', *Collected Works*, Vol. 36, p. 215; Leon Trotsky 'Introduction', *Living Thoughts of Karl Marx*, New York, 1939; Massimo Salvadori, *Karl Kautsky and the Socialist Revolution 1880–1938*, London 1979, pp. 58, 102. Also R. Laurence Moore, *European Socialists and the American Promised Land*, New York 1970; Cristiano Camporesi, *Il marxismo teorico negli USA*, Milan 1973; Harvey Klehr, 'Marxist Theory in Search of America', *Journal of Politics*, 35, 1973, and 'Leninist Theory in Search of America', *Polity*, 9, 1976; Lewis Feuer, *Marx and the Intellectuals*, New York 1969.

Civil War, the rule of capital has remained more powerfully installed and less politically contested than in any other advanced capitalist social formation. In the face of this dilemma, and given the apparent inadequacy of the theory of the American working class as an 'immature proletariat', what other perspectives are available for conceptualizing the problem of an absent political class consciousness in the United States?

One strategy might be to shift theoretical focus from the dialectic of conjunctural constraints acting upon universal processes (the global logic of class struggle and class consciousness), and to emphasize, instead, the relative permanence of the decisive sociological or cultural features that have historically differentiated the United States. This is the approach of the current of idealist interpretations of American 'civilization' from Tocqueville to Hartz, including the Commons-Perlman school of labor historiography, which has tried to locate the originality of American history in constitutive essences like the 'absence of feudalism' or the 'ubiquity of job consciousness'. From the standpoint of this liberal metaphysics, the problem of working-class consciousness is no problem at all: the political incorporation of the industrial proletariat was predestined even before its birth by the very structure of American culture — the lack of feudal class struggles, the hegemony of a Lockean world-view, the safety-valve of the frontier, and so on. Conversely, socialist consciousness is seen as the result of industrialization in the specifically European socio-historical setting littered with relics of feudalism. Traces of this grandiose but empirically suspect architectonic have tinged the writings of some Marxist writers, who have also tried to explain the specificity of the American working class in terms of some grand peculiarity of US history, such as the impact of immigration or the role of early mass suffrage.[3]

There is, however, an alternative methodology both to the old Marxist 'orthodoxy' with its faith in the eventual 'normalization' of the class struggle in the US, and to the various theories of American exceptionalism with their emphasis on the passive submission of the working class to omnipotent socio-historical determinants. First we must reconstruct the basic frames of reference for the history of the American working class.

---

[3] Cf. Louis Hartz, *The Liberal Tradition in America*, New York 1955, and *The Founding of New Societies*, New York 1964; and Selig Perlman, *A Theory of the Labor Movement*, New York 1928. An exhaustive inventory of 'single factor' theories of the exceptionalism of the American labor movement is undertaken by John Laslett and Seymour Martin Lipset (eds.), *Failure of a Dream? Essays in the History of American Socialism*, New York 1974.

On the one hand, we must discard the idea that the fate of the American working class has been shaped by any overarching *telos* (liberal democracy, cultural individualism, or whatever) or clockwork of simple, interacting causes (upward mobility plus ethnicity plus ...). All plausible explanatory variables must be concretized within the historically specific contexts of class struggle and collective practice which, after all, are their only real modes of existence. Against such positivist conceptions of a working class permanently shipwrecked on 'reefs of roast beef' (Sombart)[4] or shoals of universal suffrage (Hartz et al.), Engels, Lenin and Trotsky were absolutely correct to affirm the central role of class struggle in the making of American history and in the periodic renewal of opportunities for the transformation of class consciousness.

On the other hand, the Marxist classics tended to underestimate the role of the sedimented historical experiences of the working class as they influenced and circumscribed its capacities for development in succeeding periods. Each major cycle of class struggle, economic crisis, and social restructuring in American history has finally been resolved through epochal tests of strength between capital and labor. The results of these historical collisions have been new structural forms that regulated the objective conditions for accumulation in the next period, as well as the subjective capacities for class organization and consciousness. *The emphasis on the 'temporary' character of obstacles to political class consciousness tended to obscure precisely this cumulative impact of the series of historic defeats suffered by the American working class.* As I will argue in the present chapter, each generational defeat of the American labor movement disarmed it in some vital respect before the challenges and battles of the following period.

The ultimate, though by no means preordained, trajectory of this disrupted history has been the consolidation of a relationship between the American working class and American capitalism that stands in striking contrast to the balance of class forces in other capitalist states. It is a question not merely of the 'absence of social democracy' — although this is the most dramatic symptom — but of a qualitatively different level of class consciousness and intra-class cohesion.

Despite profound differences in national tradition as well as evident divergences in the levels of class conflict, all the proletariats of Western Europe are politically 'incorporated' — I use this term only in a highly qualified and contingent sense — through the agency of labor reform-

---

[4] For Sombart, see Jerome Karabel, 'The Failure of American Socialism Reconsidered', *Socialist Register — 1979*, London.

ism. That is, their relationship to capitalism is mediated and regulated at a multiplicity of levels (political, economic and cultural) by *collective, self-formed institutions* that tend to create and maintain a corporate class consciousness. Admittedly, in the post-war period European workers have increasingly become subject to the 'Americanizing' influence of a socially disintegrative model of class culture and consumption, yet the solidity of working-class culture is remarkable and continues to provide the infrastructure for socialist and communist politics throughout Western Europe.

The American working class, on the other hand, lacking any broad array of collective institutions or any totalizing agent of class consciousness (that is, a class party), has been increasingly integrated into American capitalism through the *negativities* of its internal stratification, its privatization in consumption, and its disorganization *vis-à-vis* political and trade-union bureaucracies. As Ira Katznelson has emphasized, the absence of '"global" institutions and meaning systems of class' in America has led to an extreme *fragmentation* and *serialization* of the work, community and political universes of the American proletariat.[5] The proposed distinction, therefore, is between *a reformist working class in Western Europe* — historically janus-faced in the irreducible tensions of its integrated and potentially revolutionary aspects — *and a 'disorganized' and increasingly 'depoliticized' working class in the United States.*

I must stress, however, that this differentiation was not inscribed, once and for all, in some primordial matrix of historical or structural conditions. If anything, this contrast has only acquired its sharpest visibility and salience during the post-war wave of economic expansion when there has been, for the first time in history, a general tendency in Western Europe — or at least the EEC countries — toward a stabilization of parliamentary democracy and the growth of mass consumption. In other words, it is precisely in the period of the most well-defined structural convergence and homogenization of political terrains that the profound differences in the historical formation of the American and European proletariats have become more striking and politically consequential. This suggests that the watershed for creating the divergence between European and American levels of proletarian class consciousness was the failure of the labor movements of the 1930s and 1940s to unify the American working class on either the economic or the political planes.

[5] Ira Katznelson, 'Considerations on Social Democracy in the United States', *Comparative Politics*, October 1978, pp. 95–96.

An analysis of this pivotal conjuncture of course requires some treatment of the accumulation of previous defeats which conditioned its outcome. The present chapter aims to be a kind of historical preface to an analysis of the contemporary crisis of class consciousness in the United States. Focusing on the changing interfaces between the economic class struggles, class composition, and the political system,[6] I have attempted to trace the chain of historic 'defeats' and blocked possibilities that have negatively determined the position of the working class in post-war society. This problematic of the 'unmaking' of the American working class is argued in three steps:

First, by examining the unique course of bourgeois democratic revolution in the United States in relation to the emergence of a factory working class and its failure to achieve any initial political autonomy.

Second, by surveying the contradictory relationship between unifying waves of labor militancy and the turbulent recomposition of the proletariat by European immigration and internal migration. In particular, I will focus on the successive failures of 'labor abolitionism,' 'labor populism', and Debsian socialism to provide durable foundations for the growth of independent class politics or to generate the sociological supports for a unitary proletarian sub-culture.

Third (in the next chapter), by considering, in magnified detail, the legacy of the class struggles of the Roosevelt–Truman era in contributing to the current disorganization and weakness of working-class consciousness and militancy in the United States.

1. The Paradox of American 'Democracy'

There have been two, 'ideal-typical' historical paths by which independent labor politics have emerged in industrializing societies. The first, embracing continental Europe, has involved the precipitation of a proletarian current in the course of bourgeois-democratic revolution. The second, later route — followed by Britain and most of its white-settler offspring (Australia, New Zealand, and Canada) — has

---

[6] A truly rigorous theoretical analysis would also have to take account of two other factors as well: first, the specificity of the political structure and party system; second, the role of pre-emptive political repression in blocking the emergence of working-class and Black radicalism. The solitary, synoptic analysis of the role of repression in deradicalizing the American labor movement is Robert Justin Goldstein's pathbreaking *Political Repression in Modern America*, Cambridge (Mass.) 1978. Burnham provides a fascinating overview of the specificity of American electoral institutions and their success in diluting working-class political power in 'The United States: The Politics of Heterogeneity'.

passed through the transformation of trade-union militancy by economic crisis, state repression, and the rise of new working-class strata.[7] In this section I will examine some of the most important reasons why the political terrain in the early American Republic was so unfavorable to the first of these processes.

In every European nation, the working classes were forced to conduct protracted struggles for suffrage and civil liberties. The initial phases of the active self-formation of the European working classes encompassed both elementary economic organization and rudimentary political mobilization for democratic rights. Every European proletariat forged its early identity through revolutionary-democratic mass movements: Chartism in Britain (1832–48), the Lasallean and 'Illegal' periods of German labor (1960–85), the bitter struggle of Belgian labor for the extension of the vote, the battle against absolutism in Russia (1898-1917).

In the face of the weakness or simple treason of the middle classes, the young working-class movements were forced to carry on the democratic struggle through their own independent mobilization. Thus the strength of proletarian radicalism and the degree of its conscious self-reliance were conditioned by both the relative social power of the bourgeoisie and the extent to which the democratic revolution had been left 'unfinished.' In a general sense, we can distinguish three kinds of national contexts in which an original coalescence of economic and political class consciousness took place: 1) against a hegemonic bourgeoisie in the context of a restricted franchise (Britain or Belgium in the nineteenth century); 2) within the framework of an on-going bourgeois-democratic revolution (France in 1848-52); or 3) in the absence or impossibility of a bourgeois-democratic revolution, against both the pre-capitalist and bourgeois ruling classes at the same time (Russia in 1905–17 — the pattern of 'permanent revolution'). The impetus of working-class militancy was different in each case, yet some mode of proletarian political independence (be it a nonviolent petitioning campaign or a centralized underground party) was a necessary prerequisite.

In the United States, on the other hand, a very different politico-juridical framework was present during the infancy of the working class. The most obvious fact, which impressed itself on every Old

---

[7] Of course, combinations of both paths are also possible as in the case of Britain which experienced first Chartism as a mass — and premier — revolutionary-democratic movement of the working class; then, after a long interlude of apparently successful incorporation of the proletariat within the two-party system, the rise of the Labor Party in response to the New Unionism, Taff Vale, wartime repression, etc.

World visitor, was the absence of residual pre-capitalist class structures and social institutions. As the Hartzian school has emphasized, the Northern colonies were a transplanted 'fragment' of the most advanced production relations and ideological superstructures of the seventeenth century: British merchant and agrarian capitalism, Puritan religion, and Lockean philosophy. Long after their official suppression in Britain, New England popular consciousness safeguarded the radical doctrines of the English Revolution and continued to translate them into practice. But no later than 1750, for example, from one half to three quarters of the adult white males in New England, including much of the artisanal population, were already exercising a local franchise. By Andrew Jackson's second term in 1832, property qualifications had been removed in all but four of the states.[8] Thus, in dramatic contra-distinction to Europe, popular sovereignty (for white males) was the *pre-existent* ideological and institutional framework for the industrial revolution and the rise of the proletariat.

Another important difference between Europe and America was the class composition of the leadership of the democratic movement. In Europe, bourgeois liberalism had (at least until 1848) generally taken a position of adamant opposition to 'democracy'. Its strategic aim was to mobilize the plebeian masses against aristocratic power without thereby being forced to concede universal suffrage. The manipulation of the English working classes by the Whigs in reform struggles of the 1820s and early 1930s was a classic case. To the extent that the bourgeois revolution actually became a 'democratic' revolution, it was because elements of the plebeian strata (urban artisans, petty bourgeoisie, declassed intellectuals, supported by the multitudes of journeymen, laborers, and sections of the peasantry) violently assumed leadership, usually in the context of a life-or-death threat to the survival of the revolution or temporizing betrayal by the haute bourgeoisie (France in 1791 or Germany in 1849). Furthermore, by the 1830s, surviving elements of this plebeian Jacobinism were rapidly being transformed, under the impact of industrialism, into a proletarian proto-socialism (Blanquism, the Communist League, etc.)

In the United States, by contrast, the commanding heights of the bourgeois-democratic 'revolution' were dominated, without significant challenge, by the political representatives of the American bourgeoisie. Thus, in a certain ironic sense, the American bourgeoisie (in a defini-tion encompassing historically specific configurations of large

---

[8] Cf. Edward McChesney Sait, *American Parties and Elections*, New York 1939, pp. 21–31; and Chilton Williamson, *American Suffrage from Property to Democracy*, Princeton 1960.

merchants, bankers, big capitalist landowners or planters, and, later, industrialists) was the only 'classical' revolutionary-democratic bourgeoisie in world history: all other bourgeois-democratic revolutions have depended, to one degree or another, upon plebeian wings or 'surrogates' to defeat aristocratic reaction and demolish the structure of the ancien regimes.

This was partly a result of the fact that the 'bourgeois-democratic' revolution in America was not an uprising against a moribund feudalism, but rather a unique process of capitalist national liberation involving, in the period from 1760 to 1860, a multi-phase struggle against the constraints imposed by a globally hegemonic British capital on the growth of native bourgeois society. It is possible to see the Revolution of 1776, for instance, as very much a civil war against Loyalist *comprador* strata, and the Civil War as a continuing revolution against an informal British imperialism that had incorporated the cotton export economy of the South in an alliance of neocolonial dependency. In the first phase, a merchant-planter coalition overthrew the obstacles to internal expansion, and in the second, an alliance of fledgling industrial capital and Western farmers created the preconditions for national economic integration.

Moreover, the American bourgeoisie was able to rely upon exceptional class alliances to consolidate its hegemony. The existence in the United States of a numerically dominant class of small capitalist farmers — a class with virtually no equivalent in mid-nineteenth-century Europe where agriculture was predominantly operated by semi-aristocratic landowners or subsistence peasants — provided secure social anchorage for an explicitly bourgeois politics celebrating the sanctity of private property and the virtue of capital accumulation. Since the ideology of the industrial bourgeoisie found such direct resonance in the entrepreneurial outlook of the majority of the Northern agrarian class, mass democratic politics did not pose the same kind of dangers as they did in most of Europe where the middle strata or petty bourgeoisie were so much weaker in the nineteenth century. In other words, while the European bourgeoisie had to fight long delaying actions (frequently in alliance with residual aristocracies) against the advance of a broad franchise which they feared would give power to workers and peasants, the industrial fraction of the American bourgeoisie, relying on the stabilizing social ballast of the farmers, was able to achieve national political dominance in 1860 at the head of the revolutionary-democratic crusade against the plantocracy and its international allies.[9]

As Perlman noted many years ago, this particular constellation of historical factors — the existence of a 'democratic' bourgeoisie and the correlative absence of an 'ancien regime' — made it much more difficult for artisans and workers to constitute themselves as an autonomous force in the politics of the antebellum era. The same factors also gave the democratic movement in America its relatively 'conservative' cast. In contrast with the anti-feudal revolutions of France or Spain, for example, there was no broad, radical assault on the legitimating institutions and ideology of society which might later serve as a model for working-class revolutionism. The plebeian colonial masses did not rise up under the leadership of their planter and mercantile 'revolutionaries' in 1776 to ignite a worldwide democratic revolution — as the *sans-culotte* followers of Saint-Just and Robespierre would aspire to do a few years later — but rather to defend the special gift of popular liberty that God and Locke had granted their Puritan ancestors. Similarly, in arousing the North in 1861, Lincoln and the Republicans vehemently rejected the revolutionary slogans of Garrison and the Abolitionists (the extension of 'equal rights' to Afro-Americans and the destruction of the slave order) to appeal, instead, to the 'preservation of the Union and Free *White* Labor'. These ideological nuances have far more than incidental significance; they testify both to the solidity of bourgeois political domination and to the inhibition of 'permanent democratic revolution' in America.[10]

All this should not be taken to mean that the artisanal or early industrial working class in America were without clearly conceived interests or articulate voices of their own. Yet, without underestimating the economic militancy of the early working class or its devotion to the struggle against 'Oligarchy', it is necessary to emphasize the structural

---

[9] It should be noted, however, that the Southern planters exercised an analogous hegemony over the small white farmers of the Southern lowlands and plains. The cement of this ideological adhesion was not so much pseudo-aristocratic paternalism as a degenerate Jeffersonian liberalism. For all their manorial trappings, 'ultras' like Calhoun stood far closer to the radical Whig tradition than to high Toryism. Appeals to states' rights and individualism were buttressed by the vision of a permanently expanding slave frontier that perpetually renewed the possibilities for small-scale accumulation and ascent into the big planter stratum. The white supremacist democracy of the Southern *Herrenvolk* iterated many of the same central themes (e.g. entrepreneurial egalitarianism) as Northern capitalist ideology.

[10] Marx's theory of 'permanent revolution', it will be recalled, was an integral element in his strategic reflections on the dynamic of the failed German democratic revolution of 1848–1850. It projected the possibility that the revolutionary-democratic movement might, under certain circumstances, 'grow over' into a struggle for a 'social republic' led by an independent worker-peasant wing. More generally, it pointed to the conditions that created the possibility of a hegemonic working-class Jacobinism as a prelude to socialism.

and cultural obstacles to any thoroughgoing radicalization of the democratic movement and to the crystallization of an autonomous proletarian politics. While American workers provided shock troops in defence of 'Equal Rights', they never created independent political movements with the influence or historical impact of Chartism or French socialism. The famous Workingmen's Parties of 1828–1832, which the young Marx celebrated as the first parties of labor, may seem an obvious exception. But the 'Workies' were a socially composite movement whose concept of the 'working man' had such catholic inclusivity that only bankers, speculators, and a few Tammany Hall bosses were doctrinally excluded. The Workingman's Movement of the 1830s undoubtedly did focus and express the concerns of pre-industrial workers, strengthened impulses towards trade-union organization, and trained laborers in the art of politics; but it never achieved more than the most preliminary level of political self-consciousness.[11]

Incipient class consciousness was blunted by two illusions: one economic, the other political. The first grew out of the prevalence of petty production and small property which created, if not the fabled Jacksonian age of universal mobility, then at least a significantly greater fluidity of class boundaries between journeymen and the layer of small entrepreneurs. The result was an ideology of 'Producerism' that mapped class relations along an axis of 'producers' versus 'parasitic money power' and conflated all strata of workers and most capitalists into a single 'industrial' bloc. This petty-bourgeois outlook, constructed from the standpoint of the sphere of circulation rather than the labor process, did not really begin to break down until the great crisis of 1873-1877 brought capital and labor into confrontation on a *national* scale for the first time.

The political illusion, closely interwoven with a false perception of class relationships, was the popular view of the state as an agency of democratic reform. The existence of a unique and more or less unrestricted white manhood suffrage imparted to the Jacksonian working class a deep belief in the exceptionalism of American society. Unlike their European brothers, who experienced both the absence of political and economic freedom, white American working men came to contrast their political liberty with their economic exploitation. In his study of the transformation of artisan shoemakers of Lynn (Mass.) into a dependent factory proletariat, Alan Dawley repeatedly emphasizes their persistent belief that they possessed 'a vested interest in the existing political system'. Whereas European workers tended to view the

---

[11] Cf. Walter Hugins, *Jacksonian Democracy and the Working Class*, Stanford 1960.

state as 'an instrument of their oppression, controlled by hostile social and economic interests, against which it was necessary to organise in separate class parties; American workers tended to cling to the illusion of an ameliorative "popular sovereignty"'.[12]

Yet it would be foolish to overstate this point.[13] The political 'incorporation' of native workers in the antebellum era had definite limits, and any attempt unilaterally to explain the deradicalization of the working class through the integrative powers of mass democracy must necessarily flounder on the contradictory implications of its own premises. Nineteenth-century labor history proved time and again that the very parliamentary illusions borne by the native working class also carried subversive potentials. In the face of increasing exploitation and class polarization, for example, the egalitarian ideology of American laborers (like the New England shoemakers) could become a powerful catalyst for collective organization (creating the New England Mechanics' Association), as well as for militant resistance (unleashing the Great Strike of 1860). European factory masters could frequently command ancestral patterns of lower-class deference and cultural subordination, but the American industrialists had to deal with 'free-born' Yankee workers who rejected paternalism and demanded to be treated as equals. From the Jacksonian period onward, the native working-class ethos of 'Equal Rights' — so deeply ingrained by the mass upheavals of 1776, 1828, and 1861 — came increasingly into collision with the emergence of the factory system and the concentration of economic power.[14]

These ideological tensions were amplified by the exceptional violence of the battle for union recognition in the United States. The precocity of working-class suffrage as an integrative force in America must be balanced against the great difficulty of Yankee trade unions in achieving durable organization. To make a comparison with the British case: if American workmen possessed an unrestricted vote over half a

---

[12] Alan Dawley, *Class and Community: The Industrial Revolution in Lynn*, Cambridge (Mass.) 1976, pp. 235, 237.

[13] As I believe Dawley does when he claims that 'the ballot box was the coffin of class consciousness'. Ibid., p. 70.

[14] Popular democratic tradition most dramatically asserted itself in the repeated justification of armed self-defence against 'tyranny'. Thus in the 1880s, when some unions began to form their own 'militias' in response to employer and state violence, the *Labor Leaf* of Detroit could advise its readers that 'every union ought to have its company of sharpshooters ... learn to preserve your rights in the same way your forefathers did'. Richard Oestreicher, 'Solidarity and Fragmentation: Working People and Class Consciousness in Detroit, 1877–1895', PhD Thesis, Michigan State University 1979, p. 280.

century earlier than their English counterparts, they also had to struggle a generation longer in the face of hostile courts and intransigent employers to consolidate their first craft unions. American labor may never have had to face the carnage of a Paris Commune or defeated revolution, but it has been bled in countless 'Peterloos' at the hands of Pinkertons or the militia.

It seems a tenable hypothesis, therefore, that widespread legal repression, especially when coupled with the impact of industrialism and cyclical crisis upon mobility and wages, might undermine the working class's fundamental illusions about bourgeois political leadership. In this context it is relevant to recall the example of a *second path* toward working-class political independence represented by the labor parties of other 'democratic' Anglo-Saxon nations, particularly where this process has involved — as in Edwardian England or post-war Canada — the breakdown of previous political incorporation within bourgeois parties (primarily Liberal Parties). Certainly, to the extent that state repression or economic depression was a midwife to the birth of labor parties (a point that I will weigh again in the following section), late nineteenth-century or early twentieth-century America possessed the ingredients in full measure. Why then — despite several partial ruptures and temporary defections — did American labor fail to take advantage of broad suffrage to forge its own political instruments? The next stage in answering this question is to shift our focus from the constitution of the political system to the historical composition of the working class itself.

II. Political Consciousness and Class Composition

The increasing proletarianization of the American social structure has not been matched by an equal tendency toward the homogenization of the working class as a cultural or political collectivity. Stratifications rooted in differential positions in the social labor process have been reinforced by deep-seated ethnic, religious, racial, and sexual antagonisms within the working class. In different periods these divisions have fused together as definite intra-class hierarchies (for example, 'native+skilled+Protestant' versus 'immigrant+unskilled+Catholic') representing unequal access to employment, consumption, legal rights, and trade-union organization. The political power of the working class within American 'democracy' has always been greatly diluted by the effective disfranchisement of large sectors of labor: blacks, immigrants, women, migrant workers, among others.

Periodically in the course of the nineteenth and early twentieth centuries, however, the search for defensive organization at the workplace produced waves of mass struggle that temporarily overrode or weakened some of these divisions, and led to the formation of a succession of avowedly unitary economic organizations of the working class. But until the 1930s — and then only under the peculiar circumstances I will analyze later — no comparable dynamic emerged on the political plane. The most victimized and disfranchised sectors of the working class had to seek political equality by their own efforts, and usually through incorporation within the multi-class coalitional base of one or the other of the capitalist parties. To the discomfort of many Marxists as well as economic determinists of the Beardian school, all recent analyses of mass voting patterns in the US between 1870 and 1932 have corroborated the persistent primacy of *ethno-religious* cleavages as determinants of party loyalty and voting preference.[15]

This contradictory dialectic of class unification/class stratification, and the corresponding tendency toward the bifurcation or disarticulation of workplace and political consciousness, needs to be examined more concretely within the specific contexts of the three waves of mass struggle that stand out as key phases in the formation of the industrial proletariat in America: 1) the early battles for trade unionism and a shorter working day, 1832-1860; 2) the volcanic postbellum labor insurgencies of 1877, 1884-87, and 1892-96; and 3) the great tide of strikes from 1909 to 1922, which was only superficially punctuated by the 1914–15 recession.

All periodizations are somewhat arbitrary and risk obscuring important continuities and causal linkages, but I believe that these three periods define integral generations of working-class consciousness shaped by common experiences of economic militancy, each culminat-

---

[15] The ethno-cultural interpretation of American voting behaviour was first proposed by Lee Benson in his major revisionist work, *The Concept of Jacksonian Democracy: New York as a Test Case*, Princeton 1961. A critical acceptance of the overwhelming evidence for the significance of this religious divide does not, of course, imply concurrence with the 'new political history's' interpretative tendency to marginalize class as a factor in American history. Whatever their theoretical pretensions, the current crop of historical voting studies only inflict fatal damage on an older Turner-Beard calculus of 'economic interest groups'. Rather than banishing class struggle from center-stage, these studies only challenge Marxists to theorize more rigorously the *refraction* of class differences through a singular American ethno-religious prism. Cf. Paul E. Johnson, *A Shopkeepers' Millennium*, New York 1978, and James E. Wright, 'The Ethno-cultural Model of Voting: A Behavioral and Historical Critique', in Allan Bogue (ed.), *Emerging Theoretical Models in Social and Political History*, Beverly Hills 1973.

ing in crises that temporarily posed the question of independent
political action. The problem at hand is to consider the roles of racism
and nativism in preventing American workers from 'seizing the time' in
the pivotal turning points of class struggle — above all 1856–57, 1892–
96, 1912 and 1919–24 — when political realignment seemed most
possible and necessary.

Labor and the Civil War

The period from 1843 to 1856 was the crucible of an explosive mix of
socio-economic transformations: the rise of mechanized consumer-
goods industries in New England, the rapid capitalization of
Midwestern agriculture, the acquisition of the Pacific Slope and the
Southwest, and the fitful booms and expansionist demands of King
Cotton. It was also an era of complex transition in social structures.
The new Western cities and towns still provided something of the
famous 'safety valve' of social mobility, but the factory towns and great
port cities of the Eastern seaboard witnessed the hardening of class
lines and the constriction of opportunities for economic independence.
The traditional artisanal working class, with its vague and fluid boundaries with the petty bourgeoisie, had been partially superseded by two
new strata of workers: first, the emergent factory proletariat rooted in
the shoe and textile industries of New England, and second, the
nomadic armies of largely immigrant labor who moved across the face
of the North, building railways and digging canals.

In this *Sturm und Drang* of labor's infancy, romantic longings for
imaginary past idylls coexisted with realistic intimations of the future.
Time and again, in a pattern which would repeat itself virtually to the
eve of the twentieth century, the labor movement was deflected by
utopian enthusiasms for monetary panaceas or free land schemes that
would roll back industrialism and re-establish an ideally harmonized,
'Republican social order' of small producers. At the same time,
however, more hard-headed militants, sensing the inevitability of economic change and influenced by the model of British labor, began to dig
in for the long struggle. From the mid-1830s onwards, journeymen in
the big port cities began to assert their separate economic interests,
organizing their own benefit societies and early trade unions. Over the
next two decades the center of gravity of this union movement began to
shift either to skilled workers in the new mechanized industries like the
cotton spinners and shoemakers, or towards the craftsmen who made
the machines, like the engineers, iron puddlers, and molders. Unfortu-

nately their efforts were rewarded by few permanent successes: the broad Ten Hour Day agitation of the 1840s rose and fell, a first generation of trade unions perished in the Panic of 1837, a second in the Depression of 1857, and, finally, on the eve of the Civil War, the most powerful trade union in North America — the New England Mechanics' Association (shoemakers) — was crushed after a long strike.

More important than this ebb and flow, however, were the residue of consciousness and embryonic class unity left behind, and the way in which this emergent 'laborism' fitted into the overall political conjuncture. As I have already indicated, the Jacksonian era had seen a growing awareness within the laboring class of the incompatibility between great concentrations of capital and the preservation of egalitarianism. Thus consciousness was only partially dissipated by the utopian fads and various Western booms. By the end of Jackson's second term, for instance, the New York 'Workies' resurrected themselves as the 'Locofoco' insurgency within the Democratic Party. Although Locofocoism represented the incorporation of the formerly independent workingmen's movements into the regular party system, it also achieved a dramatic reorientation of both parties to 'labor' as a growing voting bloc. The attempt by President Van Buren — Jackson's chosen successor and the hero of the Locofocos — to establish a ten-hour day for federal employers was a symbolic concession to this new power.

Furthermore, by the 1850s an accumulation of conditions existed for a new and more coherent crystallization of working-class, political identity. In many manufacturing towns, the decline of the autonomous artisan was almost complete, and the outlines of the new class structure were becoming increasingly apparent and disturbing. Thus, in her careful study of the industrialization of Newark crafts between 1800 and 1860, Susan Hirsch emphasizes that the 1850s were the watershed decade when inter-class mobility disappeared and 'the membership of the classes became fixed.'[16]

Coincident with this consolidation of class divisions was the eruption of new ideological issues in national politics and the breakdown of old class alliances. In 1857, just as the old party system was decomposing against the background of guerrilla warfare in Kansas, a severe economic crisis brought massive joblessness and industrial unrest to Northern cities. This conjuncture of economic and political crisis would have to have offered a propitious opportunity for American labor, or at least its advanced detachments, to protect its own leader-

<hr>

[16] Susan E. Hirsch, *Roots of the American Working Class*, Philadelphia 1978, p. 79.

ship in the political arena. In particular, it would seem to have been the moment for drawing together separate strands of democratic reform by uniting the dual issues of chattel and wage slavery.

The concept of such a *labor abolitionism* was openly advocated. Albert Brisbane, Robert Owen, Wendell Phillips, and Frederick Douglas espoused it, Marx and Engels cheered it on from across the seas, a few militant workmen tried to realize it. But in the event, it was a stillborn crusade. Despite the dramatic growth of the factory proletariat and the sharpening of the economic class struggle, no new working-men's party or locofocoist insurgency emerged in the 1850s to constitute a 'labor wing' of the Lincoln coalition. In the absence of a working class anti-slavery current, labor lost the chance to forge its own links of unity with the Black masses of the South or to create is own revolutionary-democratic political tradition.

Labor's inability to become an independent political actor in the greatest national crisis in American history was due, in part, to the fact that the initial process of industrialization had tended to *fragment rather than unify* the working class. The 'workies' of 1829–34 were able to draw upon the commonality of their artisanal culture and a fused tradition of Protestant-democratic nationalism. In the following decades, however, three powerful centrifugal forces acted to pull the labor movement apart just as the American Industrial Revolution was reaching its 'take-off' point.

1. The Urban-Industrial Frontier.

The first force was the very unevenness of industrialization and prole-tarianization in an American setting, where economic growth occurred not only through a concentric deepening around original nuclei, but also and especially through a succession of sectional developments. The new Western industrial cities (for example, Pittsburgh, Cincinnati, and Chicago after 1850) were built up almost overnight, manifesting little continuity with pre-industrial traditions or social relations.[17] This 'boomtown' characteristic of American industrialization meant that the labor movement in the United States, with the partial exception of New England valleys and the older Eastern port cities, arose without those deep roots in the artisanal resistance to industrialism which many historians have stressed as a determining factor in the formation of

---

[17] 'In most industrial regions west of the Alleghenies, the town did not precede the factory; the factory made the town.' R.H. Tawney, *The American Labour Movement and Other Essays*, London 1979, p. 57.

militant unionism and working-class consciousness. Moreover, it was this expanding urban-industrial frontier — rather than the Turnerian agrarian frontier — with its constantly replenished opportunities for small-scale entrepreneurial accumulation, that provided material sustenance for the petty-bourgeois ideologies of individual mobility that gripped the minds of so many American workers. American laborers — to a far greater extent than workers in European industrial nations — could vote with their feet against oppressive working conditions as, all too frequently, geographical mobility became a surrogate for collective action.

2. Nativism and the Cultural Division of the US Proletariat.

The second centrifugal influence — and decidedly the most disastrous obstacle to labor unity in the 1850s — was the reaction of native workers to the arrival of several million impoverished Irish and German laborers who came in a flood after the European crop failures of the 1840s. These new immigrants provided the cheap labor power for the growth of New England factories as well as the armies of raw muscle for Western railroads and Pennsylvania coalfields. They were met by the universal hostility of a native working class which rioted against them, evicted them from workplaces, refused them admission into trade unions, and tried to exclude them from the franchise.[18] Partly rooted in purely economic rivalries in the labor market (although modern labor historiography has uprooted the hoary old myth that the Irish arrived in New England textile mills as strike breakers), the Yankee-versus-immigrant polarization in the working class also reflected a profound cultural antagonism that would hinder efforts at labor unity for more than a century. It would be easy to define this cleavage as a persistent opposition between native-Protestant and immigrant-Catholic workers; yet this antinomy does not sufficiently capture the complex nuances of how, on the one hand, religion, ethnicity, and popular custom were concatenated into two rival systems — or, on the other, how they were integrated into the matrix of a global, and highly distinctive, American bourgeois culture.

The central paradox of American culture is that while Engels was correct when he labelled it the 'purest bourgeois culture', Marx was equally right when he observed that 'North America is pre-eminently

---

[18] The immigration of Irish Catholics went back to the late 1820s. By the end of the Jacksonian period there were already attacks on Boston convents and riots between rival Irish and native hand-loom weavers in Philadelphia.

the country of religiosity'.[19] In the absence of a state church or aristocratic hierarchy, secularization was not a requirement for liberalism, and America did not experience the kind of 'cultural revolution' represented by Jacobin anticlericalism in Europe. Nor did the American working class develop the traditions of critical, defiant rationalism that on the Continent were so vital in orienting the proletariat toward socialism and in establishing an alliance with the intelligentsia. Instead, the industrial revolution in America went hand in hand with the reinforcement of religious influences upon popular culture and working-class consciousness.[20]

Protestantism, for instance, was not merely a majority religion in antebellum America; it was also directly constitutive of popular republican nationalism. As Rhys Issac and others have shown, popular support for the American Revolution was the product of a 'double ideological eruption', as patriotic rebellion against Parliament was legitimated by the rise of a radical evangelicalism that translated the 'rights of man' through the idiom of perfectionist Protestantism.[21] This 'First Great Awakening' was followed by a 'Second', in the Jacksonian era, which provided the medium for the incubation of a series of Yankee moral crusades that ultimately converged in the Republican Party of the 1850s (abolitionism, free soil, and anti-popery). On the one hand, this revivalism helped forge a more inclusive and homogeneous *Northern* Protestant nationalist identity. On the other the renewal of pietism was a powerful means for establishing the social hegemony of the new industrial capitalists. Religious moralism was the most effective weapon against those arch-enemies of industrial discipline and high profits: 'drunkeness, spontaneous holidays, and inattention to work'.[22] Like the analogous English Methodism, however, evangelical religion

---

[19] Karl Marx, 'On the Jewish Question', *Collected Works*, vol. 3, p. 151.

[20] The power of religion in America has yet to wane. The US *alone* among major industrial nations experienced a powerful resurgence of religion in the post-war period; church affiliation, in fact, has climbed steadily throughout the twentieth century, from 43% in 1910 to 69% in 1960. According to recent surveys there are more than 45,000,000 'born-again' evangelical Protestants and Charismatic Catholics in the US today. Sydney Ahlstrom, *A Religious History of the American People*, New Haven 1972, pp. 951–952; and Jeremy Rifkin (with Ted Howard), *The Emerging Order: God in an Age of Scarcity*, New York 1979.

[21] Rhys Issac, 'Preacher and Patriots: Popular Culture and the Revolution in Virginia', in Alfred Young (ed.), *The American Revolution*, DeKalb 1976, p. 130; also Michael Greenberg, 'Revival, Reform, Revolution: Samuel Davies and the Great Awakening in Virginia', *Marxist Perspectives*, Summer 1980.

[22] Cf. Ahlstrom, *A Religious History*, pp. 844–845; Johnson, *A Shopkeeper's Millennium*, pp. 135-137; and Ray Allen Billington, *The Protestant Crusade, 1800-1860*, New York 1938.

could be a two-edged sword, and workingmen could appropriate its egalitarian side to advocate good, Protestant justifications for trade unionism and the Ten Hour Day. But the salient fact, in any case, is that the evangelistic fires were stoking the pietism of the Yankee working class to a white heat at the very moment when Catholic immigrants began to flood Eastern labor markets (American Catholics multiplied from 663,000 in 1840 to 3,103,000 in 1860).

The Irish immigrants of the famine generation and their successors after 1850 were bringing with them to 'the most militant Protestant nation in the world'[23] a highly distinctive and energetic variant of Catholicism. Many labor historians have characterized the religion of the immigrants as a quintessentially conservative, if not 'feudal' institution, exhibiting the 'deepest continuity with traditions of the peasantry'.[24] But this confuses the ultramontane stance of Continental Catholicism, indissolubly tied to Metternichean reaction and the rearguard defence of royalty, with the anti-monarchical and pro-republican Catholicism of the Irish lay poor. The fierce religiosity of the Irish immigrants to America was the product of a 'Devotional Revolution' in Ireland that followed in the wake of the defeat of the Revolution of 1789 and was closely associated with Daniel O'Connell's Catholic Emancipation Movement.[25] Furthermore, the vast majority of Irish immigrants were scarcely peasants in any rigorous sense of the term; rather, they were sharecroppers, marginal tenants, agricultural laborers, and seasonal navvies fleeing the genocidal consequences of colonial underdevelopment. Their revived religion was fused with a republican nationalism that had very different political implications from those which accompanied Catholic piety in French or Spanish contexts.

The key point is that the American Catholic Church which these Irish immigrants largely created and dominated was, in any comparative estimate, in the van of adaptation to liberal capitalist society. In particular, its symbiotic ties with resurgent Irish Catholicism provided it with the twin traditions of a plebeian, indeed, working class, clergy (in the 1940s Archbishop Cushing could boast to a CIO meeting that 'not a single Bishop or Archbishop of the American hierarchy was the son of a college graduate')[26] and an openness to democratic ideology via the original fusion of religion and Irish nationalism. Faced with the

---

[23] Johnson, *A Shopkeeper's Millennium*, cover note.

[24] Stanley Aronowitz, *False Promises*, New York 1973, p. 167.

[25] See Emmet Larkin, 'The Devotional Revolution in Ireland, 1850–1875', *American Historical Review*, June 1972; Bruce Francis Biever, S.J., *Religion, Culture and Values*, New York 1976.

[26] Ahlstrom, *A Religious History*, p. 1007.

challenge of the Knights of Labor in the 1880s, it was also the first national Catholic church to undertake an interventionist role in the labor movement, preserving its ideological domination through sponsorship of an anti-radical right wing in the trade unions.[27]

The ingenuity of American Catholicism, already becoming apparent in the 1850s, was that it functioned as an apparatus for acculturating millions of Catholic immigrants to American liberal-capitalist society while simultaneously carving out its own sphere of sub-cultural hegemony through its (eventually) vast system of parochial schools and Catholic (or Catholic-cum-ethnic) associations. This unique historical project embroiled the American Church in concurrent battles both against Vatican intransigents who opposed the rapprochement with 'modernity', as well as with the mainstream of American Protestantism, which feared that the Pilgrim heritage was in mortal danger from the twin (and interrelated) evils of 'Rum and Romanism'.

The important precision, therefore, is that it was not just immigration, nor even Catholic immigration *per se*, that was breaking down the cultural homogeneity of the Northern working class; but rather, from the late 1840s onward, the formation of *two corporatist sub-cultures* organized along a religious divide and operating through an enormous array of institutions and movements (ranging from the Women's Christian Temperance Union to the Knights of Columbus). Each of these great cultural-religious blocs encompassed a myriad of ethnic, denominational, and sectional sub-alignments which, in turn, possessed their own spheres of effective autonomy.[28] The radical differences between the social and cultural universes of American and most Western European workers was not the presence of ethnic or religious division, but the manner in which a multiplicity of these differences was aggregated and counterposed on a national level across a single

---

[27] The hegemony of the 'modernist' wing of American Catholicism has only been secured through constant internal struggle, and it would be mistaken to underestimate the power of the conservative hierarchy at any particular point in its history. Nevertheless, the adaptive 'Americanizers' have been the real pioneers of the Church's social and political insertion into American life. Occasionally they have also been the catalyst of change in the broader world church as well. Thus the battle of Cardinal Gibbons and the Americanists against church reactionaries over the question of the Knights of Labor paved the way for the 1891 *Rerum Novarum* of Pope Leo XIII, which brought a 'truce' between the Vatican and the liberal and labor movements. In this sense 'christian democracy' was born in the United States. See Henry J. Browne, *The Catholic Church and the Knights of Labor*, Washington D.C., 1949.

[28] Ethnicity in America is, of course, as Glazer and Moynihan have emphasized, 'a new social form' not merely a 'survival from the age of mass immigration'. Nathan Glazer and

ethno-cultural axis. The institutional complexes of 'Protestant Nativism' and 'Catholicism' operated a complex mediation between ethnic and linguistic particularisms on one level, and the general framework of national bourgeois culture on another.[29] While they were in some sense parallel agents of *acculturation* (Catholic schools imparted American nationalism and respect for property just as effectively as Protestant-dominated public schools), they were also antagonistic structures of *assimilation* (ethnic groups tended to form alliances on denominational lines, ethnic exogamy remained religiously endogamous, etc.).

Cultural division was reproduced on a political plane in the 1850s. The restructuring of the party system that took place after 1854 reflected both the increasing sectional polarization *and* the new widening of ethno-religious cleavages in the working class. Thus working-class nativism contributed to the formation of the virulently anti-Catholic, anti-immigrant 'American' or 'Know-Nothing' Party which temporarily became one of the most successful third-party movements in American history. By the middle of the decade, the majority of the Know-Nothings fused with the Free Soil Party and a wing of the disintegrating Whig Party to form the new Republican Party. The rise of the Republicans clearly represented the triumph of the most aggressive Yankee small-capitalist strata, and the party's program was a compelling synthesis of Protestant moralism, centralizing nationalism, and idealized entrepreneurial capitalism. Ironically, the Republican battle cry of 'free labor' had nothing to do with the rights of collective labor, but rather evoked the dream of escape from wage labor through individual mobility.[30]

The Catholic immigrants, in reaction, were driven to the Democratic Party which offered a *laissez-faire* toleration of religious and

---

Daniel Patrick Moynihan, *Beyond the Melting Pot*, Cambridge (Mass.) 1963, p. 16. I would add that to understand how specific ethnicities cohere and are reproduced it is essential to refer to the overall balance of class, religious, ethnic, and racial alignment. Thus, in reaction to the immigration of Irish Catholics, Irish Protestants quickly became 'Scotch-Irish'. Later, diverse communities of Serbs, Croats, Slovenians, Slovaks, Poles, and Magyars — forced to band together against discrimination and exploitation — accepted a certain ethnic commonality as 'hunkies' despite their traditional divisions and antagonisms. See Josef J. Barton, *Peasants and Strangers*, Cambridge (Mass.) 1975, p. 20.

[29] For some political historians, however, the most relevant antimonies are 'pietism' versus 'liturgism', as German high-church Lutherans in the Midwest tended to bloc with Irish and German Catholics against temperance and in support of parochial education. See Kleppner, *The Third Electoral System*, p. 363.

[30] See Eric Foner, *Free Soil, Free Labor, Free Men: The Ideology of the Republican Party before the Civil War*, New York 1970.

cultural differences. This bonding of the urban Catholic working class to the weaker and more backward sections of agrarian capital reinforced the Jacksonian pattern of alliances, in the sharpest contrast to Britain, where the working class was allied to the stronger and more modern section of the industrial bourgeoisie through the Liberal Party. The ensuing political split in the US working class lasted until the eve of the New Deal, with consequences that were inimical to the development of class consciousness. Native Protestant workers rallied to the leadership of their Protestant bosses and exploiters, while Catholic immigrants forged an unholy alliance with Southern reaction.[31]

3. Racism: The Unifying Theme

This account of the working class in the 1850s would be incomplete without discussing a third divisive force: racism. American democracy was, after all, the most spectacularly successful case of settler-colonialism and the correlative condition for 'free soil, free labor' was the genocidal removal of the indigenous population. Moreover, as Tocqueville observed, the antebellum North was, if anything, more poisonously anti-Black than the South.

An already consolidated white racism tied to the myth of a future black flooding of Northern labor markets led most native workmen to oppose social equality and suffrage for Black freedmen. From Boston to Cincinnati, the white lower classes periodically rioted, attacked communities of freedmen, hounded Abolitionists, and imposed color bars on their crafts. Northern Blacks were everywhere excluded from the universalization of manhood suffrage in the 1820s and 1830s, and on the eve of the Civil War only four states in the Union allowed freed-

---

[31] In his well-known study of Lynn, Massachusetts as a 'microcosm' of the industrial revolution in the USA, Alan Dawley has de-emphasized ethno-religious divisions in the working class as a cause of the defeat of class consciousness in the 1850s. Instead, he has argued that it was the 'timing of events' — specifically the nationalist impact of the Civil War in the context of a profound commitment to democratic suffrage — which was responsible for the political incorporation of the native working class within the Republican Party. Yet Lynn, as Dawley admits, was atypical, with 'a larger proportion of native-born workers than nearly every other major manufacturing centre in the state'. Had Dawley chosen other 'microcosms', he might have drawn different conclusions — as has Susan Hirsch, for instance, in her study of how ethno-religious conflicts in antebellum Newark brought the social order to 'ruins' in the 1850s and fatally split craftsmen into competing 'ethnic ghettoes'. Dawley, *Class and Community*, pp. 238-239; and with Paul Faler, 'Working-Class Culture and Politics in the Industrial Revolution: Sources of Loyalism and Rebellion', in Milton Cantor, ed., *American Working Class Culture*, Westport 1979, pp. 70-71; Hirsch, *Roots of the American Working Class*, pp. 106–107, 120–123.

men even a qualified franchise.[32] The rise of the Republican Party and massive Northern opposition to the *extension* of slavery contributed little to changing these prejudices. The young Republican Party carefully skirted or openly opposed the integration of Blacks into Northern society; deportation to Africa, in fact, was the favorite solution. Although segments of the native white working class, especially in New England, eventually embraced Abolitionism, they remained a minority whose opposition to slavery was most often framed within a pietistic religious ideology, rather than within a clear political analysis of the relationship between capitalism and slavery. Unfortunately more articulate and widely heard voices in the working class were those of 'labor leaders' and disgruntled Jacksonian radicals like Orestes Brownson or George H. Evans, who, in the guise of class politics, advocated an alliance of Northern labor with the slaveowners against 'capital'.

Among the immigrant proletariat, on the other hand, a section of the German workers possessed a more or less revolutionary understanding of the political implications of the slavery crisis for the future of American labor. They attempted to mobilize support for Abolitionism, and denounced the efforts of pro-slavery demagogues like Herman Kriege and the *New York Staats-Zeitung*. But these 'Red 48ers' — including the vanguard 'Communist Club' of New York — were ghettoized by language and their lack of understanding of the culture of American labor. Their heroic efforts had little impact upon the mainstream of the labor movement.

As for the Irish (already the bulk of the unskilled working class), in the 1840s William Lloyd Garrison had originated a bold strategy for building an alliance between Abolitionism and the contemporary movement in Ireland for repeal of the anti-Catholic laws. Unlike other Abolitionists, Garrison had sincere sympathies with the Irish and believed that the immigrant supporters of Daniel O'Connell in America could be rallied to a mutually beneficial united front. In response to solicitations from Garrison, the 'Great Liberator' (as O'Connell was popularly known) issued a series of ringing appeals for Irish solidarity with Abolitionism: 'I want no American aid if it comes across the Atlantic stained in Negro blood'; 'Over the broad Atlantic I

---

[32] 'At the outbreak of the Civil War only four states permitted Negroes to vote — New Hampshire, Vermont, Massachusetts, and New York; and only in New York did they constitute as much as one per cent of the population. There were 149 Negroes in New Hampshire; 194 in Vermont. In practice few could vote in Massachusetts, because of the literacy test, or in New York, because of the property qualification applicable only to Negroes.' Sait, *American Parties and Elections*, p. 42.

put forth my voice saying — Come out of such a land, you Irishmen, or
if you remain, and dare countenance the system of slavery ... we will
recognize you as Irishmen no longer'.[33]

O'Connell received a torrent of angry replies from American
Repealers decrying his support for Blacks. One letter came from an
assembly of Irish miners in Pennsylvania. After denouncing his address
as a 'fabrication' and warning that they would never accept Blacks as
'brethren', the miners added: 'We do not form a distinct class of the
community, but consider ourselves in every respect as CITIZENS of this
great and glorious REPUBLIC — that we look upon every attempt to
address us, otherwise than as CITIZENS, upon the subject of the abolition of slavery, or any subject whatsoever, as base and iniquitous, no
matter from what quarter it may proceed.'[34] The refusal of Irish miners
in an anthracite hell-hole of eastern Pennsylvania not only to
sympathize with the slaves, but to accept the implication — even from
their own national hero — that they were in America anything less
than 'CITIZENS', speaks volumes about the ideological impact of American exceptionalism and the difficulties of building a class-conscious
labor movement.

Thus, despite Garrison's and O'Connell's combined efforts,
Abolitionism failed utterly to stir the most exploited and outcast strata
of the Northern working class. Although the Irish stood loyally by the
Union in the Civil War (few as Republicans, most as 'Union Democrats') anti-Black racism grew as the rising cost of living combined with
a class-based conscription system to further increase the miseries of the
immigrant ghettoes and fuel the distorted perception that 'the Blacks
were to blame'. The great Draft Riot of 1863 — the bloodiest civil
disturbance in American history — exhibited the schizophrenic consciousness of the immigrant poor: their hatred of the silk-stocking rich
and their equal resentment against Blacks. Although attempts have
been made to rationalize the sadistic attacks by the Irish on freedmen
as the consequences of a desperate rivalry for unskilled jobs between
the two groups, this analysis has lost ground in the face of growing
evidence that Blacks had already been excluded from most categories
of manual labor and that the competitive 'threat' was totally one-sided
— directed in fact against Blacks.[35] Perhaps the racism of the Irish must
be seen instead as part and parcel of their rapid and defensive 'Ameri-

---

[33] Gilbert Osofsky, 'Abolitionists, Irish Immigrants and the Dilemmas of Romantic
Nationalism', *American Historical Review*, October 1975, p. 905.

[34] Ibid., p. 902.

[35] 'The old advocations, by which coloured men obtained a livelihood, are rapidly

canization' in a social context where each corporatist lower-class culture (native-Protestant versus immigrant-Catholic) faithfully reflected through the prism of its own particular values the unifying settler-colonial credo that made them all 'CITIZENS'.

Labor and Populism

The economic crisis at the beginning of the Civil War, and the employer offensive that accompanied it, undermined most of the remaining trade unions. But when a new unionism emerged at the end of the war, the basis for common action between native and immigrant had been strengthened by their shared experiences and sacrifices on the battlefield. Between 500,000 and 750,000 workers, almost a quarter of the male proletariat, fought for the Union; given the discriminatory draft system, a disproportionate share were Irish and German immigrants. Moreover, in the industrial boom that began in 1863 and lasted until 1873, many immigrant workers began to move out of the unskilled job ghetto in which they had been previously confined and into the construction crafts, metal trades, and other skilled sectors. At the same time, new winds of revolution from Ireland (the 1867 Fenian rising, the 1879-82 Land War) and Germany Lasalleanism and the struggle for suffrage) were politicizing immigrant workers in a more radical direction. Although violent echoes of antebellum ethno-religious conflict were still heard after Appomattox (New York's 'Orange Riots' of 1869 and 1870, the bloody feuding between 'Hibernians' and British miners in the Pennsylvania coalfields), the basic trend of labor struggles in the postbellum generation was the growing unity of the working class at the workplace and its search for more effective forms of solidarity and trade-union organization.

The Gilded Age opened an era of full-scale industrialization centered on the consolidation of a continental internal market and the growing mechanization of the capital-goods sector of the economy. The expansion of Western agriculture and railroads created an enormous appetite for machinery and iron products that was fed by the rise of a vast new industrial complex around the Great Lakes. By the end of Reconstruction, Chicago had surpassed Manchester as the world's greatest manufacturing metropolis, while the American working class

---

unceasingly and inevitably passing into other hands; every hour sees the black man elbowed out of employment by some newly arrived immigrant, whose hunger and whose color are thought to give him a better title to place; and so we believe it will continue until the last prop is levelled beneath us.' *Frederick Douglas's Paper*, March 4, 1853.

had almost doubled in size. Yet mass-production industries were still in their infancy and only a handful of factories employed more than a thousand workers. The railways were thus unique by virtue of their giant corporate size, financial resources, and enormous workforces. The railway working class, one million strong by the end of the century and alone possessing the capacity for co-ordinated national strikes, emerged as the 'social vanguard' of the entire American proletariat. It was no accident that the class struggles of each decennial business cycle between 1870 and 1900 culminated in national railway strikes supported by the riotous solidarity of hundreds of thousands, even millions of other workers and sympathetic small farmers. The Great Rebellion of 1877, the massive Gould system strikes of 1885 and 1886, and the epic Pullman Strike (or 'Debs Rebellion') of 1894: these were the flashpoints of class struggle in late nineteenth-century America.

Each of these strike waves reinforced attempts to build more broadly inclusive national labor organizations. As early as 1867, with the formation of the shortlived National Labor Union, the concept of a united workers' federation integrating both native and foreign-stock laborers had begun to win mass support. During the 1877 railroad strikes, a previously clandestine and little-known movement — patterned after freemasonry to shield it from employer repression — called the 'Knights of Labor' emerged to lead struggles in a number of states. In 1885, striking Knights on the Southwestern railroads defeated Jay Gould, the most powerful and wily robber baron of his day. As a result, unorganized workers everywhere turned toward the Order, whose membership grew to more than 700,000 in 1886. At the same time many unions began to affiliate, while of those which did not, the most important — including the crucial railway brotherhoods — were rapidly being pressed toward merger by rank-and-file sentiment. In a period when even the most skilled craftsmen had great difficulty maintaining union organization in the face of employer hostility and state violence, it was widely accepted that only a vast, inclusive movement of the entire proletariat could constitute a sufficiently powerful framework of solidarity and mutual aid to allow component unions to grow and survive. The flexible structure of the Knights provided for this aid by developing a broad range of organizational forms, based on craft (National Trades Assemblies), industry (Special Assemblies) or locality (District Assemblies).

Beyond the mere economic organization of the toiling classes, however, the Knights aspired to a more profound vision. They tapped the wellsprings of diverse laboring traditions (fraternalism, evangelicalism, 'equal rights', and mutualism) to nourish a network of solidary association that bound together workplace and community. A typical inventory of Knights-related organizations (in this case, Detroit 1885) encompassed: 'Unions, Knights of Labor assemblies, Working-men's Club Rooms, cooperative stores and factories, labor newspapers, singing societies, social clubs, political organizations, and a workers' militia(!)'.[36] But the invention that most clearly testified to the Knight's project of forging a *parallel proletarian civil society* was the Knights of Labor 'Court'. In his fundamental work on the Order's membership and internal organization, Garlock provides a description of this astonishing institution: 'Each Local Assembly had its own court whose officers were elected by the membership, in which Knights settled differences without recourse to the civil courts. Members charged one another not only with such violations of obligation to the Order as scabbing or accepting substandard wages, but for such violations of domestic obligation as wife-beating and desertion, for such violations of standards of social conduct as public intoxication or the failure to pay boarding bills'.[37] The embryonic class culture represented by the Knights not only transcended a 'pure and simple' trade-union economism, but also provided the first alternative to dominant ethno-religious sub-cultures.[38] It has been estimated that at one time or another 100,000 to 200,000 individuals served as officers in Knights' courts or local assemblies; any sampling of names reveals the land-mark reconciliation of Irish, German, and native workers that the Order had achieved. The Knights also made the first serious effort to organize the female proletariat — appointing a full-time woman organizer — and a pioneering, though feeble attempt at integrating Black laborers.[39] To the enthusiastic Engels, the rise of the Knights could be interpreted as nothing less than the American working class's first clear step towards becoming a 'class-for-itself': 'the first national organization created by the American working class as a whole ... the only national bond that holds them together, that makes their strength felt to themselves no less than to their enemies'.[40]

---

[36] Oestreicher, 'Solidarity and Fragmentation', p. 123.

[37] Jonathan Garlock, 'A Structural Analysis of the Knights of Labor: A Prolegomenon to the History of the Producing Classes', University of Rochester, PhD Thesis, 1974, p. 7.

[38] The unity of the Knights of Labor was all the more significant in face of the powerful resurgence of anti-Catholicism in the 1880s, as pietism responded to the surging Catholic birth-rate and the expansion of the parochial school system. See Kleppner, *The Third Electoral System*, pp. 216-221.

[39] Garlock, 'A Structural Analysis', p. 21.

[40] Friedrich Engels, 'The Labour Movement in America', American Preface to *The Condition of the Working Class in England*, Moscow 1977, p. 21.

The gospel of labor solidarity assumed a millenarian quality in the railway strikes and eight-hour-day demonstrations of 1886, as combined Knights and trade-union membership reached a nineteenth-century height. The world's first May Day touched off a spontaneous, month-long wave of mass marches, walk-outs, and quasi-general strikes that culminated in nationwide violence as newspaper head-lines asked: 'THE REVOLUTION?'. In the wake of the defeat of the third anti-Gould strike, however, and of the repression that followed the Haymarket Massacre, the dizzy growth of the Knights was brought to a sudden halt, and, in an atmosphere of worsening relations with the unions and internal vituperations against the Powderly leader-ship, the Order began its long slide toward oblivion. The consequent fragmentation of the labor movement also undermined the survival of the various local 'labor parties' that flourished in the brief climax of Knights' power and working-class unity in 1885–86.

The causes of the Knights' decline and the erosion of their cultural and political networks have long been an occasion for historiographic controversy;[41] and without directly entering the lists, it is worthwhile to examine several factors that would reappear in later conjunctures as obstacles to unitarian class organization. The Knights' power on the railways, for example, was undermined by the defection of the engineers, who were bribed and pampered by railway barons grown keenly aware of the unique power of this group of workers to shut down the entire economy. After 1885, the Engineers, under the right-wing suzerainty of Grandmaster Arthur, never again officially struck or came to the aid of fellow railways workers. The deser-tion of the Engineers' Brotherhood presaged the growth within the labor movement of a counter-trend towards a narrow and aristocratic conception of organization.

Another problem illuminated by the crisis of the Knights was a

---

[41] The battlelines run roughly as follows: those groomed in the 'Wisconsin' tradition of Commons and Perlman with its almost teleological conviction that Gomperism was the natural destiny of American labor have tended to view the Knights as an impossible dream — the last hurrah of an old 'utopian' reform tradition that clung to a classless ideology of 'producerism' and to the advocacy of petty-bourgeois panaceas like cheap money (Green-backism) and producer cooperatives. Other scholars, including Marxists like Foner as well as the most recent generation of Knights' historians (Garlock, Oestreicher, etc.), have argued a contrasting view of the Order; agreeing, it is true, that the Knights were burdened by ideological dead weight, but emphasizing as Engels did that the far more important dimension of the movement was its profound impulse toward a class, rather than merely craft, solidarity.

developing symbiosis between labor leadership and the patronage machinery of the Democratic Party. The Knights' archives reveal scores of rank-and-file protests against the manipulation of the Order to bolster individual political careers. Master Workman Powderly, Democratic Mayor of Scranton (Pa.) and later (Republican-appointed) Commissioner of Immigration, was only the most famous of many examples. Indeed, David Montgomery, contrasting British and American conditions, has suggested that the 'most effective deterrent' in this period to the maturation of class consciousness and the creation of a labor party was precisely 'the ease with which American working men entered elected office'.[42] The cooptation of individual labor leaders was facilitated by the revolution in American city government that occurred in the 1880s as an aspirant petty bourgeoisie of Irish — and occasionally German — extraction began to take municipal power from old Yankee elites. Beginning with the victories of Irish mayoral candidates in New York (1880) and Boston (1884), the new politicos generalized a Tammany Hall model of political brokerage based on a captive Catholic working-class vote.[43] Local trade-union leaders — especially in the Irish-dominated building trades — were often key links in cementing machine control as well as principal beneficiaries of political sinecures. The overall effect of this 'spoils system' was to corrupt labor leadership, substitute paternalism for worker self-reliance, and, through the formation of ethnic patronage monopolies, keep the poorer strata of the working class permanently divided. Finally, it is important to recognize that this tendency towards the assimilation of labor leadership by local political regimes preceded by almost a generation the precipitation of a significant trade-union bureaucracy *per se* (this would only develop on a broad scale with the rise of full-time 'walking delegates' and business agents after 1900).

It would be mistaken, however, to see the collapse of the Knights after 1887 as the end of the wave of postbellum labor militancy. In the early

---

[42] David Montgomery, *Beyond Equality*, New York 1967, pp. 215 and 208–209.

[43] In explaining the decline of the previously militant labor movement in Troy, New York, Daniel Walkowitz attributes special importance to the rise of an Irish middle class that gradually expropriated the community leadership previously exercised by the well-organized and articulate iron molders: 'Instead of the few petit bourgeois Irish shopkeepers ... who were traditionally men of the worker community, a new middle class had emerged which consisted of professionals and entrepreneurs, or men of commerce. The latter's domination of the Democratic party, and their continued involvement with the workers in French-Canadian and Irish ethnic clubs and nationalist movements, *began to diminish the working class base within the ethnic community and to shift ethnic allegiances to an inter-class axis.*' Daniel J. Walkowitz, *Worker City, Company Town*, Urbana 1978, p. 260.

1890s, the incipient trends toward the crystallization of a craft aristocracy within the working class and a bureaucracy within the trade unions were outstripped by the apparent radicalization of key sectors of labor. With the decline of the Knights, much of the fighting energy mobilized in the eighties was simply transferred to the two new movements that claimed to provide more effective frameworks for labor solidarity. On the one hand, the American Railroad Union under the leadership of Eugene Debs expressed the continuing desire of the railway workers for an inclusive, all-grades organization. A prototype industrial union, it was widely welcomed as labor's most advanced response to the challenge of the 'trusts'. The American Federation of Labor, on the other hand, was still far from the conservative monolith of business unionism that it would one day become. The child of the historic agitation for the eight-hour day in 1886, the early AFL was seen by its founders, many of them avowed socialists, as a more homogeneously proletarian organization than the Knights. At the time of Grover Cleveland's re-election in 1892, the AFL was still an embryonic coalition of national unions (including the Industrial Mineworkers), state federations, municipal trades councils, and independent locals. Its future structure and politics remained to be resolved by the conflict of ideological currents within it, including a rapidly growing socialist faction.

It was the Great Depression of 1893–96 — the worst collapse of the nineteenth century — that forced the issue of the labor movement's political identity and sounded the depths of its internal unity and cohesion. The fighting will and consciousness of a whole generation of labor militants, matured over the long cycle of struggles and movements since 1877, were tested in the series of violent battles that culminated in the American Railroad Union's boycott of the Pullman Company in 1894. What was so remarkable about the Pullman strike, distinguishing it among the three or four most climactic labor battles in American history,[44] was not only its escalation into a national confrontation between hundreds of thousands of workers and the federal government — this had also occurred in 1877 — but, rather, its unprecedented conjunction with massive upsurges of native agrarian radicalism and international labor politics.

The birth of the Farmers' Alliance in the late eighties, in a period of falling crop prices and rising rents, had signalled a radicalization of agrarian protest in the United States. Whereas previous farmer

---

[44] Other watershed labor battles were the 1919 Steel Strike, whose defeat paved the way for the collapse of trade unionism in the 1920s, and the 1936-37 General Motors Sit-down Strike, which secured the first CIO beach-head in the mass production industries.

movements, such as the various 'farmer parties' of the 1870s or the
national Grange, had tended to represent the interests of more prosper-
ous farmers, the Alliance derived an almost millenarian energy from its
roots in the poorer strata of the rural population. Especially in the
Southern cotton belt where the *ancien régime* had been recast into the
debt servitude of the crop-lien system, the Alliance by its unprecedented feat of uniting Black and white tenants had become a subversive
force of unknown potential. Furthermore, in areas of the South and
the Southwest an active cooperation existed between trade unions,
local assemblies of the Knights and the Alliance. (A frequently overlooked fact was the dynamism of Southern trade unionism in the
late eighties. New Orleans, in particular, had a powerful inter-racial
trade-union movement that made it a labor citadel by 1890.[45])

After the dramatic entry of the Alliance into politics in 1892 as the
Peoples' Party, grass-roots pressure began to build for a national
farmer-labor coalition similar to what already existed in the Southwest.
Labor Populism seemed to offer the unifying strategic vision and
breadth of organization that had been missing in the ephemeral labor
parties that had briefly flourished in New York, Chicago, and Milwaukee in the aftermath of Haymarket and the 1885–86 strike wave. At the
same time, Labor Populism seemed the natural American counterpart
to the new working-class parties then emerging in Europe and
Australia. The contemporary labor press reveals the keen interest with
which American trade unionists followed the rise of European social
democracy and Anglo-Australian laborism. Although German-
American workmen were naturally most electrified by the successes of
the SPD, it was the model of the Australian labor parties and the British
Independent Labor Party that stirred the greatest excitement in the
ranks of the AFL.

The Australian parties — the first *trade-union* rather than socialist
political parties in the world — were a direct outgrowth of the great
maritime and Queensland shearers' strikes of 1890–91. Although craft
unionists had been the first to seek political representation, it was the
impetus of the new, mass unions of pastoral workers, dockers, and
miners — reacting to economic depression and government repression
— that ruptured the bourgeois domination of the political arena and
gave the new parties their initial strength. Similarly in Britain, Keir
Hardie's Independent Labour Party (whose influence was generally

<hr>

[45] Cf. David Paul Bennetts, 'Black and White Workers: New Orleans, 1880–1900,'
University of Illinois (Champaign-Urbana) PhD Thesis, 1972; and Melton McLaurin, *The
Knights of Labor in the South*, Westport 1978.

exaggerated by its Yankee enthusiasts) was particularly oriented to the New Unions, which were most vulnerable to the increasing attacks on trade-union rights by the courts and House of Lords. It was, therefore, not surprising that it was a coalition of socialists and industrial unionists (especially the fledgling United Mine Workers) who lobbied within the AFL for independent labor political action as a riposte to government strike-breaking. At the 1893 AFL convention, they succeeded in winning majority support for an eleven-point political program copied from the platform of the British ILP (including a famous 'plank ten' which called for 'collectivization of industry'). The convention forwarded the program to constituent unions for membership ratification.

At the same time, Chicago emerged as the national center of the experiment of uniting Populism and the new labor radicalism. Even before the depression, police persecution and municipal corruption had revived Chicago labor's interest in independent politics. Then, in the face, first of government suppression of the 1894 Coal Strike, immediately followed by federal intervention against the Pullman strikers, the current of interest broadened into a mass movement. The embattled national miners' and railroad unions together with the Knights of Labor endorsed the Populists, while at a tumultuous conference in Springfield called by the Illinois Federation of Labor, a broad spectrum of unionists, insurgent farmers, and middle-class radicals met to consider the formation of a state-wide People's Party. Against the dramatic background of Debs's imprisonment and the crushing of the Pullman Strike, the delegates unified around a Populist banner and on the basis of an amended version of the eleven-point ILP platform. The key architect of farmer-labor unity at Springfield was the famous muckraker and Fabian socialist, Henry Demarest Lloyd, whose avowed strategy was to make Illinois Labor-Populism the 'spearhead of the movement to transform the People's Party into the American counterpart of the ILP'.[46] Indeed, spurred by the tireless efforts of local socialists, trade unions throughout the neighboring states of Wisconsin and Minnesota also joined the Populist crusade while simultaneously ratifying the proposed eleven points for the AFL. Lloyd was so sure that the momentum towards Labor-Populism was growing invincible that he asked Gompers to call a national conference to form a united front for the fall elections.

Gompers, meanwhile, was no less determined to defeat the socialist

---

[46] Chester McArthur Destler, *American Radicalism: 1865–1901*, New London 1946, p. 213.

challenge within the AFL and to 'restrict and terminate the alliance between organized labor and Populism'.[47] His allies included not only the more conservative craft unions, but also the right wing of the populist party. By 1894, a more conservative and anti-labor bloc of wealthier farmers from the Great Plains states ('a shadow movement imitative of populism but without organic roots in the Alliance network and its political culture') was beginning to displace the leadership of the more radical Southern and Southwestern Alliancemen.[48] With the financial resources of the silver interests (the American Bi-Metallic League) behind them, the Midwesterners hoped first to reduce the populist program to the single issue of free silver, and then to maneuver a fusion with the silverite wing of the Democratic Party. Their distaste for the radical Labor-Populism represented by the Springfield platform coincided with Gompers's.

The defeat of Labor-Populism was a tragi-comedy in several acts. First, at the 1894 Denver convention of the AFL, Gompers, supported by the conservative building trades, succeeded in preventing adoption of the ILP program, despite evidence of its endorsement by a majority of the rank and file. The AFL's repudiation of the eleven points then provided a pretext for moderate agrarians and corrupt 'machine' trade unionists in Illinois to foment a split with the Populist left wing. Many of the disillusioned socialists, in turn, followed Daniel De Leon's sectarian advice and returned to the isolated advocacy of 'chemically pure' revolutionary programs. Finally, after a bitterly contested battle between the Midwestern and Southern wings of the Populist Party in July 1896, the progressive Omaha Platform (with its several pro-labor planks) was scrapped for the sake of free silver quackery and fusion with the Democrats. The subsequent presidential election — which a year or two before had promised to be the dawn of a new era of farmer-labor political independence — demolished all third-party hopes and ushered in, instead, a generation of Republican-big business hegemony over national politics.

Underlying the debacle of 1896, however, was more than simply the successful conspiracies of Gompers and the conservative Populists to derail a radical farmer-labor coalition. Even when full allowance is made for the demoralization and confusion created by the infighting within the AFL and the Populist party, a great discrepancy remains

---

[47] Ibid., p. 183; also J.F. Finn, 'AF of L Leaders and the Question of Politics in the Early 1890s', *American Studies*, 7, 3.

[48] David Montgomery, 'On Goodwyn's Populists', *Marxist Perspectives*, Spring 1978, p. 169.

between the radicalism of the veteran trade-union militants — Debs, McBride, Morgan, etc. — and the apparent apathy or indifference of the majority of the urban and still predominantly unorganized working class. Despite the fact that Chicago in the midst of the depression was frequently described by contemporary observers as a city 'trembling on the brink of revolution', the Labor-Populists won only about twenty per cent of the potential labor vote (40,000 out of 230,000) at the height of their influence in 1894. Moreover, in a pattern of regional exceptionalism that would be repeated again in the twentieth century, the movement for an independent labor politics failed to grow in the other major urban-industrial centers outside of the Chicago-Northwestern area. Were there not, therefore, other, more profound forces acting to disrupt the advance of Labor-Populism and to deflect the development of American labor from the path traced by British and Australian labor parties?

Two factors stand out most clearly. First, the united rebellion of the Southern yeomen and farm tenants — the cutting edge of agrarian radicalism — was broken up by a violent counter-attack of the regional ruling class which counterposed 'Jim Crow' and redneck demagogism to the Farmers' Alliance and inter-racial cooperation. A vicious panoply of Black disfranchisement, racial segregation, and lynch terror was installed in the nineties to suppress militant Black tenants, to keep them tied to the land, and to prevent their future collaboration with poor whites. At the same time, the defeat of the great New Orleans General Strike of 1892 destroyed the vanguard of Southern labor and wrecked inter-racial unity among workers. Out of its ashes arose a stunted, Jim Crow white unionism on one hand, and a pariah Black sub-proletariat on the other.[49] These twin defeats of Southern tenants and workers were decisive in allowing merchant-planter reaction to block the development of a free labor market: freezing the Southern economy for more than half a century in the disastrous mold of a servile cotton monoculture.

Secondly, this Southern counter-revolution was paralleled north of the Mason-Dixon Line by a resurgence of nativism and ethno-religious conflict within the industrial working class. In the bleak depression days of the mid-nineties, many native as well as 'old' immigrant workers came to believe that burgeoning immigration was creating a grave competitive threat. (Symbolically, 1896 was the first year that Eastern and Southern European immigration exceeded that from

---

[49] Bennetts, 'Black and White Workers', pp. 554-55.

Northwestern Europe.) Simultaneously, in response to the political success of Irish Democrats in the elections of 1890 and 1892, there was a resurgence of militant anti-Catholicism led by the American Protective Association (a predominantly Scotch-Irish group that blamed the collapse on the 'flood of immigrants unloosed on America by papal agents') and the 150,000-member United American Mechanics.[50] Fatally for the hopes of labor radicals, anti-immigrant and anti-Catholic prejudice rent the unity of even those industrial unions, the miners and the railway workers, which were ostensibly the bedrock of Labor-Populism: 'Protestants were warned to avoid all unions dominated by papists, to discard the strike as a useless device, and to place no confidence in free silver. This advice made so strong an impression that Eugene Debs, the militant labor leader, and Ignatius Donnelly, the fiery Populist, called the APA an instrument designed by the railroad magnates to disorganize unions. In fact, APA-ism did have a disruptive impact on unionism, and not only among railroad employees. In the coalfields of Pennsylvania and Illinois this internecine strife checked a UMW organizing drive; in many cases it tore existing locals apart'.[51]

The Populist movement itself did little to allay the fears of the immigrant proletariat or to arrest the increasing polarization within the ranks of the 'producing classes'. Its cultural style was definitely evangelical, while its strong affinities for prohibitionism and state education reproduced classic nativist motifs. This may partially explain why so many foreign-born workers in the Midwest spurned Labor Populism at the very moment when they were moving away from the party of Cleveland and 'hard times'. Although the Republicans (briefly in 1896 the *less* nativist of the two parties) temporarily captured an important segment of the alienated Catholic working-class vote, an even larger part retreated from electoral participation altogether. The election of 1896 thus marks a profound mutation in American political culture. At a time when the European proletariat was becoming more politically engaged than ever before, the American working class was undergoing a striking electoral *demobilization* as a result of the nativist backlash (particularly the agrarian capture of the Democratic Party) and of new restrictions on the popular suffrage (Black disenfranchisement, poll taxes, and residency requirements). This combined process of exclusion/abstention dispersed the working-class vote while simultaneously creating a

---

[50] John Higham, *Strangers in the Land,* New York 1974, p. 81.
[51] Ibid., p. 82.

huge 'gap' — absent proletarian voters whom every third-party movement of the twentieth century would seek to identify and mobilize.[52]

Finally, it must be noted that the renaissance of the ethno-religious
and racial conflict at the end of the nineteenth century was intimately
connected with a far-reaching transmutation of popular ideologies. In
the face of the race terror in Dixie and the demands of US expansionism
in the Carribean and the Pacific, the old popular nationalism framed
by Lincolnian Unionism was being remolded into a xenophobic creed
of 'Anglo-Saxon Americanism' based on social Darwinism and
'scientific racism'.[53] The coincidence of this ideological torsion within
popular culture with the second major recomposition of the American
working class, fed by the new immigration, provides a context for
understanding the increasing rightward shift of the AFL after 1896
towards Jim Crow unions, immigration restriction, and narrow craft
exclusivism. Although trade unionism for the first time survived a
serious depression, the later nineties were reminiscent of the 1850s, by
reason of the intensity of the working-class dissension and fragmentation as Protestant was again mobilized against Catholic, white against
Black, and native against immigrant.

The Failure of Debsian Socialism

1. The Splintered World of Labor.

The new immigration, like the old, provided super-exploited gang
labor for extractive industries, domestic service, and construction. It
also provided on a rapidly expanding scale the armies of machine
operatives and semi-skilled laborers required by the dramatic growth,
from 1898 onwards, of the trustified mass-production industries. By
1914, when Henry Ford began to create his 'brave new world' of
assembly production at his Highland Park (Michigan) Model-T plant,
the majority of this enlarged proletariat were foreign-born workers,
more often than not politically disenfranchised and segregated — by
poverty or deliberate discrimination — into slum areas apart from the

---

[52] 'The large decline in participation after 1900 and the exceptional working-class
abstention rate today very much resemble a gap in the active American electorate that was
filled elsewhere by socialist parties.' Walter Dean Burnham, 'The Politics of Heterogeneity', p. 679.

[53] 'Never have patriotism, imperialism, and the religion of American Protestants stood
in such fervent coalescence as during the McKinley-Roosevelt era'. Ahlstrom, *A Religious
History*, p. 880.

native working class. The new coalescence of ethnicity, religion and skill produced the differentiated hierarchy depicted below (p. 42).

The origins of this hierarchy require some comment. In the first place, it is important to challenge the common assertion that immigration *per se* — 'hordes of peasants' — created an unmeltable and culturally backward heterogenity that vitiated class unity.[54] The new immigrants brought a vast array of parochial kin and village identifications with them from the old country. But the conscious decision to forge larger ethnic solidarities as the basis for communal organization in America was most often a defensive reaction to exclusion and victimization in the new country. In other words, class and ethnicity were often the bases of alternative survival strategies, and the actual impact of immigration depended greatly upon the strength and inclusivity of existing class institutions.

This point is brought out neatly in John Cumbler's contrast of the labor movements in the cities of Lynn and Fall River, Massachusetts. Lynn possessed one of the oldest and strongest trade-union traditions in America, and its working class was unified by a highly integrated relationship between leisure, work and the home. Fall River, on the other hand, lacked such cohesive, class-based community institutions, and its workforce was decentralized among relatively isolated work and residential areas. In Lynn, where the new immigration was a small, steady flow, the new arrivals were assimilated into the larger, unitary working-class community. In Fall River, by contrast, the arrival of large numbers of Portugese and Poles at the turn of the century was greeted with nativist hostility and led to 'community fragmentation into separate ethnic units of social activity'.[55]

Unfortunately, most of industrial America was more like Fall River than Lynn. Whereas the Western European class struggles of the 1880s and 1890s had spun a web of integrating proletarian institutions (ranging from workmen's clubs, cooperatives, and 'labor churches' to *casas del pueblo* and workers' educational societies), the US labor movement of the late nineteenth century, as we have seen, failed to generate a working-class 'culture' that could overcome ethno-religious alignments outside the workplace.

---

[54] Such is the gist of the so-called 'Handlin-Hofstader thesis'. Cf. Oscar Handlin, *The Uprooted*, Boston 1951, p. 217 ff,; Eric Hofstader, *Age of Reform*, New York 1955, pp. 180–184; also Aronowitz, *False Promises*, p. 164; Gerald Rosenblum, *Immigrant Workers*, New York 1973, esp. pp. 151–154; and Gabriel Kolko, *Main Currents in Modern American History*, New York 1976, pp. 68–69.

[55] John T. Cumbler, *Working-Class Community in Industrial America: Work, Leisure, and Struggle in Two Industrial Cities, 1880–1930*, Westport 1979, p. 8.

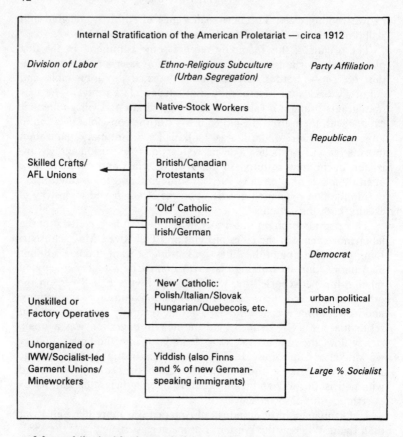

Meanwhile, inside the workplace itself, a profound recomposition of
the division of labor was reinforcing and overdetermining the effects of
the new immigration. The introduction of new mass-production technologies went hand in hand with a corporate assault on the power of
skilled labor. This offensive began on a systematic scale with the
Carnegie Company's defeat of the powerful Homestead lodges of the
Amalgamated Association of Iron and Steel Workers in 1892, and
continued for thirty years until the defeat of the railway 'systems federation' strike in 1922 established the supremacy of the open shop. As
industrial management broke the power of craftsmen and diluted their
skills, however, it carefully avoided 'levelling' them into the ranks of the
semi-skilled. Precisely to avoid such an explosive homogenization of
status, the companies wooed demoralized skilled workers with piece-

rates, bonuses, savings schemes, and 'profit-sharing'. Where craftsmen had traditionally seen themselves as the natural leadership of the laboring class, the corporations now promoted new social norms — especially the 'pride' of home ownership and membership in patriotic associations — that encouraged symbolic assimilation with the petty bourgeoisie. Drawn primarily from native and old-immigrant backgrounds, the skilled workers were purposely mobilized as an indispensable buffer against the organization of the unskilled.

The new immigrants, in turn, were 'frozen' into the ranks of the unskilled. The frenetic geographical mobility of the newcomers — as they were ceaselessly uprooted by the tides of the business cycle or returned home with their small savings — contrasts with their decreasing occupational mobility. In one carefully studied Slavic steeltown, for instance, the rate of upward mobility on the job ladder underwent a drastic decline from thirty-two per cent in 1888 to only nine per cent in 1905.[56] Within the plants themselves, the labor process was increasingly organized on the basis of ethnically and linguistically segregated work-groups supervised by unsympathetic native craftsmen or foremen. Again, however, the impact of the heterogenization of the workforce depended on whether or not a unifying counter force of trade unionism existed. In the coalfields of Pennsylvania, for example, the industrially organized Mineworkers succeeded after long struggles in forging a polyglot labor force into a militant membership. In those fiefdoms of 'industrial feudalism' (the steeltowns of Pennsylvania), on the other hand, where the craft unions had been crushed between 1892 and 1901, the workers seemed hopelessly divided.

This industrial caste system was reproduced in the rigid segregation and fragmentation of working-class residential life. By 1910, the American industrial city had developed a strikingly different social physiognomy from that of European factory centers. On both continents the building of street-car systems and elevated/underground railways had given powerful impetus to increasing spatial segregation. In Europe this took the form of further class polarization as proletarian 'east ends' and red *arrondissements* glared across a widening social-spatial gulf at bourgeois west ends and fashionable *faubourgs*. In the United States, by way of contrast, increasing class segregation of housing was overlaid by simultaneously expanding ethnic differentiation. Thus Buffalo, Cleveland, Chicago, Detroit, and Pittsburg all acquired after 1890, a characteristic *tripartite* spatial division between 1) middle-class suburbs, 2) a zone of decent, older housing (often

---

[56] John Bodnar, *Immigration and Industrialization*, Pittsburg 1977, p. 56.

single-family) occupied by native workers and some 'old' immigrants, and 3) an inner core of tenements, shabby apartments, and over-crowded boarding houses that provided dormitories for the new immigrant proletariat. Further transposed upon the belts of working-class residence was a grid — almost microscopically detailed in some cities — of ethnically and linguistically differentiated neighborhoods, 'each with an institutional life of its own'.[57]

Mediating this complex residential and workplace polarization between the native/skilled and immigrant/unskilled workers, were the 'old' foreign-stock Catholic workers, Irish and German. This inter-mediary stratum, particularly its Irish component, held an ambivalent but pivotal place within the internal structure of the working class. On the one hand, the Irish were partially integrated into the more privileged segment of the proletariat by their successful penetration of the skilled trades and by their disproportionate weight in the emergent trade-union bureaucracy. (Karson has discovered, for example, that no fewer than sixty-two AFL unions had Irish Catholic presidents in the 1906–18 period.)[58] Many of them also lived in the same 'better off' neighborhoods with the native skilled workers. On the other hand, they were linked to the new immigrants by economic status — since a majority of the Irish (especially the new arrivals) were still, in 1910, unskilled laborers or transport workers — as well as by their domina-tion of the two central institutions upon which a majority of new immigrants were vitally dependent: the Catholic Church and the Demo-cratic patronage machines in most industrial cities.

Finally, standing outside of the principal sub-cultural alignments of the working class were several exceptional groups of Central and East-ern European immigrants. Although every nation sent its exiled radicals across the Atlantic, the predominant languages of Marxism in America have been German and Yiddish.[59] The employers' blacklists and Bismark's anti-socialist laws forced new generations of German-Lassalleans, anarchist followers of Jonathan Most, and Marxists to follow the footsteps of the 'red 48ers' who had emigrated to the United

---

[57] Ibid., p. 14; also O. Zunz, 'Detroit en 1880: espace et ségrégation', *Annales*, 32, 1, January–February 1977; Josef Barton, *Peasants and Strangers*, Cambridge (Mass.) 1975, p. 18.

[58] Marc Karson, *American Labor Unions and Politics: 1900–1918*, Carbondale 1958, pp. 221-224.

[59] The third language would probably have been Finnish. Far-left Finnish laborers left their indelible mark across the Northwest from the Mesabi iron mines to the Astoria fisher-ies, and the Finnish Socialist Federation organized a unique mass emigration of loggers and miners to the Karelian Soviet Republic in the early 1920s.

States. In the late nineteenth century these revolutionary German workmen — from whose ranks came the Haymarket martyrs Spies, Engel, and Fischer — created their own extraordinary German-speaking cultural apparatus of gymnastic societies, rifle clubs, educational circles, and socialist beer gardens. They also played the major role in building such important unions as the Brewers, Cigar Makers, and Bakers. For several generations they were the left wing of the labor movements in Chicago and St. Louis, but without question their greatest accomplishment was making Milwaukee the strongest citadel of socialism in America from 1910 to 1954.

The other great concentration of immigrant radicalism was the Lower East Side of New York, where a million Jewish and Italian immigrants were crammed into the densest tenement district in the world. One of the unexpected after effects of the Russian Revolution of 1905 was to provide the Lower East Side with an exiled cadre of brilliant young Labor Bundists and Jewish Social Democrats. In a remarkably few years they had organized a mass base of fifty thousand or so Yiddish-speaking socialist voters who crusaded for garment unionism and provided the backbone of left-wing opposition to Tammany Hall.

2. The Twin Souls of American Socialism

The aspiration of Debsian socialism was to unify and represent this divided and culturally multiform American proletariat. In the wake of the Panic of 1907 and the Supreme Court's draconian attacks on trade unionism (the Danbury Hatters and the Buck's Stove and Range cases — the American equivalents of Taff Vale), there was a powerful surge of working-class votes towards the Socialist Party, despite Gompers's attempt to steer labor into a *de facto* alliance with the Democrats. Yet by the high point of 1912, the party was being torn apart by internal schisms and ideological divergencies. The crisis of the party, of course, had many causes, but above all it reflected the contradictory dynamic of the class struggle in the Progressive era.

The years between 1909 and 1913 marked a watershed in the history of the international labor movement. In the United States, as well as in Britain, Germany, France and Russia, they saw the outbreak of violent 'mass' strikes and the entry of new strata of unskilled workers into the class struggle. Beginning with the rebellion of immigrant steel workers in McKees Rock (Pennsylvania) and sweated New York garment workers (the Shirtwaist Strike) in 1909, the supposedly 'unorganizable' immigrant proletariat erupted in militant upheaval. Supported by the

Industrial Workers of the World and the Socialist organizers of the garment unions, the new workers launched strike after strike across a spectrum of mass-production industries from textile to auto. Simultaneously the AFL — already hard-pressed by the so-called 'Employers' Mass Offensive' of 1903–1908 — had to fight bitter, rearguard battles against the degradation of their crafts by dilution, Taylorism, and speed-up. The longest and most epic of these struggles was the spectacular forty-five month fight of the railway shop crafts against the introduction of scientific management on the Harriman lines in 1911-15.

Unlike the strike waves of the 1877–1896 period, however, the mass strikes of the early twentieth century largely failed to unify native and immigrant workers. Failing to unite the defensive fights of skilled labor and the organizing campaigns among the new immigrants, the movements tended to assume divergent and, all too frequently, antagonistic postures. The split within the working class became so profound that some Socialist writers regularly wrote of the 'civil war' in labor's ranks, while IWW organizers complained that the AFL unions were deliberately undermining and sabotaging the strikes of the immigrant proletariat.

This discord between the struggles of the craft unions and unorganized immigrants was carried into the Socialist Party in the form of a conflict between its reformist and syndicalist wings. The reformists, led by Victor Berger from his German Socialist bastion in Wisconsin, were committed to a program of Bernsteinian gradualism exemplified by mild civic meliorism and sporadic criticism of Gompers's leadership of the AFL. They possessed no strategy nor any visible commitment to the unionization of the unorganized, and were generally indistinguishable from the AFL mainstream in their support for racist immigration restrictions. Berger, moreover, was a declared white supremacist. As for the attitude of the right wing toward the new immigrants, Sally Miller provides this characterization of the 'model' Milwaukee party: 'While theoretically it was deplorable that organized labor was restricted to the skilled, in practice the Milwaukee socialists were comfortable with skilled German union men and scornful of unskilled new immigrants. The partnership they envisioned with labor was one of Germans and natives almost exclusively.'[60]

In contrast, the Socialist left wing — many of whom angrily withdrew from the party after Big Bill Hayward was purged in 1912 — adopted an almost exclusively industrial perspective that focused on the allegedly

---

[60] Sally Miller, 'Milwaukee: Of Ethnicity and Labour', in Bruce Stave (ed.), *Socialism and the Cities*, Port Washington 1975, p. 45.

immanent revolutionary potential of the immigrant and unorganized workers. They repudiated the AFL as a hopeless cause and concentrated their energies on building the One Big Union. Although these left socialists played invaluable supporting roles in the wave of immigrant strikes in basic industry, their syndicalism proved to be only a temporary tactical palliative for the needs of the unorganized factory proletariat. The IWW could exemplify fighting solidarity at the workplace but it had almost nothing to say about the political problems of slum communities caught up in complex dependencies upon the powers of church and patronage. It is not surprising that of the great strikes of this period, with the exception of the campaign in the New York garment unions, none left either durable union organization or led to any local victories for Socialist candidates.

It is hard to avoid the conclusion that neither of the two major tendencies of American socialism in 1912 offered a realistic strategy for uniting the working class or co-ordinating trade-union strategy with socialist intervention in the urban political arena. The reformists had no plan for building industrial unionism, while the revolutionaries saw no point in attempting to influence skilled workers or in contesting Gompers's domination of the AFL. Similarly, neither the 'sewer socialism' of the right (whose municipal programme was often — as Walter Lippman pointed out — indistinguishable from progressivism) nor the apoliticism of the syndicalist left met the need for a socialist political solution to the urban crisis and the plight of the slum proletariat. At every level the strategic perspectives of American socialism remained contradictory, embryonic, and unsynthesized.

On an organizational plane, the party never attempted to meld its different social components into an organic whole; in reality American socialism remained a series of ethnically and linguistically segmented socialisms. The most important socialist electoral strongholds were ethnically homogeneous constituencies: Germans in Milwaukee, Scandinavians in Minneapolis, Jews in Manhattan, Pennsylvania Dutch in Reading. The leadership of the party kept the separate language organizations of the smaller ethnic socialisms at a distance from one another and from the levers of power within the party: 'The immigrant socialists were the Party's transmission belt to the new immigrant workers. But the Party never set this transmission belt in motion. Instead, partly motivated by nativism and racism and worried by their politics, it kept these immigrant socialists adrift, failing to integrate them.'[61]

[61] Charles Leinenweber, 'The American Socialist Party and the "New Immigrants"', *Science and Society*, Winter 1968, p. 25.

Perhaps the gravest failing of the party, however, was its utter inability to penetrate the core of the industrial working class: the old and new Catholic immigrants. Compared to the dominating Irish presence in the AFL, for example, Irish radicals — although they included such fiery organizers as Elizabeth Gurley Flynn, William Z. Foster and James Cannon — were a beleaguered handful. Of the several million Poles concentrated in the industrial heartland, perhaps two or three thousand at most were affiliated with the right-wing Polish Socialist Federation. Meanwhile *Il Proletario* moaned that 'in a city that numbers 650,000 Italians [New York] there are a couple of hundred socialists registered with the party'.[62] While some historians have claimed that the opposition of the Catholic church effectively precluded any mass radicalization of Irish, Polish or Italian laborers, the reasons would seem more complex. Italian immigrants to Argentina, after all, were the builders of a radical labor movement, while Polish immigrant miners in the Ruhr were quite susceptible to revolutionary agitation. Perhaps that temporary sojourner in American socialism, James Connolly, was right when he argued against Daniel De Leon that anti-clerical, anti-papist propaganda in an American context would always be mistaken by Catholic immigrants as another species of nativism.

Connolly may have had in mind the *Appeal to Reason*, the spectacularly successful (750,000 subscribers) socialist journal from the cornbelt, which declaimed virulently against both the Catholic church and the new immigration. Another kind of argument has been made by Melvyn Dubofsky in his study of the failure of the Socialist Party to reach the New York Irish: he points out that the 'Irish immigrant link to the Democratic machine, well established by the end of the nineteenth century, was at floodtide in the Progressive era when Boss Charles Murphy grafted modern social reforms onto the old wardheeling Tammany structure'.[63] The implication is that the Irish workers, by virtue of their relatively privileged access to trade-union organization and political patronage, were little tempted by the entreaties of a predominantly Jewish socialist movement which, if it ever came to power, might dismantle the traditional Hibernian job trust at city hall.

One of the tragedies of the Socialist Party was that its bitter

---

[62] *Il Proletario*, quoted in S.M. Tomasi and M.H. Engel (eds.), *The Italian Experience in the United States*, Staten Island 1970, p. 192.

[63] Melvyn Dubofsky, 'Success and Failure of Socialism in New York City, 1900-1918: A Case Study', *Labor History*, Fall 1968, p. 372.

factional battles contributed so little to the recognition or clarification of these underlying strategic contradictions. Debs, almost alone at times, seemed to have a strong intuitive grasp of the fact that socialism could never hope to win the American working class politically unless the internal unity of the class could be grounded in some common direction of struggle. He hoped that the movement for industrial unionism might provide such a unifying practice — answering the needs of both craftsmen and operatives — and, for that reason, he came to reject the dual unionism espoused by the syndicalist left wing. In this spirit he issued a somewhat quixotic call in 1914 for the formation of an industrial union 'center' based on an alliance of the Eastern (UMW) and Western (WFM) miners, which could lead organizational campaigns in the mass-production industries and establish an alternative pole to Gompersism.[64] Although Debs's Appeal was ignored, its spirit was resurrected in 1917, when the Chicago Federation of Labor under the militant leadership of John Fitzpatrick and Edward Nockels decided to flaunt narrow craft shibboleths and to pool resources for a bold organizing drive in the stockyards. With William Z. Foster as chief organizer and abetted by the government's fear of wartime strikes, 100,000 packinghouse workers in Chicago and neighboring cities were unionized in a historic victory over the big packers in 1918.

The next year, with the faint-hearted and unreliable support of the AFL leadership, Foster and Fitzpatrick attempted to carry the methods of the stockyard campaign to the steel valleys of Pennsylvania and the mill neighborhoods of South Chicago. The steel industry was the front line of the open shop in America, and it was universally recognized that its organization was the strategic key to the entire industrial working class. Although the House of Morgan had wiped out the last vestiges of craft unionism a decade before, Foster and Fitzpatrick found hope in the growing unrest of the immigrant steelworkers who labored seven days a week, twelve hours per day in the deadly mills for poverty-level wages. Despite the vacillating attitude of the skilled native workers and the complex problems of craft territoriality (no less than 24 AFL unions claimed jurisdictions in steel), several hundred thousand, primarily immigrant, steelworkers heeded Foster's strike call against the most powerful industrial monopoly in the world. The Slavs and Italians held firm for three months against the 'cossack

---

[64] Daniel De Leon, of course, was the premier theorist of 'revolutionary industrial unionism', except that in his fervid sectarian conception this entailed winning the working class to the Socialist Labor Party's tiny 'socialist unions', rather than working within existing unions.

terror' of the state police and company guards, but in the end the strike was betrayed by the craft unions and undermined by the growing climate of anti-radical, anti-foreign hysteria in the country.

As one historian has put it, 1919 was the 'turning point ... which didn't turn'.[65] It was the failed test of native labor's ability to unite with the immigrant proletariat. The defeat of the steelworkers' organizing drive marked the end of the remarkable insurgency of Eastern and Southern European workers that had rocked industry since 1909. Faced with a tidal wave of nativist reaction, led by the rise of the Ku Klux Klan in midwestern industrial states, the 'new' immigrants retreated into the sanctuaries of ethnic community until the Depression triggered a second, even more militant upsurge. As for the skilled workers, the 1919 defeat opened the way for a broad employers' offensive that rolled back the wartime gains of the AFL and established the open-shop 'American Plan' upon the ruins of the once mighty mineworkers and railway shop unions.

In this period of general retreat, however, a last great outburst of popular radicalism flared across the Northwestern tier of states from Illinois to Washington. The Farmer Labor Party movement of 1919–24 drew energy from a number of centers of resistance, including the militant city labor federations in Chicago, Seattle and Minneapolis, embattled coalminers in Southern Illinois, immigrant iron miners in Minnesota, and the semi-socialist Non-Partisan Leagues in the Dakotas.

Attempting to fill the vacuum left by the factional disintegration of the Socialist Party in 1919, the third-party movement aimed to unify a fightback against the bosses' offensive, government repression, falling crop prices, and the coal depression. After a number of false starts and premature initiatives, the powerful Farmer Labor Party of Minnesota, already in control of its state's government, assumed leadership of the movement to regroup the various popular blocs into a new national party. Although the movement had to blend a diversity of ideologies ranging from Republican progressivism to Bolshevism, it made great strides in mobilizing labor support in neighboring states. At this point, on the very eve of the founding convention, Gompers (in a repeat performance of his earlier sabotage of Labor-Populism) and the railway brotherhoods intervened to wreck the embryonic new party. Red-baiting the Minnesota movement for allowing Communist participation, they convinced the venerable progressive statesman, Robert LaFollette,

[65] David Brody, *Labor in Crisis — The Steel Strike of 1919*, Philadelphia and New York 1965, cover note.

to refuse nomination and a third-party ticket, and thereby scuttled the electoral strategy that farmer-laborites had hoped would unite the new party. Although LaFollette ran on an independent ticket endorsed by the AFL in the 1924 presidential elections, actual labor support was desultory and paved the way for the AFL's return to its old non-partisan bunker.

It would be difficult to exaggerate the magnitude of American labor's defeat in the 1919–1924 period. For almost a decade, the corporations were virtually free from the challenge of militant unionism. In the interlude of the 'American Plan' employers accelerated the attack on worker control within the labor process, the new mass-production technologies advancing side by side with new forms of corporate management and work supervision. The totality of this transformation of the labor process — first 'Taylorism', then 'Fordism' — conferred vastly expanded powers of domination through its systematic decomposition of skills and serialization of the workforce.[66] Already by the end of the First World War, the capitalist class in United States (especially in the advanced sectors of the 'Second Technological Revolution': vehicles, electrical machinery, chemicals, and other consumer durables) was perhaps a generation ahead of its European competitors in the degree to which skilled labor had been subordinated and fragmented in the labor process. At the same time, however, the revolution in production and the post-war debacle of the AFL was weakening the material props of craft consciousness. The 'Fordist' integration of mass production was setting the stage for the emergence of the CIO and the rebirth of industrial unionism.

---

[66] The productivity revolution represented by the new labor processes resulted in an almost 50 per cent increase in industrial production between 1918 and 1928, while the factory workforce actually declined by 6 per cent. Thus, as Stan Vittoz has pointed out, the traditional dependence by American industry on a continual influx of low-cost immigrant labor never returned after the war, and big business raised only half-hearted opposition to the successful nativist campaign for immigration restriction in the early 1920s. Vittoz, 'World War I and the Political Accommodation ᵒᶠ Transitional Market Forces: The Case of Immigration Restriction', *Politics and Society*, Vol. 8, No. I, 1978, p. 65. These developments are discussed in greater detail in chapter 3 below.

2

The Barren Marriage of American Labor and the Democratic Party

On the eve of the New Deal's inauguration in the winter of 1933, the auto industry in Detroit was stunned by an energetic and well-planned walkout at the Briggs Auto plant. Following three and one half years of nearly catastrophic unemployment and paralyzed inaction by the American Federation of Labor, the Briggs strike signaled the revival of industrial militancy. This 'Lexington and Concord of the auto rebellion', as it was later typed, was fought for two demands that would be central in most early New Deal strikes: company recognition of rank-and-file-controlled shop committees, and the limitation of the authority of foremen and line supervisors.[1]

Seventeen years later, and in the wake of hundreds of local strikes as well as two nationwide walkouts (1937 and 1946), the United Auto Workers signed the so-called 'Treaty of Detroit' with General Motors. The 1950 contract with its five-year no-strike pledge symbolized the end of the long New Deal/Fair Deal cycle of class struggle and established the model of collective bargaining that prevailed until the 1980s. On the one side, the contract conceded the permanence of union representation and provided for the periodic increase of wages and benefits tied to productivity growth. On the other, the contract — by affirming the inviolability of managerial prerogatives, by relinquishing worker protection against technological change, and by ensnaring grievance procedure in a bureaucratic maze — also liquidated precisely that concern for rank-and-file power in the immediate labor process that had been the central axis of the original 1933–37 upsurge in auto and other mass production industries. As *Fortune* slyly put it at the time: 'GM may have paid a billion for peace ... It got a bargain'.[2]

The long route from the informal shop-floor democracy of the first

---

[1] On the Briggs Strike, see Roger Keeran, 'Communists and Auto Workers', University of Wisconsin, PhD Thesis, 1974, pp. 102–15.

[2] *Fortune*, July 1950, p. 53. For an analysis of the 1950 GM contract, see Frank Emspak, 'The Break-Up of the Congress of Industrial Organizations (CIO), 1945–1950', University of Wisconsin, PhD Thesis, 1972, pp. 364–65.

Briggs strike to the boardroom wheeling-dealing of the 1950 settlement, and the corresponding dilution and displacement of rank-and-file demands which this entailed, has usually been ascribed to the gradual bureaucratization of the new industrial unions. This transformation was accelerated, it has been argued, by wartime government intervention, and consolidated with the final metamorphosis of formerly militant labor leaders into the postwar era's 'new men of power'.[3] Whether emphasis is placed on the repression of the labor left or simply the operation of a Michelsian 'iron law of oligarchy', the triumph of bureaucratism has usually been seen as the determinant event in the dissipation of activism at the base.

This view has obscured the deeper, less unilateral dialectic between the ossification of industrial unionism into a bureaucratic mold and the changing content and trajectory of mass militancy. The CIO was not, as it has often been popularly depicted, the product of a single, heroic upsurge of working-class ardor. On the contrary, the new industrial unions were formed by highly uneven, discontinuous movements of mass organization which mobilized different strata of the proletariat. As I showed in Chapter One the CIO was the heir to a contradictory legacy. On the one hand it inherited the accumulated defeats of earlier eras: the deep divisions between sectors of the working class, the absence of a unifying nexus of common proletarian institutions, the obscurantism of Gompersian craft unionism, and the forced marriage between the Catholic working class and the Democratic Party. On the other hand, it received the unquenched fire lit by the Wobblies, and the Knights of Labor before them, which burned on in the small, but unbroken, cadres of revolutionary workers in unorganized mines and mills. It has been all too easy for the contemporary American left, still obsessed by the intractable enigma and charisma of the thirties, to believe that the trajectory of this process was predetermined by the deep structures of American history. It has been easier still to believe that all was possible, that the working class of the thirties and forties, like the characters in a Clifford Odets play, were there waiting, in raw militancy and spontaneous class instinct, for the 'correct' revolutionary cue.

A more cautious assessment of the CIO's conflicting possibilities and determinancies must focus on precisely this tension between the received condition of its emergence and the new terrains opened up by the creative impudence of struggle. The inevitability of the bureaucratic

[3] For the earliest statements of this position, see Harold Mitchell, 'Union Structure and Democracy', *Enquiry*, January 1943; and C. Wright Mills, *New Men of Power*, New York 1948.

incorporation of the new unions; the counter-potentials of mass radicalism and a labor party — these are questions that must be situated in relationship to the internal logic of the seventeen-year wave of class struggle from Briggs to the 'Treaty of Detroit'. The first step is to identify the key conjunctures in the history of the CIO which crystallized certain balances of forces while simultaneously annulling others. In fact, four periods stand out clearly as integral, constitutive phases in the formation of the industrial unions:

1. THE FIRST UPSURGE, 1933–37: The original rebellion of the unorganized industrial proletariat, starting with the 1933 'NRA' strikes and culminating in the sitdown 'fever' of winter/spring 1937. This was arguably the highwater mark of the class struggle in modern American history.

2. LABOR'S CIVIL WAR (I), 1937–41: Beginning with the 'Roosevelt Recession' in the summer of 1937, the CIO's great offensive suddenly ground to a halt in the face of growing unemployment, renewed employer terrorism, and most of all the increasingly effective competition of the class-collaborationist AFL.

3. THE SECOND UPSURGE, 1941–46: A second phase of CIO expansion came with the defense-induced industrial recovery of late 1940 and early 1941. After a series of new mass strikes in 1941 (Ford, Goodyear, Bethlehem, and Allis-Chalmers), official trade-union action was suspended for the sake of a wartime 'no-strike' pledge ameliorated by government-imposed unionization of war industries. This incipient statification of the industrial unions provoked an explosive wave of wildcat militancy through 1943–45, until the restoration of bureaucratic hegemony with the great 'safety-valve' strikes of 1946.

4. LABOR'S CIVIL WAR (II), 1947–50: The postwar organizing strategy of the CIO (public employment, retail, 'Operation Dixie,' and so on) collapsed in midst of a new employer-state offensive (Taft-Hartley in 1947) coupled with Cold War bloodletting within the CIO itself — the purge of left-led unions, mass blacklisting, and wholesale intra-CIO raiding. The result was a new stagnation of CIO growth and further gains by the AFL.

In the argument that follows, I employ this periodization as a framework for attempting to reconstruct the internal dynamics of CIO militancy in relation both to the actual and the *potential* development of political consciousness within the industrial working class.

I. From Briggs to Flint

The original period of the CIO's formation — 1933–37 — has been incomparably better studied than its wartime expansion; yet the historiography of this heroic period has tended to become so encrusted with mythology and *idées fixes* that certain crucial features have all but disappeared from the historical landscape. In particular, there are three aspects of labor's 'great upheaval' that need to be set far more sharply in relief:

First, the majority of the militant base for the new unionism was provided by second-generation workers, sons and daughters of the 1900–1920 'new immigrants', whose activation as trade unionists went hand in hand with their mobilization as the electoral bulwark of the New Deal. As Samuel Lubell has argued, 'the real revolutionary surge behind the New Deal lay in ... [the] coupling of the depression with the rise of a new generation which had been malnourished on the congestion of our cities and the abuses of industrialism.'[4] In 1930, there were twenty-five million of these second-generation Americans; together with their parents they constituted a third (forty million) of the white population and a majority of the working class. Although native-stock and Irish-origin leaders still tended to exercise a disproportionate weight in the general staffs of the unions and organizing drives, the CIO's early grassroots were the second-generation workers in the steel mills, anthracite mines, packinghouses, coke ovens, foundries, and auto assembly lines. Their relationship to the twenties boom was similar to that of Black workers to the 'affluence' of the sixties: dazzled by the sights and smells of a banquet in which they were never allowed to participate. Occupationally frozen in semi-hereditary unskilled and menial slots, forced to bear the brunt of urban poverty and hard times, but no longer limited by their parents' language or peasant superstitions — this second generation was ripe for rebellion.

Secondly, when the industrial uprising finally began in 1933, it was not primarily concerned with wages or even working hours. The underlying thrust was surprisingly non-economistic: in a majority of cases the fundamental grievance was the petty depotism of the workplace incarnated in the capricious power of the foremen and the inhuman pressures of mechanized production lines. It must be recalled that in 1933 the typical American factory was a miniature feudal state where streamlined technologies were combined with a naked brutality that was the envy of fascist labor ministers. In Ford's immense citadels

---

[4] Samuel Lubell, *The Future of American Politics*, London 1952, p. 29.

at Dearborn and River Rouge, for example, security chief Harry Bennett's 'servicemen' openly terrorized and beat assembly workers for such transgressions of plant rules as talking to one another on the line. In the huge Goodyear complex at Akron the majority of workers were pitted against a paramilitary 'flying squad' of company favorites and stoolpigeons. But the most totalitarian settings were undoubtedly the grim steel towns of Ohio, Pennsylvania, Illinois, and Indiana — the 'little Siberias' of Aliquippa, Weirton, Steelton, Duquesne, and so on — where steel barons like Tom Girdler and Benjamin Fairless exercised untrammeled local dictatorships. As Mayor Crawford of Duquesne once put it, 'Jesus Christ couldn't speak in Duquesne for the American Federation of Labor'.[5] Thus it is not surprising that the deepest impulse of the early industrial strikes was the fight for democratization at the workplace and civil liberties in company towns. In one of the few community-focused studies of the rise of the CIO, James McDonnell has shown how Buffalo industrial workers in the early thirties were preoccupied with the establishment of union contracts and seniority as restraints upon the unbridled power of management. This quest for a degree of workplace control took specific forms in different industries: in Buffalo steel mills, for example, the overriding grievance was the foreman-controlled hiring 'shape-up,' while for auto workers it was the indiscriminate speed-up on the assembly lines.[6]

Thirdly, this rebellion (even at first in the mines) owed nothing to the benevolent hand of John L. Lewis or other official leaders. The most striking aspect of the early thirties insurgency was the defiant autonomy of (usually clandestine) plant committees from any of the official apparatuses. Liberal hagiography, with its attribution of a decisive progressive role to the paradoxical Lewis (in earlier and later reincarnations, the *bête noire* of the left) has traditionally confused matters by its need to see the formation of the CIO as a historic, unmitigated step forward in the 'march of trade unionism'. In maintaining this position, it has tended to confuse the process by which militancy developed at the base with the very different causation and interests involved in the internal crisis of the old AFL bureaucracy. To weigh events more accurately, we need to keep one crucial fact in mind: *the original Committee for Industrial Organization (CIO) was an alliance of dissident trade-union bureaucrats, with important financial resources and friends in high places, created for the purpose of capturing an already existent mass movement of*

---

[5] J. Raymond Walsh, CIO *Industrial Unionism in Action*, New York 1937, pp. 51–2.

[6] James R. McDonnell, 'The Rise of the CIO in Buffalo, New York: 1936–42', University of Wisconsin, PhD thesis, 1970, pp. 35–46.

industrial shop committees and rebel locals — a movement with dangerous embryonic proclivities toward an anti-Gompersian model of 'class struggle unionism'.

A brief reprise of the emergence of the CIO may clarify why the intervention of the Lewis-Hillman wing of the AFL bureaucracy, supported by Roosevelt and Secretary of Labor Perkins, was ultimately a Greek gift to the rank and file movement involved.

Following the passage of the neo-corporatist National Recovery Act of 1933 (with its famous Section 7-A asserting, with a calculated ambiguity, the 'right of labor to representatives of its own choosing'), a wave of strikes broke out like summer lightning across the industrial heartland. With the exception of garment and coal-mining, where rank and file spontaneity was soon harnessed to the rebuilding of the power of established bureaucracies, the leadership of these 'NRA strikes' was provided by two species of unofficial vanguards.

On the one hand, there were the implanted nuclei of revolutionary cadres, the most important of which were the Communist Party's factory cells, its separatist 'third period' unions affiliated to the Trade Union Unity League, and, perhaps most significantly, its Slavic, Finnish, Magyar, and Yiddish language federations and cultural organizations which gave it privileged access to the first and second-generation 'new immigrants'.[7] There were also the much smaller, but locally important bands of Trotskyists, Wobblies, and American Workers' Party members ('Musteites') as well as the trade-union membership of the old Socialist Party.

On the other hand, informal groupings of highly skilled workers conserved and transmitted neo-syndicalist craft traditions of a more radical inflection than the AFL mainstream. Including highly paid machine makers and peripatetic maintenance technicians, these elite strata tended to be loosely supervised and, by virtue of their mobility or

---

[7] Communist Party membership almost doubled from 1933 to 1935 (14,000 to 27,000), but its real influence was greatly amplified by its radical publications within the various ethnic communities. In 1930, the CP published no fewer than eight foreign language *daily* papers in Finnish, Yiddish, Russian, Lithuanian, Croatian, Hungarian, and German. Some historians have belabored the overwhelmingly foreign-born composition of American Communism (90 per cent at its founding in 1919, still 80 per cent fifteen years later) as the reason for its alleged peripheralization, but this assessment must be balanced against the actual composition of the industrial working class itself. In 1933, for example, the factory proletariat was still 60 per cent foreign-born or second-generation 'new immigrants'. If anything, the Party's membership corresponded to the contemporary make-up of the class and gave it indisputable advantages over more 'Americanized' groups like the Musteites (American Workers' Party) who had great difficulty penetrating ethnic proletarian milieux. For statistics, see Nathan Glazer, *The Social Basis of American Communism*, New York 1961.

58

vantage point in the labor process of mass industry, were uniquely placed to provide leadership and coordination to the organizing efforts of operatives and line workers. Drastic wage-cutting in the late twenties, followed by the impact of the Depression, drove broad sections of this skilled aristocracy in mass production industry to reject the craft exclusivism and nativism which had proven so divisive in the industrial strikes of the 1909–1922 period. Instead, groups of craftsmen played catalytic roles in the organization of the NRA strikes. The outstanding early representative of this insurgency of skilled workers against 'Fordism' was the Detroit-based Mechanics' Educational Society of America (MESA), which was composed primarily (although not exclusively) of tool and die makers under the influence of British shop-stewardist traditions. In the fall of 1933, MESA, uniting with groups of semi-skilled workers, successfully struck contract tool and die shops in the Detroit area and created the first union beachhead in the auto industry.[8]

By late 1933 to early 1934, these advanced detachments of radicals and rebel craftsmen had begun to cement alliances with strategic groups of second-generation semi-skilled workers who, in turn, mobilized the hidden strengths of informal workgroups and ethnic networks. The enlarged shop committees sought further linkages with other plants in the same city or industry. The search for solidarity at both city-wide and industry levels produced a flood of new applications for AFL charters (forcing the CP to abandon its dual unions at the end of 1934), as well as a dramatic reinvigoration of somnolent city central labor councils. At the same time, this renaissance of unionism — David Brody considers this period to be the high point of mass participation in the labor movement[9] — posed an excruciating dilemma for the AFL's dominant right-wing troika of Hutchinson, Frey and Woll, and to the craft 'job trust' which they represented (respectively the construction, metal and printing trades). Their problem was finding a way of keeping control over the new unionism while simultaneously preventing its materialization into either of the two subversive forms traditionally opposed by the conservative craft bloc: mass industrial unions or their functional homologues, broadly inclusive and independent city labor movements. The Executive Council's solution was to force the new

---

8 On the seminal role of the 'autonomous worker' in the rise of the CIO, see Ronald Schatz, 'Union Pioneers, the Founders of Local Unions at General Electric and Westinghouse, 1933–37', *Journal of American History*, 66, 1979, esp. p. 595.

9 David Brody, 'Labor and the Great Depression: The Interpretative Prospects', *Labor History*, 13, spring 1972, p. 242.

unionists into temporary 'federal locals' subject to future redistribution among craft internationals, and to invest dictatorial control over organizing campaigns in basic industry to 'expert' (inept and alcoholic) AFL functionaries appointed by President Green.

The entry of the AFL apparatus immediately acted as a dampening force upon the rank-and-file movements in industry. What the auto, rubber, steel, and electrical insurgents demanded was a militant plan of battle against the corporations which aimed at the earliest possible national walk-outs, backed by the resources of the AFL. Green's plenipotentiaries, on the other hand, exercised every ounce of guile to derail the strike movements and to reach accommodations with management and the government. In auto, for example, the machinations of chief organizers Collins and Dillon, together with the AFL's acquiescence in an intolerably pro-employer formulation of the industry's NRA code, sparked an open revolt of the local shop committees who went ahead, under the influence of the left, to prepare the basis for an independent auto workers international. In rubber and electrical, similar ruptures took place between militant rank and filers and their appointed 'leaders'. In steel, however, the AFL's sabotage of the great 1933–34 movement for an industry-wide strike led to a more permanent demoralization as tens of thousands of millhands made an exodus from federal locals and Amalgamated lodges.

In the meantime, the forged ties of solidarity at the local level found explosive expression in three successive city-wide strikes which rocked Toledo, Minneapolis and San Francisco in 1934. In each case, the struggle of a leading sector of local workers (auto, truckdrivers, and maritime), under the leadership of avowed revolutionaries (Musteites, Trotskyists and Communists), catalyzed massive violent confrontations between labor and capital. The national AFL responded to these upheavals with disclaimers and denunciations, while Tobin of the Teamsters dispatched goons to strikebreak against the radical drivers in Minneapolis.

By the time that John L. Lewis got around to delivering his legendary right-cross to Big Bill Hutchinson's chin at the 1935 AFL convention — symbolically precipitating the exit of the future CIO unions — broad sections of the industrial grassroots were already either deeply alienated from the AFL leadership or in open revolt. Even more ominously, there was a visible *radicalization* of the rank-and-file movement expressed both by the growth of left-wing groups, and, especially, by their ability to lead masses of workers in broad struggles like the 1934 strikes. Moreover, the left's capacity to act as an alternative pole of leadership was greatly enhanced by the *de facto* industrial united front between the Communists and Socialists which emerged in 1935 and lasted, at least in auto, until March or April of 1937.[10] Although this brief season of left unity was only a passing fancy of the Communists (then en route from the sectarianism of the third period to the sycophancy of the popular front), it was a vital factor in the next and most dramatic phase of the rebellion in industry: the sitdown wave of 1936–37.

In the year between the summers of 1936 and 1937, the shop committees in auto, rubber and electrical — along with kindred rank and file movements in maritime — launched a sustained offensive that was quite unequalled in American history for its tactical creativity as well as its demonstration of the power of the collective worker in modern industry. By uniting the skilled and unskilled, the native and the foreign-born, these strikes 'created a solidarity that hitherto eluded American workers.'[11] At the root of the success of this strike wave, which breached for the first time the main bastions of capital (General Motors, US Steel, General Electric and Chrysler), were two invaluable resources. One was the recovery, or, perhaps, reinvention, of those radical tactics based on rank-and-file solidarity and initiative which the Wobblies had pioneered in the previous generation: the sitdown strike and the mass picket. The other crucial variable was the quality of strategic leadership and inter-plant coordination which was supplied by the left, particularly the Communists. Unlike the top-down generalship which unfortunately became all too typical of the CP's trade-union 'influentials' after 1938, the Communist strike leaders of 1936–37 (Mortimer and Travis in auto, Emspak in electrical, and so on) were genuine tribunes of the rank and file, who worked with relentless energy to expand and deepen mass participation in strike organization. It is no exaggeration to claim that a fecund synthesis was temporarily achieved between the highly participationist and egalitarian tradition of struggle derived from the Wobblies, and some of the best elements of American Leninism's emphasis on organization, discipline and strategy.[12]

---

[10] On this ephemeral united front, see Joseph Starobin, *American Communism in Crisis: 1943–57*, Princeton 1977, p. 38; and Staughton Lynd, 'The United Front in America: A Note', *Radical America*, 8, July–August 1974.

[11] Melvyn Dubofsky, 'Not so "Turbulent Years": Another Look at the American Thirties', *Amerika Studien*, 24, I, p. 8.

[12] Unfortunately, this 'synthesis' was only achieved temporarily on a practical plane; no important attempt was made to theorize the lessons of the sitdowns or to appreciate the strategic importance of defending the autonomy and democracy of the shop committees. In an interesting contrast between the early CIO and the British shop stewards' movements

The results were staggering: an epidemic of sitdown strikes beginning in rubber in 1936, then taken up by the autoworkers in their epic GM strike of winter 1937, and finally exploding in the spring fever of 1937 as some 400,000 workers staged 477 sitdowns.[13] Mighty corporations seemed to fall like dominoes before such prodigies of rank-and-file energy as the ingenious capture of 'Fisher Number Four' or the *eleven*-mile-long picket line at −9° which the rubber workers staged at the Goodyear complex in 1936. By directly encroaching upon the sanctity of corporate property and providing workers with a premonitory revelation of their collective power, the sitdowns seemed to be transforming proletarian consciousness and dissolving old indoctrinations. Social surveys among militant rubber workers in Akron, for example, showed a 'distressing' absence of respect for corporate property as well as the strength of a group ethos that valued human rights over property rights.

The goal of the secessionist bureaucrats led by Lewis and Hillman was to dam this torrent of mass militancy and to rechannel it into pacific tributaries under their command. Their model of industrial unionism was Lewis' own United Mine Workers (UMW), which banned radicals and whose constitution provided for 'tight central control, limited local autonomy, and minimized rank-and-file participation'.[14] Where prior industry-wide organization of shop committees or union nuclei was lacking, as in steel and meatpacking, this structure was summarily imposed. Both the Steel and Packinghouse Workers' Organizing Committees (SWOC and PWOC) were strictly top-down operations, headed by handpicked lieutenants of Lewis from the UMW who supplanted existing local leadership. As Bert Cochran has observed, 'there were no conventions, no elections, no autonomous locals or districts'.[15] In the industries where such a *coup de main* was impossible (i.e. where some coalesced national framework already existed: auto, rubber, electric and oil), Lewis created a dual structure

---

of the First World War, David Brody points to the absence in the thirties of a sustaining 'syndicalist' ideology concerned with problems of workers' control or functional shop leadership. See 'Labor History and Rank and File Militancy', *Labor History*, 16 Winter 1975.

[13] In 1937, sitdowners included hospital workers, trash collectors, gravediggers, blind workers, engineers, prisoners, tenants, students, and baseball players. The fundamental study is Sidney Fine, *Sitdown*, Ann Arbor 1969; while an interesting new left evocation of the experience is Jeremy Brecher, *The Sitdown Strikes of the 1930s*, Root and Branch Pamphlet No. 4, Charlestown (Mass.) 1972.

[14] Lorin Lee Cary, 'Institutionalized Conservatism in the Early CIO: Adolf Germer, A Case Study', *Labor History*, 12, Fall, 1972, p.494.

[15] Bert Cochran, *Labor and Communism*, Princeton 1977, pp. 100–01.

of field representatives and regional directors. The CIO staff worked hand in hand with New Deal officials to promote 'responsible' negotiated settlements and to suppress the rampant use of the sitdown strike. Ironically, it was Adolf Germer, the former leader of the socialist opposition in the UMW, whom Lewis entrusted with the mission of squelching the sitdowns soon after their first outbreak in Akron at the end of March 1936. With the collaboration of the Department of Labor, Germer tried to end the strike, but the rank and file, already soured by its earlier experiences with AFL organizers, 'remained suspicious of all but their own local union officer', and shouted Germer down at a mass meeting.[16] After a few more trying months in Akron, Germer followed the sitdown epidemic to Detroit, where he was the highest ranking CIO representative at hand for the beginning of the historic General Motors strike. Bypassing Germer's objections and his petty obstructionism, however, the Socialist and Communist leadership at Flint and Cleveland forced the GM showdown upon Lewis as a virtual *fait accompli.*

The success of the rank-and-file leadership in retaining its autonomy and initiative during the Flint strike contrasts with events a few months later. By March 1937, Lewis was able to abort a repeat attempt of the GM sitdowns at Chrysler, foiled a proposed general strike in Detroit, and, by the end of the spring, brought the sitdown wave to a halt. Although the onslaught of a second depression in summer 1937 helped dampen mass militancy, other more directly political factors contributed to the sharp decline of strike momentum and the assertion of greater control by the CIO bureaucracy. First, Lewis commanded indispensable financial resources drawn from the treasury of the UMW — a decisive advantage over the relatively impoverished federations of shop committees. Secondly, and more importantly, the secession of the CIO leadership from the AFL coincided with a fateful recomposition of Roosevelt's political coalition that favored a new collusion between the state and the industrial unions. Until the middle of 1935, FDR had managed to draw support both from the majority of the unions and from the so-called 'progressive' wing of capital (advocates of greater corporatism, including the management of GE, US Steel, the Rockefeller oil interests, and even the President of the US Chamber of Commerce). He balanced this conflictual alliance by offering the AFL a more or less pro-union interpretation of NRA codes in lighter (and Northern) industries, as well as more energetic relief measures; to big business, on the other hand, he ceded an interpretation of the NRA codes in heavy

---

[16] Cary, p. 494.

industry which — as we have seen in the cases of steel and auto — buttressed the 'company unions' that had been thrown up as road-blocks to genuine organization.[17] This political juggling act worked for a time but as rank-and-file insurgency in the plants continued to grow regardless of the codes, corporate capital began to re-evaluate its support for the New Deal. It was this mass desertion of business from the administration in 1935 that drove a *reluctant* Roosevelt temporarily into the arms of Lewis and the CIO insurgents. With an attenuated base of business support (now primarily composed of anti-Wall Street segments of Western and Southern entrepreneurs), Roosevelt needed the powerful electoral bulwark that the surge of four million workers into the CIO during 1935–37 offered. Lewis and Hillman, in turn, needed the charisma of Roosevelt's backing and the clout of his political-judicial support to bring the rank and file into line. Thus, in the brief halcyon days of Roosevelt's and Lewis's relationship in 1936, the CIO created Labor's Nonpartisan League (LNPL) to mobilize support for Roosevelt and help make up the deficit in campaign financing left by the defection of Democratic bankers and businessmen. Roosevelt reciprocated by allowing the pro-CIO liberals in the Labor Department and the National Labor Relations Board to provide the new unions with tacit support.

Nevertheless, it is highly unlikely that Lewis and Hillman could have so easily consolidated their control without aid from a third source, the Communist Party. Almost immediately after the stunning victory at Flint, the CP began to discard the residue of its working relationship with the Socialists and to turn towards a new alliance with Lewis (and later, after Lewis's resignation in 1940, with Murray and Hillman). Again it was a cold-blooded marriage of convenience: the bureaucratic integration of the CIO was an incomparably easier matter with Communist complicity, and Lewis also needed the kind of superb organizing talent which they seemed to possess in abundance. On the other side, the CP's turn toward Lewis, under the rising star of Earl Browder, was a logical part of a broader maneuver to legitimize the Communists as the left-wing of the New Deal coalition. In time they would have to pay a terrible price at the hands of their erstwhile allies for this 'center-left coalition'. Meanwhile, the Party's work in the unions began to take on a totally new character as the exigencies of intra-bureaucratic struggle assumed priority over the defense of rank-and-file democracy or the creation of a mass socialist current in the

---

[17] For a contemporary analysis see Louis F. Budenz, 'After the Strike — What?', *Common Sense*, September 1935, p. 10.

unions. Communist criticism of Lewis (and later of Murray) ceased, the call for an independent labor party was muted, and by 1938 the party's factory cells and plant papers were abolished.[18]

The full import of these new alignments was revealed in the organiz- ation of the campaign against hold-out 'Little Steel' in 1937. The Communists contributed at least a third of the organizers for the Steel Workers Organizing Committee (SWOC), but abstained from attempts at recruitment or at criticism of the autocratic Lewis-Murray leader- ship, even when, at the end of the campaign, all Party members were summarily purged from the staff.[19] Tactically conservative and deter- mined to keep a tight rein on local strike committees, SWOC eschewed sitdowns and prepared for a long, conventional walkout. This played into the hands of the shrewd and ruthless Tom Girdler, generalissimo of the Little Steel employers, who launched a preemptive lockout, barricading forces of scabs and heavily armed company guards inside the mills. Girdler's 'reverse sitdowns' were reinforced with a recipe of massive anti-union propaganda, middle-class vigilantes, and terrorism against picket lines drawn from the so-called 'Mohawk Valley Formula' (after the strategy that Remington Rand Corporation had used to defeat the CIO in upstate New York). Lewis, in turn, counted on FDR and New Deal state officials (newly elected with the backing of LNPL) to overcome the steel barons' systematic and blatant defiance of the Wagner Act. When Democratic Governor Davey of Ohio sent the national guard into the steel towns of Canton, Massillon, and Youngs- town, they were welcomed as 'brotherly heroes' by the SWOC strikers. The guardsmen, in return, launched a reign of terror reminiscent of the suppression of the 1919 Steel Strike which virtually drove SWOC under-

[18] Starobin, *American Communism in Crisis*, p. 36; and Emspak, 'The Break-up of the CIO', p. 49. After the war, leading CP trade-union strategists undertook bitter self-criticism for their failure to sustain the Party's influence within the CIO rank and file. Thus trade union secretary Roy Hudson was forced to admit that the CP had disastrously underem- phasized union democracy for the sake of supporting Murray and Hillman, while electrical workers' leader Dave Davis confessed that even the CP-led unions were infected by 'rampant bureaucratism'. In a more recent memoir, John Williamson — a principal archi- tect of the CP's strategy of the 'left-center coalition' within the CIO — outlined what he believed were the Party's three fundamental errors: (1) failure to build socialist conscious- ness in the unions; (2) failure to keep building a CP mass base in the unions; and (3) failure to build a left current within the AFL. He further observed that it was the weakness of the CP's implantation in the trade union rank and file that ultimately made the Party so vulner- able to McCarthyite persecution (Cf. Roy Hudson in *Political Affairs*, 24, July 1945, p. 605; Dave Davis, cited in Starobin, *American Communism*, pp. 96–8; and John Williamson, *Dangerous Scot*, New York 1969, p. 156.)

[19] Cochran, *Labor and Communism*, pp. 100–01.

ground in Ohio. Meanwhile, the even more 'pro-labor' Governor Earl of Pennsylvania, who in earlier months had supported the CIO's fight to establish civil liberties in the Allegheny and Monongahela valleys, also backtracked into a repressive stance. The key to the behavior of these Democratic politicans, of course, was the attitude of the administration in Washington. Roosevelt, shifting ground to rebuild support from business circles as well as with the anti-CIO leadership of the AFL, cynically repaid his electoral debts to the CIO by playing the role of Pontius Pilate in the aftermath of the bloody Memorial Day (1938) massacre of striking steelworkers in South Chicago. While Lewis was busy defusing rank-and-file anger inside SWOC, which was pushing for a general strike in Chicago, FDR declared 'a plague on both houses' and coolly distanced himself from the CIO. The combined result of Lewis's bureaucratism, the CP's new-found moderation, and FDR's betrayal was the defeat of SWOC and the crashing halt of the CIO's offensive in industry.[20]

II. The Labor Party That Never Was

The awakening of class solidarity that welded together industrial workers in the struggle for unionization was replicated on an electoral plane as a tendential political unity of working-class constituencies previously fragmented by religious and racial division. The New Deal landslide victory of 1936 marked, for the first time, the supersession of the traditional ethno-religious patterning of the Northern electorate by a clear polarization of workers and capitalists between the Democratic and Republican parties. This political recomposition was primarily a product of the rise of a second-generation ethnic-proletarian voting bloc augmented by the conversion of formerly Republican Blacks and many native Protestant workers.[21] A contradictory double movement was involved in this realignment of political axes: on the one hand, as an expansion of the Democratic Party's active base, it contributed to a spectacular reinforcement of capitalist political hegemony; on the other, to the extent that it tended to unify the working class politically, it created new potentials for eventually undermining this same bourgeois party duopoly.

While conventional political history has stressed the irresistible tide

[20] Cf. Art Preis, *Labor's Giant Step*, New York 1964, 67–71; J.B. Widick, 'Question of Trade Union Unity', *New International,* January 1938, p. 15; and Walsh, CIO, p. 181.

[21] See Kristi Andersen, *The Creation of a Democratic Majority, 1928–1936*, Chicago 1980.

of the first movement, the left of the thirties, dubious about the New Deal's capacity to cure the ills of American capitalism, was much more impressed with the opportunities created by the second. It was the consensus of the left that the rise of the CIO was finally producing, where the Knights of Labor and the Industrial Workers of the World had failed, the successful cellular structure and strategic imperative for a labor party. The emergence of the new industrial unions, while largely buttressing the Democrats, also coincided with a dramatic ferment of alternative political movements and labor-oriented third parties. In Minnesota, for example, the 'radical' Farmer-Labor Party consolidated its dominance in 1934–36 with the election of a Governor and two US Senators, while in Washington and Oregon the labor-based Commonwealth Federations (emulations of the social-democratic Cooperative Commonwealth Party of Canada) captured their state Democratic Parties for several years. In California, Upton Sinclair's 'EPIC' movement promised to redistribute the wealth, and in Wisconsin the Lafollette dynasty continued its reign through the powerful Progressive Party (later fused with the state's farmer-labor movement).[22] Simultaneously, the surge of industrial unionism, confronted with the challenge of corporate and state repression, became unavoidably politicized. In 'feudal' steel towns, as we have seen, political mobilization for democratic rights was a virtual precondition for union organization. Similarly in auto centers, the sitdown strikes spurred UAW militants to campaign against corporation-dominated local governments. In Lansing and Jackson, Michigan, for example, UAW 'flying squads' did double duty picketing and

---

[22] The Progressive Congressman from Wisconsin, Thomas R. Amlie, was the spark-plug of efforts in 1934–36 to unite all the third-party currents into a single movement preparatory to the launching of a new national party in 1936 or 1940. Under the successive titles of the 'League for Independent Political Action', the 'National Farmer-Labor Party Federation', and finally the 'American Commonwealth Federation' (ACF), Amlie, John Dewey, Paul Douglas and other 'progressive liberals' tried to win the adhesion of innumerable farm organizations, trade unions, and statewide third parties to their program of 'production for use'. At its inaugural conference in Chicago in 1935, the ACF, backed by numerous groups, including the garment and textile workers' unions, predicted it would win five to ten million votes in the 1936 elections and the presidency itself by 1940. Unfortunately, the linchpin of its entire strategy was the sponsorship of the powerful Minnesota Farmer-Labor Party, and when FLP Governor Olson threw his support to FDR and the Democrats in 1936, it squelched the national hopes of the ACF. See Selden Rodman, 'A Third Party by March?', *Common Sense*, January 1935, pp. 17–8; Thomas R. Amlie, 'The American Commonwealth Federation: "What Chance in 1936?"', *Common Sense*, August 1935, pp. 6–9; and Millard Gieske, *Minnesota Farmer-Laborism: The Third-Party Alternative*, Minneapolis 1979, pp. 206–8, 220–21 and 244.

ballot counting, while in Flint and Saginaw the union stewards were also organized on a residential basis, creating a powerful ward organization. Local after local of the auto, electrical and garment workers voted support for the concept of a labor party in a groundswell of political independence that discomfited Lewis and Hillman. A Gallup Poll conducted in August 1937, following the sitdown wave, showed that at least 21% of the population supported the eventual formation of the national farmer-labor party.[23]

Why, then, did this convergence of politicized trade-union militancy and third-party experimentation fail again — as in 1894 and 1919[24] — to produce any lasting synthesis? Two interrelated explanations have been advanced. One is that the 'leftward' turn of the New Deal in 1935 stole the thunder and co-opted the popular *raison d'être* of the insurgent political movements. The other is that, contrary to the strike-breaking of Cleveland and Wilson, Roosevelt's tacit support for the CIO in 1936–37 allowed him to appear as the savior of industrial unionism. Both of these explanations have obvious kernels of truth. There can be no doubt, for instance, that the broad reforms of FDR's 'second hundred days' in 1935 constituted a powerful gravitational force that pulled contemporary radicalism much closer to the orbit of the Democratic Party. One example was the increasingly intimate alliance between the Minnesota Farmer-Labor Party — supposedly the main stalking-horse of a national third party — and the New Deal. Another was the unprecedented creation of the American Labor Party in order to channel New York's significant radical vote toward support for the regime in power (FDR and Mayor La Guardia). Even Labor's Nonpartisan League, nominally the independent political expression of the CIO, was little more than a captive campaign apparatus for Roosevelt and selected pro-labor Democrats. Finally, in regard to the use of the state's coercive apparatus, Staughton Lynd is unquestionably correct to emphasize the shrewdness of Roosevelt's strategy of deradicalizing the sitdown wave through sympathetic federal mediation rather than through the draconian presidential repression that had been the ultimate weapon of previous administrations.[25]

But this line of analysis loses much of its cogency when it is generalized beyond the immediate conjuncture of 1935-37 and the honeymoon of FDR and the CIO. The satellization of the LNPL and the

---

[23] Donald R. McCoy, 'The National Progressives of America, 1938', *The Mississippi Valley Historical Review*, XLIV, June 1957, p. 76.

[24] See above, chapter 1.

[25] Lynd, 'The United Front,' pp. 30–31.

farmer-labor movements, for example, was emphatically not the same as their actual absorption into the Democratic Party. Most contemporary Marxists, counting on the crisis of the New Deal and the eventual replacement of Roosevelt from the right, still visualised them as the foci of a future realignment to the left (1940 was the popularly predicted date). Precisely such a crisis of reform ensued in mid-1937, with the onset of the second slump and the increasing defiance of the National Labor Relations Board by an intransigent sector of capital (Ford, Dupont, Little Steel, and so on). Roosevelt's attempts at shoring up the New Deal with an exemplary 'purge' of congressional reactionaries and his strategy of packing the Supreme Court were both dramatic failures; in 1938, following the decimation of liberals in the fall elections, a resurgent bloc of Republicans and 'Bourbon' Southern Democrats actually took control of Congress away from New Deal liberals. This shift in the national political balance, combined with FDR's overriding desire to win support for an increasingly interventionist foreign policy, pre-empted further reform initiatives or new concessions to labor. More than that, it led to a drastic cut in public relief in 1939 (which sparked widespread strikes and riots) and, as we have seen, renewed state repression of strikes and organizing drives. Lynd's assertion that the CIO never experienced the 'stage of radicalizing confrontation with state power' must certainly be qualified by the widespread strike-breaking of New Deal governors, exemplified in the terrorization of the SWOC in late 1937.[26]

Thus by 1937–39, the crucial integrative props of Rooseveltian Democracy — economic restoration, social reformism, and suspension of state repression — were openly in crisis, and seemingly propitious conditions again existed for the further growth of local labor or farmer-labor movements and their eventual national coalescence. The traditional view of certain Marxist currents has been that 1938 was the most advantageous opportunity for revolutionary politics in the twentieth century. The puzzle, however, is how to explain why 1938 was actually a year of unmitigated disaster for third-party and labor party hopes, which instead of growing at the expense of the New Deal's crisis, virtually collapsed. In Wisconsin and Minnesota, for example,

---

[26] The unleashing of the national guard against SWOC was merely the climax of five years of repressive attacks by Democratic state governors. In 1934, for example, a national textile workers strike was broken by a massive mobilization of guardsmen from Rhode Island to Georgia. In 1935 alone, the militia was employed in 73 strikes in 20 states, 'a majority of them under Democratic "New Deal" administration'. Needless to say, Roosevelt made no attempt to use his executive powers to curb strike-breaking by his local allies and supporters. See Preis, *Labor's Giant Step*, p. 96.

the Progressive and Farmer-Labor Parties suffered the devastating losses of both governorships and a reduction in their combined congressional delegations from twelve to four. In Washington, the Commonwealth Federation was dislodged from its command of the state Democratic Party, and in California, the EPIC movement quietly disappeared from the scene. Meanwhile, the UAW's 'Vote Labor' campaign in the Detroit municipal elections of 1937 — the CIO's most ambitious foray into local politics — lost by a surprising margin ('100,000 and 200,000 workers who are registered voters did not vote'), while the LNPL's desultory performance in the 1938 elections cast doubt on its continued viability.[27]

The AFL Resurgence

The key to this paradox of declining third party fortunes was the veritable 'civil war' which broke out between the AFL and the new unions in 1937–38. It was not just a question of labor disunity, but rather of an extraordinary resurgence of right-wing trade unionism allied in informal, but decisive ways with the contemporary offensive of capital. On a local level, the AFL colluded with employers to pre-empt CIO organizing drives by signing toothless, 'sweetheart' contracts or even the chartering of company unions. At the same time, the national AFL Executive, long anxious to tame the power of central labor councils, ordered a thorough purge of the CIO from local labor bodies. In a post-mortem on the failure of SWOC, J.B. Widick blamed AFL President Green for splitting strategic central labor councils in Detroit, Cleveland and Akron 'precisely when labor solidarity was indispensable to prevent the "Little Steel" defeat from turning into a rout'.[28] On the West Coast, the AFL Teamsters countered the CIO's famous 'March Inland' from its waterfront base with a wave of violence and secret agreements with employers. Even bloodier guerrilla warfare erupted on the New Orleans' docks between AFL and CIO longshoremen, while Southern open-shop supporters gleefully circulated the AFL's red-baiting diatribes against the industrial unions.[29]

---

[27] Hugh T. Lovin, 'The Fall of Farmer-Labor Parties, 1936–38', *Pacific North-West Quarterly* 62 January 1971; Gieske, *Minnesota Farmer-Laborism*, p. 272; George Tselos, 'The Minneapolis Labor Movement in the 1930s', University of Minnesota, PhD Thesis, 1970, pp. 418–79; and Ben Fischer, 'The Lessons of Detroit's Labor Campaign', *Socialist Review*, January-February 1938, p. 17.

[28] Widick, 'Question of Trade Union Unity', p. 15.

[29] Frey, for example, publicly claimed that 'the CIO policy was determined in the headquarters of the Communist Party in Moscow', while the anti-semite Wharton (Machinists)

The strange bedfellows of the AFL and big business also cooperated on a political plane to defend their collusive contract-making by demanding the amendment of the Wagner Act to 'guarantee to the employer "free speech" to express his union preference'. This dangerous attempt to re-legalize company unionism was typical of an AFL strategy which, in its frenzy to stop the growth of the CIO proved more Pyrrhic than Machiavellian. The AFL's political endorsement policy, as adopted by its 1937 convention, placed it in opposition to any candidate sympathetic to the CIO.[30] By thus splitting the labor vote, the AFL effectively undermined the base of state third-party movements, city-wide labor tickets, and the left wing of the New Deal. In 1938, the AFL withdrew from the Minnesota Farmer-Labor Party, the Oregon Commonwealth Federation, and the New York American Labor Party, while severing its remaining links with Labor's Nonpartisan League. Simultaneously, the AFL worked to defeat Mineworkers' leader Tom Kennedy in his gubernatorial bid in Pennsylvania, and radical congressman Maury Maverick in Texas. (In some cases, however, the AFL's endorsements were so odious — as in the case of Green's support for right-wing Governor Merriam in California — that its local affiliates rebelled and temporarily united with CIO unions.)

The AFL's fratricidal mania was self-destructive to the extent that it undermined the political leverage of the entire labor bureaucracy on the eve of World War Two. As we shall see later, labor's disunity precluded the negotiation of the kind of 'tripartite' political participation in the war economy that Gompers had partially achieved during World War One and which the British Labour Party won after 1942. At the same time, however, the AFL did manage to grow rather spectacularly in the late thirties, and by 1940 had recouped most of its membership and financial losses from the CIO schism. Although part of this growth was built on the flimsy support of sweetheart unionism, another part reflected the re-emergence of militancy in the ranks of the AFL itself. Unlike the strike movements in mass production industry, however, the new combativity of the AFL lacked any broad resonance

---

characterized his opponents as '... Lewis, Hillman, Dubinsky, Howard and their gang of sluggers, communists, radicals, and soap box artists, professional bums, expelled members of labor unions, outright scabs and the Jewish organizations with all their red affiliates', Walsh, CIO, p. 215.

[30] See Herbert Harris and David Denson, 'Is Green Digging Labor's Grave?', *Common Sense*, February 1940, pp. 4-5. Many liberal congressmen also blamed the AFL for the initial defeats of the Fair Labor Standards Act. See William H. Riker, 'The CIO in Politics, 1936–40,' Harvard, PhD Thesis, 1948, pp. 106–7.

since it was constrained within a narrow and tightly controlled economism. Faced with the CIO challenge, the larger AFL unions like the
Machinists, Carpenters, Meatcutters, and Teamsters launched new
organizing campaigns and adopted quasi-industrial structures and
jurisdictions.[31] But these membership drives failed to generate the sustained rank-and-file activism that accompanied the emergence of
industrial unions like the UAW. The modernization of the AFL after
1937 took place through an enlargement and recomposition of the
bureaucracy itself — a process typified by the rise of young turks like
Jimmy Hoffa in the Teamsters, who gave old-fashioned business
unionism a new aggressiveness (with tactics borrowed from radicals or
the CIO) without changing one atom of its social and political conservatism.

It would be mistaken to assume, however, that the rightward and
divisive posture of the AFL in the late thirties was exclusively the result
of its ossified bureaucracy defending its traditional sinecures. Equally
important was the fact that the *ancien régime* ultimately drew its solidity
from the relative conservatism of its predominantly skilled, native-
Protestant and 'old immigrant' membership. It was, moreover,
precisely this stratum of the working class which was most susceptible
to the ideological and cultural pressures of the petty bourgeoisie. The
relative social gravity of the middle strata and the degree of perme-
ability between its lower levels and the upper sections of the working
class have both been unusually high in the United States — perhaps
higher than in any other industrial country. An adequate theoretical
approach to the history of labor in the thirties would have to chart the
course of the various movements and perturbations of the different
middle strata and their mediating impact upon the development of
working-class consciousness (and vice versa). Suffice it to say, that while
middle-class insurgencies of the first Roosevelt administration tended
in a generally 'populist' direction that politically buttressed the New
Deal, after 1937 there was a profound middle-class counter-reaction to
the CIO and the growth of the left.[32] This anti-CIO, anti-radical backlash, incessantly fanned by the press and the corporate media,

---

[31] Brody believes that 'in the long run, adaptive old-line unions such as the Teamsters
and the Butcher Workmen, once they had come under the stimulus of the events of the
Great Depression proved to be more effective vehicles for expansion than the militant
industrial unions'. David Brody, 'Labor and the Great Depression,' p. 237.

[32] The repudiation of the New Deal by the middle classes was in part a reaction to the
stirrings of protest after the 1936–37 victories in the most submerged sections of the working class: women, Blacks, service and retail workers, employees of small business, and farm
labor. Particularly dramatic was the collapse of the Rooseveltian farm alliance in the late

contributed to the retrenchment of the AFL bureaucracy and provided it with a broad patriotic sanction for opposing the new industrial unions. At the same time, the resurgence of the AFL in the context of the rightward shift in national politics put the CIO leadership under increasing pressure — especially after the Ladies Garment Workers and the Milliners union rejoined the AFL in 1940 in protest at the dominant 'center-left' alliance within the CIO. Under siege, Lewis and Hillman clung even more desperately to their links to Roosevelt and the shrunken liberal wing of the Democratic Party.

Increasingly, uncritical support for Roosevelt also came from the Communist Party which, decked out in its new image as 'twentieth-century Americanism,' took popular-frontism to such extremes as the endorsement of the Kelly-Nash machine in Chicago, which was directly responsible for the 1937 massacre of steel strikers, and of the infamous anti-union regime of Boss Hague in New Jersey. The syco-phantic policies of the Communists did little, however, to broaden their base in the industrial working class. Although the party reached the zenith of its popular influence in this period, with perhaps 75,000 members and a periphery of more than 500,000, a majority of its growth came from an influx of second-generation Jewish white-collar and professional workers. Between 1935 and 1941, the non-blue-collar component of party membership jumped from barely 5 per cent to almost 45 per cent, while the New York component more than doubled from 22.5 per cent to nearly 50 per cent.[33] As Nathan Glazer has pointed out in his study of the party's changing social composition: 'During the thirties the party was transformed from a largely working-class organization to one that was half middle class ... even though the party had increased five-fold since the late twenties, there had been no such increase in the cadres in important industries. The party strength in the unions — except for maritime and longshore and the white-collar unions — was not a mass-membership strength. It was based on organizational control.'[34] While the Communist Party was undergoing

---

thirties, an event not unrelated to widespread processing and trucking strikes as well as to the CIO's attempts to organize field hands. Ironically, the New Deal's own agricultural policies, which favored planters and large farmers, produced a political frankenstein in the form of the immensely powerful and militantly anti-liberal Farm Bureau Federation. The Bureau, which enjoyed governmental sponsorship through the Agriculture Department's Extension Service, became the organizer of rural resistance to New Deal policies and played a major role in bringing about the conservative congressional victories of 1938 and 1942.

[33] Glazer, *American Communism*, pp. 114, 116.
[34] Ibid.

this paradoxical process of simultaneous growth and relative 'deprole-tarianization', the rest of the left was near collapse. The Socialist Party, unable as always to give its trade-union interventions any strategy or coherent leadership, virtually disintegrated in a series of factional splits and defections after 1936, while the Trotskyists were seriously weak-ened by major doctrinal schisms in 1940. The curious result was to give the CP a resonance in national politics and a hegemony on the left that was quite unequalled since the heyday of the old Socialist Party in 1910–12, while at the same time the party was becoming more detached from strong roots in the newly-unionized industrial working class.

The weakness of the labor left as a mass ideological current, and its dangerous over-dependence on bureaucratic alliances with 'center' forces, was vividly demonstrated by the Roosevelt Administration's success in repressing and isolating CIO radicals on the eve of the 1940–41 rearmament boom. First, with the active support of the Minneapolis employers, President Tobin of the Teamsters (the most outstanding AFL Democrat and friend of FDR) cashed in his political debts with the White House and obtained massive federal sedition prosecution of the Trotskyist leadership of Drivers' Local 544 — the nerve-center of labor militancy in the Northwest. (Ironically the Communists, who would later be decimated by the Smith Act, supported its initial application against their Trotskyist factional opponents in Minneapolis.) Then, in the summer of 1941, the Communists were evicted from the strategic aircraft industry, after Roosevelt ordered the Army to break the North American Aviation strike (Inglewood, California) led by Wyndham Mortimer, the hero of the 1936–37 Flint strike. *Here was the ostensible 'Pullman' of the New Deal: federal bayonets versus twelve thousand militant rank-and-file workers.* But unlike in 1894, there was neither massive national solidarity with the blacklisted workers, nor any political break with the administration. Instead, the CIO leadership (Murray and Hill-man since the resignation of Lewis in 1940) eagerly collaborated with Roosevelt's strike-breaking in the dual hope of weakening the Communists within the CIO while simultaneously gaining administra-tion support for the 'top-down' unionization of the defense industry. The Communists, for their part, mounted only a desultory campaign of defense; their temporary tangent of militancy since 1939 was broken by the invasion of Russia, as the party returned to virtually uncritical adu-lation of Roosevelt and Murray in the fall of 1941.

74

III. WWII: Wildcats and Hate Strikes

After nearly four years of trying to hold the fort against the attacks of employers and the rival AFL, the CIO regained the initiative in 1941.[35] As industrial production revived under the stimulus of Lendlease and rearmament, previously organized workers struck on a broad front for the first wage increases since 1937. Leading the way were Lewis' indomitable Mineworkers, whose solidarity and tenacity in successive strikes was probably unexcelled in American history. Striking in direct defiance of Roosevelt and his ill-fated Defense Mediation Board, the UMW set important precedents by winning the union shop and eliminating traditional Southern wage differentials. Meanwhile, workers in holdout, openshop industries again began to respond to CIO organizing drives. Ford and Bethlehem Steel were the most important of these anti-CIO employers; within weeks of one another in spring 1940, however, both capitulated to offensives of the UAW and SWOC. The great Ford strike, in particular, recalled the heroic days of Flint, with its mass picketing, flying squads, and — a new and distinctively American invention — encircling mammoth blockades of strikers' cars. Although the repression of the North American strike was an ominous sign, the general tempo of summer-fall 1941, in the wake of the breakthroughs at Ford and Bethlehem, was a strong upbeat of rank-and-file energy with clear refrains of the 'spirit of 37'.

This Indian summer of mass militancy was brought to an abrupt halt by the bombing of Pearl Harbor. Rank-and-file labor was quickly shackled by the restrictions of a wartime no-strike pledge and the regressive wage ceilings of the so-called 'Little Steel Formula'. The advent of the war was also the catalyst for far-reaching transformations in the organization of the labor force and the role of the state in the economy.

First, there was an 'unprecedented recomposition of the working class' as millions of rural immigrants, women, and Blacks entered the industrial labor market. It has been estimated that more than fifteen million Americans moved from one city, state or region to another in search of employment between 1940 and 1945. Four-and-one-half

---

[35] CIO membership doubled in 1937 in the wake of the sitdowns, and again in 1941 after the breakthroughs at Ford and Bethlehem. Between 1938 and 1940, however, the CIO's numbers had declined as a result of the depression in basic industry and the employers' counter-offensive. Meanwhile, the AFL, as we have seen, steadily recuperated its strength through backdoor deals with employers and by recruitment drives in less hard-hit transport and construction industries.

million permanently moved from the farm to the city. Underlying these great wartime migrations was the 'pull' of a new industrial revolution in the South and Far West, and the 'push' of accelerating agricultural mechanization and the collapse of cotton tenancy in the Southern Blackbelt. The burgeoning arms economy was midwife to both processes, as new concentrations of industrial labor emerged almost overnight in California aircraft plants or Southern shipyards, while older manufacturing centers underwent drastic metamorphoses in their social composition. Particularly striking was the rapid proletarianization of the Black population as a result of a new and ongoing exodus northward, which between 1940 and 1945 reduced the percentage of Black men employed in agriculture from 41 per cent to 28 per cent, while simultaneously doubling the percentage of Black workers in the total manufacturing labor force (from 5.9 per cent to 10.1 per cent). Similarly, millions of women gained entry for the first time to formerly male-exclusive citadels of mass production and heavy industries. The magnitude of the shifts involved can be gauged from the example of wartime Detroit, where by late 1942, almost 200,000 male workers were conscripted into military service and 750,000 new workers entered the labor-force: this number included 352,000 rural immigrants, 135,000 women and 60,000 Blacks. The confluence of these trends produced a dramatic, and, as we shall see in a moment, decisive change in the social base and consciousness of industrial unionism.[36]

Secondly, the war catalyzed a conflictual restructuring of the historic relationships between organized labor, capital and the state. The previous estrangement of the dominant fractions of corporate capital from the New Deal was superseded by intimate collaboration, as the flower of Wall Street became the economic warlords of Washington, while leading reformers were being exiled to minor administrative posts. The reigning congressional alliance of Republicans and right-wing Democrats was reinforced by the rise of a bureaucratic cabal of 'dollar a year' corporate executives and bellicose Southern Democrats in command of the war economy. In contrast to World War One, when the army had been obdurately uncooperative with business's efforts to coordinate procurement and production, the generals and the admirals

[36] See James Green, 'Fighting on Two Fronts: Working Class Militancy in the 1940s', *Radical America*, 9, 4–5, p. 27; Jay Mandle, *The Roots of Black Poverty*, Durham 1978, pp. 84–85; Roger Keeran, 'Everything for Victory: Influence in the Auto Industry During World War II', *Science and Society*, XLIII, Spring 1979, p. 7; and Nelson Lichtenstein, 'Ambiguous Legacy: The Union Security Problem During World War II', *Labor History*, 18 Spring 1977, p. 224.

now entered into a new and permanent collusion with war contractors and their political agents. The emergent 'military-industrial complex' succeeded where the NRA had failed in melding the political and economic ingredients for state monopoly capitalism.[37]

But this new coordination between private accumulation and the imperialist state required a level of labor productivity and industrial peace which could only be secured through the willing collaboration of the trade-union bureaucracy. Interestingly, the CIO leadership on the eve of World War Two (and under the influence of Catholic corporatist theories) submitted precisely such a plan for permanent harmonization of the interests of capital and labor through an integration of collective bargaining with scientific management. The proposal that Philip Murray took to Roosevelt in December 1940 as a basis for the organization of defense production advocated the formation of 'industrial councils' which would allow unions to participate in various aspects of plant management while encouraging a common interest between workers and the front office in raising productivity. Murray made the argument — later expanded by Walter Reuther — that the greater the degree of formal union 'partnership' with management and government, the more effective the control which the union leadership could exercise over disruptive or subversive 'minorities' in the rank and file.[38] The political clout of the CIO, however, had been too badly eroded by internecine fighting with the AFL and desertions within its own camp (including the all-important UMW in 1942) to win much support for this industrial council scheme. Instead, the labor movement as a whole, including the AFL, paid for its disunity by exclusion from the summit levels of the war economy as well as by its continuing weak and largely ineffectual influence upon Congress. Like the Wilson administration of

---

[37] The vanguard of the new symbiosis between government and big business was the Committee for Economic Development (CED) founded in 1942 by a phalanx of top corporate leaders under the sponsorship of Commerce Secretary Jesse Jones. The CED was a tireless missionary in the business community, ceaselessly trying to convert the medium-sized entrepreneurial strata to the virtues of stronger state intervention — sans welfare — on behalf of private investment. Similarly, the CED lobbied for the wartime tax amortization privileges and the Defense Plant Corporation subsidies which pumped billions of dollars of public monies into the reconstruction of the fixed-capital base of American industry. See Norman D. Markowitz, *The Rise and Fall of the Peoples' Century*, New York 1973, pp. 63–64; Gerald T. White, *Billions for Defense: Government Financing by the Defense Plant Corporation during World War II*, University (Alabama) 1980; and Philip Burch, Jr., *Elites in American History*, New York 1980, pp. 72–3, 386–88.

[38] The industrial council scheme might be taken as an American prefiguration of the postwar German system of industrial 'co-determination' (*Mitbestimmung*). Its direct antecedent was the AFL's self-defeating enthusiasm for scientific management in the 1920s as a

1917-18, FDR's third term mouthed the rhetoric of a 'tripartite' war effort, but its real commitments were revealed by the demotion of labor to a minor role in the key War Production Board, while billions of dollars-worth of prime contracts were being awarded to notorious violators of the Wagner Act.

The defeat of the CIO's call for 'industrial democracy' was partially mitigated, however, by the War Labor Board's reluctant concession of a generalized 'maintenance of membership' (quasi-union shop) and automatic union dues check-off in the summer of 1942. As Nelson Lichtenstein has shown in a careful study, the administration was above all concerned to shore up the position of the labor bureaucracy in face of internal union decomposition and the consequent loss of control over the workforce.[39] Increasing restiveness against the no-strike pledge among war workers (especially in the strategic shipyards), as well as the re-emergence of Lewis as an independent and possibly rebel pole in the labor movement, compelled the government to reinforce the power of Murray and company. The result was a social contract that 'conscripted' war workers into unions while at the same time denying the unions any authentic capacity to represent the economic interests of their members. 'Maintenance of membership' thus helped produce a dramatic increase in unionization, but with entirely different consequences from the struggles of the early thirties, since workers were now organized by the state into unions, rather than organizing themselves.[40]

Simultaneously, the turbulent recomposition of the workforce was breaking down many of the social networks and primary workgroups which had been the autochthonous roots of the CIO. Militancy was in a

---

bridge to labor-capital cooperation. Murray elaborated his ideas, with the help of Morris Cooke, in *Organized Labor and Production: Next Steps in Industrial Democracy*, New York 1942. This reorientation of CIO strategy was continued in Clinton Golden and Harold Ruttenberg, *Dynamics of Industrial Democracy*, New York 1942. Golden and Ruttenberg, high officials of the Steelworkers, offered management a bundle of olive branches ranging from cessation of wildcat strikes to CIO cooperation in raising productivity in return for the establishment of the closed shop. For them 'industrial democracy' meant 'worker participation in management as an outlet, improving productivity and reducing costs.' See Milton Derber, *The American Idea of Industrial Democracy, 1865–1965*, Urbana 1970, pp. 370–73, 377 (Reuther), and 380–82 (Golden and Ruttenberg quote).

[39] Lichtenstein, 'Ambiguous Legacy', pp. 228–235.

[40] 'The 1940s did not witness the striking transformations in class consciousness that occurred during the Depression, when there was a "making" of a white, male working-class identity that did not exist as coherently in the 1920s. In fact, the war years brought a great influx of blacks and women into the working class. But this period did not see a significant integration of these newcomers into the conscious working class or its institutions'. (Green, 'Fighting on Two Fronts', p. 28.)

sense displaced upwards into the layer of veteran secondary union leaders — stewards, committeemen and local officials — while the base became more anomic, volatile and transient. As a direct consequence, the class struggle within the war plants regressed to a more primitive level of sporadic, semi-spontaneous outbursts. These flare-ups nonetheless acquired a cumulative dynamic of their own as inflation and declining real wages continued to stir mass discontent. The catalytic agent that transformed this simmering unrest into an explosion was, predictably, Lewis's coal miners. The least affected by shifts in the labor force or the turmoil of wartime migration, the UMW rank and file exerted continuous pressure on Lewis to keep up the fight against the employers. In the face of a particularly determined wildcat strike by Pennsylvania anthracite miners in 1943, that for the first time in a decade challenged his control, Lewis was forced to lead the UMW into an open rebellion against the no-strike pledge. After four general walkouts in defiance of Roosevelt's threats to draft strikers and send the army into the coalfields, the mineworkers won their demand for 'portal to portal' pay. Although viciously calumniated by the press, the UMW victory electrified rank-and-file workers in war industries. 'By 1944 as large a proportion of the work force were taking part in work stoppages as at the height of the sitdown strikes seven years before'.[41] The rebellion was particularly extensive in rubber and auto where it took the form of successive waves of wildcat strikes. While 'all Akron rose in revolt' against the no-strike pledge and the international leadership of the rubber-workers union, more than half of the UAW membership joined an unauthorized walk-out of some variety in 1943.[42]

The CIO was thrown into an acute crisis. With the support of the War Labor Board, the bureaucracy attempted to isolate and punish individual militants: in rubber alone, hundreds of shop stewards were purged and blacklisted. But conditions on the shopfloor — particularly the nearly complete breakdown of grievance procedures — continued to fuel the wildcat movement. As national trade-union executives became virtual representatives of the government, the secondary leadership increasingly took up the complaints of the rank-and-file and began to coordinate resistance to the no-strike pledge. In rubber, this new layer of rebel leaders took control of key Akron locals, while in auto, Briggs Local 212, led by the fiery Emil Mazey, became a national

---

[41] Lichtenstein, p. 234.
[42] Cochran, *Labor and Communism*, p. 202.

rallying point for insubordinate shop stewards and local officials.[43]

Politically, this rebellion of the local leadership was translated into new enthusiasm for the concept of a labor party. There was a pervasive sense in union ranks that the New Deal had collapsed and that the country was caught in a wave of reaction, exemplified by the passage of the anti-labor Smith-Connally Act in 1943. In the UAW the Mazey-ites, with supporters in fifty locals, were the most committed to the creation of an independent labor party. In 1943, they took over the almost moribund Michigan Labor's Nonpartisan League, revitalized it, and changed its name to the Progressive Labor League with the declared purpose of creating a state labor party as soon as possible. The Dubinsky (ILGWU) wing of the American Labor Party in New York, which was engaged in a fierce battle with the Hillman–CP 'left wing', was advocating a state-by-state expansion of the ALP. Dubinsky had not the slightest desire to challenge FDR's national leadership, but he was dissatisfied with the sycophantic subservience of the ALP to the New York Democratic Party. He envisioned a multiplicity of state labor parties which would allow the trade-union bureaucracy to exert more forceful and independent leverage vis-à-vis local and state Democratic apparatuses. Although Dubinsky and the UAW dissidents were motivated by different visions (Mazey and his friends were much further to the left — peripherally influenced by Trotskyism), their mutual interests in fostering a more independent labor politics propelled them in a similar direction.[44] Clearly this renewal of third-party agitation, connected as it was with the massive grassroots upheaval against the bureaucratization and incipient statification of the unions, offered the best prospects since 1937 for the reconstitution of a socialist current in the working class.

Tragically, no large, industrially implanted left cadre were available to co-ordinate the struggle against the no-strike pledge and to nurture the various seedlings of independent political action. The Communists possessed the only left organization of sufficient size and resources, but they were adamantly opposed to the wildcat movement and to its political offshoots. The CP had moved so far to the right since 1941 in support of the war effort, that the traditional left-right spectrum no longer accurately measured the real differences between factions of the CIO. The Browder leadership surpassed the most reactionary layers of the bureaucracy in its advocacy of speed-up and piecework; and when

---

[43] Lichtenstein, pp. 235–237; see also his University of California PhD Thesis (1974), 'Industrial Unionism Under the No-Strike Pledge', pp. 371–73.

[44] Lichtenstein, 'Industrial Unionism', pp. 432, 536–53.

rank-and-file workers struck for higher wages or against inhuman conditions on the assembly lines, the party was the first to defend the no-strike pledge.[45] It also consistently supported the Murray–Hillman leadership in its efforts to crack down on 'divisive' third-party currents within the CIO. In Michigan, the Communist-dominated Industrial Union Councils fought tooth and nail against Mazey's attempts to float a state labor party, while in New York the CP collaborated with Hillman in reducing the ALP to an uncritical and purely dependent appendage of the regular Democratic Party.[46] Finally, in 1944, Browderism reached its *reductio ad absurdum* with the formal dissolution of the Party and the adoption of the so-called 'Teheran Line' with its illusions of a permanent pacification of the class struggle and a postwar Soviet-American alliance.

The Communists' abdication of leadership opened the way for anti-communist forces within the CIO to manipulate rank-and-file unrest to their own factional advantage. The later postwar destruction of the CIO's trade-union influence can only be understood against the background of its isolation from wartime strike currents and its dependence upon inter-bureaucratic politics. Within the important United Electrical Workers (UE), for example, anti-Communist dissident James Carey and his Jesuit-led allies from the American Catholic Trade Unionists (ACTU) (who modeled their organization on CP factory cells) profited from grass-roots dissatisfaction with the Communist-dominated international leadership. In the UAW, the explosive issues of incentive pay and speed-up — both of which were defended by the Communists and their allies in the Addes-Frankensteen faction — provoked a deep split in the leadership. The Reuther faction alone reoriented itself to the rebellion of the locals and outflanked the Communists and their center allies by appearing as the most militant wing of the national leadership. From 1943 onward, the Reutherites inexorably gained ground at the CP's expense, while also recruiting key rebels like Mazey. Reuther's leadership of the 113-

---

[45] Cochran, pp. 210–11. Typical CP wartime leaflet: 'Advocates of strike threats or strike actions in America in 1945 are SCABS in the war against Hitlerism, they are SCABS against our Armed Forces, they are SCABS against the labor movement', (Cited in Keeran, 'Everything for Victory', p. 23.)

[46] Lichtenstein, 'Industrial Unionism', pp. 544–53. A short-lived labor party, growing out of the Michigan LNPL and inspired by the successes of the Canadian CCF in the 1944 Ontario elections, was launched as the Michigan Commonwealth Federation under the chairmanship of Matthew Hammond, an old MESA activist and president of the fourth largest UAW local in Detroit. See Judah Drob, 'Report on Michigan Commonwealth', *Enquiry*, 2 Fall 1944, pp. 19–24; and Mary and Willard Martinson, 'Commonwealth in Michigan', *Common Sense*, June 1945, pp. 13–14.

day General Motors strike in 1946 was the ultimate masterstroke in this strategy of channeling rank-and-file energy for factional ends. It provided a 'safety-valve' for the accumulated anger of the auto workers while simultaneously consolidating Reuther's organizational hegemony and dismantling the rank-and-file caucus movement which had provided leadership to the wartime wildcats.[47]

The weakness of left influence over wartime labor militancy also diminished one of the few counterweights to the pervasive and growing racism of the white working class in the war plants. At the beginning of rearmament, Blacks had been universally excluded from defense jobs, and it was only after the rise of the 'March on Washington Movement' in 1941 organized by a Black trade unionist, A. Philip Randolph, that Roosevelt reluctantly signed an executive order against job discrimination. Although real job equality was never remotely achieved, significant numbers of Black workers did obtain footholds (usually the worst jobs) in aircraft, vehicle assembly and shipbuilding, where they often worked side by side with newly proletarianized whites from the rural South and Southwest. The result was that the wartime insurgence against working conditions and the no-strike pledge often overlapped with racist attacks on the new Black workers. Between March and June 1943, over 100,000 man-days were lost in a wave of 'hate-strikes' against the upgrading of Black workers. One of the largest occurred at the Packard Works in Detroit during April 1943, when 25,000 whites struck 'in retaliation for a brief sitdown of Blacks protesting their not being promoted'.[48] Two months later, all of Detroit erupted into anti-Black pogroms and riots which took thirty-four lives. A year later, and following innumerable other incidents in shipyards and rubber plants, a massive racist outburst in Philadelphia, sparked by the refusal of white streetcar employees to work with Blacks, forced FDR to send 5000

---

[47] Thus, despite the pivotal role of rank-and-file leaders in the organization of the wartime strike wave, no current with an articulated 'shop-stewardist' perspective survived into the postwar period. Still, employers and union bureaucrats were convinced by the experience of the wartime wildcats that industrial stability required the replacement of voluntary rank-and-file representatives by more 'responsible' full-time officials. The 1946 auto contract, for example, replaced working shop stewards (one per twenty-four workers) with full-time union 'committeemen' (representing hundreds of workers). This tendential decomposition and bureaucratization of rank-and-file leadership, together with the anti-communist purges of the late forties, was a major factor in the erosion of militancy in the postwar period. In contrast to the British case, where the war re-invigorated the shop steward movement with decisive repercussions for the postwar class struggle, American unionism became even more singularly distinguished by its high density of bureaucrats and relatively low density of shop-floor activists. (See Chapter 3, p. 117.)

[48] Cochran, pp. 221–223.

federal troops to restore order. Anti-Black virulence also undermined the CIO's attempt at its greatest political coup — UAW leader Richard Frankensteen's campaign for the mayoralty of Detroit in 1945. Frankensteen's predicted victory was snatched from under his nose by the defection of white auto workers protesting the CIO's endorsement of the federal Fair Employment Practices Committee.[49] Other examples could be given of how wartime labor militancy was infiltrated by racism; unlike the 1933-37 strike wave which had produced a profoundly unifying dynamic within the factory working class, the 1943–45 strikes vented frustration and anger without socializing the new workers in a common 'culture of struggle' or assimilating their racial and sexual divisions. The racism of the white industrial working class would remain — as we shall see later — the Achilles heel of the CIO's efforts to transform national politics.

IV. The CIO's Political Action Committee

Thus far, we have been primarily concerned with the various unsuccessful attempts to build a third party on the basis of industrial unionism, and have skirted the question of the CIO's actual relationship to the Democratic Party. For some commentators, however, the watershed in American labor history was the trade union movement's entry into the Democratic Party as its liberal pole. It has even been argued that the debate about the unique 'failure of Socialism' in the United States is spurious to the extent that the Democratic Party itself has become a surrogate social democracy. David Greenstone, in one of the few studies which has explicitly focused on the interrelationships between trade-union militancy and political mobilization, takes the nuanced position that the labor-Democratic coalition has constituted 'a partial equivalence to the social-democratic-trade-union alliances in much of Western Europe'.[50] Michael Harrington has more explicitly proposed that there exists a full correspondence or functional homology between the labor wing of the Democrats and European social democracy: 'The most bizarre fact of all: that there is a mass social democratic movement in America today in a pro-capitalist, anti-socialist disguise.'[51]

---

[49] Philip Foner, *Organized Labor and the Black Worker*, New York 1974, pp. 221–223; and James Caldwell Foster, *The Union Politic: The CIO's Political Action Committee*, Columbus (Mo.) 1975, p. 59 (the Frankensteen campaign).

[50] J. David Greenstone, *Labor in American Politics*, New York 1969, p. 361.

[51] Michael Harrington, *Socialism*, New York 1972, p. 132.

How reasonable is this 'bizarre fact'? Has the integration of the trade-union movement into the Democratic Party produced, even tendentially, a peculiarly American version of social democracy in capitalist garb? A brief critical sketch of the history of the CIO's troubled alliances with the Roosevelt and Truman regimes will clarify the extent to which labor succeeded in instrumentalizing its vital political objectives through the Democratic Party.

The political alliance between the CIO and the Democrats dates, of course, from the formation of Labor's Nonpartisan League in 1936; but the real institutional coalescence of the two only permanently took hold in 1944, with the launching of the Political Action Committee (PAC) as the CIO's new campaign apparatus. The PAC was created in response to parallel crises in the party and the CIO. On the Democratic side, the party had suffered a serious defeat in the 1942 Congressional elections with the defection of most of the Midwest to the Republicans. Within the reduced New Deal alliance, the urban vote was correspondingly more crucial than ever, but, as Clark Clifford warned Roosevelt in a secret 1943 note, the big city Democratic machines were in 'profound crisis' and could no longer reliably guarantee the delivery of the ethnic working-class vote.[52] The debilitation of the machines was partially due to the atrophy of their patronage resources following the increasing federalization of relief and employment, and partially due to the success of industrial unionism in weakening traditional dependencies between workers and wardheelers. Roosevelt and his chief politicos thus attached priority to the creation of a trade-union political apparatus which could compensate for the increasing electoral deficiencies of the boss system, while also extending Democratic hegemony to the newer industrial centers in the South and West.

On the CIO side, a great deal of soul-searching had taken place in the wake of the humiliating failures of its congressional lobbies and its relative marginalization in the councils of the war economy. The need for a new political strategy was given special urgency in June 1943 with the passage of the Smith-Connally Act authorizing presidential takeovers of strike-torn industries and banning direct union political contributions. The worst suspicions of Murray and Hillman were aroused by the knowledge that 'the AFL's chief lobbyist, John Frey had secretly allowed a number of pro-AFL congressmen to vote with the majority in overriding President Roosevelt's veto.'[53] They saw the specter of an AFL-conservative alliance armed with the power to

---

[52] Cochran, p. 237
[53] Foster, *The Union Politic*, p. 12.

hamstring or even roll back industrial unionism. At the same time they were disturbed by the pro-labor party rumblings within their own ranks, particularly to the extent that these were coming from the same dissident corners responsible for the wildcat movement. The essence of the CIO's political problems, as the Executive Board saw it, was its failure to politicize deeply its membership. Voter non-participation was notoriously high in the industrial working class, and the wartime recomposition of the labor force made the situation even worse. A pre-election survey of UAW locals in Detroit revealed that barely 30 per cent of the membership was registered to vote.[54] The goal of the CIO in establishing PACs on a national and local basis was to create a new 'CIO voter' whose adherence to the New Deal wing of the Democratic Party would become as natural and reliable as that of a British laborite or European social democrat. The PACs aimed to achieve this through massive voter registration campaigns and the creation of a permanent army of precinct workers.

Leftists and liberals welcomed the PAC as a 'revival of the popular front' and 'the last great hope of the New Deal'. Although a few dreamed from time to time that the PAC might ultimately create the nucleus of a future labor party, the more widely embraced view was that it was the vehicle for establishing liberal supremacy within the Democratic Party. The CIO leadership, the Communists, and a broad spectrum of 'progressives' all agreed that the formation of the PAC was part of a process of realignment that would eventually rally labor, New Dealers, and progressive Republicans into a single liberal party, while forcing Bourbon Democrats and the Republican mainstream to regroup in a second, conservative party. It was generally held that such a realignment was the indispensable precondition for resuming the march of reform and breaking through the intractable roadblock that had been created by the collusion of Southern Democrats with the Republicans since 1938.

The CIO invested tremendous energy and resources into building the PAC, and great claims were made for its role in the Democratic success of 1944. The new grassroots campaign machinery with its tens of thousands of campaign workers was indisputably vital to the demo-crats, but the CIO gained surprisingly little in exchange. This was partially due to the PAC's reluctance, under Hillman's leadership, to go into the trenches to defend the New Deal or to extract any meaningful *quid pro quo* from Roosevelt. Specifically, the struggle between the right and liberal wings of the Democratic Party had become focused on

---

[54] Riker, 'The CIO in Politics', p. 163.

Vice-President Wallace's quest for renomination. Wallace — an odd fish even by the standards of American politics — had emerged as the champion of beleaguered New Dealers; almost alone in the administration he continued with religious zeal to defend regional planning, to make populist attacks on monopoly, and to advocate the CIO-sponsored proposal for an 'Economic Bill of Rights'. With FDR in failing health, the Southern conservative wing (which supported Byrnes) and the big city machines (who supported Truman) were united in their opposition to Wallace's renomination as heir apparent. Although the stakes were clear, the CIO leadership hesitated to challenge the power of the machine bosses openly, and, as Markowitz observes, 'Hillman made no attempt to apply pressure on Roosevelt for the Wallace candidacy'.[55] The result was tacit CIO endorsement of Senator Truman, protégé of the corrupt Pendergast machine in Kansas City, and the defeat of Wallace.

The PAC's failure to defend Wallace was the prelude to a series of further defeats over federal reconversion policy, as the supposedly 'progressive' 79th Congress repeatedly gave way to the corporations on tax policy and disabled welfare and employment legislation.[56] Tax concessions were particularly significant, since they allowed corporations that showed losses after the war — as a result of strikes, for instance — to claim rebates from their wartime excess profits tax. This was little more than a publicly financed war-chest for the corporate showdown with the unions that was universally anticipated after V-J Day. The attack on labor, however, was to take a different form from the employers' offensive at the end of World War One. Rather than seeking to roll back unionism in mass production industries altogether, as had the earlier 'American Plan', the strategy of big business in the Truman years pivoted around the containment of industrial unionism within institutional constraints that harmonized collective bargaining with the restoration of managerial control over the labor process. At

---

[55] Markowitz, *Peoples' Century*, pp. 97–98. According to Markowitz, the 1944 Convention 'was primarily an example of Roosevelt's failure to transform the Democratic Party into a liberal-labor party ... The Truman victory was the nadir of Rooseveltian politics'. (116).

[56] The contrast with Britain under the Labour government puts the failure of the PAC in sharper relief: 'Even when wages were good, the American worker did not receive the protection afforded ... his British counterpart: a guaranteed forty-hour week, programs for reemploying displaced workers, separation and relocation pay, preservation of peacetime seniority for those transferring to war work, and an updated social security program'. (Paul Koistinen, 'Mobilizing the World War II Economy: Labor and the Industrial-Military Alliance', *Pacific Historical Review*, 42, 1973, p. 469.)

Truman's ill-fated National Labor–Management Conference in October 1945, the business delegation, while accepting the utility of collective bargaining in the abstract, 'placed managerial inviolability at the center of its program for postwar labor relations'.[57] Over a decade of intermittent rank-and-file guerrilla warfare, spiced with sitdowns and wildcats, had eroded the formerly despotic powers of foremen and line supervisors. Rejecting the CIO's warmed-over pleas for more 'industrial democracy', the front-line corporations in auto, steel and electrical manufacture adopted a plan of battle which, by maintaining a hard position on wages, aimed purposefully to provoke long, draining strikes to deflate grassroots militancy. Ultimately the corporations hoped to force the unions to accept a tough trade-off between wage increases and control over working conditions. In particular they wanted strong curbs on the role of rank-and-file leadership, the restriction of the right to strike, and long, multi-year contracts.

The explosion, when it came in the late fall of 1945, was bigger than any previous strike wave in American history, and it wreaked havoc with relations between the CIO and the Democratic Party. In the year after V-J Day, over five million workers hit the picket line, and by the end of January 1946, the industrial core of the economy was virtually at a standstill as the auto, steel, electrical and packinghouse workers were simultaneously on strike. As Art Preis points out, 'for the number of strikers, their weight in industry and duration of struggle, the 1945–46 strike wave in the U.S. surpassed anything of its kind in any capitalist country, including the British General Strike of 1926'.[58] In contrast to 1936–37 or even 1941, however, there was minimal rank-and-file initiative in the organization of the strikes. The corporations generally did not attempt to run scabs, and the CIO bureaucracy was in firm control of day to day tactics. Indeed, as we have already seen in the case of Reuther and the GM strike, there was a deliberate strategy to use the strikes to let off steam in the ranks while centralizing further the power of the national union leaderships. In the one case of 'run-away' militancy — the several city-wide stoppages led by militant local CIO Industrial Councils — the Executive Board clamped down ruthlessly, stripping the Councils of their autonomy and eliminating their local democratic control.

[57] David Brody, 'The New Deal and World War Two', in John Braeman, et. al. (eds.), *The New Deal: The National Level* (Volume One), Columbus 1975, p. 286. Cf. Derber, *Industrial Democracy*, pp. 394–399; and Barton Bernstein, 'The Truman Administration and Its Reconversion Wage Policy', *Labor History*, VI, 1965, pp. 228–230.

[58] Preis, *Labor's Giant Step*, p. 276.

Truman responded to the labor movement's plea for support by enjoining the miners, threatening to conscript the railroad workers, and calling for broad repressive powers. This anti-labor stance, reminiscent of Wilson's sharp turn in 1919, coincided with a purge of Wallace (now Secretary of Commerce) and other former members of the New Deal inner circle. As a result, the political strategy of the CIO and their liberal supporters was temporarily thrown into chaos. Murray was briefly and uncomfortably forced, for the only time, into opposing the administration, while his erstwhile Communist allies, shedding their longheld position that the Democratic Party was '*the* popular front', were gingerly exploring the possibility of a left-liberal third party supported by units of the PAC and its non-labor affiliates. Not to be outflanked by the Communists, Walter Reuther, Norman Thomas, John Dewey, and a host of other putative social democrats came together in May 1946 as the shortlived 'National Educational Committee for a New Party'. Neither the Communists nor the social democrats, however, proposed an immediate political break with the Democrats; instead, they counted on PAC successes in the 1946 congressional elections to shift the balance of power to the progressive pole. But millions of workers, alienated by Truman's return to government strike-breaking and his failure to control the rising cost of living, ignored the pleas of the PAC and boycotted the congressional elections of 1946. In the face of the PAC's inability to demarcate itself clearly from administration, the 'new labor voter' proved chimerical. With the participation of a mere 30 per cent of the electorate, CIO candidates were crushed, and the first Republican Congress since Hoover took office over the decimated ranks of the New Deal Democrats. In stark contrast to the contemporary accomplishments of Attlee's Labour government in Britain, the first postwar US congress set aside earlier promises of an 'Economic Bill of Rights' in order to concentrate on the passage of the Taft–Hartley Act of 1947 and the salvation of anti-Communist regimes in Greece and China.

The Taft–Hartley Act codified the employers' aims of deradicalizing the CIO and of legally suppressing the most effective weapons of labor solidarity. It accomplished the former by imposing the requirement of anti-communist disclaimers for trade union officials, and the latter by outlawing sympathy strikes, supportive boycotts, wildcats and mass picketing (the sitdown had already been banned by the Supreme Court in 1938). Taft Hartley also renewed the Smith–Connally Act's prohibition against union campaign contributions, in a clear attack on the operations of the PAC. Recognizing the gravity of the threat posed by the implementation of Taft-Hartley, Lewis's miners and the Commun-

88

ist-led United Electrical Workers immediately proposed a campaign of non-compliance augmented by mass mobilizations and, perhaps, even a general strike.[59] Murray and the other CIO chieftains were thus confronted with the dilemma of crossing two rubicons at once: on the one hand they had to decide whether to defy Taft–Hartley and lead the industrial unions outside the pale of the National Labor Relations Act; on the other, they had to choose whether to support the popular front groundswell behind Wallace which, with the support of the Communists, was becoming a movement for a third party.

In the event, however, they declined either to go back into the streets or to join with the embryonic third-party forces. Instead, they chose to reconsolidate their shaken alliance with Truman and the national Democratic Party, allowing the CIO in the process to become an integral component of the administration's escalating anticommunist crusade. Many different pressures were operating to force Murray and the CIO 'center' to repudiate their longtime allies on the left. In an era of bureaucratic retrenchment, for example, there was no longer the same practical need for the Communists and their particular skills at mobilization and propaganda. The principal historian of the PAC has argued that Murray's transition to open, militant anti-communism in 1948, and his temporary alliance with the Cold War liberals of the Americans for Democratic Action (ADA) were basically pragmatic maneuvers to derail the Wallace movement, which he saw threatening PAC's efforts to lobby for a legislative repeal of Taft–Hartley. 'A liberal, Democratic President was the CIO's foremost objective for 1948. Rejection of the Communists and acceptance of the ADA was but a means to achieve that end'.[60] Following the same logic, the CIO's one-sided and obsequious tie to the Presidential level of the Democratic Party — like Gompers's earlier reliance upon Wilson — bound it naturally to the twists and turns of American foreign policy from the ephemeral 'one world' enthusiasms of the Teheran Conference period to the nuclear imperialism of the late forties.

But there were deeper reasons for the sudden riptide of anticommunism which pulled asunder the decade-old 'left-center' alliance

---

[59] Lewis, once a strong advocate of state intervention and reliance upon the Democrats, had since 1940 become increasingly disenchanted with the role of the government in industrial relations. By 1947 he had become a solitary champion of the return to strict Gompersian *laissez-faire*, favoring the repeal not only of Taft–Hartley, but of the Wagner Act as well. See Melvyn Dubofsky and Warren Van Tine, *John L. Lewis*, New York 1977, pp. 475–476.

[60] Foster, *The Union Politic*, p. 92.

within the CIO. The integration of the unions into the Cold War consensus was correlated with a far-reaching rearticulation of the cultural universe of the American working class. The Second World War, in particular, was a watershed of enormous importance — comparable to the 1890s[61] — in reforging blue-collar identity. Earlier I contrasted the immanently solidaristic and perhaps even social-democratic thrust of the CIO with the recharged conservatism of the AFL, as well as with the anomie and racial conflict produced by the wartime recomposition of the industrial working class. By themselves these divergent ideological currents only denoted the contradictory possibilities of the period and the highly unsettled, transitional state of proletarian consciousness. What ultimately created the basis for a new cultural cohesion within the postwar American working class was the rise of wartime nationalism. It must be recalled that 'Americanism' had previously served as a watchword for successive nativist crusades, as broad strata of the 'new immigrants' stubbornly clung to their old ethnic identifications and patriotisms, refusing to submit to a coercive cultural assimilation. Even the savage official jingoism of the First World War, far from welding together a nationalist unity within the working class, further divided it through its antagonism to the Germans, alienation of the Irish, and persecution of more radical immigrant groups. The significance of the new nationalism that had been incubated in the thirties and fanned to a fever pitch by the war mobilization was that it was broadly inclusive of the *white* working class (Blacks, Mexicans and Japanese-Americans need not apply) and, moreover, was propped-up by powerful material supports. The latter included the job-generating capacities of the permanent arms economy, and, in a more general sense, the new structural position of the American working class within a postwar world economy dominated by US capital. With the adoption of peacetime universal military service in the late 1940s — whose burden fell almost entirely on working-class youth via a system of class-biased educational and occupational deferments — the American state acquired a potent instrument for inculcating patriotic, anti-radical and pro-authoritarian attitudes in each generation of workers.

Ironically, 'progressives' and popular front leftists were among the most zealous missionaries of the new nationalism. Unlike the First World War, when there was courageous and massive resistance to militarism by the Socialist Party and the IWW, the majority of the left of the forties uncritically supported Roosevelt's wartime leadership. The

[61] See Chapter 1, pp. 37-39.

Communists, in particular, outdid themselves in twisting anti-fascism into a *raison d'être* for promoting official chauvinism — to the point of actually supporting the 'relocation' of the entire Japanese population of the West Coast into concentration camps in 1942. The CP's attempt to manipulate a camouflage patriotism, like its abdication of leadership in the wartime wildcats, only further disarmed the left before the CIO bureaucracy once the new nationalism was redeployed in 1946–47 as a virulent anti-communism.

Cold War jingoism had its most dramatic impact and sunk its deepest roots in precisely those sectors of the working class that had previously been most insulated from patriotic hysteria. Frequently overlooked in analyses of the postwar working class was the alarming impact of the Red Army's entry into Eastern Europe upon the Slavs and Hungarians who composed perhaps half of the CIO membership. The left-wing ethnic organizations which had played such a heroic role in the early organization of the CIO, and which had been one of the most important sources of socialist influence on the industrial working class, either collapsed or were marginalized by a huge recrudescence of right-wing, anti-communist nationalism in each ethnic community.[62] This recasting of ethnic culture in a fanatical anti-communist mold, and its insertion into a new national patriotic consensus, was largely catalyzed through the Catholic Church and the myriad organizational tentacles (ranging from ACTU to the Knights of Columbus) it extended into the daily life of the Catholic working class.

When Philip Murray and his chief adviser, Andrew Biemiller, sat down to design a new strategy for the PAC in 1948, their first consideration was how to recapture the Slavic and Catholic working-class vote. To accomplish this they emphasized the CIO's strong support for the Marshall Plan and in general for Truman's anti-communist foreign policy. At the same time, they made the insistent pragmatic appeal that only the re-election of the purportedly chastened Truman would guarantee the passage of long blocked social legislation and the repeal of Taft–Hartley. Through herculean efforts involving armies of trade-union precinct workers, the PAC, together with the AFL's newly formed Labor's League for Political Education (UPE), mobilised the (relatively) largest class vote in American history and gave Truman his seemingly

---

[62] This rightward drift of ethnic nationalism had been foreshadowed in 1939 by the traumatic impact of the Russo-Finnish War in alienating most of the Finno-American working class from its traditional socialist sympathies. For the collapse of farmer-laborism in its former Finnish bastion of the Eighth Congressional District of Minnesota, see Gieske, *Minnesota Farmer-Laborism*, p. 298.

impossible victory over Dewey. The embattled Communists, on the other hand, joined with a rump of popular-front liberals behind Wallace's quixotic campaign against the Cold War. Unable to rally rank-and-file support even in the unions which they still led, they attracted barely 3.5 per cent of the CIO vote.[63]

If the Democratic victory of 1948 was the labor movement's most stunning electoral success, it was also the most hollow. The supposed mandate for a 'Fair Deal' which had been given to Truman and the 'liberal' 81st Congress proved to be a license for compromise and dilution of the reform program. As proposals for national health insurance were simply shelved (where they remain today), Truman sided repeatedly with private construction interests to transform the Housing Act of 1949 into a subsidy for business and middle-class home owners, rather than the public housing program for the working class which the CIO had originally envisaged. Meanwhile, in the classic pattern of FDR's second administration, Truman yielded to the congressional power of the Dixiecrats and began to sacrifice liberal items in his domestic program to secure Southern support for his Cold War policies. Not surprisingly, the first to go were the much vaunted civil rights reforms promised in the 1948 Democratic platform; next was the repeal of Taft--Hartley, the first priority of the PAC program. As the outbreak of the Korean War closed down shop on domestic reformism and brought the Nixons and McCarthys to power in Washington, the CIO found itself once more outside in the cold and empty-handed.[64]

While the CIO bureaucracy was losing the legislative battle in Washington, some of the largest industrial unions were being bled white by labor's 'second civil war' — the struggle between the right and left wings of the CIO. The reluctance of the CIO mainstream to accept John L. Lewis's proposal for mass action against Taft–Hartley is more understandable when it is recognized that many of the same unions were actually exploiting the anti-communist provisions of the act to raid other left-led CIO unions. In 1948, the UAW launched major piratical forays against both the Farm Equipment Union and the United Electrical Workers (UE). After the 1949 expulsion of eleven allegedly Communist-controlled unions from the CIO, these raids turned into a cannibal feast. The most tragic case was the forced dismemberment of

[63] Markowitz, *Peoples' Century*, p. 281.
[64] See Harvey Sitkoff, 'Years of the Locust', in Richard S. Kirkendall, *The Truman Period as a Research Field: A Reappraisal, 1972*, Columbia (Mo.) 1974, pp. 95–104. Sitkoff points out that the military-industrial complex created during World War II was consolidated by Truman's corporate-dominated economic cabinet (Snyder, Harriman, Allen, and so on) pp. 87–90.

the UE, the third largest union in the CIO and traditionally one of the most militant. In 1948, the UE had been able to negotiate from a position of strength, representing all the workers in the electrical manufacturing industry; by 1953, after five years of raids and the chartering of a rival international, some *eighty* different unions had parcellized the UE's jurisdiction and were bargaining for a membership only half the size of the 1948 UE rank-and-file. While raiding was in progress, employers were given a free hand to conduct long-sought purges of the militant local and secondary leaderships. On a single day in Chicago, for example, three electrical companies fired more than five hundred UE officials and stewards (and were later upheld by the NLRB under provisions of Taft–Hartley).[65]

The fratricide within the CIO was also the principal cause of the collapse of 'Operation Dixie', its Southern organizing campaign. When it was launched in 1946, Murray called it the 'most important drive of its kind ever undertaken by any labor organization in the history of this country'.[66] The original strategy had envisioned a two-stage process of mobilizing Southern workers: first concentrating organizing efforts against key regional open-shop employers, followed by the political consolidation of the new recruits into local PACs. Implicit in this second stage of 'Operation Dixie' was an ambitious attempt to reshape the national balance of political forces by overthrowing Bourbon power through massive voter registration and the cultivation of a Southern labor electorate. But Operation Dixie barely got off the ground before it was embroiled in the CIO's internecine feuds and anti-communist purges. The crisis came to a head in Alabama when Murray's own Steel Workers tried to break a local of the leftish Mine, Mill and Smelter Workers that represented militant Black iron miners around Birmingham. Anti-communism blended with overt racism as the white Steel Workers leadership terrorized rank-and-file iron miners and prevented Black CIO members from voting.[67] Similar scenarios were enacted in textile and tobacco, and, as Emspak has noted: 'Instead of devoting resources to organizing new people, the

---

[65] Emspak, 'Break-Up of the CIO'. pp. 355–58.

[66] Quoted in F. Ray Marshall, *Labor in the South*, Cambridge (Mass.) 1967, p. 254.

[67] Marshall, pp. 258–260; and Nell Irvin Painter, *The Narrative of Hosea Hudson*, Cambridge (Mass.) 1979, pp. 308 and 329–334. Hudson was an astonishingly brave Black Communist who weathered two decades of beatings, jailings and blacklisting in the Alabama labor movement. In his opinion, 'the steelworkers' leadership wasn't lukewarm on fighting for the rights of the Negro people. It was worse than lukewarm'. (329) In addition, he emphasizes the exclusion of Blacks from the Alabama CIO Executive Board and PAC's refusal to register Blacks to vote in Gadsden and other industrial towns (pp. 331–34).

CIO devoted its efforts to disorganizing existing unions. In effect the civil war within the CIO spelled the end of any substantive organizing in the South'.[68]

V. The Balance Sheet

In 1952, following Eisenhower's defeat of Stevenson, Jack Kroll, the head of the PAC, sent Walter Reuther a confidential memo in which he sketched a dismal balance sheet of the CIO-Democratic alliance. According to Kroll, the CIO, despite its heroic and expensive exertions for the Democratic Party, still found itself bargaining 'much as it would with an employer'. He pointed out that unlike the British TUC's relationship with the Labour Party, the CIO did not possess a single vote in the inner councils of the party, nor any voice in its day to day operation. Its relationship to the congressional Democratic Party was even worse, since Southern conservatives, rather than Northern liberals, held the levers of power in the House and the Senate: 'Thus, the congressional branch of the party could be completely opposed to pro-union legislation, even though the national convention, the democratically-chosen voice of the party, had gone on record as favoring such legislation'. Kroll cited the particularly galling example of Dixiecrat support for anti-union 'right to work' legislation. In sum Kroll argued that the situation had become 'intolerable' and that the CIO should scuttle the status quo as soon as possible for a new political policy more congruent with its interests. His recommendations — never debated — ranged from abandoning politics altogether to concentrating on running CIO members for office.[69]

Kroll's pessimistic assessment was disingenuous to the extent that it elided the material advantages that the labor bureaucracy exacted from the coalition (political appointments and local patronage power), but it otherwise remains a compelling confession of the bankruptcy of the Democratic road to labor reformism. The harnessing of industrial unionism to renovate the vote-gathering machinery of the Democratic Party was an effective instrumental relationship in one direction only. This fundamental disequilibrium in the process of power brokerage which so frustrated the CIO leadership was the inevitable result of the absence of three factors that were the necessary preconditions for any 'social-democratization' of the Democratic Party: (1) labor unity; (2) a

---

[68] Emspak, p. 301.
[69] Foster, *The Union Politic*, pp. 199–200.

94

class realignment of the political system; and (3) the elusive 'CIO voter'.

As we have seen, the 'civil wars' between the AFL and CIO, and later within the CIO itself, undermined every attempt to establish a liberal bloc in American politics or to develop the basis for independent political action by labor. Without minimizing the purely political or inter-bureaucratic aspects of the schism between the AFL and CIO, the underlying determinant was still the persistence of those divisions between the craft and mass-production workforces that had polarized the American proletariat since the turn of the century. As we have seen, the surprising resurgence of the AFL in the late thirties behind the banners of labor-patriotism and anti-communism exploited the residual prejudices of the native and old-immigrant stock workers against the second-generation ethnic laborers in the mines and factories. Working-class disunity was further augmented by the pervasive white racism which all too frequently subverted wartime industrial militancy into 'hate strikes' against Black newcomers. Finally, the Cold War dramatically strengthened the hegemony of Catholicism and right-wing ethnic nationalism in broad sectors of the industrial working class.

Yet these centrifugal tendencies within the labor movement might not have been decisive if the CIO had preserved the momentum of its earlier organizing drives. The stark reality was, however, that industrial unionism was only a partial success, and that its defeats were as fateful as its victories in shaping the subsequent history of the labor movement. The anti-communist inquisition within the CIO, in particular, produced a staggering series of losses: the 'deunionization' of the electrical and textile industries,[70] the destruction of promising beachheads in the tertiary, professional and agricultural sectors, and the collapse of 'Operation Dixie'. These reverses, in turn, had long-range effects on the structure of both the working class and of the trade-union movement in the 50's and 60's.

First, the failure to extend union organization to the rapidly expanding female clerical proletariat and to Southern workers in general formed the basis for a new hierarchization and segmentation of the working class. Henceforth, the old ethno-religious dimension of working-class stratification, although scarcely abolished,[71] lost primacy to racial and sexual divisions in the workforce. Similarly, skill differen-

---

[70] Some indicative statistics: textile unionization fell from 20 per cent in 1948 to 7 per cent in 1962, while overall trade union membership in the rapidly industrializing South declined from 43.1 per cent of non-agricultural workers in 1953, to 29.5 per cent in 1964. Marshall, pp. 299, 302.

[71] The internal structure of the American working class still preserves the visible traces of its earlier stratification. The unionization of basic industry allowed workers of 'new immigrant' stock to rise above subsistence level and to attain the social norm of consump-

tials became relatively less important overall than union organization and the incorporation into the generalized norm of mass consumption from which most Blacks, Southern workers and female breadwinners were excluded.

Secondly, the powerful solidaristic principles of the original CIO increasingly gave way to the 'new model' business unionism which the Teamsters, Machinists, and other large AFL unions had pioneered in the late thirties out of an unholy amalgam of craft and industrial union principles. In his *False Promises*, Stanley Aronowitz has demonstrated how craft exclusivism and segmentation re-established themselves within the postwar CIO unions. Especially destructive of intra-union solidarity were the establishment of separate elections for different skill categories, of separate departmental seniority lists (particularly discriminatory against Blacks and women), and of percentage (rather than 'flat rate') wage bargaining. The result was the reinforcement of 'the social divisions within the factories based on ethnicity, race, and sex' so that 'the solidarity achieved during the CIO drive two decades earlier was destroyed'.[72] This erosion of the distinctive identity of the industrial unions, as well as the relative stagnation of their growth, cleared the way for a political, and then organizational rapprochment with the AFL which was as much a surrender to the legacy of Gomperism as a victory for trade union unity.[73]

Labor disunity also contributed to the failure of the strategy of electoral realignment which a majority of social democrats and labor reformers had embraced in preference to building an independent labor party. As we have seen, relations between the two wings of the labor movement were at their nadir in 1937–38, precisely when Roosevelt tried to rally liberals in his sole attempt to dislodge the most reactionary wing of the Democratic Party. But the Democratic right

tion represented by home ownership and the private automobile. By every other measure, however, their social mobility has been agonizingly slow; in the steel industry, for example, Slavic foremen and supervisors only began to appear in numbers during the early 1960s. The retarded occupational mobility of ethnic white industrial workers has variously been a spur to coalition-building wih even more victimized Black and Hispanic workers, and on other occasions, the stimulus to ferocious resistance to the upgrading of non-white labor. See John Bodnar, *Immigration and Industrialization*, Pittsburg 197, pp. 146–7.

[72] Aronowitz, *False Promises*, New York 1973, p. 182.

[73] The AFL entered the merger negotiations from a position of strength. Since 1953, its share of national union membership had increased from 62 per cent to 64 per cent, while the CIO's had actually fallen from 23 per cent to 20 per cent. This balance of forces was reflected in the dominance of former AFL officials on the unified Executive Council (17 ex-AFL versus 10 ex-CIO), as well as in key political action, lobbying, and foreign policy units. See Graham K. Wilson, *Unions in American National Politics*, London 1979, pp. 7–11.

wing easily weathered Roosevelt's half-hearted purges, and through its new alliance with congressional Republicans, actually buttressed its power. This congressional united front of Bourbons and Republicans held the balance of legislative power for most of a decade after 1937, and provided the indispensable political machinery for the increasingly bold corporate counter-offensive against the CIO. In order to congeal a majority around their foreign policy initiatives, both Roosevelt and Truman were forced to woo the Democratic right with compromises on social programs and civil rights. Thus from 1938 onwards, the maintenance of a bipartisan consensus in support of American imperialism overrode the exigencies of social legislation or political reform. By accepting the discipline of the Cold War mobilization, the unions and their liberal allies surrendered independence of action and ratified the subordination of social welfare to global anti-communism.

Although the CIO made periodic attempts to outflank the Democratic right by organizing its own popular alliances with working farmers and sympathetic liberal professionals, it failed to make a sustained attack on the citadel of right-wing political power: the rotten-borough system of the South. The entire edifice of Democratic conservatism, as well as the interlinked corporate and Cold War political alliances which it sustained, ultimately rested on the linchpins of Black disenfranchisement and the poll tax.[74] In the one-party system of the deep South, a kind of Jacksonian revolution in reverse, reacting to the threat of populism in the 1890s, had taken the vote away from the majority of the laboring population — white as well as Black. In the 1938 congressional elections, for example, forty-three Southern congressmen were elected without a *single* oppositional vote, twenty-six fought an opponent armed with fewer than a hundred ballots, while in twenty-nine districts less than four per cent of the electorate voted. These beneficiaries of the 'white primary', the property qualification, and the two-dollar poll tax, in turn, controlled one-third of the standing committees in Congress and held veto-power over reform legislation.[75]

The enfranchisement of the Southern masses should have been the key to the recomposition of the Democratic Party and the consolidation

---

[74] Blacks found the New Deal bittersweet at best. Although they had decamped from the Republican Party en masse in 1936 to support FDR, they discovered that the Democratic Party remained as white supremacist as ever. Even his own wife's entreaties failed to persuade Roosevelt, ever conscious of his Southern flank, to endorse anti-lynching legislation, much less to support Black voting rights. As a result, fewer than 250,000 new Black voters were added to the electorate in the thirties. See George B. Tindall, *The Emergence of the New South*, Baton Rouge 1967, p. 557.

[75] Dee Brown, 'The South's Belated Revenge', *Common Sense*, April 1938, pp. 15–17.

of a liberal-labor congressional majority. But the problem of suffrage was inextricably bound up with the existence of those two other pillars of class rule in the South: Jim Crow and the open shop. Only a massive unionization campaign closely coordinated with full support for Black civil rights could have conceivably generated the conditions for inter-racial unity and a popular overthrow of Bourbon power. The abandonment of 'Operation Dixie' in the face of systematic repression and the CIO's own internal Cold War contradictions was an almost fatal blow to the once bright hopes for such a labor-based rebellion in the South. At the same time, the national CIO's gradual backtracking on civil rights (a trend again intimately connected with the rise of anti-communism) left the Black movement even more vulnerable to the racist backlash which swept the country in the late forties.[76] This dis-articulation of the labor and Black movements had devastating consequences for both. Its immediate result was to give the ancien regime in Dixie a new lease on life and to allow the Dixiecrat secession-ists of 1948 (who bolted the regular ticket in protest over Truman's civil rights platform) to triumphantly re-establish their power in the Democratic Party during the early 1950s. In the long run it made the civil rights revolution incomparably more difficult and bloody, rein-forced white working-class racism, and forced Black liberation into a more corporatist mold.

Finally, there is the problem of the 'union voter'. The ultimate *raison d'être* of PAC was the politicization of the CIO membership to produce a reliable and disciplined electorate. To achieve this, PAC tried to convince industrial workers that the labor alliance with liberal Democrats was the best political representation of their class interests. It failed to do so in two ways. First, because the Democrats did not usually represent the workers' interests, even their most short-term, defensive interests.

---

[76] Black leaders complained about the absence of Black representation on the national union executives, the CIO's support for avowedly racist candidates in the South, and its failure to mobilize its forces in the fight against the postwar lynch terror. Their central grievance, however, was the CIO's failure to defend the modest wartime gains of Black workers during the period of reconversion. The national CIO leadership rebuffed a Communist-sponsored proposal to adjust seniority lists so that lay-offs would not dispro-portionately victimize Blacks. The result, of course was that Blacks — and women — remained 'the last hired, but first to be fired'. Furthermore, by the time of the expulsion of the left-led unions, the CIO's civil rights stance was losing all but its rhetorical substance. This abdication by the CIO was, in turn, a factor in the inability of Blacks to regain any economic ground during the Korean War boom. See Williamson, *Dangerous Scot*, p. 165; Ray Marshall, *The Negro and Organized Labor*, New York 1965, pp. 46–49; Foner, *Black Worker*, p. 287; and Foster, *The Union Politic*, p. 287.

Repeated experiences of disillusionment and programmatic failure produced cycles of working-class abstentionism and withdrawal from the political system, as in 1942 and 1946; only the threat of complete liquidation of previous reforms provoked high levels of working-class electoral participation, as in the highly-polarized presidential races of 1936 and 1948.[77]

But the PAC also failed because it misunderstood the nature of the bonds that attached the European working-class voter to his party. It is not, after all, merely a felicific calculus of self-interest that translates membership in a labor movement into a profound, hereditary commitment. Even the most anemic labor or social democratic party in Western Europe harvests the working class's deep cultural self-identification with its institutions. To reproduce European-style political class loyalties in the United States was to assume the replication of a similar set of primary identifications with union and party. There were, of course, moments in the thirties and forties when the struggle for industrial unionism seemed to be creating an alternative culture and a new mode of daily life. The sight of the Women's Auxiliary driving the police off the streets of Flint, or the sound of ten thousand Ford strikers singing 'Solidarity Forever', were experiences that transcend the smug equations in latterday textbooks on the 'Dynamics of Wage Determination'. But the overall character of trade-union militancy in the 1930s and 1940s was defined, as Dubofsky has recently emphasized, by the limited, episodic participation of most industrial workers.[78] The wartime recomposition of the working class introduced a basic discontinuity which was reflected in the contrasting internal dynamics and political resonances of the 1934–37 and 1943–46 strike waves. Add to this the persistence of labor disunity, and it is clearer why CIO militancy

---

[77] Indices of the unions' failure to create a cohesive and activist labor electorate: The National Director of COPE (the AFL-CIO successor to PAC and LLPE) estimated in the late fifties that less than 40 per cent of the union membership was registered to vote, while a similar survey by the Amalgamated Clothing Workers in several states found only 20–30 per cent registered. (Sidney Lens, *Crisis of American Labor*, New York 1959, p. 298). In a 1970s comparative study of auto workers around the world, William Form surveyed members of the UAW Oldsmobile local in Lansing, Michigan. He discovered that fully 60 per cent of the rank-and-file disagreed with the political recommendations of COPE and generally did not believe that the union should endorse candidates. Moreover, 40 per cent were registered either as Republicans or 'independents' (William H. Form, *Blue-Collar Stratification*, Princeton 1976, pp. 146–47.) These studies could be interpreted as corroborative evidence for C. Wright Mills's thesis that the two-party system tends inevitably to 'depoliticize' the working class by denying adequate representation of its immediate interests. (Mills, *New Men of Power*, pp. 269–270).

[78] Dubofsky, 'Not So Turbulent Years'.

lacked the experiential power and coherence to create the embryo of a new working-class 'culture'. What was created, instead, was a new nexus of relations and alliances in the workplace that provided sufficient unity to ensure the effectiveness of the union, while outside the plant the working class continued to find its social identity in fragmentary ethnic and racial communities, or in a colonized leisure.[79]

The political strategy of the CIO actually contributed to this attenuation of militancy, as the subordination of the unions to the Democratic apparatus reciprocally conditioned and reinforced the canalization of shopfloor activism into a new legal labyrinth of time contracts, government mediation and legislative lobbying. It was, ironically, John L. Lewis, the original architect of the CIO's subordination to the New Deal, who played the role of a lonely Cassandra to the trade-union bureaucracy in the late forties — reminding them that the real political influence of the unions was ultimately anchored in their capacity to mobilize and sustain mass action at the point of production. Accordingly, he advocated a fighting response to the passage of the Taft–Hartley Act. By relying on backroom lobbies and campaign support for the Democrats instead, the CIO leadership willingly conceded the last vestiges of its political independence and demobilized the rank-and-file militancy that was the source of its own political leverage.[80]

In the absence of unity with the Black movement and a revitalization of rank-and-file participation, the trade unions became the captive political base for an anti-communist 'liberal' wing of the Democratic Party, whose capacity to enact substantive reform was permanently constrained by both the weight of the Democratic right wing and the exigencies of Cold War bipartisanship. The New Deal capture of the labor movement broadened the base of the Democratic Party, but it scarcely transformed it into an analogue of European laborism or social democracy. Indeed, what has been more striking than the discrepancy between labor's role in electoral mobilization and finance, and the meager legislative rewards it has received in return? The survival of Taft–Hartley and the stunting of the welfare state in America are among the most eloquent monuments to labor's failure to 'functional-

---

[79] For intricate analyses of the complex interfaces between industrial unionism and ethnic politics, see Peter Friedlander, *The Emergence of a* UAW *Local*, Pittsburgh 1975; and William Kornblum, *Blue Collar Community*, Chicago 1974.

[80] For a trenchant interpretation of the contemporary crisis of the American labor bureaucracy, see Robert Brenner, 'A New Social Democracy?', *Against the Current*, Fall 1980.

ize' its most vital day to day interests through the Democratic Party.[81]
Even the apparently spectacular revival of organized labor's political
clout during the Kennedy–Johnson administrations in the 1960s now
appears in perspective as a false spring, followed by successive electoral
debacles in the 1970s and a new fragmentation of the trade union
movement.

If the political influence of the AFL-CIO reached an apogee under
Lyndon Johnson's 'Great Society' in the mid-sixties, it was largely
because the labor bureaucracy rode the coat-tails of the civil rights
movement. The militancy of Blacks created political conditions for a
renewal of social reform for the first time since the late forties, while
catalyzing a dramatic surge of unionism in the public sector. The
virulent anti-communism and bellicosity of the AFL-CIO Executive,
however, split up the alliance of liberal forces as the Democratic party
polarized into hawkish and dovish factions in 1968. Following the AFL-
CIO's failure to endorse McGovern's anti-war candidacy in 1972, the
more 'liberal' unions like the Oil Workers and the public employees
(AFSMCE) followed the earlier example of the Auto Workers (which left
the AFL-CIO in 1967) and re-established independent electoral apparatuses. In the 1976 presidential election, the campaign committees of
these unions joined with the UAW to form the 'Labor Clearing House',
a clearly defined liberal caucus linked to the Kennedy wing of the
Democratic Party. Meanwhile, AFL-CIO chief George Meany had been
secretly negotiating with both the Nixon and Ford regimes about the
possibility of COPE's return to a Gompersian strategy of bipartisan brokerage — a gambit which subsequently collapsed in the wake of
Watergate and the general hardening of the economic class struggle in
the 1970s. In 1978, COPE attempted to rally the increasingly divided and
sclerotic trade union movement in a massive lobbying effort for labor
law reform legislation. As we shall see in the next chapter, the defeat of the
COPE drive by an overwhelmingly Democratic congress was organized
labor's worst political reverse since the failure to repeal Taft-Hartley in
1949, and signalled its declining weight in a rapidly changing and
rightward-moving Democratic Party. COPE's further failure in 1980
to stem the Reaganite tide in the industrial heartland was only an
ironic anticlimax as half the rank-and-file stayed home while another

---

[81] 'In 1949, after more than four full terms of Democratic Party rule, the United States
ranked last among industrial capitalist states in social welfare expenditures (44 per cent of
GNP).' (Ira Katznelson, 'Considerations on Social Democracy in the United States',
Comparative Politics, October 1978, p. 84).

quarter voted their lunch pails against a Democratic recession. If an emergent right-wing 'majority' is displacing the old New Deal coalition as the fulcrum of the American electoral system — a hypothesis that will be examined in detail in chapters 4 and 5 below — it is only because forty years of marriage between labor and the Democrats have produced a politically dispirited and alienated working class.

3

The Fall of the House of Labor

In January 1946, Henry Ford II rose at the conference of the Society of Automotive Engineers in Detroit to announce that the class war in the United States had ended: 'We of the Ford Motor Company have no desire to "break the unions", or to turn back the clock ...' Instead, the Ford heir intoned, 'we must look to an improved and increasingly responsible leadership for help in solving the human equation in mass production'. 'Industrial relations', he said, should be conducted with 'the same technical skill and determination that the engineer brings to mechanical problems.'[1]

In the following decades, Ford's hopes for a 'business-like' evolution of industrial relations seemed entirely fulfilled. Administered by a priestly order of arbitrators, mediators and conciliators, collective bargaining constituted a main support of the post-war social order. According to the gospel of Cold War liberalism, promulgated by Galbraith, Hofstadter and Bell, collective bargaining fine-tuned the countervailing influences of management and labor, while expanding the ambit of interest-group democracy into the workplace itself. Moreover, as the editors of *Fortune* pointed out in their famous capitalist manifesto of 1951, the system of private contractual relations between labor and capital, dependent upon only minimal state intervention, represented a particularly 'American' solution to the 'problems of class struggle and proletarian consciousness'.[2] Everywhere during the 1950s and 1960s, progress was reputedly being made on the industrial front, testified to in voluminous academic reports on the 'maturation' of the bargaining system.

The general faith in the inevitable forward march of American industrial relations was so confident and firmly consolidated behind ivy-covered walls, that when the system began to collapse in the early 1980s, many of its chief ideologues denied even the symptoms. Thus John Dunlop, Harvard emeritus, former Secretary of Labor and author of the classic Parsonian analysis of industrial relations as a social

---

[1] Quoted in Howell John Harris, *The Right to Manage*, Madison 1982, p. 146.
[2] See 'The U.S. Labor Movement', chapter four of *USA: The Permanent Revolution*, New York 1951.

'subsystem', refused to acknowledge that the spread of 'concessionary bargaining' following the Chrysler givebacks of 1979 constituted a fundamental change in the labor–management climate. As late as 1982, on the eve of the second wave of concessions in auto and trucking, he assured *Business Week* with magisterial authority: 'It is *not* a major new era and that I am willing to sign my name to.'[3]

But by late 1983, with the Reagan 'recovery' in full swing and a further wave of concessions and wage deceleration cutting through the vitals of the AFL–CIO, even academics had to admit what rank-and-file workers knew firsthand: a veritable earthquake was crumbling the old labor 'peace'. With one-third to one-half of their memberships lost to plant closings, imports or automation, the core industrial unions have surrendered, bit by bit, many of the strategic gains they had won over the last forty years. In industry after industry, the hard-won wage 'patterns' that guaranteed contractual uniformity and preserved effective solidarity between workers in different firms are being destroyed, their place taken by a savage new wage-cutting competition. Within firms, multi-tier wage concessions, which allow employers to pay up to fifty per cent less to new hires, are eroding inter-generational solidarity, ensuring, in the guise of protecting the privileges of seniority, that older workers are more vulnerable to replacement to exactly the extent that younger workers are made more exploitable. Meanwhile, on picket lines, workers in major industries who have chosen, or been forced, to resist the concessionary tide are confronted, for the first time since the 1930s, with scabs, billy clubs and the National Guard. Finally, beyond concessions lies the specter of rapidly approaching deunionization. In such traditionally organized industries as mining, trucking, construction, meatpacking, timber products and electrical manufacture, employers are increasingly seeking decertification of their local unions or are opening new non-union plants and subsidiaries.

Corporations are now regularly breaking unions and 'turning back the clock' on a scale not witnessed since the American Plan offensive of the early 1920s, when the National Association of Manufacturers, in co-ordination with a Republican administration in Washington and local employers groups, wiped out half of the membership base of the AFL in four years. What is happening today is actually more startling, since it also necessarily involves the denaturation or outright capture of

---

[3] Interview with John Dunlop, *Business Week*, April 19, 1982, p. 36. In contrast, John Kilgour, author of the American Management Association's handbook on 'union prevention', had no doubt that a 'new era' had begun in 1975 with the hardening of management attitudes. (See *Preventive Labor Relations*, AMA Book, New York 1981, p. 323 et passim.)

the entire bureaucratic apparatus — ranging from the National Labor Relations Board to industrial tripartite committees — which had ostensibly institutionalized and 'guaranteed' perpetual labor–management harmony. As the old system of industrial relations is torn apart, American management is baring something of its real soul. As Howell John Harris has emphasized in his important study of the origins of collective bargaining, the majority in management has always held to an attitude of conservative 'realism', and remained unreconciled to the principles of unionism, dealing with unions only as a 'necessary evil'.[4] Moreover, it is becoming increasingly clear that there never was a peaceful settlement of the American class war, much less a 'social contract' between labor and capital, but rather an armed truce which lasted only as long as: 1) the deepening of internal mass demand was the primary engine of capital accumulation; and 2) unions could sustain a credible threat to resume the *offensive* against capital. When both of these conditions were eroded by far-reaching political and economic changes (to be discussed in greater detail in chapter five), and in the balance of class power, a thoroughgoing crisis of the institutional forms of collective bargaining became inevitable.

But, to recall an oft-quoted observation of Gramsci's, 'the Crisis consists precisely in the fact that the old is dying and the new cannot be born'. Although there has been a noisy trumpeting in the editorial pages of the business press, announcing a new age of worker 'participation' in industry based on quality of worklife groups (QWL), employee stock ownership plans (ESOPs), new intra-plant communications networks, gains-sharing wage mechanisms, and more humanistic management practices, nothing seems less likely than a rapid emergence of a new stabilization of industrial relations. For the alleged cornerstone of this new order — as well as, correlatively, of new 'qualitative' union demands — is the exchange of old worker prerogatives and rights for guaranteed job security: a new 'social contract' supposedly exemplified by the lifetime employment practices of non-union, high-tech corporations in the electronics and computer sectors. But by the third year of the Reagan expansion, these sectors were already in deep recessions, and the 'lifetime' employees of Apple, Hew-

---

[4] See Harris, pp. 26–32, 133–35, 154–56, 198–99. Harris shows how the difficulties of researching the corporate record had led historians writing in the 1960s, like Kolko and Weinstein, to suppose that corporate liberalism was the 'hegemonic' ideology of post-war business, when in fact it was only the most well-advertised. His correction of the record, based on pioneering research and interviews, invites a thorough rethinking of the so-called 'corporate-liberal synthesis'.

lett-Packard and Texas Instruments were hitting the bricks with pink slips in their back pockets. Like other workers, they were discovering that this is an era of many *quids* but few *quos*.

Just as the birth of the new is proving chimerical, so the dying of the old continues unmercilessly; American labor has entered a maelstrom of uncertain structural changes and unequal social struggles. In subsequent chapters, I will examine the ramifications of this crisis at the levels of class formation and national politics. For the moment, however, it is important to focus on the historical and comparative specificity of the American industrial relations 'system' that is currently under siege. Moreover, in order to understand the current management offensive, it is first necessary to consider why and how a separate apparatus of labor relations arose in the first place. That is to say, it is necessary to investigate the specific institutional forms in which the wage relation has been reproduced in different epochs of American capitalism.

The Socialization of the Wage Relation

As every reader of *Capital* knows, the wage relation is always more than the simple sale of labor-power. It comprises, first, the prehistory of that sale: how labor has been dispossessed of productive property and the means of subsistence. It encompasses, secondly, the organization of the labor market: whether labor confronts capital as an atomized mass or as a unified agent with some measure of control over the reproduction of skills and the restriction of competition. Thirdly, the wage relation consists of the historically variegated, and increasingly complex, forms in which variable capital is advanced: as direct wages, indirect wages, deferred wages, or 'social wages'. Finally, the wage relation is also determined by the actual forms of the reproduction of labor-power: the waged and unwaged, capitalist and pre-capitalist components, as well as whether this reproduction is organized through private-familial or collective consumption. During the last hundred years in the United States, the global or socially 'average' wage relationship has undergone several transformations that correspond to its increasing socialization in three successive regimes of accumulation: 1) *competitive capitalism*, from the Civil War to the Great Depression of the nineties; 2) *unorganized corporate* or *monopoly capitalism*, from 1900 to 1935–40; and 3) *organized corporate capitalism* or '*Fordism*', from approximately 1940 to 1975. Further discussion of the economic details of this history is reserved for later chapters. Here, it will only be necessary to give a brief sketch of the history of wage forms from the competitive to the Fordist stage.[5]

As we have seen, class relations in industrializing America were not tempered by the residual paternalism of a landed gentry, nor by the intervention of an administratively powerful state apparatus. There were no Disraelis or Bismarcks to lay conservative foundations for welfarism, nor were there, *pace* Hartz, powerful parties of anti-liberal reaction acting in the name of pre-capitalist social solidarities. Nowhere in the world was the sale of labor-power conducted under conditions of such savage 'freedom' of the market as in the non-Southern parts of the United States. Nor, until the First World War, was there any attempt to ameliorate this *laissez faire* wage relation by providing social insurance or protective legislation. All attempts to mobilize the reformist potential of mass suffrage for this purpose were blocked by the weight of a petty-bourgeois electorate (including nominally 'populist' farmers), ethno-religious cleavages in the working class, and, later, by the AFL's willful aversion to social legislation. In this competitive stage of accumulation, where the power of employers was measured by the number of Pinkertons they could hire, wage and price depreciation cyclically produced immiseration. Astonishingly, no organized social provision, beyond occasional soup lines or the odd local workhouse, existed for the relief of the unemployed, despite their great numbers in the three post-bellum depressions. Instead, the armies of tramps that periodically foraged the land in hard times were the most dramatic expression of a labor market organized on pure principles of Sumnerian liberalism.

To the extent that any regulation of the wage relation on a national scale occurred during this period, it was accomplished through immigration policy, the labor injunction, and the Republican tariff. The US 'open door' of immigration was not only the chief mechanism for elastically expanding the domestic labor market in response to the

---

[5] Here, and throughout the following chapters, I will have recourse to the terminology of the *école de régulation* — the international current of Marxist political economy associated with the studies of Aglietta, Boyer, Mistral, Lipietz, DeVroey and others. In contrast to Anglo-American usage, which conventionally discusses 'Fordism' as a more comprehensive application of scientific management to the labor process, these authors are primarily concerned with analyzing the articulation between mass production and mass consumption which is the pivot of structural coherence within the postwar 'intensive' or 'Fordist' regime of production. See, especially, Michel Aglietta, *A Theory of Capitalist Regulation*, London 1979. My own critical review of the original 1976 French edition of this book appeared as 'Fordism in Crisis', *Review*, II, 2, Fall 1978.

demand for unskilled labor, it was also a central pillar of the world economy, ensuring the absorption of the Old World's supernumerary masses and their potentially revolutionary threat. The labor injunction, in turn, was the iron heel of a system of judicial review which relentlessly translated liberal values of unrestrained market exchange, including the first anti-trust legislation, into anti-labor law, aimed particularly at attempts to conduct national strikes or to organize industrial unions. Finally, as James Huston has explained, 'by the 1870s it was apparent that the Republicans rested all their hopes for a contented working class upon the operation of a high tariff wall'.[6]

However, as the rapid growth of trusts in the late 1890s centralized capital into huge, new productive complexes, the limits of social Darwinism as a means of wage regulation became apparent. In this *unorganized corporate* regime of accumulation — characterized, on the one hand, by the uneven development of corporate market power and of federal economic regulation, and, on the other, by the revolutionary transformation of productivity without a concomitant expansion of social purchasing power — the problems of labor turnover, restriction of output, and plant morale became major obstacles to realizing the potential of the new system of production. The limits of simple Taylorism as a program of systematic deskilling through detailed work and incentive wages were quickly reached even before 'scientific management' had been adopted by but a few corporations. However attractive were the aims of atomizing workgroup solidarity and transferring the mental content of skill to management, particularly as a strategy for diluting the power of traditional craftsmen in the labor process, managers were at the same time aware that efficiency irreducibly depended, in the last instance, upon some measure of voluntary intellectual collaboration by the workforce in production, and some mobilization of the powers of workgroups as social units. Although mass production on a corporate scale gave capital revolutionary new techniques for coercion, it simultaneously heightened the need to discover new sources of consensus beyond the old and idiosyncratic paternalism of family firms.

---

[6] James L. Huston, 'A Political Response to Industrialization: The Republican Embrace of Protectionist Labor Doctrines', *Journal of American History*, vol 70, no. 1, June 1983, p. 55. Labor attitudes toward protection, of course, have gone full cycle from the early AFL's support of the tariff, through the CIO's endorsement of free trade (adopted by the united AFL–CIO in 1955), to the recent return to protectionism by the AFL–CIO under Kirkland.

Welfare Capitalism or Collective Bargaining?

On the eve of World War One, two experimental solutions to this larger problem of regulating the wage relation while reinforcing coercion with consensus had appeared. On the one hand, the landmark agreements signed between Sidney Hillman's garment workers and the key firms in the men's apparel industry (followed by similar agreements in the hosiery industry) offered a model for a comprehensive industrial relations system built on long-duration, collectively bargained contracts that stabilized industry-wide competition and offered workers elements of social security. On the other hand, Henry Ford inaugurated at Highland Park his famous 'five dollars a day' system, which tried to subsume every aspect of the reproduction of labor-power, including the management of the worker's household budget, under a system of authoritarian productivism. Ford was one of the first industrialists to recognize that company 'welfarism', in the absence of state provision, was not merely a duty of industrial seigneuralism, but a functional prerequisite and source of high productivity. At the same time, it is necessary to emphasize the excluded middle: the remarkable absence in the United States during this period of any strong advocacy, except in academic and professional circles, of a model for the socialization of the wage relationship based on the direct and universal assumption of social security by the state — a system already in place in Asquithian England and Wilhelmine Germany (not to mention the socialistic paradise of New Zealand!)

During the First World War, powerful supporters of the industrial collective bargaining model, like Felix Frankfurter on the Mediation Commission or Frank Walsh on the National War Labor Board, were able to encourage industrial organizing campaigns in meatpacking and steel. With trade unions' organizational strength raised to an unprecedented level by wartime tripartism, it appeared possible for a brief moment that the AFL might assume a central role in the political economy of American industry. However, the rollback of unionism following the short but vicious depression of 1921, and the epochal defeat of the railroad shopmen in the same year, along with the restriction of immigration, gave large corporations maximum freedom in shaping industrial relations. While a majority of small and medium-sized firms remained obdurately fixed in the liberal, competitive framework, most mass production industries did attempt more or less ambitious experiments in Fordist-style self-organization. Life insurance schemes, company pensions and stock purchasing plans became increasingly common, while new, 'scientific' personnel practices looked at the totality of worklife and home economy. Recognizing the inherent limits of a 'drive system' that functioned through the petty despotism of a 'foremen's empire' and galvanized union sentiments, some of the larger companies experimented along lines pioneered by the Rockefellers with satellite employee self-government through works councils and company unions. A few of the most profitable firms with the greatest oligopolistic market power even attempted to follow Procter and Gamble's landmark initiation of job security.

American welfare capitalism of the 1920s was much admired by capitalists everywhere (although nowhere more avidly than in Japan, where it was extensively copied, becoming the model to which Japanese business fatefully returned in the early 1950s after the anti-communist purge of the labor movement), and superficially appeared to be unassailable. But the system had two insurmountable contradictions as an industrial relations scheme adequate to a regime of intensive accumulation. First, the facade of happy employee consensus and representation was undergirded by daily terrorism exercised by foremen and company security departments (or even internal vigilante organizations, as at Goodyear). 'Scientific personnel management', with its superb confidence in the capacity of American salesmanship to win over the worker as well as the consumer, had not supplanted, but had only been awkwardly married to the drive system.

Secondly, welfare capitalism was fundamentally a 'micro' approach to the 'macro' problem of coordinating effective demand to rising productivity. A few of the more farsighted, 'progressive' capitalists like Gerard Swope of General Electric, and to some extent Herbert Hoover, understood that the hothouse growth of consumer durable production in the 1920s was endangered by the very marginal returns accrued in the wages of semi-skilled labor in relation to massive increases in productivity. Swope in particular was alive to the distinction between the strategy of using putatively high weekly wages to mobilize an intensified work effort, and to the global macroeconomic role of these wages as demand (before Keynes, there was no shortage of theorists of underconsumptionism, *à la* Hobson). Moreover, with the sudden Ford layoffs of 1927, and the thunderclap of depression in 1929, Swope and other welfare capitalists experienced acutely the fundamental contradiction in the new corporate capitalism's attempt to organize a high productivity economy inside a liberal, nineteenth-century state.

Hoover's attempt to organize a voluntary program of corporate wage maintenance and work-sharing had collapsed by 1931, and with it fell most of the pretensions of a 'people's' capitalism. The larger employers, some eagerly, others reluctantly, scrapped their welfarism, cut wages and returned to supervisorial autocracy. In this situation, and with the specter of drastic state intervention or popular uprising on the horizon, Swope attempted to preserve the self-organized model of welfare capitalism with a bold proposal that business should voluntarily undertake to create its own macrostructure of wage and price regulation. Under his plan, comprehensive trade associations, supported by federal relief and nationalized workmen's compensation, would stabilize wages in order to halt the downward deflationary spiral and restore the conditions for an enterprise-centered regulation of the workforce. Swope's plan, of course, was metamorphosed, with amendment, into Roosevelt's National Recovery Administration.

The underlying premise of the NRA — that the complex diversity of interests among American capitalists could be orchestrated into sectoral and global consensuses through voluntary compliance with the cartel-like NRA trade codes — was a vain illusion. It turned into a dangerous threat, in the eyes of most employers, with rank-and-file labor's avid usurpation of the ambiguous guarantee of collective representation in section 7A (originally intended as a modus vivendi between local market, AFL craft unionism and captive company unionism) to organize new industrial unions. In the wake of the corporate backlash that followed the failure of the NRA, it was left to labor and its liberal allies, without any active support from FDR, to steer the Wagner Act through congress in 1935. The Wagner Act — prefigured by Coolidge's Railroad Labor Relations Act of 1926 — provided a legislative charter for union organization and the legal continuation of the National Labor Relations Board established under the NRA. It did not however, compel employers to reach any agreement with unions[7] and, in the absence of strong enforcement powers against unfair labor practices, proved relatively toothless in the face of the extra-legal opposition immediately mounted by such hard-core anti-union employers as the 'Brass Hats' of Little Steel, Chrysler Corporation, Dupont and Sears.

As we saw in the previous chapter, the militarization of the economy was the *deus ex machina* that resolved the tense labor-management impasse of 1940–41 and allowed further progress towards a national system of industrial relations. A complex parallelogram of forces, involving the CIO's partial successes, the AFL's conservative machin-

---

[7] While upholding the constitutionality of the National Labor Relations (Wagner) Act in 1937, the Supreme Court emphasized: 'The Act does not compel agreements between employers and employees. It does not compel any agreement whatever. It does not prevent the employer "from refusing to make a collective contract and hiring individuals on whatever terms" the employer "may by unilateral action determine ..."', 301 U.S. 1 (1937).

ations, the political revival of the 'progressive' wing of management (represented, above all, by the Business Council-sponsored Committee for Economic Development), and the wartime powers of the Executive — all in the context of booming production and guaranteed profits — was required to win the acquiescence of the majority of corporate 'realists' in collective bargaining as the basis of the wage system. (In a moment I will return to the case of the hold-out companies that maintained the non-union welfare capitalism model.)

The National War Labor Board became the seedbed for the creation of the institutional and substantive order of collective bargaining. Its wage procedures laid the basis for later industry-wide patterns, while on the shopfloor it universalized grievance procedures and established the practice of final arbitration. Its precedents and rulings founded a 'common law' for plant-level labor relations, while it consolidated the basis for internal labor markets organized on the principle of succession by seniority. Moreover, its large staff of administrators and arbitrators provided the indispensible cadre of 'impartial' experts — loyal first and above all to an ideology of moderate collective bargaining and conflict resolution — who would administer the postwar system and spread its gospel in the universities.

By 1945, therefore, a half-built framework had been constructed for the operation, for the first time in the history of US labor, of an autonomous sphere of 'industrial relations'. The Wagner Act, as amended by Taft–Hartley, provided a legislative foundation for the consolidation of the existing frontier of union organization, while circumscribing and rendering difficult any new advance of organization, particularly in the South or in low-wage industries. The NWLB, on the other hand, had pioneered the rules and processes for integrating worker self-organization into the factory order without conceding any fundamental prerogatives of management control beyond the seniority system. Still missing, however, was a precise definition of the scope of bargaining and the form of the wage relation adequate to a mass consumption economy.

The articulation of collective bargaining with the political economy was fought out in the three great wage rounds of 1946, 1948 and 1949. Although Lewis's coalminers were, as usual, the first in the door, winning pensions in 1946 and health benefits in 1949, it was the protracted struggle between the autoworkers and General Motors that cast American labor relations in their postwar mold. As the Editors of *Fortune* interpreted it, the ultimate Treaty of Detroit was a basic 'affirmation ... of the free enterprise system': First, the autoworkers accepted 'the existing distribution of income between wages and profits as "normal" if not as "fair"'. Second, by explicitly accepting 'objective economic facts — costs of living and productivity — as determining wages,' the contract threw 'overboard all theories of wages as determined by political power, and of profit "as surplus value"'. Finally, 'it is one of the very few union contracts that expressly recognize[s] both the importance of the management function and the fact that management operates directly in the interest of labor'.[8]

At the same time, the 1950 General Motors agreement established the decisive 'macroeconomic principle of the progressive wage by providing an 'annual improvement factor' (i.e. productivity share) of three per cent along with a cost of living adjustment tied to the consumer price index. Furthermore, the contract also ratified the principle of private supplementation of pensions and health insurance. As these basic contractual provisions were replicated in other master contracts and 'key bargains' during the Korean War, a series of bargaining patterns emerged, covering most of the manufacturing core of the economy, as well as much of mining, transportation and construction, which provided the indispensable function (that previous company welfarism and self-organization had been unable to achieve) of guaranteeing the wage level and making it invulnerable to deflation. In tandem with the seniority system and internal promotion within the plant, the wage system thus established for the core economy, and for the core only, became relatively immune to cyclical layoffs and the tides of the labor reserve army.

American Industrial Relations and International Fordism

The 'deep structure' of the postwar boom was the expansion of the internal markets of the three metropolitan zones (North America, Western Europe and Japan) through the co-ordination of mass consumption with continuous productivity increases. The integral linkage of this co-ordination was provided by the new socialization of the wage relation achieved, at least partly, through the struggles of the American working class. In all the advanced capitalist societies, this socialization had three generic characteristics: 1) the more or less extensive substitution of some form of collective bargaining for the individual wage contract; 2) the more or less extensive insulation of the

---

[8] Editors of *Fortune*, *USA: The Permanent Revolution*, p. 94.

real wage from deflation through arbitrary wage competition, and the linkage of the nominal wage to the advance of *social* productivity (rather than merely individual effort); and 3) the collective provision of social security and some more or less extensive social 'safety net'. In every other respect, however, the institutional forms through which this socialization of the wage relation was achieved differed across the OECD zone. It is not merely that there are different industrial relations 'systems' in the various social formations, but the very nature and scope of what constitutes 'industrial relations', as distinct from social security or state administration, differ as well. To understand better what the old order of American industrial relations has been until recently, it is useful to attempt to situate its specificity in an international grid (see Table 3.1.)

The overarching specificity of the American system, of course, derives from the absence of independent political representation for labor within national or state politics. Partially because of this, American unions have never possessed the corporate rights accorded by European or Japanese legal codes which recognize their integrity as organizational entities. In the United States, collective bargaining is legally derived from a classically liberal concept of individual consent to representation. Despite the mass struggles of the 1930s, the word 'union' does not appear in either the Wagner or Taft–Hartley Acts. Because its legitimacy is therefore based on individual consent, the rights of American unions under law are provisional and revocable; anti-union campaigns on the right are thus always waged in a Jeffersonian language of the 'rights of individual workers'.

Secondly, as Derek Bok has emphasized[9], the United States is unique in excluding millions of workers from the ambit of basic labor and social legislation. Indeed universal social legislation is virtually unknown in the United States. In the first place, this represents the historic success of Southern and rural capital in excluding agricultural labor from any of the entitlements of New Deal reforms. But domestics, supervisory personnel, charitable workers, small shop employees, and even many college professors are also excluded from one coverage or another. As late as 1971, fully half of the labor force lay outside NLRA jurisdiction, while a quarter were not fully eligible for the minimum wage, unemployment insurance or workmen's compensation. Moreover, the vast majority of the US labor force who are in non-union firms

---

[9] Derek Bok, 'Reflections on the Distinctive Character of American Labor Laws', *Harvard Law Review*, vol 84, no. 6, April 1971.

Table 3.1

The Socialization of the Wage Relation: A Taxonomy of Ideal-Types

Regime of Accumulation	Form of the Wage Relation	Mode of Industrial Relations	Role of the State
1. Liberal Capitalism	simple, individual sale; elastic real wage; competitive labor market organized by labor-reserve army; free immigration.	*despotic paternalism* on enterprise basis	guarantees 'freedom' of wage contract and ensures competitive labor market.
2. Unorganized Corporate Capitalism (transitional form)	notionally determined via employee representation schemes; indirect or deferred welfare component; nascent internal labor markets; restricted immigration.	*'welfare capitalism':* corporate self-organization of productivist welfare; satellite representation schemes; in few cases, lifetime employment	fundamentally unchanged.
3. State Organized Corporate Capitalism ('Fordism')	increasing nominal wages follow productivity. large, universal social wage component.	(developed and segmented labor markets) *Northern European Model:* some direct state administration of collective bargaining; works representation; extensive 'bottom line' contracts negotiated by peak bargaining.	(1) strong state provision of welfare; corporatist structures.
		(2) *British/Belgian Model:* collective bargaining is basically unregulated by state or law.	strong state provision of welfare; weak corporatism.

(3) *North American Model*: decentralized bargaining with extensive private superstructures supported by complex judicial review; legislative regulation of right to strike	smaller, less universal social wage; larger role of forced savings via deferred wages	weak and differential state provision of welfare (except education); no corporatism;
(4) *Japanese Model*: modified welfare capitalism with sub-ordinate enterprise unionism;	smaller, universal social wage; forced savings through enterprise level insurance schemes	weak provision of welfare except education; extremely powerful imbrication of capitalist interests groups, the financial system and state administration, thus only titular tripartism

have absolutely no 'just cause' protection against arbitrary dismissal — a noticeable contrast to Europe.

Thirdly, as we saw in the last chapter, social legislation in the United States is remarkably stunted, so that the arena of collective bargaining has been compensatorily widened to include the negotiation of welfare provisions. What in Europe devolves to the working class as a social wage based on citizenship rights is available in the United States only as deferred wages negotiated by private contract between specific groups of employers and their workers. The net result is that collective bargaining in the United States has a much narrower constituency than in Europe, while its agenda has been much broader and more comprehensive.

Whereas in England there has been, until recently, no legal regulation of collective bargaining, and in several European countries, including the German Federal Republic, there is no legal control of its procedural aspects, in the United States there has been an evolving, detailed specification of the bargaining process. A separate administrative agency, the NLRB, with powers tantamount to judicial review (i.e., the ability to develop case law by analogy with precedent litigation) but with weak enforcement powers, has jurisdiction over union organization pursued under the Wagner Act. Only in the United States are there judicial principles of majority rule, exclusive representation, and representation elections, as well as the specific determination of legal forms of representation, their scope, the nature of bargaining unit and so forth. Until Thatcher's recent industrial relations legislation, the United States has also been virtually unique in its detailed regulation of the right to strike.

In Northern Europe, where the contract is usually binding, and in Britain and Belgium, where it is not, the contract has generally provided a short-term minimum base for further elaboration by local units. Contracts are generally negotiated at a 'peak' level between employers associations and national unions (or union federations or coalitions). In the United States, on the other hand, the contract is binding and of long duration (from two to five years). It usually contains no-strike provisions, is non-extensive, and, above all, is extremely detailed in its specifications: fixing the actual, not merely the minimal, conditions. Moreover, the supervision of the contract involves a complex web of regulations. In contrast to European or antipodean labor courts, the control of the apparatus of arbitration is private and involves a much expanded role of union staff experts, personnel managers and outside arbiters. To operate this system and to maintain a far more decentralized galaxy of individual contracts (over 125,000) has entailed the growth of union officialdom into a bureaucratic stratum qualitatively larger than in any other capitalist society. By 1962, for instance, there were 60,000 full-time, salaried union officials in the United States (one for every 300 workers), as contrasted to 4,000 in Britain (one for 2,000) or 900 in Sweden (one for 1,700).[10]

In summary, nowhere else have 'industrial relations' (i.e. the regulation of the bargaining process) been spun-off with the same sub-systemic autonomy and institutional self-interest as in the United States. Nowhere else has there developed such a dense mass of private 'common law,' nor so extensive a substitution of legal bureaucratization and arbitration for administrative state intervention or a public judiciary (as in the Australian system of labor courts). The driving logic of the system has been the collusion of union officialdom and management to prevent any 'statization' of collective bargaining or, for that matter, the emergence of any 'dual power' such as that achieved in post-war Britain by the strength of independent shop-steward organization.

Boulwarism: The First Knell

During the Korean War years, collective bargaining in the United States rapidly developed an elaborate institutional carapace, whose apparent solidity was fetishized by industrial relations theorists into the idea of an irreversible 'maturation' of labor relations and economic democracy. In reality, of course, the entire structure of post-war indus-trial relations was profoundly contingent. In the first place, it depended upon the trade union movement's maintenance of a satisfactory momentum of new organization, as well as their ongoing ability to mobilize existing memberships for contractual and electoral cam-paigns. Yet the immanent characteristics of the system — i.e., the fundamental shift of power from rank-and-file to staff, the non-univers-ality of bargaining, the segmentation of labor markets, etc. — estranged grassroots involvement and fostered an inertial attitude toward organizing.

Similarly, the legislative and juridical parameters of the system, however logical and rationally motivated they appeared, were shaped by volatile balances of political power. The subordination of labor to the larger coalition of interest groups within the Democratic Party, and

---

[10] Seymour Martin Lipset, 'Trade Unions and Social Structure, II', *Industrial Relations*, February 1962, p. 93.

the persistent inability to realign that power-structure toward a simulacrum of laborism or functional social democracy, grievously narrowed the trade-union bureaucracy's bargaining power. A conservative Congress in 1944, inflamed by the mineworkers' stubborn militancy, almost repealed the NLRA; a personal intervention by Senator Taft, of all people, was necessary to prevent the euthanasia of the infant bargaining system.[11] Moreover, basic labor law — the Wagner Act as amended by Taft–Hartley and Landrum–Griffith — contained plentiful provisions that could be developed in an aggressively anti-union direction: for instance, the 'right to work' legislation that has made union organization doubly difficult in Sunbelt states.

But even more importantly, collective bargaining, which itself provided certain basic conditions for capital accumulation, was in turn directly dependent on other conditions. These latter might be called the 'golden age' parameters of American capitalism. Paramount was the secure oligopolistic position of unionized manufacturing industries in an economy that was driven forward by a dynamic consumption of wage-good durables and housing, informally protected by a huge US productivity differential. Other parameters were the regulated status of transport, communications and utilities, which complemented unionism's restraint of wage competition through the support of profit and price levels, and the stable flow of revenues to defense and highway construction, key union sectors. Conversely, any slowing of mass consumption, import penetration of the domestic market, deregulation or decline in defense spending would directly undermine and destabilize bargaining structures and progressive wage agreements.

If from the onset of the modern era of bargaining, the possibility of its collapse was inscribed in the contingency of its conditions of existence, there were from the beginning more active agents to engender its dissolution, consciously and systematically working for a return to liberal or welfare-capitalist forms of wage regulation. Besides the archaic mass of non-union small employers, the agricultural interest, or the retail sector, an important group of large industries had resisted unionism through the aggressive development of sophisticated systems of employee control. Extremely capital-intensive, continuous flow industries like oil refining and chemical manufacture repelled unionism by competitively matching union wage rates (labor comprising only five per cent or so of their production costs) while developing an

---

[11] For detailed references, see Theodore St. Antoine, 'The Role of Law', in Jack Stieber, et. al. (eds.), *U.S. Industrial Relations, 1950–1980: A Critical Assessment*, Madison 1981, pp. 159–6u.

ability, through conscious overstaffing, to run plants for long periods solely with management personnel.

A more interesting model, however, of non-union industrial relations was the business machine empire originally put together in 1911 by Charles Flint, 'the father of the conglomerate', and then taken over by the Watson dynasty during the 1920s. In an age that witnessed heroic power struggles between productivist engineer-managers (both GM's Wilson and GE's Swope were electrical engineers) and Wall Street investment bankers, IBM was characterized by the dominance of the sales staff and its particular outlook. Indeed, in a sixty-year history without a single hour lost to an industrial dispute, IBM has engaged in a sustained experiment in adapting the methods of 'supersalesmanship' to control of its workforce. It has been able to do so, of course, because of a unique growth and profit record that has allowed the company to offer semi-guaranteed lifetime employment. On this basis in the 1950s, the Watsons sought to counter the GM model of industrial relations — in which the company ceded to the union a measure of organizational legitimacy within the plant (stewards frequently have office facilities within larger plants, the unions have bulletin boards, etc.) — with a slick refinement of Ford-style authoritarianism. A historic step was the salarization of the entire production staff in 1959, in a conscious attempt to refashion plant life around a white collar ethos. Continuous, systematic opinion surveys were used to monitor morale, while the famous 'open door' was established to allow employees to appeal directly to top management in lieu of grievance procedure. Moreover, contemporary IBM-watchers were struck by the 'extreme attention the company pays to internal communications':[12] a plethora of internal newsletters, videotaped addresses, an *Izvestia*-style company magazine, and paranoiac control over bulletin boards.

Already in the 1950s, IBM's striking success in preserving a union-free corporate environment was attracting a cult following in business schools. For most frontline managers, however, the features of guaranteed employment security and universal salarization seemed like dangerous or unaffordable concessions. A more relevant model of hegemonic management, sharing the IBM emphasis on 'communications' and control of plant society, but eschewing its exotic features, was the

---

[12] Nancy Foy, *The IBM World*, London 1974, p. 122. IBM has also been highly successful in transferring its personnel methods to overseas subsidiaries. IBM France rejected strike action in May 1968, while ASTMS succeeded in organizing only ten of two thousand employees at the IBM plant at Greenock on the 'Red Clyde' during the 1970s. Interestingly, the only strike against IBM occurred at its Japanese plant!

comprehensive strategy adopted by GE in the aftermath of the great electrical strike of 1946, and popularly known by the name of GE's new personnel manager, Lemuel Boulware.[13] More than any single influence, Boulwarism nurtured the anti-union corporate counter-culture which, through the rise of the conglomerate empires in the late 1960s, became the common sense of management by the late 1970s.

During the 1920s and 1930s, under the leadership of Owen D. Young and Gerard Swope, General Electric had been the most visionary of progressive managements, the closest approximation to Veblen's dream of engineers in power. In 1926, Young and Swope, seeking to stabilize employment and attract skilled labor, had met with President Green and offered to recognize a union if the AFL would organize it on industrial lines similar to the GE employee representation plan. (The astonished Green declined, undoubtedly for fear of compromising the craft jurisdiction principle.) As I have noted, Swope was a master theoretician of corporate welfarism. Before 1935, GE had already instituted pensions, unemployment benefits, a seniority system, and other prerogatives won elsewhere by arduous collective bargaining. As Ronald Schatz has pointed out in his study of the electrical workers, GE concluded an amicable company-wide contract with the left-led United Electrical Workers, CIO — in contrast to the stubborn resistance of Westinghouse and RCA.[14]

The 1946 strike, when the UE for the first time shut down every plant in the electrical industry, was a turning point. With a new upper management composed of executives from GE's home appliance division replacing the Edisonian duo of Young and Swope, the company undertook a comprehensive reversal of its formerly benign attitude toward the union and launched a crusade to reclaim control of the shopfloor. Boulware, a pioneer in market research and founder of the Marketing Executives Society, was brought in to establish a new hard-line labor relations strategy that would reassert the ideological authority of management. Borrowing freely from anti-union agitprop previously developed by Dupont, Boulware deployed the latest marketing methods to win GE's workers to the company side. As he explained 'This program of ours is a job marketing program. It is an adaptation from the consumer marketing process. ... The job market and

[13] See Herbert Northrup, *Boulwarism: The Labor Relations Policies of the General Electric Company*, Ann Arbor 1964. Northrup was a former colleague of Boulware's, so his account is highly sympathetic.

[14] See Chapter 4, 'The Silk Glove of the Company', in Ronald Schatz, *The Electrical Workers*, Urbana and Chicago, 1983.

product markets deal with the same people and the same considerations'.[15] His seriousness about the latter proposition was evident from the integrated way in which GE marketed the free enterprise system to its workers and light bulbs to the public. Ronald Reagan was rescued from the downward spiral of his acting career to promote both, in myriad plant appearances as well as on the GE television show. (In many senses, Boulwarism represents the pre-history of Reaganism.)

GE's ideological offensive, of course, was abetted by the CIO's expulsion and calumniation of the UE for being Communist, followed by the vicious raiding that destroyed unitary unionism in the electrical industry. 'Freed from the constraint of a powerful nationwide union', as Schatz explains, 'GE and Westinghouse executives set about redesigning jobs, manufacturing facilities and the internal structure of management'.[16] The essence of this strategy was the decentralization of production from older, larger Northeast factories to newer, smaller factories in the border states, the South and West. Between 1955 and 1960, GE opened twenty-five new plants in Sunbelt areas — Roanoke, Phoenix, St. Petersburg, etc. — only four of which were unionized.[17] Meanwhile, in the older organized plants Boulware dealt with the unions through 'take it or leave it' final offers accompanied by massive publicity and direct appeals to the workforce. Where General Motors, in its attempt to manage a restive rank-and-file, came to recognize its investments in the UAW's maintenance of a militant image — often colluding in the kind of stage-managed charade of class struggle described by William Serrin in his famous exposé of the 1970 contract round[18] — GE frontally challenged the unions' legitimacy. Above all it laid siege to the privileged communications position of stewards in plant society, undermining their role whenever possible, and circumscribing their mobility and access to the membership.

The Management Offensive of 1958–63

Boulwarism, in short, was a sophisticated strategy of gradual deunioni-

---

[15] Quoted in Northrup, p. 25.

[16] Schatz, p. 232.

[17] See discussion in *Fortune*, August 1960. GE also followed a deliberate strategy of sociologically segmenting its workforce: 'Some plants have mainly men; others are as high as 85 per cent female; the population of some plants is old, of others very young'. (Northrup, p. 5).

[18] See William Serrin, *The Company and the Union*, New York 1973.

zation, an internal undermining of the collective bargaining system. Initially confined to the electrical industry, where Westinghouse followed GE's lead, Boulwarism gained widespread popularity in the last, troubled biennium of the Eisenhower administration, as embattled corporations struggled to save profit levels. The recession of 1957–58 marked an end to the brief era of labor-management good feeling that had accompanied the Korean War boom. Under the conservative influence of Arthur Burns, Eisenhower retreated from his earlier mild Keynesianism and slowed the economy with reductions in federal spending. At the same time, industry was facing its first serious wave of foreign competition, as steel imports exceeded exports for the first time in 1958, and smaller, cheaper foreign cars like the Volkswagen made their debut on the American market. In this suddenly chilled economic environment, a majority of corporations looked toward major reductions in their unit labor costs.[19] The problem as they generally saw it was two-fold. First, the cost of living adjustments in most contracts had been too successful as stabilizers in the recent recession; companies strove to restore a greater measure of wage flexibility, if not competitiveness. Secondly, and more importantly, big manufacturers were bedevilled by the persistence of a regime of 'fractional bargaining' on the shopfloor whereby work-groups, abetted by restrictive work rules, used the grievance process to extract additional, extra-contractual concessions from lower-level management. Although the basic idea of judicial grievance processing under the time contract was to make the lower-level union leadership into responsible agents of plant administration, far too many stewards and committee people remained tribunes of their rank-and-file constituencies.[20] The solution, as adumbrated in lock-step fashion by contemporary managements in diverse industries, was a significant speed-up of production to be achieved by the introduction of new automated technologies (like numerical control) along with a diminution of union shop-floor power: restrictive work rules and fractional bargaining were to be abolished. In

[19] Management was also attempting to displace the costs of burgeoning managerial overheads onto production workers. In the decade between 1947 and 1957, non-production personnel, especially in sales and supervision, increased by fifty per cent, to one-fifth of the total manufacturing workforce, while salaries, as a proportion of total labor costs, soared from a quarter to a third. Data suggests the emergence of a 'salary squeeze' (see further discussion in Chapter Five below) on profits, partially due to more intensified sales competition in lieu of wage competition, that was compensated by speedup on the shopfloor. For contemporary discussions of the startling rise in white-collar manufacturing costs, see *Fortune*, April 1957, and June 1958, (esp. pp. 203–04).

[20] For the classical discussion of 'fractional bargaining', see James Kuhn, *Bargaining in Grievance Settlement*, New York 1961.

the context of these concerns, Boulwarism, with its hard bargaining stance and its strategy of management hegemony within the plant, as well as its implicit 'Southern strategy' of new investment, became the charter for the management offensive of 1958–62.

It is generally forgotten how close American industrial relations came to a raw re-opening of the class war in those years. In late 1957, with hardliner John Leary installed as its personnel director, Chrysler resumed its private crusade against the auto workers with a sweeping attack on work standards. At US Steel, where open shop advocate R. Conrad Cooper was appointed vice-president for personnel, the human relations approach to industrial relations went into eclipse, while Chairman Blough praised Boulwarism and talked ominously of 'rolling back unionism'. [21] The new corporate militancy also brought greater employer solidarity: to prevent the unions from 'whipsawing' one company against another, the Big Three automakers formed a united front in 1958 and openly canvassed the idea of a general lockout. A similar entente was achieved by the steelmakers in 1959, while the six largest airlines set up a mutually subsidized fund to spread equally the costs of lockouts or strikes.

1959 brought what the AFL–CIO called 'some of the worst storms in trade-union history'. [22] Bogged down in internal jurisdictional disputes, with its legislative program a total failure and the venality of its leadership under public attack by the McClelland Commission, the Federation was ill-prepared to meet the management offensive head on. In industry after industry, the management attack on work rules and wages provoked long strikes. The meatcutters battled Swift, the Western miners fought the copper bosses, the rubber workers conducted the most bitter industry-wide strike since 1937, and the East Coast longshoremen were restrained only by Taft–Hartley. Union strikers in Kentucky were shot, while in North Carolina eight leaders of the textile workers were imprisoned. The Eastern Front of the contract round, however, was the steel industry, where Chairman Blough's determination to eliminate the 'local practices' clause in the steel contract, which enjoined the incentive system and prevent arbitrary speed-up, led to an epic 116-day strike, ended only by the Supreme Court's willingness to uphold a Taft–Hartley injunction and presidential candidate Nixon's pressure on the steelmakers.

[21] Quoted in George Strauss, 'The Shifting Power Balance in the Plant', *Industrial Relations*, I, 3 May 1962, pp. 81–83.

[22] See Herbert Northrup, 'Management's "New Look" in Labor Relations,' *Industrial Relations*, I, 1 (October 1961), pp. 20–22.

The last year of the Eisenhower administration, with unemployment figures at a postwar high and weekly purchasing power declining, witnessed further management offensive and union retreat. The railroad and electrical machinery industries scrapped cost of living adjustments, while the UAW lost two important battles in the aircraft industry (leading to decertification at Sikorsky). The historic event of 1960, however, was the three-week GE strike. Unlike the steel industry the year before, which made no effort to keep plants open, GE aggressively tried to break the strike by keeping production going and encouraging back-to-work movements: a tactic that predictably produced violence while revealing the internal disarray of the GE unions. Carey of the IUE, the largest of the GE unions, sued for peace after a majority of his locals had broken ranks and returned to work. A.H. Raskin called it 'the worst setback any union has received in a nationwide strike since the war'.[23] GE's victory included not only its regained control over the wage payment system — cutting the COLA and introducing incentive pay (a prerequisite to further speed-up) — but also its spectacular demonstration of the efficacy of Boulwarism in demoralizing and dividing the union. Industrial relations theorist Arthur Ross, writing a year later, said that the biggest question in the American labor movement was 'will the GE strategy be applied elsewhere?'[24]

1960s: The Uncertain Direction of Industrial Relations

Perhaps it is a misleading counterfactual exercise to speculate whether

[23] Quoted in *New York Times*, October 25, 1960, p. 31. A particularly vivid example of how GE's strategy of plant decentralization was intended to apply political leverage in labor struggles is provided by the case of its Philadelphia switch-gear plant during the 1960 strike. Because the Philadelphia police refused to act energetically to keep the plant open during the strike, GE ran full-page ads attacking Mayor Richardson Dilworth and threatening to move the switch-gear works, as well as a key missile research plant, elsewhere. In response Mayor Dilworth charged GE 'with political coercion and intimidation of municipal governments as a weapon for the settlement of strikes'. According to the mayor, GE had warned that it had 'more than 160 plants in 135 cities and that this strike would give the company an excellent opportunity to judge the friendliness of city administrations toward employers. These gentlemen also said that GE could and would reorganize and relocate plants following the strike in accordance with the co-operation given GE during the strike'. (From John Herling, *The Great Price Conspiracy: The Story of the Anti-Trust Violations in the Electrical Industry*, Washington, D.C. 1962, pp. 155–56.)
[24] Arthur Ross, 'Prospects for Industrial Conflict', *Industrial Relations*, I, 1, October 1961, p. 60.

Boulwarism would have been generalized and collective bargaining destroyed if the Kennedy-Johnson boom had not relieved the pressure on profits. What is more important is that the flare-up of industrial conflict between 1958 and 1963, accompanied by prefigurative signs of union-busting, demonstrated the brittle vulnerability of the institutional structures of collective bargaining to any shift in the 'golden age' parameters of accumulation. The incident also revealed the instability of the system on the shop floor, where local unions and rank-and-file work groups resisted the imposition of speed-up and rule changes, subverting the routinized procedures of contract implementation whenever possible. Indeed, the existence of an autonomous space for shopfloor activity — no matter how restricted it might appear in comparison to English shop stewardism or Italian dualism — was the central contradiction in the system that provoked during the 1960s two diametrically opposed attempts at reform.

On the one hand, the Kennedy administration, determined to unfetter military spending and induce a military-Keynesian expansion of the kind theorized by Leon Keyserling during the Truman years, proposed to establish a national incomes policy, based on wage and price guidelines, to control the inflationary side-effects of a big defense boom. To secure labor and management collaboration, as well as to restore confidence in the shaken system of collective bargaining, Secretary of Labor Arthur Goldberg, the first labor lawyer (steelworkers) to occupy that office, organized what was intended to be a peacetime version of the War Labor Board: the President's Advisory Commission on Labor-Management Policy. More significantly, Goldberg, with the strong support of Justices Douglas and White on the Supreme Court, sought to greatly expand the power of the NLRB.[25] Whereas the Eisenhower NLRB had pursued a *de minimus* doctrine of restricted jurisdiction, the Kennedy NLRB was intended to be a major innovatory agency. The goal, already adumbrated by Justice Douglas in his pioneering labor decisions of the late 1950s, was to create an overpowering regulatory and legal framework for forcing union members to accept unlimited grievance arbitration in exchange for abjuration of the right to strike.[26]

---

[25] Kennedy's chair of the NLRB, Frank McCulloch, was a conveniently close friend of Douglas's. The domination of the administration's labor policy by labor lawyers was completed with the addition of Harvard's Archibald Cox (later of Watergate fame) as chief labor advisor. (For contrasting views of the period, see James Stern, 'The Kennedy Policy: A Favorable View', *Industrial Relations*, vol 3, no. 2, February 1964; and David Carper, 'Kennedy and the Unions', *Dissent*, Winter 1962.)

While the Kennedy administration was trying to move toward an arbitral system of industrial relations subordinated to national wage guidelines, union members themselves were beginning to revolt against their loss of control on the shopfloor. Management's largely successful speed-up offensive was everywhere worsening working conditions, while union collaboration with Kennedy led to a virtual stagnation in wages.[27] Every major ex-CIO union (with the sole exception of the democratic and militant packinghouse workers), as well as the miners, teamsters and postal workers, was eventually challenged at some time between 1963 and 1973 by a major internal insurgency. Contract rejections, a statistical rarity before 1962, soared to one-eighth of all contracts in 1968, while wildcat strikes reached a postwar record.[28] Despite the complex range of particular grievances and histories, the opposition movements universally echoed demands for aggressive strike action to combat speed-up and to raise wages. The first major upheaval occurred in Goldberg's old union, the steelworkers, where President MacDonald had virtually surrendered the union's wage-setting powers to government guidelines. A broad coalition of dissident national staff, rebellious local leaderships, and rank-and-file reformers supported A.W. Abel's successful challenge based on an eight-plant program that promised to return control of basic policy to the membership and upgrade local agreements. In the following years, the entry of hundreds of thousands of young workers, many of them veterans of Vietnam, raised the temperature of industrial relations and forced national leaderships like the UAW to initiate 'safety-valve' strikes to contain the pressure for action.

In the end, however, neither the federal government nor the union rank-and-file were able qualitatively to enlarge their power or freedom

---

[26] The Warren Court, led by Justice Douglas, had already moved in the 1957 *Lincoln Mills* case to nationalize labor law by asserting the prerogative of federal jurisdiction. The same case also created federal policy by finding that arbitration was the 'quid pro quo' for an agreement not to strike. The primacy of the private arbitral process was further buttressed in the so-called *Steelworkers Trilogy* of 1960, where Douglas established a division of labor between courts and arbitration that favored the latter (while leaving considerable confusion about the boundaries between the expanded jurisdictions of arbitration and the NLRB). At the time, this state-supported strengthening of private industrial jurisprudence (especially over and against the union rank-and-file) was seen as a shrewd solution to the problem of ensuring greater economic discipline around national wage-and-price goals without resorting to administrative or juridical statization per se. (For historical overviews, see R.W. Fleming, *The Labor Arbitration Process*, Urbana 1965; Katherine Stone, 'The Postwar Paradigm in American Labor Law', *Yale Law Journal* 90, 1981; and Karl E. Klare, 'Labor Law and the Liberal Political Imagination', *Socialist Review*, 62, 1983.)

of action within the collective bargaining system. LBJ quickly abandoned the guidelines experiment, as well as the attempt to sponsor tripartism, in favor of old-fashioned wheeling-and-dealing with individual unions and companies. Although the Supreme Court did continue to restrict the powers of rank-and-file action in favor of arbitral authority, culminating in the partial restoration of the labor injunction in the controversial *Boys Market* case of 1970, there was no parallel enforcement of management's obligation to accept arbitrators' rulings. Meanwhile, the labor revolt burnt itself out in the last days of the Great Boom without radically altering the direction of the trade-union movement. In contrast to Western Europe, where the insurgencies of 1968–73 led to profound upheavals that set new agendas for the labor movement and recomposed its activist leadership, the American rank-and-file struggles did not succeed in re-orienting the unions towards 'qualitative' demands, nor did they produce a distinct new layer of worker-militants. As often as not, the defeat of local insurgencies, or, conversely, their immediate cooption into the status quo, only left enduring legacies of frustration and demoralization.

The Failure of Union Organization

In 1973 the liberal-optimist advocates of collective bargaining celebrated the landmark 'Experimental Negotiating Agreement' signed between the steelworkers union and the major employers led by US Steel. After five years of strike turbulence unmatched since the end of the war, the ENA seemed to signify a resumption of labor-management 'institution building' without undue government intervention or rank-

---

[27] 'It is striking that every econometric wage equation devised by scholars so far — and this now includes at least a half-dozen studies embodying different production and labor-management variables — substantially overpredicts the rate of wage increase in the last several years ... What is striking is not that the rate of wage increase was lower than in ... the early 1950s, but that the rate of wage increase was lower by over 2 per cent than the equations based on the postwar relationships would have predicted'. (Otto Eckstein, quoted in Irving Beller, 'Economic Policy and the Demands of Labor', *Dissent*, May-June 1967, p.266.) Manufacturing wages in fact grew much slower between 1960 and 1965 than even the guidelines allowed (2.2 per cent per annum versus 3.2 per cent), while, alone among major industrial countries, unit labor costs in the United States fell substantially. All this despite the fact that salaries of non-production personnel were increasing rapidly, while their productivity was declining. (See Jerome Mark and Elizabeth Kahn, 'Recent Unit Cost Trends in US Manufacturing', *Monthly Labor Review*, September 1965, pp. 1056–66.)

[28] See Richard Herding, *Job Control and Union Structure*, Rotterdam 1972, p. 263; Sid Peck, 'Trends in American Labor', *New Politics*, Spring 1974, p.21.

and-file protest. Conceived as an alternative to strikes and consequent hedge buying and import inroads, the union abdicated under the Agreement the right to engage in company-wide strikes in return for a 3 per cent annual floor under wages and improved supplementals. Significantly, in the spirit of the 'Douglas Doctrine', both parties agreed to the central role of arbitration in ensuring peaceful conciliation of their respective demands. Warmly endorsed by President Nixon, the Agreement was promoted as the future of bargaining.

But if would be a shortlived future, for the artificially contrived boom that Arthur Burns had engineered to re-elect Nixon was bringing the long post-war wave of growth to a close in the sharp recession of 1974–75. In the next five years all the 'golden age' parameters of stable collective bargaining would unravel and lose their integrated coherence. But long before the unions confronted the full force of new low-wage competition at home and abroad, they had to deal with the consequences of their failure to organize the new working class created by the vast expansion of the workforce between Kennedy and Carter.

The AFL–CIO itself has estimated that its component unions succeeded in recruiting only two million of the thirty-five million new workers added to the labor force between 1960 and 1980. If the great gains in the public sector during the 1960s (the only significant new organizing since the Korean War) are deduced, there was a net decline in the absolute level of private-sector unionism — the manufacturing unions alone losing three-quarters of a million members in the early 1970s.[29] Although, as we shall see, this can be ascribed largely to corporate counter-organizing and illegal activity, the AFL–CIO, even in the best of times, has been a no-growth machine, relying, as Mike Quill often used to point out, on contracts to automatically organize new replacements for old members being lost. Highly publicized organizing campaigns by the Industrial Union Department failed because the major international unions repeatedly refused to meet their commitments: each union, in the rational spirit of business unionism, carefully discounted the cost effectiveness of investment in the drive *vis à vis* the success of its rivals. As the 1980s would again show with a new eruption of inter-union rivalries, it was often more 'profitable' for large established unions to raid other unions for new members rather than invest in costly organizing campaigns whose fruits might accrue to other unions.[30]

---

[29] See George Hildebrand, 'The Prospects for Collective Bargaining in the Manufacturing Sector, 1978–1985', in Stieben, *US Industrial Relations, 1950–1980*, p. 88.

[30] To give some recent examples, AFSCME, SEIU and CWA have been engaged in bitter

An inertial AFL-CIO Executive, unmoved by the pleadings of Reuther or public-sector leaders like Wurf, simply failed to confront the sweeping changes in the occupational and industrial order that occurred after 1963. With primary labor market jobs in manufacturing, and even, after 1974, in the public sector, relatively stabilized, the great expansion of new jobs took place in lower-wage, secondary sector employment. But the AFL-CIO, which as Stanley Aronowitz has pointed out 'has abandoned the organization of the working poor',[31] made no significant effort to unionize the largest and most rapidly growing sector of semi-skilled labor in the economy: millions of women clericals in banking, insurance, health and education.

Not only did the AFL-CIO have desultory and declining successes in organizing within the rapidly industrializing urban areas of the Southeast and Southwest, but it egregiously failed to co-ordinate the efforts of individual unions fighting plant relocation in right-to-work states. During the 1960s, a majority of corporations resorted to the radical socio-spatial strategy pioneered by GE and the non-union sector in the 1950s: building smaller factories for greater managerial control (500 employees was often reckoned optimum); decentralizing them in weakly-organized regions of the Sunbelt or the Midwestern rural periphery; recruiting workforces (farmers or housewives) without previous union experience; and implanting, from the beginning, the manipulative structures of the 'communications' model of personnel management geared toward worker individualism.

Although this strategy has occasionally backfired — as in the case of the memorable rebellion at GM's ruralized super-assembly plant in Lordstown, Ohio — it was more often successful, resulting in a new union-resistant geography of American industry. United States capital has gone furthest to break up the power of urban-union industrial agglomerations. As Lonsdale and Seyler point out, 'without a minimum of formal federal policy on the matter, the United States has probably experienced more decentralization, and, in effect, nonmetropolitan industrialization, than any major industrial nation, capitalist or socialist'.[32] With cheap energy as a key factor in allowing

---

rivalries for public employees in the Midwest, while the steelworkers have invaded UFCW's retail food jurisdiction (signing contracts for $2 an hour less), and the Seafarers and UAW are poaching on the construction trades. The teamsters, communications workers, service workers, public employees (AFSCME) and autoworkers all claim almost unlimited organizational jurisdictions.

[31] Stanley Aronowitz, *Working Class Hero*, New York 1983, pp. 88–90.

[32] Richard Lonsdale and H.L. Seyler (eds.), *Non-Metropolitan Industrialization*, Washington, D.C. 1979, p. 5.

industry to disperse in the search of malleable, non-union labor, non-metropolitan manufacturing increased faster or as rapidly as metropolitan production in every region except the West, and nearly ninety per cent of new manufacturing jobs were created outside the old unionized Heartland (see Table 3.2).

Table 3.2[33]
Geographical Growth of Manufacturing Employment, 1962–78

	Northeast	North Central	South	West
Non-metropolitan	+100,000	+564,000	+1,000,000	+190,000
Metropolitan	−600,000	+400,000	+1,000,000	+550,000
	Heartland		Sunbelt	
Total	+464,000		+2,740,000	
% Total Δ	14%		86%	

Nowhere, however, has the AFL–CIO's failure to keep up with the changing geography or structure of employment been so blatant as its inability to get any foothold in the burgeoning semi-conductor and computer industries. Great new productive complexes have been created without a single union card carrier. In a manner reminiscent of the non-union origins of Hollywood, the agricultural Santa Clara Valley, south of San Francisco, was selected by the legendary 'Fairchild Eight' in 1955 as the site for their semi-conductor division in a deliberate attempt to escape Bay Area unions and tap cheap rural labor markets. By the late 1970s, Silicon Valley had mushroomed into 1,500 non-union firms and 200,000 unorganized workers; the single largest open shop in North America.[34] Its Eastern counterpart, the non-union electronics and high-tech strip along Route 128 in Massachusetts, has also been unorganized, since the steelworkers gave up an initial attempt in the middle 1950s. Incredibly, unions waited until the early

---

[33] Claude Harron and Ronald Holling, 'Industrial Development in Non-Metropolitan America', in Lonsdale and Seyler, pp. 62–78.

[34] The Silicon Valley, of course, is also an extreme case of the emergent tendency toward an occupational structure polarized between highly paid scientific professionals and low-wage production workers. While electrical engineers frequently earn $80,000 and up, assemblers in the semi-conductor industry (75 per cent women and 61 per cent minorities) start at $5.22 per hour, rising to $8.82 on the highest job step. Moreover, most of the printed circuit board and component companies are old-fashioned sweatshops, paying a minimum wage of $3.35 and hiring undocumented workers or Southeast Asian refugees. (See exposé in *San José Mercury News*, November 5, 1984, 4C).

1980s before mounting any serious organizing effort in either area; equally astonishing, the first major organizing drive against IBM was only announced by the Communications Workers in the middle of 1985.

But organizing of any kind became progressively more difficult from the early 1970s. Where unions had once regularly expected to win seventy per cent of representation elections they now found themselves losing a majority, especially in larger plants.[35] Part of the problem was the wave of conglomerate mergers in the late 1960s which shifted tactical bargaining power to the side of management as conglomerates — without a single vulnerable node of production — were able to whipsaw unions, cross-subsidize struck facilities, or even divest themselves of organized units entirely. Attempts by the Industrial Union Department of the AFL–CIO to respond with company-wide organizing campaigns or coalition bargaining were in turn frustrated by NLRB bargaining-unit rulings that make it difficult or impossible to confront conglomerates as a whole. The greatest obstacle to new organization, however, was the increasing willingness of employers to resort to illegal resistance. Advised by a burgeoning number of union-busting consultants, who reminded managers that it took the logjammed NLRB years to process unfair labor practices, companies discovered that it was relatively inexpensive to discharge unionists or simply refuse to bargain. The notorious examples of J.P. Stevens, Litton Industries and Dupont were simply the tip of the iceberg of employer illegality: in 1978–79 alone over 30,000 individual cases of management unfair labor practices were reported, sixty per cent involving the discharge of employees for union activity, usually organizing. Indeed it has been estimated that between five and ten per cent of pro-union voters in recent representation elections have been victimized by the employer.[36]

---

[35] See Barry Hirsch and Mark Berger, 'Union Membership and Industry Characteristics', *Southern Economic Journal*, D. 3 January 1984, p. 668; and Mike Goldfield, 'The Decline of Organized Labor: NLRB Decertification Election Results', *Politics and Society*, Spring 1982.

[36] 'Perhaps the most remarkable phenomenon in the representation process over the last quarter century has been an astronomical increase in unfair labor practices by employers'. While in 1957 the NLRB had ordered 922 employees reinstated after illegal dismissal, in 1980 the number rose to 10,333. The number of discriminatory discharge cases submitted to the Board, 90% related to organizational campaigns or first contract negotiations, now averages almost 20,000 annually, or ten per cent of the union votes received in organizational campaigns during the early 1980s. (See Paul Weiler, 'Promises to Keep: Securing Workers' Rights to Self-Organization Under the NLRA', *Harvard Law Review*, 96, 8, June 1983, pp. 1780–81).

Even when companies had been forced to accept union representation victories, there was no longer any certainty in the 1970s that management would accept the rules of collective bargaining. Increasingly, companies followed in the hardball tradition of Boulware and continued to pressure the unions, looking for the earliest possible opportunity to decertify. Dow Chemical, for instance, decertified fifteen plants between 1966 and 1976, using the IBM tactics of comprehensive salarization and the promotion of job enrichment. The annual number of decertification elections, 583 in 1978–79, increased twenty-fold over the early fifties, while, according to an IUD study, over one-third of newly organized units deunionized within five years.[37] As anti-unionization became deunionization, the specter arose that employers under traditional contracts might begin to import methods of illegal resistance and union-busting. The first major industry case came in construction.

The Failure of Corporatism

During the 1970s, the 3.5 million member Building and Construction Trades Department (BCTD) remained the most powerful bloc in the AFL–CIO and the mainstay of trade-union conservatism. The bargaining power of the building trades was based on their ability to monopolize craft labor within localized construction markets, where they typically negotiated with employers at the association level. Having lost a majority of home building to non-union small contractors, the strength of the BCTD was in industrial, commercial and government construction.

During the 1970s, the stability of these bargaining structures came under serious threat from several quarters. First, the adoption of new building technologies involving extensive use of prefabricated structures, like precast concrete, eroded the boundaries of traditional skills and introduced a larger semi-skilled component into the labor force. Secondly, the union's traditional spatial monopoly on skills was challenged by the rise of giant non-union contractors, like Brown and Root or the Daniels Corporation, who operated scab armies on a national level, and by an aggressively anti-union federation of small and medium-sized commercial builders, the Associated Builders and

---

[37] Harvey Juris and Myron Rookin (eds.), *The Shrinking Perimeter: Unionism and Labor Relations in the Manufacturing Sector.* Lexington (Mass.) 1980, p. 61.

Contractors, Inc. (ABC), which sponsored its own training schemes for non-union workers.[38] These forces came together to dominate whole fields of new commercial construction, including most shopping mall development in the South and West. Their threat to the unionized industry was redoubled by the formation of the Construction Users Roundtable, representing the largest industrial corporations along lines pioneered by the American Plan in Construction during the 1920s. The Roundtable's purpose, in concert with the ABC, was to reduce building costs, arrest wage drift, and encourage skill dilution. It demanded a low-wage rationalization of commercial construction via the suppression of premium pay, the reduction of helpers' and apprentices' wages, the substitution of semi-skilled labor for craft whenever possible, and a radical elimination of restrictive union rules.[39] Large unionized builders, like the Fluor Corporation, responded to the pressures of the Roundtable and the competitive threat of the ABC by going 'double-breasted' with their own non-union subsidiaries.

The construction trades unions' counter-strategy was to involve the federal government in reforming the industry's bargaining structures along the lines of European tripartism. Already under Phase Two of Nixon's NEP, John Dunlop, chairman of the committee on wage stabilization in the construction industry, had successfully experimented with tripartite wage councils. Although these were abolished after the end of controls in May 1974, Dunlop convinced Meany and BCTD head, Georgine, that a greater centralization of bargaining on regional and national scales with government involvement was necessary to avoid a further deterioration of construction unionism on a local level. Appointed Secretary of Labor by Ford, Dunlop met with the BCTD and the contractors through the first half of 1975, proposing a sweeping settlement which he hoped might become the industry's equivalent of steel's no-strike Experimental Negotiating Agreement. What he offered was a quid pro quo in which the unions would accept a statutory prohibition against unauthorized strike action (which would have enabled corporations to obtain a new form of injunction against wildcat strikes), in exchange for the industry's accession to so-called *common situs* picketing, which would allow a union to picket an entire building site in a dispute involving a single contractor. Furthermore, a

---

[38] For the assault on union control of apprenticeship and the provision of skill, see Howard Foster, 'Industrial Relations in Construction: 1970–77' *Industrial Relations*, 17, 1, February 1978; and Howard Foster and Herbert Northrup, *Open Shop Construction*, Philadelphia 1975.

[39] See D. Quinn Mills, 'Construction'. in Gerald Somers (ed.), *Collective Bargaining: The Contemporary American Experience* (IRRA) Madison 1980, pp. 89–91.

national three-party commission would be established with a mandate to promote centralized bargaining by imposing regional or national guidelines on local contracts.

Both bills passed Congress with the support of the AFL–CIO and were sent to Ford for signature. In the meantime, however, an unprecedented coalition of business groups and right-wing activists came together to demand a veto. In short order, New Right media wizard Richard Viguerie deluged the White House with over 700,000 oppositional telegrams and letters.[40] By December, most of the unionized contractors had repudiated the agreement as well, and Ford's veto was assured. Dunlop promptly resigned.

Far from dissuading Meany that corporatism was politically impossible, the failure of the Dunlop plan only encouraged the Federation to reintroduce the package in the first Carter Congress. This time, however, construction bargaining reform bills were followed by a labor law reform bill. Unlike earlier union campaigns to repeal the reactionary provisions of the Taft–Hartley Act, labor law reform only looked for a preservation of the industrial relations status quo by reinforcing the NLRB's powers to halt the epidemic of employer illegality. In tandem with construction reforms, labor law reform represented the maximum thrust of the AFL–CIO's fundamentally conservative response to the crisis of the labor movement. Just as the construction package was tied together by the sacrifice of the rights of local members to strike, so, too, labor-law reform was completely geared to support a top-down public relations approach to union organization, with little provision for the rights of rank-and-file unionists. Moreover, as the *New York Times* forced Meany to admit at the time, the AFL–CIO had no actual plans for any major new organization.[41]

In the event, the AFL–CIO's strategy was not to take the offensive nor even to lead a legislative battle against business; the reform legislation had been purposely moderated to solicit corporate cooperation. In line with Dunlop's concept of tripartite negotiation, the real objective of the AFL–CIO was to use its political influence in an overwhelmingly Democratic Congress to induce business to join in rebuilding a consensus in support of collective bargaining. The vehicle for promoting this consensus was the Labor Management Group that had been reassembled by Dunlop, Meany and Reginald Jones of GE on the precedent of previous administrations' advisory commissions. This private body, chaired by

[40] Richard Harwood, *The Pursuit of the Presidency, 1980*, New York 1980, p. 34.
[41] 'Meany Says Labor Has No Plans for Organizing Drive', *New York Times*, February 23, 1978.

Dunlop, was intended to constitute a kind of economic shadow cabinet — indeed, Carter naively hoped that it would quietly generate a 'social contract' to deal with inflation and the problems of business regulation. On the AFL-CIO side, Murray Finley of the Clothing Workers claimed that the Group had a tacit understanding: 'Labor would support free enterprise, and business would support a strong, democratic labor movement'.[42] It was to the corporate members of the Group that Meany looked for support for labor law reform.

Instead, as both Douglas Fraser and Lane Kirkland complained at the time, the business members responded with smiles and 'class war'. The Business Roundtable, to which the corporate members of the Group also belonged, far from lauding the reforms, opposed them with one of the most extravagant lobbying efforts in history. Created from a merger of the Construction Users Roundtable and the corporate Labor Law Study Committee (formed in 1965 to oppose 14-B repeal), the powerful Roundtable contributed to the defeat of *situs* picketing in 1977, and then stopped labor law reform in the Senate, where it was filibustered to death. The destruction of its legislative program in the Democratic Congress was the biggest debacle in the AFL-CIO's history.[43]

In retrospect, it is clear that Meany and Dunlop ignored the fundamental power shifts that were occuring in both the economy and the political system. On the one hand, the AFL-CIO and its academic allies overestimated their influence in the Carter Administration and Congress. It was delusive to believe that labor could dramatically reassert its clout within the political system without any significant reinvigoration of its own grassroots. On the other hand, they drastically underestimated the lobbying power of business. The emergence of the Roundtable marked a quantum jump in the political organization of the largest corporations, uniting most of the 200 largest firms for the first time in a single peak association. With tactical initiative in the economy and Congress slipping to the corporations, there was simply no important constraint to induce them to take the corporatist ideas of Dunlop or the AFL-CIO seriously. They were becoming free, for the first time in the postwar era, to reshape industrial relations in their own image.

---

[42] Quoted in *Business Week*, August 14, 1978, p. 80
[43] See Kim McQuaid, *Big Business and Presidential Power*, New York 1982, pp. 301–2. The entire Georgia Democratic congressional delegation voted against the earlier *situs* bill, unquestionably with the President's permission.

The End of the Golden Age

1978 was the first year of Reaganomics. A congress two-thirds controlled by Democrats endorsed the legislative agenda of the Business Roundtable by freezing social spending, deregulating the transport and phone industries, and supporting Carter's move to higher interest rates.[44] This resort to a monetarist management of the stagflationary crisis accelerated the erosion of the 'golden age' parameters of American industrial relations. Throughout the core mass-production economy — where unionization had previously stabilized wage competition — labor costs *per se*, rather than just unit labor costs, again became the decisive variable in corporate balance-sheets. Moreover, as we shall explore in greater detail in Chapter Five, the standardized mass consumption of the 1950s and 1960s was being transformed, through a new bimodal income redistribution between working poor and middle strata, into a more stratified network of markets, with an increasing proportion of cheap wage-goods supplied from East Asia.

This restructuring of the American economy away from the Fordist model was led by four trends which sealed the fate of the old regime of industrial relations. *First*, the nearly autarchic American economy was open to foreign imports during the 1970s. Although the internationalization of the US domestic market is usually presented as an inevitable, automatic consequence of sheer market forces, nothing could be further from the truth. The dramatic integration with the world market was politically encouraged by a coalition of forces led by the largest US banks and science-based industries, together with traditional export interests. For the most technologically advanced corporations, ranging from GM to the newly unregulated AT&T, the opening of the economy was a necessary extension of their own evolution into globally-integrated industries. In their efforts to achieve world-level economies of scale made possible by *internal* international divisions of labor, these multinationals have had to radically reorient cost calculations based on traditional oligopolistic, home-market niches. On the one hand, they are in the course of dramatically automating and rationalizing their US production and office facilities. Unlike predominantly home-centered industries, the primary concern of these firms is not so much to cut wages as to cut their workforces through robotization and global subcontracting. On the other hand, this internationalizing core of adv-

---

[44] See *ibid.*, pp. 302–5.

anced industries has also been in the vanguard of efforts to reduce the social overhead costs of production in the United States. That is to say, as they have traded national oligopoly for world industry status, they have become increasingly concerned with reducing costs of inputs that are not internationally competitive, including health provision, communications, domestic transport, construction, as well as safety and environmental regulation.

In this way the new international conditions of competition have fueled the corporate-sponsored movement for deregulation — the *second* major underlying trend in the current crisis of industrial relations. The careful *ententes cordiales* between unions and employers in trucking and air transport have been replaced by ruthless downward spirals of wage cutting and deunionization, most often in the wake of expansion by non-union operators based in the Southeast or Southwest. The near-destruction of the National Master Freight Agreement is perhaps most significant since it has provided wage leadership for a constellation of distributive, processing and wholesale industries linked to truck transport. Moreover, the decline of the Teamsters' ability to control the movement of highway-transported goods has weakened the strike power of myriads of other spatially-localized unions.

The role of Sunbelt-based companies is a *third* major factor in the new competitive equation. In retrospect, it can be seen that the postwar defeat of Southern labor organization (and, correlatively, the failure of the labor movement to become a civil rights movement) was the Achilles heel of American unionism. The right-to-work states have allowed American capital a unique internal mobility, leaving a vast economic space for the evolution of 'Southern strategies' and the crystallization of new non-union sectors. In virtually every industry the supposedly 'marginal' periphery of non-union production has in fact been the redoubt from which, during the 1970s, major assaults have been launched against wage levels and bargaining patterns. We have already noted the case of construction, where the ABC group together with large scab firms like Brown and Root have reshaped the commercial and industrial building industries. In meatpacking, to which I shall refer again, an aggressive non-union newcomer, Iowa Beef Processors, has virtually destroyed the bargaining structure of the industry, becoming the dominant firm in the process. In the airline industry, deregulation has allowed anti-union, sunbelt-based competitors like Delta and Texas Air to establish the competitive standards for the industry, leading to wage cuts and concessions in every other carrier. In steel, the analogous role of spoiler has been played by the new 'minimills', processing scrap with non-union workforces, while

Michelin's non-union complex in South Carolina contributed to the shutting down of tire production in Akron. In the retail industry, union chains have been forced on the offensive against their employees because of pressure from non-union giants like K-Mart and Super Valu. These examples could easily be multiplied, as the emergence of a new non-union sector, typically facilitated by conglomerate mergers and corporate 'double breasting', has reintroduced competitive labor markets.[45]

The *fourth* major trend has been the increasing popularity of deindustrialization as a deliberate financial strategy. Those major industrial oligopolies least advantaged to restructure their production internally — above all the home-bound US steel industry — have instead divested their old capital base to become conglomerates in search of new profit centers in oil production, financial services or military manufacture. Their principal tactic has been to use the threat of plant closure to bully unions into massive wage and benefit concessions which provide cash-flow for reinvestment in new fields followed by closure of the very plants the concessions were supposed to save. Such was the case when US Steel extorted a billion dollars of wage concessions from the steelworkers, which it promptly used to buy Marathon Oil in 1983. In other examples, concession-generated profits have been kept in the industry, but used to shift production overseas or towards the Southeast: this has been the fate of 'give-backs' offered by the rubber workers and Northwest loggers. The political weakness of organized labor can be measured, not so much by the defeats of Carter or Mondale, but by its unhappy failure to pass any enforceable legislation against arbitrary plant closures or the asset-stripping of the old industrial base.

Union Busters in Power

Reaganism has shattered any illusion that the government structures of labor relations possess an institutional integrity or autonomy beyond the dominant ideological currents of the day. The principal state and judicial instruments of labor policy — the Supreme Court, the NLRB, and the administrative and regulatory agencies of the Department of Labor — have been motivated to reverse thirty-five years of policy and

---

[45] For an overview, see Charles Craypo, 'The Decline of Union Bargaining Power', in Michael Carter and William Leahy (eds.), *New Directions in Labor Economics and Industrial Relations*, Notre Dame and London 1981.

accepted procedure. It is not just that the administration has struck sharp blows against labor — as in the destruction of the air-controllers union or in its attacks on the postal workers — but that it has created an executive and judicial framework most conducive to the new accumulation strategies of capital. By partially 'deregulating' labor relations along with banking and transportation, Reagan has paved the way for more rapid capital flight, plant closure, deunionization, and the proliferation of all manner of new sweated industries. In the process he has also eliminated, temporarily or permanently, the judicial supports upon which the practice of bureaucratic trade unionism has vitally depended for over a generation.

To begin with, Reagan slammed the door of the Labor Department in the AFL-CIO's face, despite the latter's belief that the department and its many sinecures were the property of the labor movement. He thus broke the Republican tradition of awarding the department to a representative of the construction trades (e.g., Republican Secretaries of Labor Durkin, Brennan and Dunlop), instead appointing a brazen flunkey of the Teamsters Union with innumerable connections to organized crime. Under Donovan's tenure (ended in 1985), the Justice Department has moved aggressively to reverse labor reforms by administrative fiat: exempting certain categories of federal contractors from minimum wage provisions; weakening affirmative action requirements; cutting Occupational Safety and Health Administration standards; removing seventy-year-old restrictions on child labor and home work; replacing CETA with a low-cost job training bill; and, through elaborate amendment, virtually overturning the Davis-Bacon Act (which dictated the prevailing rate for federal construction). Moreover, to help cover the tracks of union-busting, the Bureau of Labor Statistics closed down several of its time-series related to reporting strike activity and the status of smaller businesses.

Meanwhile, the NLRB, whose institutional autonomy had generally been respected by previous Republican administrations, was awarded to representatives of the Heritage Foundation (Robert Hunter), the National Right to Work Committee (lawyer Hugh Reilly), and the Business Roundtable (corporate lawyers Donald Dotson and Patricia Diaz Dennis). In 1980, Hunter (former chief aide to Senator Orrin Hatch, the leader of the anti-labor-law-reform filibuster) drafted the Heritage Foundation's recommendations on labor policy to Reagan. The document outlined the issues that have become the chief ideological concerns of the present NLRB: 'repeal of those NLRB provisions which establish collective rights as paramount to individual rights', the removal of judicial antitrust exemption for unions, and the return of the power to initiate labor law to the states.[46] Like other Reagan-appointed deregulators in charge of regulatory agencies, the new NLRB under Chairman Dotson has pursued a targeted list of precedents to be overturned. By 1984, they had succeeded in reversing ten major rulings of previous boards. In the name of the supremacy of 'individual' rights, they have limited the right to leaflet, provided for the dismissal of strikers engaged in 'loud verbal conduct', and ruled against individual employees protesting unsafe working conditions. They upheld complains against unions nearly ninety per cent of the time, while denying half of the unfair practices charged against management.[47]

Most importantly, however, the Reagan NLRB, with the support of the Burger Court, has created broad legal justification for the runaway shop and concessionary bargaining. The cornerstone of the new doctrine is the notorious *Milwaukee Spring* case of 1984 which, by reversing earlier NLRB judgments, found that employers need not bargain over plant closure and relocation to non-union sites if the closure does not 'turn' on labor costs. In cognate rulings the Board has allowed employers to contract out work without bargaining with unions, and supported their right to reopen contracts to demand concessions.

Unions, on the other hand, have been denied the right to information about their employer's non-union operations, even when work is being shifted there. The Burger court has added its own capstone to these decisions with the 1984 ruling in the *Bildisco* case: financially troubled companies can now void their union contracts through bankruptcy law, even when they are not actually on the verge of failure.

Collective Bargaining in Reverse

These rulings, of course, have only followed in the wake of the new corporate offensive itself. Although the employer reopening of contracts to demand favorable modifications had become increasingly common during the 1970s on a local union level, particularly in cases involving older manufacturing plants, it was the three successive waves of wage and benefit concessions at Chrysler from 1979 to 1981 that opened the floodgates to reverse bargaining on company-wide and, ultimately,

[46] James Berstein and Lawrence Gold, 'Mid-Life Crisis: The NLRB at Fifty', *Dissent* Summer 1984, p. 216.

[47] *Ibid*; see also report on NLRB in *Business Week*, June 11, 1984.

industry-wide levels.[48] In rapid order, the Chrysler precedent was followed by the rubber and meatpacking industries, then, as the Federal Reserve's monetarism contributed to the worst recession since 1938, Ford and General Motors forced the reopening of the 1979 auto contract. During the first half of 1982, almost sixty per cent of unions engaged in bargaining had to accept real wage freezes or reductions in their new contract, while the overall trend of wage increases decelerated for the first time in forty years.[49]

The first year of the Reagan 'recovery' witnessed a further escalation of employer demands. Although many industrial relations experts, led by John Dunlop, had predicted a return to 'normal' bargaining practice once the downturn was over, 1983 was what the Bureau of Labor Statistics called 'the first year of negative average adjustment for major settlements.'[50] Without a single meaningful guarantee against further disinvestment or plant closing, the steelworkers, under an ailing and disoriented leadership, conceded ten per cent wage cuts, the suspension of the COLA, and sweeping work rule revisions. (A few months later US Steel announced the closure of twenty mills). The copper industry, traditionally tied to bargaining trends in steel, tried to replicate these take-backs, provoking at Phelps Dodge one of the longest and most bitter struggles since the 1930s. Meanwhile, industries tied to the auto pattern, including aerospace and farm equipment, aggressively pushed through the opening created by the previous year's auto concessions. After seven months of picketing Caterpillar, the longest company-wide strike ever waged by the UAW, the union managed to save the COLA but was forced to forego wage increases; IAM and UAW memberships in the aerospace industry, on the other hand, chose to ignore their internationals, returning to work on the basis of 'two-tier' packages that cut the wages of new workers. In spite of comfortable profit levels, Greyhound forced a seven-week strike on its drivers to take back fifteen per cent of wages, a target reduction that was also achieved

---

[48] See Peter Henle 'Reverse Collective Bargaining?', *Industrial and Labor Relations Review*, 25, 3 April 1973. In the twelve examples between 1970 and 1972 that Henle cites, the threat of plant closure was used to introduce sweeping changes in work practice quite as much as to reduce wages.

[49] For excellent overviews of the contemporary period, see Jane Slaughter, *Concessions and How to Beat Them*, Labor Notes Book, Detroit 1983; and Kim Moody, 'Stumbling in the Dark; American Labor's Failed Response', in Mike Davis, et. al. (eds.), *The Year Left 1985*, New York and London 1985.

[50] George Rubin, 'Collective Bargaining in 1982', *Monthly Labor Review* (henceforward, MLR), January 1983, p. 28; and 'Research Summaries', MLR, June 1983, pp. 39–40.

by several airlines, but which paled in comparison to forty to sixty per cent wage concessions extorted from meatcutters.

Far from recovering their bargaining strength as the economy resumed growth, most unions experienced a virtual collapse of their wage power. The Reagan boom was the first upturn in modern American economic history not accompanied by a substantial increase in wages. In the second year of the expansion real wages were actually falling, as the three per cent growth in compensation chased four per cent inflation. Within a remarkably short period, the management offensive had achieved total flexibility in the real wage, thereby inadvertently weakening one of the main supports of mass purchasing power. The trend is likely to be a long-lasting one to the extent that larger wage patterns have been irreversibly fragmented.

Wage-setting since the 1960s had been profoundly influenced by the spread of escalator clauses and COLAs which promoted increased homogeneity and patterning of contractual provisions within, and often between, industries. In 1964, the traditional pacesetting role of the auto and steel contracts for metal fabrication industries had been replicated in the transport and distributive sectors by Jimmy Hoffa's master national agreement in interstate trucking. As a result, union bargaining in key sectors was orchestrated into a triennial periodicity partially disassociated from the pulses of the business cycle, and union wages tended to become centralized via pacesetters and the generalization of comparable COLAs. Although COLAs in 1978 covered only 9.5 per cent of the total labor force, they included three-quarters of manufacturing plants with more than a thousand workers.[51] Thus for unions in strong labor-market positions, the informal spread of pattern bargaining was tantamount during the 1970s to the protection against inflation offered in some European countries by official national wage indexation, although under American conditions it also led to a dramatic widening of the wage gulf between unionized workers and the unorganized majority.

It is not surprising, therefore, that concessionary bargaining has been oriented not only toward wage reductions, but also toward the fragmentation of the wage pattern, the desynchronization of the bargaining cycle, and, in some cases, to the elimination of broadly inclusive COLAs. One major employer after another has sought to break out of industry patterns in order to take competitive advantage of local concessions. The decline of multi-employer bargaining has spread

<hr>

[51] See 'Collective Bargaining in 1984', MLR, January 1985.

from auto (where Chrysler, despite historically high profits in 1984, had managed to preserve its differential wage advantage) to a host of other industries, including grocery, timber, trucking (where almost half of the major employers have broken with the unified bargaining process of the Master Freight Agreement), airlines, aluminum, copper, farm implement, and meatpacking. Finally, in May 1985, twenty-six years of co-ordinated steel bargaining was ended (the ENA had died the year before), partially as result of the USW's failure to hold the line around the anti-concession policy it had adopted in 1983. By allowing local unions to grant off-pattern settlements to a number of smaller steel producers, the international undermined the *raison d'être* for compliance by the larger producers.[52]

If on a macroeconomic scale this decomposition of pattern bargaining arrests wage drift and makes wages as a whole more susceptible to deflation, on a microeconomic scale it drastically reduces the impact of union strike action and intensifies competition between unionized workers by making it easier to shift production between plants. As a result, the worst settlements in an industry, or company, increasingly become the standard of wage determination. The ultimate trajectory, excluding deunionization *tout court*, is toward a system of highly individuated plant-level or firm-specific contracts with increased wage differentiation at every level from the industry to the plant department. In the worst case scenario, precedents for which already exist, the traditional role of the union 'patriotically' supporting its industrial sector against other sectors and foreign competitors degenerates into a simulacrum of Japanese enterprise unionism, where each local union is mobilized against every other in a war of all against all.

The Shrinking Perimeter of Unionism

Another possible fate for labor under the nascent neo-liberal regime of industrial relations is exemplified by the reconversion of the meatpacking industry from a high-wage to a low-wage sector. Meatpacking provides a perfect example of how the combined forces of conglomerate ownership and non-union competition have dramatically turned back the clock that Henry Ford II promised would only move forward. After a generation of struggle, the 'lords of the stockyards', as Brecht called them, were forced into agreements with the militant CIO Packinghouse

---

[52] See Jacoby, *Industrial Relations Research Association 37th Conference Papers.*

workers and the AFL meatcutters in the 1940s. The respective master contracts in beef and pork packing remained stable until the 1960s when, in the wake of the industry's decentralization from its old urban centers, the non-union Iowa Beef Processors entered the scene. IBF, like its imitator, Missouri Beef Processors (or MBPXL), radically challenged the traditional division of labor in the industry by introducing a new technology of frozen beef, machine-cut by semi-skilled, non-union operators. Defeating no less than nine successive strikes and organizing campaigns, IBP had acquired such a dominant position in the beef side of the industry, that several of the largest old-line packers left beef entirely.[53] With beef wages depressed to sixty per cent of the contractual level in pork, and with the largest packers absorbed by powerful conglomerates (in IBP's case, Armand Hammer's Occidental Petroleum), the defenses around union wages in pork packing began to crumble as well.

The employers' offensive in pork packing is significant because of the ruthless and ingenious tactics used by the packers. Rather than waging war by attrition as in other industries, the pork packers successfully overthrew the master contract by *coup d'état*. Esmark, for example, sold off its Swift division to new owners, but retained thirty five per cent of the stock. Wages in the reorganized company were cut by half. Morell, a branch of United Brands, extorted large concessions from its workers and then subcontracted slaughtering to Greyhound, which owned Armour, who sold it to Con Agra, which promptly deunionized it. Meanwhile, Wilson took direct advantage of the bankruptcy laws by invoking 'chapter eleven', closing down, and reopening the next day with wages cut by forty per cent and restrictive workrules eliminated. The union's appeals to the Reaganized NLRB fell on deaf ears.

In the related case of the timber products industry, high to low-wage conversion was achieved through geographical relocation and union disunity. Louisiana-Pacific, worried about lower-cost Canadian competition, decided to shift production from the Pacific Northwest to new mills in the South where wages and benefits were fifty per cent less. In order to minimize the labor-costs of restructuring (supplementary unemployment benefits, etc.) and to rationalize its residual operations in the Northwest, it forced the Carpenters (one of three major unions in timber) out on strike. After a long violent strike, lasting almost two years, the Carpenters were broken at twelve mills by strike-breakers and company harrassment. In bolting from the

---

[53] Over 350 meatpacking plants closed during the 1970s — a dramatic index of the turmoil in the industry. (See Rubin, MLR, January 1983, p. 30)

multi-employer pattern that had been established in 1980 to prevent wage-cutting from becoming a major competitive factor, L-P has now destabilized the whole industry, ensuring further employer efforts either to shift production Southward or to reduce Northwest union wages to Louisiana and Mississippi levels.

In other unionized industries, employers have taken advantage of a sympathetic political climate to reestablish the open shop. In construction the momentum toward deunionization has increased under Reagan, as the volume of non-union plant construction has quadrupled from 1970s levels. According to *Business Week*, 'nearly 400,000 skilled workers have abandoned unions because locals could not find them jobs'.[54] The ABC continues the largest union-busting operation in the country, recently having set up a network of law firms in one hundred cities to advise builders on how to evict unions or to set up non-union subsidiaries. At the same time, the president of the association of large unionized contractors has threatened that without sweeping concessions by the unions the entire industry will be deunionized within a decade, with crafts reorganized along industrial lines. Meanwhile, the construction industry's practice of combining union and non-union operations has spread to the trucking and coal mining industries. Most of the twenty largest unionized trucking firms, who together account for half of the membership under the Master Freight Agreement, have bought up non-union systems. In mining, where union membership has plummeted from seventy to forty per cent of the workforce over the last decade, with attendant loss of union leverage in bargaining, many of the largest firms are 'double-breasted', including Dupont's Consolidation Coal Company, which usually acts as the industry pacemaker in industrial relations.

Overall, Reagan's first term witnessed a decline in the density of unionization that was unprecedented in the postwar experience of any OECD nation: the only comparable antecedent, apart from fascism in Europe, was the US Open Shop of the 1920s. Private sector unionization, which stood at a meridian of nearly thirty-five per cent in 1953, has plummeted from a fifth to a sixth of the labor force — the smallest percentage in any advanced industrial society. As Chart 1 illustrates, the contrast with the Canadian experience is dramatic: from 1940 to 1965, unionization in both countries was synchronized in trend; from 1965, however, there has been a sharp divergence, accelerating since 1975.

---

[54] *Business Week*, February 4, 1985, pp. 52, 54.

Chart 1[55]
Union Density: 1935–1985 (app.)

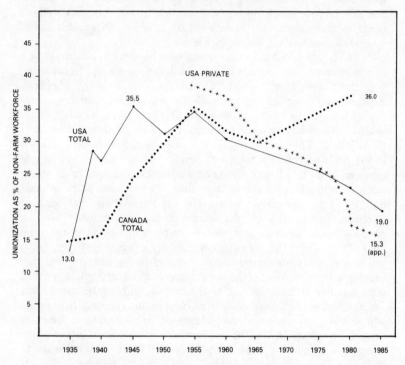

Although part of the American decline is attributable to the new job mix created by rising, unorganized service employment (up five million from 1980–84), and stagnant or declining employment in more organized goods-producing sectors, a significant share involves the direct replacement of union jobs via union-busting or plant relocation. Bureau of Labor Statistics analyses reveal that, whereas the goods-producing department of the economy suffered a net job loss of 800,000, mostly in manufacturing, during this period, unionism in the

---

[55] Compiled from the Department of Labor, *Handbook of Labor Statistics*; Larry T. Adams, 'Changing Employment Patterns of Organized Workers', MLR, February 1985; and Canadian data from Weiler, 'Promises to Keep'. Different time series are only roughly approximate and should be treated with caution; for a good discussion of the problems of measuring union density and comparing it internationally, see footnotes in Weiler.

department fell by two million; the difference being the 'creation' of 1.1 million non-union jobs. Union decreases were particularly sharp (see Table 3.3) in mining (forty-three per cent) and in newly unregulated industries — transportation, utilities and communications — where unionism slipped by a quarter.

Table 3.3[56]

Percentage of Union Membership Among Wage and Salary Workers

	1980	1984	% decline
All industries	23.0	19.1	17
Private sector	20.1	15.6	22
GOODS-PRODUCING	30.5	24.5	20
Mining	32.0	17.9	44
Construction	30.9	24.3	21
Manufacturing	32.3	26.5	18
Durable Goods	34.8	28.0	20
Non-Durable	28.5	24.2	15
SERVICE-PRODUCING	13.5	10.6	21
Transportation, utilities, and communications	48.4	39.6	18
Wholesale and retail trade	10.1	8.2	19
Finance, insurance and real estate	3.2	2.7	16
Service	8.9	7.2	19
Government	35.9	35.9	0

To understand the current status of unionism it is useful to imagine the American labor-force roughly divided in half. One half, including goods-producing industries along with transportation and government, is weakly organized, about thirty per cent; the other half, including services, trade and financial services — is basically an open shop (only seven per cent union). Within the weakly organized half of the economy, moreover, the only sector of unionism demonstrably able to hold its own is the public sector, which in 1984 for the first time became the largest single contingent of the trade union movement (5.661 million versus 5.302 million in manufacture and 2.146 million in transportation-communications) — a shift which will probably have increasing consequences for the AFL-CIO's internal balance of power as

[56] Data from Adams, p. 26.

well. Yet even within the state sector, the organized share has only been maintained by vigorous new recruitment in the face of the sweeping privatization of public services sponsored by the Reagan administration at all governmental levels.[57]

It is likely that this decline will continue and perhaps even accelerate in some sectors like construction and trucking. The US trade-union movement has yet to pass through the eye of the storm. The plunge in membership caused by the 1980–82 recession, followed by the offensive power of management through the subsequent recovery, presages even harder times when the economy again goes into a downswing, or some of the landmines in the financial system explode. Unionism is probably not headed toward extinction but toward a kind of Babylonian captivity in a system of decentralized industrial relations dominated by the corporations and conditioned by the great mass of unorganized labor outside. As union bargaining power declines, it is also likely that union leaders will embrace political alliances with their corporations to demand greater protectionism or restriction of immigration. In the face of the real challenge of a new international division of labor, quasi-racialist calls to defend American standards and products may be the easiest and most demagogic way out for embattled trade-union bureaucrats. Certainly there are many precedents, including the AFL's ill-fated alliance with the American Legion and the Taylor Society during the 1920s, or the AFL–CIO's current bed-sharing with the military-industrial complex.

At the same time, it would be delusory to imagine that the decline of union wage power will lead to some new rearticulation of industrial relations along a 'neoliberal' model. The success of the current management offensive is destroying the foundations of the political economy of Fordism, without establishing any new linkage between the transformation of the conditions of production and the growth of effective demand. The partial desocialization of the wage relation depresses mass purchasing power and creates further segmentation in the working class. The great danger, of course, is that concessionary

---

[57] Reagan sold Conrail and increased contracting out in the Pentagon and throughout the Executive branch. Equally important, the reduction of direct aid to cities and counties spurred them to seek non-union private suppliers of service. As Stuart Butler of the Heritage Foundation explained: 'Local governments had to redefine their role and maintain the same levels of service with less federal funds. They had to either raise taxes, which was politically unacceptable, or look at alternative service providers to do their job less expensively'. (quoted in NYT, May 29, 1985, p. 9) The most controversial of these 'alternative service providers' are the growing numbers of private prisons and security services contracted to state and local government, as well as the Immigration Service.

bargaining, by weakening the unions' role in the regulation of the economy, invites the return of some of the central contradictions of the old liberal regime of accumulation, including underconsumptionism.

Disenfranchising the Future

There are, however, not a few academic observers, as well as some unionists, who see a silver lining in the dark cloud of current industrial relations. In their recent book, *The Next Industrial Divide*, Piore and Sabel argue that the assault on the contractual order, by weakening job control via seniority and giving more scope to experiments in work organization, is inadvertently fostering elements of a new system of 'flexible production', which with union support might return labor to a golden age of craft autonomy and competency.[58] In a kindred but more realistic spirit, Stanley Aronowitz has argued that crisis bargaining might win 'qualitative' demands that would not be available in periods of economic expansion. Invoking the positive heritage of the 'reciprocal bargaining' advocated by Sidney Hillman, he has pointed to the IAM contracts with Eastern Airlines and Pan Am as important steps forward toward an American analogue of German *Mitbestimmung* supported by a 'new communications model of unionism', where the membership has access to financial planning information and participates in company investment decisions. He contrasts the option for 'reciprocity' with the 'futile' alternatives of 'subordination or intransigence'.[59]

Among the unions themselves, the UAW has come closest to advocating that the current crisis of bargaining can be turned to labor's advantage. It approached the crucial 1984 negotiations with an extraordinary air of self-confidence, announcing, according to a leading spokesman, 'We're going directly for a say in the investment function of the corporation. We want all sourcing decisions to be negotiated with us. We want veto power. We want joint determination across the board'.[60] In the event, the UAW's experiment in 'strategic bargaining' led

[58] See Michael Piore and Charles Sabel, *The Second Industrial Divide*, New York 1984. The authors specifically point to the innovations in work design that GM was able to undertake in its unorganized Southern plants in the 1970s (pp. 243–44), as well as to non-union 'high-technology industrial districts' (p. 286 passim) like Silicon Valley. Although the book struggles to maintain a sympathetic attitude toward unionism, it sees the post-war system of mass-production collective bargaining as a fall from the nascent work paradise of the American Plan (p. 124 passim).

[59] See 'Two, Three, Many Greyhounds?', *Nation*, December 17, 1983, pp. 325–26.

[60] UAW spokesperson Peter Laarman, quoted in David Moberg, 'Unions seek job security, but bosses still want cutbacks', *In These Times*, August 8–21, 1984, p. 10.

to a historic settlement with GM in which they attained almost none of these 'qualitative' goals. Instead, the UAW has given the company a free hand in investment and automation in exchange for a 'job security bank' which provides guaranteed employment to senior workers in the face of job changes originating from automation or outsourcing. (This precarious guarantee provides absolutely no protection, on the other hand, against the effects of recession or foreign competition.) In addition, the union reversed its historic advocacy of greater equality in wages by accepting lump-sum payments in the second and third contract year that will not raise the base rate of payment. This drift towards a new inegalitarianism was also visible in the negotiations around GM's proposed 'Saturn Project'. Despite ferocious complaints from skilled-trades dissidents who claimed the deal was tantamount to the destruction of the seniority principle, the union accepted a compromise whereby Saturn workers would be salarized à la IBM at eighty-five per cent of average wages, with employment guarantees for eighty per cent of the workforce.[61]

Although it is too early to tell whether the 1984 auto contract is the 'Second Treaty of Detroit' advertised by the industry and the union, it is certainly a disturbing harbinger of the extent to which concessionary bargaining has eroded the principles of even the most progressive large unions. For the 'bottom line' of the GM settlement was the UAW's willingness to relinquish defense of its job base in return for some security provisions for senior members that could be negotiated without a national strike. In abandoning its custodial responsibilities toward employment, the union was breaking faith not only with a quarter million laid-off autoworkers, who now have no chance of being rehired, but also with the working class of cities dependent on the multiplier effects of auto employment. No group will be hurt worse than the Black inner city of Detroit — an ironic fillip to the UAW's efforts to build the 'progressive alliance'.

Nor are the contract's provisions to protect currently employed workers more than a slender reed in a very strong wind. As confidential GM documents leaked by the union during the contract round reveal, the company is planning over the next few years to cut 50,000 jobs through robotization, another 40,000 through outsourcing and foreign co-production. With a predicted attrition from retirements of yet another 40,000 workers over the same period, 50,000 jobs remain to be

---

[61] Ibid.; and see Moberg's further analysis, *In These Times*, September 26–October 2, 1984.

redeployed or pensioned by the $1 billion job bank.[62] With a recession looming and import penetration predicted by the Commerce Department to grow to one-third of the market by 1987, most of these jobs will probably be lost without any obligation on the company's part beyond a traditional unemployment settlement.[63]

The Faustian deal that the autoworkers and other unions are trying to cut involves the sacrifice of the rights of new workers in exchange for precarious protections for older members. One of the most widespread versions of this trade-off is the so-called 'two-tier' wage agreement. It originated in the retail food industry during the 1970s as unionized employers reacted to the growing competitive pressure of non-union warehouse stores. Under some concessionary agreements made by the United Food and Commercial Workers, new hires are started at less than half the rate of older workers. As the system has been generalized throughout the airlines, trucking, and aerospace industries, it has typically involved wage reductions of fifteen to forty-five per cent.[64] In 1984, the Reagan administration succeeded in imposing a twenty-five per cent below standard two tier on the Postal Service.

The success of multi-tier wage deals, far from giving security to older workers, has only promoted their rapid replacement. Under some food industry contracts signed in the late 1970s, for example, a majority of employees are now on the bottom tier.[65] Wage discrimination encourages substituting part-time employees working for the lower rate for full-timers. One of Greyhound's main demands, for example, was for a free hand in hiring part-timers. Involuntary part-time workers constitute the fastest growing segment of the labor force — more than six million workers earning an average forty per cent an hour less than their full-time counterparts.[66] According to a survey conducted by the Business Council at the start of the upturn in 1983, most manufacturers indicated that they were not planning to rebuild previous staffing levels as production returned to capacity. Instead, they reported extensive plans for new automation combined with greater use of temporary labor to deal with production surges.[67] In the 'high tech' factories of Silicon Valley, a third of the workforce are hired as temporaries, how-

---

[62] Ibid.

[63] *Dun's Business Monthly*, July 1985, p. 19.

[64] *Business Week*, April 8, 1985, pp. 70–71.

[65] *Business Week*, February 6, 1984, p. 17.

[66] *Business Week*, April 1, 1985, pp. 62–63.

[67] Reported in NYT, May 16, 1983, pp. 1, 8; see also, Peter Nulty, 'Will the Big Guys Hire Again?', *Fortune*, April 30, 1984. GE, for one, estimates that half of its present US workforce will be eliminated by robots by 1990. (See *Business Week*, June 14, 1982, p. 61).

ever full time their real status, in order to avoid payment of benefits and supplementaries. Casualization has gone so far in the food processing and retail food industries that the UFCW reckons that half of its members now consists of part-timers.[68] Another union with a large percentage of seasonal and part-time workers, the Teamsters, eagerly takes their dues money while moving at their 1982 Convention virtually to disfranchise them from any voice in internal union affairs.

Meanwhile, involuntary part-time work has spread so extensively among the credentialled strata in health care and education that whole new categories of underclass professionals have come into existence. Hospitals, faced with competition from cost-conscious HMOs, have defended profit levels by replacing full-time nurses with part-timers: a practice which in Minneapolis hospitals led to entire casualized wards and the biggest nurses' strike in American history during the spring of 1985. Colleges, aided by a Supreme Court decision that ruled most private institution faculty outside the ambit of the NLRA, have so vigorously replaced full-timers that today more than a third of all college teaching is conducted by 'adjuncts' or 'visiting' lecturers. Predictably, the Reagan administration has done its bit towards promoting a second tier in the civil service by ruling that federal agencies could employ workers as 'temporaries' for as long as four years.[69]

These new inequities — which veteran labor activist Sidney Lens has characterized as the 'worst setback for unions in a half-century'[70] — are a social time-bomb for the labor movement, menacing any attempt at renovation or renewal. In early 1985, the AFL–CIO executive, with unusual fanfare and national press coverage, welcomed a report it had commissioned from Harvard professor James Medoff on 'The Changing Situation of Workers and Their Unions'. The essence of the Medoff report was that the future of the labor movement depended on sustained and energetic publicity to sell unionism to the unorganized workforce. Whatever the good intentions of the report, any new advertising of the virtues of the AFL–CIO must fall afoul of the organization's estrangement from much of its membership. At a time when a militant, broad concept of solidarity is most necessary for the survival of the movement, the *sauve qui peut* attitude which is being adopted by so many union leaders and by parts of the older membership is a certain recipe for further defeats. In an economy based on historically

---

[68] *Business Week*, April 8, 1985, pp. 70–71.
[69] *Business Week*, April 1, 1985, pp. 62–63.
[70] See 'US Labor Needs Solidarity Too', *Nation*, January 14, 1984

segmented labor markets, the union alternative to new organization has all too frequently been to raise further barriers to any mobility between primary and secondary sectors. Now, with the primary sector itself under siege, unions have closed in around the *laager* of the seniority system, abandoning the unemployed, betraying the trust of working-class communities, and treating young workers as expendable pawns. Such a blinkered, Maginot-like defense of existing employment privileges risks the creation of a reactive anti-solidarity, as the unemployed become strike-breakers, or the second-class citizens of the lower wage tiers decertify unions that have failed to represent them. Curious as this may seem to anyone familiar with the long history of labor militancy in the US, the union movement may be in process of abandoning the majority of the American working class. The short and medium-range political consequences of this self-immolation on the part of the unions will be the subject of a subsequent chapter. In the present context, it is quite enough to observe that the immediate economic consequences for all but a handful of US workers are nothing short of disastrous.

Part Two:
The Age of Reagan

4

The New Right's Road to Power

In 1980, the worst nightmares of the American left appeared to come true. Like some shaggy beast of the apocalypse, Reaganism hunkered out of the Sunbelt, devouring liberal senators and Great Society programs in its path. With the fortieth president's popularity seemingly immune to the misfortunes of his regime, most surviving liberals soon abandoned any pretense of opposition, becoming a tame fringe bordering the administration's solid center of welfare cutting and military spending. With the complicity of a craven media, public discourse has been commandeered by a gaggle of post-liberals, neo-conservatives and new rightists pandering to grotesque inversions of positive discrimination for the middle classes and welfare for the corporations. Indisputably, a seismic shift rightwards has occurred at every level of American politics, with grim implications for the future of women, minorities and the labor movement. It is far less clear, however, whether the less than thirty per cent of the electorate who elected and re-elected Ronald Reagan have actually inaugurated the long-awaited 'Republican majority', or, by demolishing the last integuments of the New Deal political order, only brought the endemic crisis of the party system to a new precipice.

Subsequent chapters will explore the far-reaching shifts in class formation and the international economy that have prepared a favorable social terrain for Reaganism; they will also consider the direction of the current politico-economic realignment and the possible futures that may evolve from it. Our primary focus will be on the emergence of what might be called the 'broad right', sustained by a logic of 'over-consumptionism', and personified by the neo-liberal succession in the Democratic Party, as much as by Reaganism *per se*. But before any larger overview of Reaganism and American politics is possible, it is first necessary to retrace the genealogy of the old liberalism's gravedigger, the New Right. In part, this is a task of reconstructing the inner history of modern Republicanism as a struggle between organized interest groups representing different fractions of capital in relation to the emergence of a 'Fordist' regime of accumulation based on a collectively-bargained wage system. It also demands an accounting of how progressive popular movements of the 1960s were replaced in the 1970s by counter-movements of the right, which, through elaborate political brokerage, became articulated with aggressive elements of the capitalist offensive to constitute a new political coalition. Finally, it will necessarily entail a consideration of the political technologies and modes of mobilization that have so singularly favored the rise of this New Right coalition, shaping a political arena incomparably more congenial to conservative populism than to social democracy. Like many another tawdry tale in American culture, this one begins in Southern California.

Politics California Style

It is hardly surprising that California politics provided the primitive accumulation of conditions for the emergence of the New Right and the presidential ambitions of Ronald Reagan. California, as everyone knows, is the prefigurative laboratory for national political trends: its internal antinomies usually anticipate the form and content of social conflicts elsewhere. It is sufficient to recall Berkeley, Watts or Delano, which literally and symbolically heralded the movements of the late sixties, or Orange County, the antediluvian suburb universally recognized as both the birthplace and promised land of the New Right. The rabid polarization of the Southern California suburbs against the campuses and ghettoes, together with iron-heeled power of the corporate growers, created a ripe political context for new modes of right-wing mobilization. Indeed, one of the most important sequences of experiences through which the New Right came to recognize its power was the series of referenda that united a middle-class and white working-class backlash against integrated housing (1964–65), abolition of the death penalty (1965, 1976), the rights of farm labor (1972), school busing (1979) and property taxes (1978).

Essential to the orchestration of these right-wing, single-issue movements was the availability of plebiscitary mechanisms that maximize the impact of large inputs of money and advertising. California stands in another premonitory relationship to national politics as the first place in which traditional party apparatuses were superseded by new technologies of political manipulation. As Arthur Hadley has noted, California was 'the first state in which the traditional functions of the party broke down'.[1] More precisely, they were reformed out of exist-

---

[1] Arthur T. Hadley, *The Invisible Primary*, Englewood Cliffs 1976, p. 76.

ence. The California Progressives, composed of middle-class *enragés*, wanted to put political power beyond the reach of either organized labor or the Southern Pacific Railroad. In their crusading period between 1907 and 1912, they struck mortal blows against the state's corrupt party system by introducing the initiative and referendum, adopting cross-filing in primaries (which allowed Republican voters to participate in the Democratic primary and vice versa), and placing most state jobs in civil service.

The next stage in California's political revolution occured in 1934 when the celluloid power of Hollywood was mobilized by Louis B. Mayer to defeat Upton Sinclair's radical EPIC ('End Poverty in California') movement in the gubernatorial election. At about the same time, Whitaker and Baxter (or Campaigns, Inc. as they were also called) became the first public relations firm in the world to specialize in professional campaign management. They were so successful in blocking Governor Earl Warren's health insurance legislation during the 1940s, that they were hired by the American Medical Association to organize the largest peacetime advertising campaign in history to defeat Truman's national compulsory health insurance program. Meanwhile, Robinson and Company, of San Francisco, had virtually transformed the initiative and referendum processes into a private monopoly. Claiming in 1949 to have masterminded ninety-five per cent of all such votes over the previous thirty years, Robinson guaranteed to qualify any initiative for the ballot (it required at least 250,000 signatures) for $75,000. Moreover, this pioneer predecessor of Richard Viguerie and the political direct mail industry, also offered direct mail to all of California's five million voters for another $180,000.

The vaunted Progressive system of 'direct democracy' proved in practice to be an almost ideal instrument for the perpetuation of the power of California's ruling groups. Having largely supplanted the formal ability of party bosses to broker nominations or dispense patronage, the emergent system of California politics opened the way for any group of wealthy backers to attempt to valorize some celebrity-commodity as political capital. The 'perfect' candidate no longer needed to be found in a log cabin; he could be manufactured on a Hollywood set. By the 1960s, both parties had discovered the alchemy of cultivating the political homunculus, but the Republicans would remain the more skillful in surrounding their synthetic candidates with grassroots supporters and causes. In California itself, the right wing's almost total domination of the initiative and referendum system provided an agitational machinery *par excellence*. Successive single-issue campaigns, ranging from anti-busing to the Jarvis tax crusade, generated hundreds of thousands of new names for the direct mail list, enlisted thousands of new right-wing activists, and produced bumper crops of highly visible new candidates.

Almost twenty years have passed since Ronald Reagan was catapulted into the governor's mansion in Sacramento by a wave of anti-student, anti-Black reaction.

In the interval, national politics, particularly at the senatorial and presidential levels, have assimilated several of the most distinctive aspects of what used to be called California's 'anti-politics'. First, the number of states nominating presidential candidates through direct primaries has more than doubled during the last twelve years (see Table 4.1); less than a quarter of convention delegates are still selected by the traditional methods of party caucus or state convention. This has radically displaced the strategic locus of the nomination battle from the smoke-filled room to the television studio. For both incumbents and challengers, campaigning has become a virtually permanent process (Reagan, for example, campaigned almost uninterruptedly from 1976 onwards), requiring unprecedented financial resources and mass-media exposure. To appreciate the relative novelty of this approach, it should be recalled that the first candidate to seek his party's presidential nomination by focusing on primaries was Estes Kefauver in 1950. Interestingly, Kefauver, the hard-fisted hero of Senate anti-crime hearings, was also the first presidential candidate to establish a national following through extensive television coverage. And to confirm how thoroughly this process is now in place, recall that the last candidate to achieve nomination *without* fighting his way through the primaries was Hubert Humphrey in 1968, who was selected in the old-fashioned way by party bosses and lobbyists behind the closed doors of the national convention.

Table 4.1
Recent Changes in Presidential Nomination Process[2]

	Number of States Holding Primaries	Percentages of Delegates Selected in Primaries	
		Democratic	Republican
1968	17	38	34
1972	23	61	53
1976	30	73	68
1980	36	76	76

This synergy of primaries and television was the first step in the creeping 'Californization' of national politics. The second step was Congress's October 1974 reform of campaign financing, which drastically limited the maximum amount of individual donations and established a system of matching funds. Ironically, these so-called 'Watergate reforms' produced the opposite result from their declared goal of 'democratizing' the electoral process and reducing the influence of large donors. Instead, a massive shift of power was accomplished away from traditional partisan structures (limits were also imposed on direct party funding) to corporate-dominated Political Action Committees (PACs) and the proprietors of direct mail technology. The proliferation of PACs has become, as Adlai Stevenson Jr. has emphasized, 'a revolutionary element in American politics'.[3] Historically, the 'political action committee' had been invented, and more or less exclusively utilized, by trade unions and other groups dependent upon grassroots financing and support. By restricting corporate lump-sum donations, however, the 1974 reforms compelled corporations to canvass contributions aggressively from their managements and employees. At the same time, corporate PACs learned to tap truly vast constituencies through the services of specialized direct mail firms. As we shall see later, large-scale direct mail solicitation was one of the most important innovations of the 1964 Goldwater campaign. Its current master practitioner is an ex-Goldwaterite and unrepentant admirer of Joseph McCarthy named Richard Viguerie, whose three hundred non-union employees send out more than 100 million pieces of mail each year, using some 300 mailing lists that contain the names of more than 25 million Americans.

The power of right-wing PACs has been amplified by their increasing concentration on the financing of single-issue campaigns and political referenda. This kind of focused single-issue funding, when backed by the awesome money power that the corporate PACs can deploy, has become the linchpin of the new politics. First, it has established a new, direct link between corporate interest groups and mass single-issue constituencies. This link, moreover, tends to by-pass traditional party

[2] Morris P. Fiorina, 'The Decline of Collective Responsibility in American Politics', *Daedalus*, 109, 3, Summer 1980, p. 29. The expansion of presidential primaries was a direct by-product of the 'New Politics' movement within the Democratic Party which sought to redress the defeat of the 'doves' at the bitter 1968 Convention by breaking the power of machine bosses and hawkish labor bureaucrats through a reformation of the nomination process. Under the threat of court action, the less centralized and more amateurish Republican Party apparatus was also 'opened up'.

[3] Quoted in Alan Crawford, *Thunder on the Right*, New York 1980, p. 45.

organization, relying instead upon the direct mail operators and right-wing campaign activists. Secondly, the accumulation of lists of individual contributions, conveniently stored on computer tapes, can be combined and retrieved for use in general elections. Reagan's 1980 campaign, for instance, made very effective use of lists containing the names of gun owners, 'right-to-lifers', members of the American Medical Association, Cuban exiles, anti-pornography zealots, policemen, opponents of the Panama Canal Treaty, and so on. Thirdly, successful candidates tend to become autonomous of party discipline to the extent that they submit themselves to the 'servicing' of PAC special interests. As the aggregative and mediative functions of the party apparatuses are eroded, the PACs increasingly confiscate the ability to define political agendas and to mold public discourse. Finally the liberal–labor wing of the Democratic Party has been disastrously outflanked by the political revolution it inadvertently helped to foster with the Watergate reforms. Viguerie's well-known boast that the 'liberals are eight to ten years behind us in developing the technology of politics'[4] was stunningly reconfirmed in 1984. A virtually computerized Republican election machine out-registered the Democrats, who were hoping to bring millions of new anti-Reagan voters to the polls, delivering instead millions of additional conservative votes. At the same time, this technical and financial gap has been aggravated by the liberal inability to mobilize as many *activists* as the other side. The Republicans have perversely become the more populist party. The aging battalions of the New Deal have been defeated quite as much by the infantry charges of the New Right rank and file as by the deafening media cannonades of its advertising wizards.

From Old Guard to New Right

This transformation of the electoral process has been accompanied by far-reaching changes in the internal power structures of the two parties, which in turn have tended to reflect the political realignment of different socio-economic constituencies. The most consequential of these changes for understanding the rise of Reaganism has been a rather complex double movement which, since 1968, has brought a relatively 'peripheral' fraction of capital to power in the Republican Party, while moving the political representatives of the 'core' fraction into a more

---

[4] Quoted in the *Guardian* (New York), May 1, 1981, p. 5.

bipartisan — or perhaps one should say: *transpartisan* — relationship to the party system. This has not involved a fundamental 'power shift' between the 'Cowboy' capitalists of the Sunbelt and the 'Yankee' financiers of the Northeast, as some writers have hypothesized;[5] rather, it has entailed the establishment of a delimited, and probably unstable, consortium of power and interest between the different groups. In order to understand the implications of this development, it is necessary briefly to rehearse some salient facts about the character of the American party system, in particular, the role of different capitalist class-fractions.

The American political system differs radically from other parliamentary democracies. It is wrong to imagine that it can be analyzed as a special variety of European politics *minus* a working-class party; equally, the positional signifiers 'right-left-center', which in Europe automatically condense stable congruences of class and ideology, are often inapplicable, if not positively misleading, in describing American political alignments. Central and exceptional characteristics of American party politics include: the subordination-integration of organized labor within one of the capitalist parties; the political segmentation of the proletariat and middle strata by racial and ethno-religious conflict; the singular weight and episodic militancy of the petty bourgeoisie; the distinctive complexity and fluidity of the internal structure of the big bourgeoisie; and the importance of regional polarizations within a federal political structure.

These last two factors are especially important in understanding the internal politics of the modern Republican Party and are closely related to one another. Regional conflicts have often refracted the prolonged struggles for power between different capitalist fractions, while the successive appearance of industrial 'frontiers' has created opportunities for the emergence of new regional centers of capital. In contrast to the geo-financial centralism of other capitalist countries,[6] the dominance of Wall Street has always been qualified by competition with financial centers in Cleveland, Chicago, San Francisco and, more recently, Los Angeles and Houston. As a result, the privileged access to national government enjoyed by older sections of the bourgeoisie has been rep-

---

[5] See Kirkpatrick Sale, *Power Shift: The Rise of the Southern Rim and Its Challenge to the Eastern Establishment*, New York 1979.

[6] Between Jackson's overthrow of the Second Bank of the United States in 1836 and the establishment of the Federal Reserve System in 1913, there was no 'central bank' in a European sense. This bred financial anarchy and instability at times, but also put Western banks under a looser Eastern rein. Similarly, the still unrepealed prohibitions against interstate chain banking have afforded a measure of protectionism to regional financial centres.

164

eatedly challenged by the assault of newer, regionally-based capitalist groups — a conflict facilitated by a relatively decentralized political system that permits consolidation of local citadels of capitalist power on a state or municipal basis. These complex struggles between capital have tended to shape competing coalitions of interests within the bourgeoisie. At the level of national politics, it is possible to distinguish a traditional *core* fraction of finance capital, as well as successive *peripheral* fractions in opposition.

For most of this century, the presidential level of the Republican Party has been dominated by its so-called 'Eastern Establishment' or — as conservatives have called it since 1940 — the '*Liberal* Eastern Establishment'. The historic power of this wing corresponds to its social composition: encompassing most of the 'Boston-Wall Street' network of finance capital with the exception of German-Jewish banking capital (traditionally Democratic). Between McKinley and Hoover,[7] the economic and politically hegemonic instance within this bloc — and, thus, for US capitalism as a whole — was the power of the great investment banks and, above all, the House of Morgan. The investment banks had been the chief conduits of the European capital that helped finance the US industrial revolution in the nineteenth century, and they used their financial might to carry out a vast restructuring of the American economy between 1898 and 1902. What they created might be described as an *unorganized corporate capitalism* based on the control of the investment banks over a spectrum of infrastructural and industrial monopolies. Although the sweeping trustification carried out by Morgan was a precondition for mass production, the inherently *rentier* character of investment bank dominance (which extorted monopoly rents and speculative profits from the most technologically advanced industries via control of money, utility costs, railway rates, and certain inputs) was a positive fetter on the emergence of a 'Fordist' regime of intensive accumulation. Although some capitalists in the advanced sectors supported the Democratic Party (Henry Ford in the early years), most rallied behind the Rockefeller-Standard Oil forces in the Republican Party. Self-financed by oil profits, the Rockefeller empire had escaped financial control by the investment banks and, as the second largest capital group in America, was well-positioned to

[7] In 1896, the Republican Party became truly the majority party of big business as the so-called 'Gold Democrats' (including the leading Eastern Democratic capitalists) lost control of their party to a fusion ticket of Populists and petty-bourgeois Silver Democrats. McKinley's subsequent defeat of Bryan is generally reckoned to have 'realigned' the party system, ushering in almost forty years of Republican dominance of Congress.

lead the attack on Morgan power. Ironically, it was the Democratic New Deal landslide in 1932 that created the conditions for both the economic and political recomposition of the Republican core fraction.

First, a series of sweeping reforms (Glass-Steagall Act of 1935, Public Utility Holding Company Act of 1935, Chandler Act of 1935, etc.) dismantled investment bank control over capital markets, railroads, utilities and communications (ATT escaped Morgan domination in 1940). This removed the chief obstacle to the hegemony of the most advanced industrial corporations and, later, their associated *commercial* banks. Secondly, the seven main capital groups, which in 1938 controlled two-thirds of the assets of the 200 largest corporations, became increasingly integrated via a labyrinthian network of interlocking directorships and shareholdings, creating a more unified material 'general interest' between the groups. Thirdly, with the coming of the Second World War, core capital definitively abandoned its protectionist swaddling clothes for imperial robes. The reconstruction of international free trade within an American imperium became its overriding goal. Roosevelt's policies of a bipartisan war cabinet and corporate control within the state structures of the war economy firmly established the basis for postwar continuity of core dominance — regardless of the party in power — in the strategic Cabinet positions controlling foreign policy, defense and the macro-economy. Fourthly, the re-organization of power within the core capitalist bloc cleared the way for the political accommodation of *weak* versions of collective bargaining and welfare expenditure. Thus in 1940, the 'Eastern Establishment' raised a liberal flag with the nomination of Wendell Willkie in a deliberate attempt to win over part of the urban New Deal electorate (farmers had already returned to the Republican fold in 1938). For the next quarter-century, all Republican presidential candidates (Dewey, Eisenhower, Nixon in 1960) adhered to the core program of corporate internationalism and critical toleration of New Deal reforms.

The first mass current in American politics to self-consciously call itself the 'Right' was the loosely-knit opposition wing of the Republican Party which emerged in 1938 under the leadership of Senator Taft of Ohio. Its financial nucleus was a constellation of protectionist Midwestern banking and industrial interests (including the lords of 'little steel') who were ultramontane in their loyalty to McKinleyism and fanatical in their opposition to both the New Deal and liberal-internationalist Republicanism. This peripheral capitalist bloc also attracted support from the flotsam and jetsam connected to the old rentier strata, as well as from the shopkeepers of a myriad small-town 'Main Streets' who had little use for the federal government and even less for Eastern bankers. Its distinctive resonance was its blending of anti-Rooseveltian intransigence with a fierce nationalism — frequently misnamed 'isolationism' — that urged the pursuit of Manifest Destiny in the Caribbean and Pacific, while rejecting American involvement in European intrigues. Taft's unceasing criticism of the hated 'Eastern Establishment' and American aid for Britain also gave him a purchase upon those German immigrant constituencies of Wisconsin and the upper Midwest that had formerly supported Lafollette Progressivism. Taft exploited this mid-continental power base to become Senate leader and to gain control of the Republican National Committee, but the presidential nomination eluded him. Despite his support from the party 'regulars', Taft's presidential drives were sabotaged four times between 1940 and 1952 by shrewd injections of Eastern money and the defection of right-wing allies.

The Republican Right was also internally divided by differences which emerged in the 1945-49 period over the Truman administration's policies for containing Communism in Western Europe. 'Old nationalists' like Taft stuck fast by the credo of 'Fortress America' and 'Asia First', but the so-called 'new nationalists' like Vandenberg, Nixon and Knowland joined forces with Eastern Republicans and Democrats in a bipartisan bloc to support the Truman Doctrine and the Marshall Plan. The victory of the Chinese Revolution in 1949, however, reconciled the splintered Right and allowed them to recapture the profitable politics of anti-Communism from the Democrats (exploiting the theme of 'who betrayed China?'). The soaring popularities of General McArthur and of grand inquisitor Joe McCarthy seemed to portend a coming right-wing Thermidor, but by 1954 both had severely discredited themselves by reckless attacks on Republican moderates and the sacrosanct figure of President Eisenhower.[8] With their decline and Taft's death, the influence and cohesion of the Right began to wane. At the same time, however, conservative Republicans remained restive over Eisenhower's failure to build the grassroots strength of the party; and the situation became critical when the 1958 midterm elections returned the greatest Democratic gains since 1934. Between 1958 and 1963, a 'New Right' began to crystallize within the Republican Party which, while ultimately recuperating much of the Taft social base, differed significantly in its socio-economic profile and political strategy from the disappearing old guard. Whereas Taftism was an expression of the provincial Babbitry of the Midwest, the New Right was typified

---

[8] Cf. Michael W. Miles, *The Odyssey of the American Right*, New York/Oxford 1980; and David Caute, *The Great Fear*, London 1978.

by the entrepreneurs and suburban elites of the emergent 'Sunbelt'. Its power structure, as we shall see, was a new peripheral capital fraction, which shared both traditional right-wing interests in the Pacific Basin, as well as the Eastern Establishment's obsession with the Middle East. While the popular culture of the Old Right had been rooted in 'America First-ism' and pervasive anti-semitism, the New Right scavenged much of its identity from the growing backlash against the civil rights movement. Finally, the New Right, unlike the Old, was genuinely a *movement* with ideology, discipline, cadre and an impressive willingness to exploit new political technologies.

The Goldwater Legacy

As the battle for the Republican succession heated up in early 1960, conservatives — old and new — confidently assumed that Vice-President Nixon would pick up Taft's fallen mantle and chase the moneylenders of Wall Street from the temple of the GOP. When Nixon instead contrived an electoral pact with Nelson Rockefeller (the Eastern Establishment incarnate and the *bête noire* of the right), conservative anger was articulated by a then virtually unknown senator from Arizona, Barry Goldwater, who called it 'the Munich of the Republican Party'. Goldwater's subsequent *jihad*-cum-presidential-campaign has often been dismissed as a great aberration in the fundamentally centrist and consensualist movement of American politics (he did, after all, lose by *sixteen* million votes). Since November 1980, however, the Goldwater crusade has retrospectively taken on a new significance: Reagan's victory, it is now clear, was built upon its institutional and political legacy.

Many contingent factors — Rockefeller's divorce, Scranton's indecisiveness, Nixon's 1962 gubernatorial defeat, Lodge's late start, etc. — contributed to Goldwater's stunning upset of the Eastern Establishment at the 1964 convention, but the decisive element was undoubtedly the superior organization of the Goldwater camp. Whereas Taft's old guard was still fundamentally a network of courthouse cliques, the Goldwaterites were a *cadre* of middle-class, mostly college-educated, activists with a transcendent commitment to a right-wing ideology and political agenda rather than to the Republican Party *per se*. They were also a financially independent movement, succeeding in the supposedly impossible feat of mounting a national campaign against the Democrats without support from the Eastern Establishment (most of whom decamped towards Lyndon Johnson). As we shall see,

the great postwar boom — particularly the disproportionate share of
military spending received by the South and West — raised new
centers of financial power in Los Angeles, Houston and Denver; and
Goldwater was bankrolled by many of the same 'angels' who would
later elevate Reagan. More innovatively, Goldwater 'was the first major
political candidate for whom supporters conducted a large-scale
campaign to solicit political contributions through the mails.'[9] The
extensive mailing lists that William S. Warner collected for Goldwater
were a revolutionary step forward in emancipating the right from
dependence on the Eastern Establishment and in providing the
resources for it to survive and grow as a network of institutionalized
single-issue movements and multipurpose umbrella groups. The
organizational originality of the Goldwater effort, and its radical depar-
ture from Republican tradition, is vividly revealed by a comparison of
its financial base with that of Eisenhower's 1952 campaign (Table 4.2).

Goldwater's grand design in 1964 combined two ambitious
schemas; the 'Southern strategy' and the 'hidden Republican majority'. The first assumed that the growth of massive white resistance to
the civil rights movement since 1954 had opened a huge potential
breach for right-wing Republicans in the formerly 'solid South'; while
the second argued that the GOP had lost thirteen per cent of its voters
since 1940 because, in nominating moderates, it had failed to offer a
real alternative to an alleged 'silent majority' of conservative voters. The
testing of these assumptions in the heat of battle produced traumatic
lessons which became codified in subsequent right-wing campaigns.
The 'Southern strategy' was a qualified success to the extent that five of
Goldwater's meager six victories were in states of the Deep South
(Louisiana, Mississippi, Alabama, Georgia and South Carolina). The

Table 4.2[10]

	Number of contributors	% of donations over $500
Eisenhower (52)	37,500	88%
Goldwater (64)	1,000,000	28%

[9] Crawford, p. 46.
[10] From Stephen Hess and David S. Broder, *The Republican Establishment*, New York 1967, pp. 59–61.

'hidden Republican majority', on the other hand, proved to be a deadly delusion, as Goldwater's doctrinal fidelity to conservative ideology (for example, in Appalachia he condemned anti-poverty measures, in Florida he attacked medical aid for the elderly, and so on) alienated millions who had voted for Nixon in 1960, giving Johnson the largest plurality in history. At the time, many liberals and establishment Republicans believed that the New Right had been effectively annihilated as a serious political force; in fact, the organizational apparatus survived intact, and thousands of conservative activists learned salutory lessons which they would apply in the campaigns of the seventies. First, 1964 demonstrated the suicidal folly of attacking vastly popular New Deal reforms, like Social Security or the TVA, which benefited the middle classes quite as much as the working classes. Secondly, the abrupt practical refutation of the latent majority thesis sharpened the focus around the problem of *winning over* elements of the Democratic coalition and encouraged many conservatives to concentrate on bipartisan single-issue campaigns with a rightist dynamic, rather than on frontal ideological clashes.

The general crisis of the Great Society in 1968 produced a renaissance of right-wing activism. The Southern strategy became a 'Northern strategy' when George Wallace invaded Yankeeland in the wake of three years of ghetto insurrections and white backlash. Although Wallace principally represented the politics of white supremacy, he also liked to expound on 'our populist struggle' against the 'twin exploiters, the corporate establishment of wealth and the leftist education-welfare establishment'. Some ex-Goldwaterites like Kevin Phillips and Patrick Buchanan began to argue that a new right-wing majority might be built by using anti-elitism to channel class hostility against a parasitic 'new class' lodged in the universities and government bureaucracy. Phillips attempted to theorize the lessons of the Goldwater campaign and the Wallace movement in his book *The Emerging Republican Majority*, which proposed a precise electoral blueprint for utilizing racism and 'status resentment' to realign white Northern ethnics and Southern rednecks behind a neo-populist GOP. Although the book was ignored by Nixon (to whom Phillips had offered it as a kind of contemporary *Prince*), the galleys made the rounds of the Republican National Committee and left a deep impression on most of the future managers of the 1980 campaign.

Phillip's interpretation of the New Right as latterday Jacksonianism was just one of the new permutations of conservative philosophy as the once powerful coterie of Burkean intellectuals around the *National Review* (including such 'effete snobs' as William Buckley) were pushed aside in favor of more popular and philistine programs. By the beginning of Nixon's imperial presidency it was necessary to distinguish a confusing cluster of New Rights, as ex-Goldwaterites mated and multiplied in a fruitful array of movements and organizations. Although a certain continuity was represented by the American Conservative Union (founded in 1964 to institutionalize the Draft Goldwater movement), a new organizational pole emerged in the early seventies under the troika of Coors, Weyrich and Viguerie. Coors, a wealthy Colorado brewer who had de-unionized his plants after one of the longest strikes and boycotts in American history, teamed up with conservative activist Paul Weyrich and direct mail wizard Richard Viguerie to found the Committee for the Survival of a Free Congress (CSFC), an alternative to the American Conservative Union's political fund. By 1976, the CSFC, together with other New Right PACs coordinated by Viguerie, were 'raising more money than the Republican National Committee and its House and Senate campaign committees combined'[11]. Simultaneously, the sustained, systematic expansion of single-issue movements under right-wing control was creating an unprecedented array of interlocking organizations and constituencies, ranging from 'law and order' interest groups (Americans for Effective Law Enforcement, National Rifle Association, etc.) to 'new Cold War' lobbies (American Security Council) or politicized fundamentalism (Rev. Jerry Falwell's Moral Majority).[12] The largest and most effective category of single-issue groups, however, were those devoted to the defence of the sanctity of white suburban family life, including dozens of mass anti-busing movements, Phyllis Schlafly's anti-ERA Eagle Forum, Anita Bryant's anti-gay-rights campaign, and — largest of all — the 'Right to Life' crusade. Significantly, several of these single-issue blocs — the pro-Cold War, anti-busing and anti-abortion movements in particular — mobilized widespread support from classical New Deal blue-collar constituencies, thus demonstrating that social conservatism, racism and patriotism provided powerful entrées for New Right politics where Goldwaterite economic conservatism had dismally failed. As Viguerie

---

[11] Crawford, p. 47.

[12] Fundamentalism has enjoyed an extraordinary renaissance in the United States over the last generation. While liberal Protestant churches have declined, a group like the Southern Baptists gained no fewer than two million members between 1965 and 1975. Today there are at least 45 million fundamentalists, and all three presidential candidates in 1980 declared themselves to be 'born again' Christians (although Reagan ultimately won 61% of the fundamentalist vote). A far right-wing 'electronic church' comprising 36 wholly religious TV stations and 1,300 religious radio stations is claimed to reach a weekly audience of almost 100 million (Crawford, pp. 159–61).

explained in 1981: 'It was the social issues that got us this far, and that's what will take us into the future. We never really won until we began stressing issues like busing, abortion, school prayer and gun control. We talked about the sanctity of free enterprise, about the Communist onslaught until we were blue in the face. But we didn't start winning majorities in elections until we got down to gut level issues.'[13]

Sunbelt Barons and Hollywood Cowboys

The broadening of the New Right's organizational base was accompanied by a consolidation of its links with the new peripheral fraction of predominantly Southern and Western capital. The original nucleus of Sunbelt entrepreneurs who had financed Goldwater were reinforced in the late sixties and early seventies by new levies of Texas oil millionaires, Florida real-estate speculators and California construction contractors. The Vietnam War boom accelerated industrialization throughout the Southern zone of the United States, while the 1971 and 1974 recessions stimulated capital flight from the unionized Northeast to the relatively 'union-free' environments of the Confederacy and Southwest/Mountain states. The seventies witnessed the most rapid and large-scale shift in economic power in American history.

While overall manufacturing employment tended to decline slightly this was 'due entirely to changes in the North, where almost one million jobs were lost between 1970 and 1977. Vigorous growth in the South, by contrast, created more than 200,000 new jobs in manufacturing over the period'.[14] Whereas 3,500,000 Southerners (86 per cent black) had fled northwards or westwards in the twenty years up to 1960, the seventies saw the same number of immigrants (mainly white) heading south in less than half this time-span. Meanwhile, the great Southern California boom resumed after a short aerospace depression at the end of the sixties, and both Los Angeles and Houston began to flex their new muscles as international financial centers. The Sunbelt's economic clout also benefited from the late-sixties merger wave (the biggest in American history), which saw many regionally-based firms attain footholds in the *Fortune* '500'.

Although many of the most distinctive industries of the Sunbelt —

[13] Quoted in the *Guardian* (New York), April 1, 1981, p. 5.
[14] Robert Estall, 'The Changing Balance of the Northern and Southern Regions of the United States', *American Studies*, 14, 3, p. 370.

aerospace, electronics and the super-oil firms — are constituents of core capital directly controlled by Eastern finance groups, the power of regional capital was also greatly expanded in the last decade. A partial inventory of the leading backers of the New Right (including members of Reagan's 'Kitchen Cabinet') is revealing: oil exploration (Henry Salvatori, Leon Hess, Ed Noble, Norton Simon); construction (J. Robert Fluor); tourism/recreation (Barron Hilton, Walter Knott, J. Willard Marriott); agribusiness/real estate (Jack Wrather, William Wilson, Charles Wick, William French Smith, Irvine Corporation); supermarkets (Theodore Cummins); textile (Roger Milliken), plus such singularities as Coors, Holmes Tuttle (world's largest automobile dealer) and Justin Dart (Kraft Cheese and Tupperware). Interestingly, large military contractors and defense firms, although integral to Reagan's victory, do not stand out in the power structure of the New Right; owned or satellitized by core capital, they have usually been found in the retinue of Establishment Republicans or hawkish Democrats like 'Scoop' Jackson of Washington (also a favourite son of the AFL–CIO). Nor are the pioneering capitalists of Silicon Valley, the 'high-tech' entrepreneurs or latterday Henry Fords, particularly represented in the New Right elite. What, then, are the common structural characteristics that permit us to speak of this apparent smorgasbord of special interests, ranging from Knott's Berry Farm to Coors Beer, as a distinct 'class-fraction'?

First is the prevalence of single-family control (*de facto* or *de jure*) and an obsession with preserving financial and managerial independence. Secondly, many are particularly labor-intensive, and all are rabidly anti-union and anti-welfare. Thirdly, in contrast to Old Right Midwestern manufacturers (with their protectionist, internal market orientation), these New Right capitalists are expansionist, with particularly well-defined interests in the Middle East, and to a lesser extent in Mexico/Central America. Fourthly, they are all deeply tied by complex networks of investments, hidden share-holdings, and direct activity to Sunbelt land and mineral speculation. One of the secrets of their cherished financial autonomy has been their ability to realize enormous profits in commercial real-estate markets and oil leases. They are a quasi-rentier bloc with substantial objective interests in the maintenance of boom conditions in the Sunbelt and in the preservation of inflated land and resource equities. Finally, precisely because of their intrinsic dependence upon hothouse economic conditions and high growth rates, they also have an overriding interest in ensuring that federal transfer mechanisms — above all, defense spending — continue disproportionately to favor Sunbelt states. As Table 4.3 demonstrates,

Table 4.3
Federal Taxes, Expenditures and Net Flow, North and South, 1976[15]

	Federal Taxes	($ million) Federal Expenditures	Net Flow
North	151,367	118,657	−32,710
South	89,732	102,346	+12,614

differential fiscal flows ironically privilege those areas where anti-statist rhetoric is most strident.

The internal power structure of the New Right, therefore, is dominated by an alliance of entrepreneurial rather than corporate capitalists, centered for the most part in the primary and tertiary sectors, with vested interests in regional land/resource speculation, hyper-militarization and a filibustering attitude towards the Third World. They stand out sharply from both the increasingly archaic Midwest manufacturing stratum as well as from the transnational leviathans of the East — not least because of their different relationship to the inflationary dynamic of the economy. While inflation has threatened manufacturing capital as a whole with increasingly high replacement costs of fixed capital (while devalorizing older energy-intensive technologies), it has tended to promote growth in the primary and tertiary sectors of the Sunbelt and to yield huge speculative boondoggles. It is no wonder that, as we shall see later, the New Right has been more enamored with supply-side economics, with its reflationary implications, than with a purist monetarism with deflationary consequences.

It was only logical that the 'frontiersmen' of Sunbelt capitalism would seek a square-shouldered, macho-mannered political represent-ative of their own ideal-type. Moreover, the survival of the New Right, in the face of its own rampant factionalism and centrifugal self-inter-ests, required a single, charismatic leadership. Despite his genuine popularity among the Republican electorate and his ruthless determin-ation to control the party, President Nixon was never an acceptable *führer*-figure for most of the New Right. In their eyes he was the apost-ate twice over, in bed with the Rockefellers, and the one who had 'sold out' Taiwan and imposed wage and price controls when no Democrat would have dared. (Part of the dementia behind CREEP and Watergate may have been an expression of Nixon's recognition that he lacked

---

[15] Estall, p. 379. Cf. Table 5.3, p. 195.

adequate legitimacy and backing from either pole of his own party.) In contrast, much of the New Right's grassroots was charmed by the image which had been built round Reagan (thanks to state-of-the-art political advertising), and the 'permanent candidate's' campaign (he first announced his presidential ambitions in 1968) gained steadily in momentum and direct-mail dollars. Reagan was not, however, the first choice of most of the key New Right capitalists nor of the strategic troika of Coors-Viguerie-Weyrich. Their hero was John Connally — Nixon's Treasury Secretary, former Governor of Texas and no mere Hollywood cowboy. It was their plan to support him against Ford and Reagan in 1976, but the taint of Watergate was indelible (a point proven for a second time in 1980).

In 1968, a loose alliance of right-wing forces captured control of the Republican Party apparatus from the Eastern Establishment. In the wake of Watergate, however, the latter made a vigorous counterattack: Ford was 'induced' to appoint Rockefeller Vice-President, Kissinger was given a second lease on life (to the disgust of the New Right), and in 1975, the conservatives lost control of the Republican National Committee. This 'liberal captivity' of the GOP was largely blamed by the New Right on Goldwater's reluctance to support right-winger Dean Burch of California for the Republican Chairmanship. Goldwater's 'treason', following Nixon's apostasy, raised fears among the New Right as to whether *any* conservative candidate could be immune to seduction by the Establishment or vouchsafed from making concessions to the center. These tensions exploded at the 1976 convention when Reagan chose the liberal Schweiker rather than the conservative Crane as his running mate in an obvious bid for broader support. The doyens of the New Right fulminated, and Weyrich warned the Reaganites that if their leader was ever elected, the New Right would be 'out'.[16] Nonetheless, in a display of discipline that was a portent of things to come in 1980, the New Right grassroots held firm for Reagan. Indeed, they almost unseated the incumbent President, something hitherto reckoned nearly impossible in modern conditions, and as impressive a feat as Goldwater's nomination twelve years before.

It is illuminating to compare the relative situations of the New Right and the Eastern Establishment on the eve of the 1980 campaign. According to Alan Crawford, the New Right — narrowly defined by close ties to nodal organizations like the CSFC and the National Conservative PAC — emerged from the 1978 midterm elections with control of

---

[16] Quoted in Crawford, p. 118.

ten per cent of Congress (40 Congressmen, 10 Senators).[17] In the Senate this represented a five-fold increase since 1972 and was significantly attributable to support from single-issue voters. In terms of financial power, the New Right had an unequalled and frightening mastery of direct mail technology. Geographically, however, the New Right remained primarily a sectional phenomenon, with a particularly strong concentration of representation in the Mountain states (six of ten senators) as well as islands of power in California, the Midwest and Dixie. Significantly, its geographical boundaries tended to coincide with the most concentrated distribution of Mormonism and evangelical Protestantism: the new 'burnt-over' districts of the Sunbelt most likely to sustain a politics of moral revanchism. Although the New Right's single-issue blitzkriegs had been successful in the more industrialized areas of the country as well, they also tended to leave more ephemeral political traces. The heavily Catholic and ethnic electorate of the Northeast, while susceptible to the appeals of a 'pro-family' social conservatism, was generally repelled, as the Goldwater campaign demonstrated, by traditional economic conservatism. Any hope for the New Right to escape from its Sunbelt ghetto depended on its ability to discover an economic demagogy that was equally acceptable to Western entrepreneurs and Eastern skilled workers and professionals.

Meanwhile, the 'Eastern Establishment' within the Republican party had become both more conservative and organizationally diffuse. Although Ford and Bush were nominal standard-bearers of the moderate wing, they scarcely stood in the same direct and intimate relationship to the core as had Rockefeller and Scranton, the main Establishment candidates in the sixties. To a profound degree, the 'core' had disengaged itself from a specific or permanent commitment to a particular wing of the Republican party or even to the GOP *per se*. With the presidency in virtually uninterrupted crisis from 1965 onwards, and with a general weakening of the role of regular party apparatuses in the face of the 'new politics', the political articulation of core interests became increasingly dependent on the strengthening of *parastatal* rather than partisan institutions. First, as a result of Vietnam and the world economic crisis, there was a massive reinforcement of the 'bonding' between the key corporate foreign and macroeconomic policy organs (the Council on Foreign Relations, Committee for Economic Development, and so on) and their corresponding depart-

---

[17] Ibid, p. 267. The congressional penumbra of the New Right — its softcore sympathizers and more or less consistent allies — would probably have included in 1978/79 another one hundred members of the House and a further dozen senators.

ments and cabinet positions in Washington. In the same spirit, David Rockefeller's Trilateral Commission represented an unprecedented (and largely unsuccessful) attempt to create a network of bipartisan support for what was intended to be a unified program of the core's domestic and transnational interests. Secondly, the new linkage between PACs and single-issue politics spurred an expansion and reorganization of corporate lobbies and employer associations. The 'interest group' level of American politics became more important than ever, while simultaneously becoming less dependent upon partisan affiliation. The number of corporate PACs exploded from a mere 89 at the end of 1974 to 954 in January 1981, while a powerful new alliance of the largest corporation — the Business Roundtable[18] — was organized to coordinate congressional lobbying.

It is important to note, however, that the spectacular successes of the Business Roundtable and corporate PACs — like their defeat of labor-law reform or their gutting of Carter's proposed Consumer Protection Agency — have been achieved around a relatively 'easy' axis of issues (anti-labor, anti-regulation, and to some extent, pro-'new Cold War') that has encouraged unity within the core, and between it and peripheral capital. (Indeed, mainstream corporations have found it increasingly useful to deploy the New Right as shock troops in confrontations with the AFL–CIO or environmental groups.) Yet major macroeconomic issues like reindustrialization, energy policy and protectionism have resisted any spontaneous or symbiotic corporate consensus. Moreover, the persistent syndrome of crisis at the executive level and rapid turn-over of policies have produced a generalized sense that the difficult work of arbitrating a medium- or long-term economic strategy requires, first of all, a restabilization of the regime, backed by a durable electoral mandate. Despite the success of the core in conducting politics at a parastatal or interest-group level, it was inevitably brought back to the problem of shaping a new political equilibrium at a time when the electorate itself was becoming distinctly 'dealigned' from party structures and traditional loyalties. The forces of the Establishment, quite as much as the New Right, were thus confronted with the puzzle of how to find the center of gravity for a new coalition. The answer once again came from California.

---

[18] The Roundtable's exclusiveness, together with its political pragmatism, have provoked the retaliatory formation of the 'American Business Conference' by a constellation of medium-sized, high-growth companies that are ideologically aligned with the New Right. See Kim McQuaid, 'The Roundtable: Getting Results in Washington', *Harvard Business Review*, May/June 1981.

The Politics of Stagflation

The missing link between the New Right and a new majority was provided by Howard Jarvis and the Proposition 13 movement in California. The wave of tax-cutting crusades which followed the victory of Proposition 13 in 1978 surpassed the success of all other single-issue movements. In an almost simultaneous reflex, every potential Republican candidate immediately declared himself for fiscal liberation, and an ecumenical 'truth squad' including Ford and Reagan was organized to tour the country. But while politicians of all stripes, including most Democrats, were eager to bask in the reflected glory of rampant tax slashing on a municipal or state level, few of those with establishment links were prepared to endorse unreservedly fiscal panaceas on a national scale where they might turn into inflationary Frankensteins. The rational timidity of Carter and Ford, however, proved their undoing in 1980 when they confronted the onslaught of Reagan's supply-side janissaries. In the final round, Carter ended up running on a budget-balancing platform that must have seemed grimly Hooverian in the depressed industrial centers of the Northeast, while Reagan (who delights in comparisons with FDR) was able to appear Rooseveltian with his promise of fiscally-induced 'reindustrialization'. The traditional roles of the parties were reversed in another way as well: for the first time in modern history the Republicans mobilized a larger army of campaign workers than the Democrats.[19] With his Sunbelt flanks secure and perhaps as many as a million volunteers at hand, Reagan was effectively able to concentrate the final phase of his campaign on the older industrial states. When the smoke had cleared, the Democrats had lost more than a quarter of self-described 'liberal' voters and almost half of trade-union households.

Whatever may have been the dimension of purely negative 'protest votes' directed against Carter personally and especially at his handling of the 'hostage crisis' in Iran, the success of Reagan and other conservative candidates in the industrial states owed most to the clever downplaying of anti-union rhetoric and the systematic accentuation of the pro-growth aspects of the supply-side program. Moreover, it was the New Right component of the Reagan coalition that had become the most militant advocate of the non-Euclidean economics of Laffer, Kemp and Wanniski. In their mass conversion to fiscal neo-populism (not unreminiscent of Bryan's free silver panacea), they have simultaneously

---

[19] See Andrew Mollison, 'How Reagan Plans to Win', *New Leader*, 8 September 1980, pp. 3–4.

poached from the liberals (the Kemp-Roth tax scheme was inspired by Kennedy's 'New Economics') and stolen thunder from Wallace (all polls corroborated white working-class *ressentiment* against welfare recipients).[20] It remains to be explained, however, why the New Right was apparently so successful in mobilizing the support of many white workers for a redistributive strategy victimising minorities, public-sector employees and low-wage workers.

The stagflation of the 1970s transformed the objective terrain and subjective discourse of politics in America in a way which encouraged the growth of right-wing neo-populism. While traditional depressions have tended to achieve a levelling effect in the composition of the working class, stagflation worked oppositely, deepening and exaggerating intra-class differentiation. Where differentials have tended to be as historically great, and labor market segmentation as extreme, as in the United States, protracted stagflation produced chasms of inequality between working-class strata. In the 1970s, for instance, the wage differential (not including supplementals) between steelworkers and apparel workers virtually doubled; or in absolute terms, where the difference between their wages in 1970 was $83, in 1980 it was $277![21] This has led some analysts to go so far as to suggest the existence of a tendential 'Brazilianization' of the American social structure, as it polarizes not only between classes, but *within* classes, to create opposing camps of inflationary 'haves' and 'have-nots'. The consequent fragmentation of the class structure facilitated the recomposition of politics around the selfishly 'survivalist' axis favored by the New Right: 'The complexity of the "restratification" of the working class has aggravated the tendency in American politics for class issues to become lost in a welter of sectoral and stratum divisions. This, in turn, has helped promote a politics that is not only more than usually self-interested and short-sighted, but also centered increasingly on a narrowed range of "social" issues, especially those of home and family. Where relative prosperity or impoverishment may hang on the timing of a house purchase or the fact of working in (say) the aerospace rather than the auto industry or having been born in 1940 rather than 1950, the sense of commonality of experience and needs disintegrates.'[22]

As we shall see in more detail in the next chapter the divisive impact

[20] See Ben Bedell, 'Reagan and the Workers' Vote', *Guardian* (New York), November 26, 1980, p. 5.

[21] *International Herald Tribune,* January 25, 1981.

[22] Elliott Currie, Robert Dunn and David Fogarty, 'The New Immiseration.' *Socialist Review* 54, November–December 1980, p. 26.

of stagflation upon the working class was further abetted by the dramatic reversal in the levels of activism sustained by the left and right respectively. As the movements of the sixties declined, new movements of the right surged forward. Black power and women's liberation were eclipsed by middle-class militancy, as unprecedented numbers of white-collar, professional and managerial strata became active in single-issue campaigns or local politics, often abandoning their old party affiliations en route. Although a radical minority of these movements acted to recycle the personnel and concerns of the New Left, the mainstream flowed rightward with strong overtones of racial and sexual backlash. This 'greening' of American politics effectively disfranchised the poor, while simultaneously ensuring that the new activism of the middle classes acted as a ventriloquism for the voices of corporate PACs and New Right lobbies.

In the absence of pressure from the left, the momentum of conservative activism has pushed the 'center' many leagues rightward. Much has been written about the collapse of liberalism among congressional Democrats since Reagan's inauguration, but well before the election, leading figures on the Democratic 'left' were staking out new homes further right. It should be recalled that it was Frank Church, not Jesse Helms, who orchestrated the outcry against Soviet troops in Cuba (who had been there since 1963), while George McGovern was supporting revival of the B-1 bomber project and Alan Cranston was proposing ingenious ways to transfer social spending to the Pentagon. Like the GOP, the Democratic Party has also undergone profound transformations in its internal power structure: as the influence of the trade-union movement declines and big-city machines disappear, an increasing number of Democratic congressmen have become dependent upon corporate PACs and correspondingly sensitive to the pressures of New Right single-issue campaigns. Most suburban Republicans and Democrats have become virtually indistinguishable, and, as the votes over budget cuts during Reagan's first term illustrated, the support of conservative Democrats provides the regime with a functional majority in the House as well as in the Senate.[23] Several years ago, the United Auto Workers organized a conference to explore the prospects for a

---

[23] The Democratic strategy seems to be to outflank the Republicans from the right. Already during Reagan's first year in office, the chief budgetary spokesman for congressional Democrats, Rep. Dan Rostenkowski (Chairman of the House Ways and Means Committee), proposed to cut top-strata tax rates by 50% to 70% — 'an idea the White House rejected out of fear that it would be viewed as giving too much to the rich'. (*Business Week*, April 20, 1981, p. 79).

new 'Progressive Alliance' based on labor, minorities and women; little or nothing came of this initiative. Indeed, it was probably almost a decade too late to resurrect successfully the New Deal coalition. It is chastening to recall Irving Howe's warning in 1964 that the failure of the labor movement strongly to ally itself with Blacks was enabling the New Right 'to enter its "take off" phase'.[24] Seventeen years later it landed ...

---

[24] Irving Howe, 'The Goldwater Movement', in *Steady Work*, New York 1966, pp. 224–25.

5
The Political Economy of Late-Imperial America

The fate of America's imperial power under Reagan is curious. Forty years after the Red Army inadvertently ensured that the American Century rather than the Thousand Year Reich would be the hegemonic system of capitalist rule in the mid-twentieth century, the mechanisms of that rule are undergoing profound but paradoxical restructuring. On the one hand, the New Cold War has called forth an overreaching program of geo-military expansion that aims at nothing less than omnicompetent US interventionism guaranteed by a space-based nuclear supremacy. On the other hand, the burden of this military Keynesianism has strained the financial system to the point of crisis and contributed to the virtual destruction of the competitive position of American manufactures. In another set of paradoxical contrasts, to be explored in the next chapter, most of the conventional indices of US economic superiority, especially those reflecting international competitiveness, appear to be in steep decline, yet American domestic consumption more than ever constitutes the dynamic center of the world market.

The overall trend is toward an unprecedented *disarticulation* of the military, political, industrial and monetary instances of American hegemony. Whereas in the older Cold War era, American world power was based on a coherent interlacing of nuclear monopoly, monetary sovereignty, domestic reform, and national productivity sustained by mass purchasing power, today this configuration is increasingly disassembled: military build-up appears as a surrogate for, not a correlate of, economic growth, and the ability to consume becomes more detached from the actual movement of productivity. Some power resources appear to be increasing within the system, while others appear to be declining. Moreover, new or previously marginal historical actors, ranging from politically insurgent middle-strata and entrepreneurial elements in the American Sunbelt to suddenly explosive religious-nationalist movements in the Third World, play enhanced highly original roles in a world system formerly defined by predominantly bilateral struggles between labor and capital, or capitalism and state socialism.

The purpose of this chapter is to try to identify the social forces and circumstances that have brought about the transition to Reaganism and a newer, but not necessarily 'higher', stage of American imperialism. My central hypothesis is that the historical era defined by the equation of 'Americanism' with democratic capitalism — that is, by the progressive expansion of bourgeois democracy and mass consumption under the aegis of the United States — is approaching its terminus. The root cause of this crisis, I will argue, is only partially located in the internal contradictions of the labor-process and profit cycle of the 'Fordist' regime of accumulation that has been the institutional order of postwar metropolitan growth. Fully as important as the gradual exhaustion of the sources of productivity and profitability in the old system of accumulation have been the politically imposed limits on geographical expansion — represented in this account primarily by the defeat of reformist capitalism in Latin America — and to its domestic deepening, in the United States, with the halting of the 'Second Reconstruction'. The 'pure' logic of the system has, to so speak, been over-determined and overridden by, first, successful resistance among the oligarchical strata in the class structure of a large part of the semi-industrial periphery, and, secondly, by mobilization of a heteroclite coalition of sub-bourgeois strata in the United States. The result, I shall argue, is both a 'structure of crisis' and a nascent politico-economic coherence, as what I term the logic of 'overconsumptionism' increasingly directs the restructuring of American hegemony. But before considering the emergence of this new Americanism without Fordism, it is first necessary to recall how the original system of US hegemony, domestically and internationally, was organized in its postwar golden age.

I. Atlantic 'Ultra-Imperialism'?

The postwar era of American hegemony was inaugurated by a 'revolution from above' in the 1945–50 period that reconstructed the power of the West European bourgeoisies along a new axis of liberalism and interdependence with US global power, while simultaneously purging and disunifying the European labor movement. The crucial precondition, of course, was the unique techno-military advantage attained by the United States in the summer of 1945: the great historical contingency of the atomic bomb was joined to the more predictable results of the full-scale mobilization of the productive forces of the giant American economy (which *doubled* its industrial capacity between 1940 and

1945). By any accounting, August 6 1945 must be reckoned the commencement of the 'American Century', as the destruction of Hiroshima removed the constraints of power-sharing negotiated by the Allied triumvirate at Yalta.

The bipolar world which emerged after Hiroshima was, in a perverse sense, the realization of Kautsky's prophecy of 'ultra-imperialism' stood on its head. Kautsky had claimed to see, through the smoke and ruin of World War One, an emergent new order, dominated by the United States, where the logic of monopoly would transform the violence of inter-imperialist rivalry into a pacific collusion for the purpose of exploiting the non-industrial world.[1] In the event, it was rather the global logic of counter-revolutionary violence which created conditions for the peaceful economic interdependence of a chastened Atlantic imperialism under American leadership. Although the Bretton Woods institutions — the World Bank and IMF — are often portrayed as the foundations of the post-war system, their interventions only became consequential at the end of the reconstruction period in the late 1950s. First and above all, it was *multi-national military integration*, under the slogan of collective security against the USSR, which preceded and quickened the interpenetration of the major capitalist economies, making possible the new era of commercial liberalism which flowered between 1958 and 1973.

In concentric accretion around the central fortress of the US National Security State, successive presidential initiatives and 'doctrines', responding to the shifting geopolitical storm-centers of revolution and nationalist insurgency, erected an interlocking structure of military alliances, aid programs and nuclear tripwires. From the Chapultepec Pact of 1945 (which created a Western Hemisphere military alliance) to the Manila Pact of 1954 (which organized SEATO), an ultra-imperialist military-economic order was forged, linking together in forty countries the outposts and contingents — imperial or mercenary — to their ultimate headquarters in the White House.

This quasi-absolutist centralization of strategic military power by the United States allowed an enlightened and flexible subordinancy for its principal satraps. In particular, it proved highly accommodating to the residual imperialist pretensions of the French and British — the mock-heroic secession of the *force de frappe* and the enduring myth of the 'special relationship'. This flexibility has been grounded in the

---

[1] See Massimo Salvadori, 'The Hypothesis of "Ultra-Imperialism"', in *Karl Kautsky and the Socialist Revolution, 1880–1938*, London 1979, pp. 181–202.

particular disjunction of economic and military power, and expenditure, which the structure of American hegemony has permitted. The Yankee legions on the Elbe and along the DMZ, together with the nuclear umbrellas that protect them, made it possible for the European and Japanese economies to provide, respectively, high social-welfare overheads to integrate labor, and vast trade and agricultural subsidies to preserve international competitiveness — with each keeping up a strident ideological mobilization against communism all the while. In other words, the major allies, with the signal exception of Britain and its high per capita military outlays, have reaped the social-conformist fruits of militarism without having to pay the real market price.

On the American side, analysts have frequently alluded to the trade-offs between the costs of the permanent arms economy and the low relative levels of welfare provisions and employment security. Yet this has seldom ruffled a public opinion trained since Lend-Lease to equate military expenditure with job creation and general prosperity. Even those sections of capital outside the lush gardens of the defense industry have gained from the innumerable spin-offs and multiplier-effects of the military budget, including the vast state subsidization of research and development. Finally, as *hegemon*, the United States has been uniquely able — by virtue of specific conjunctural circumstances — to 'cash in' its integrative military supremacy for enhanced economic advantages. An outstanding example of such an operation, of course, was Nixon's and Kissinger's manipulation of the Arab bourgeoisies' military dependence on the United States to reassert American control over both oil and petro-dollars, to the detriment of European and Japanese production costs and trade balances.

Origins of the NATO State System

It was only within a framework of bourgeois stability and inter-imperialist pacifism, guaranteed by American nuclear supremacy, that the old Wilsonian project of the 'liberalization' of European (and now, also, Japanese)[2] capitalism was actually accomplished in the early Cold War years. Political liberalization was the precondition for economic liberalization, and it is important to recall that, excepting the brief and unstable interlude between Versailles and the march of the Blackshirts,

---

[2] For an interesting survey of the history of postwar capitalism that includes a good, comparative account of the Japanese transition to a high productivity economy, see Philip Armstrong, Andrew Glyn, and John Harrison, *Capitalism Since World War II*, London 1984.

the post-1945 period was the first full cycle of normative parliamentary democracy upon a universal franchise in West European history (the Iberian fascist states, of course, remaining significant exceptions to this otherwise general rule). The achievement of controlled democratization was essential to the dynamic of American hegemony, and, in particular, to the ability of Washington to counterpose its own ideological universal to the challenge of socialism.

First, however, we should identify the two major obstacles that had previously made a full-scale parliamentary politics so atypical or unstable in the greater part of *Mitteleuropa* and the Mediterranean Basin. One was the relative weight and militancy of the local labor movements, predominantly Marxist or anarchist in orientation. The other was the persistence of much of the sociological and political debris of late absolutism.[3] Time and again, a *sub-hegemonic* bourgeoisie, incapable of creating its own mass parties or reconciling its own internal schisms, allied with a tenacious aristocracy (often supported as well by an ultramontane peasantry or ruined *mittelstand*) to overthrow democratic institutions seemingly too conducive to radical or reformist labor movements. This particular fragility of European political capitalism was, of course, directly related to the meagreness of the 'welfare surplus' available as a resource for class conciliation. The latter, in turn, was an expression of the general underdevelopment of coherent capitalist relations of production and consumption: i.e., the prevalence of pre-capitalist agriculture, strength of rentier strata, inefficient and cartelized heavy industries, mass underconsumption, and so on.

An American project to intervene in the reshaping of European capitalism was first elaborated during World War One as part of the Wilson administration's attempt to merchandise 'democratic' war aims to the skeptical American and weary Allied publics. Wilson's Fourteen Points of 1917 — a specific riposte to the peace appeal of the Russian Revolution — universalized the ideology of American Progressivism (previously distinguished by the self-veneration of national exceptionalism and a strong aversion to European involvements) via a messianic

---

[3] For a provocative analysis, see Arno Mayer, *The Persistence of the Old Regime*, London, 1981. Significantly, during the century of British hegemony over the world economy, there was typically a collusion between English capitalism and the backward social strata of Europe. The contrast with the strategy of American hegemony is decisive. After the domestic Jacobin scare of the 1790s and the threat of Napoleon's Continental System, the British bourgeoisie forsook any ambition to be revolutionary missionaries of capitalism in Europe itself. Cobdenite liberalism might be encouraged among the creole classes in the Antilles or Rio de la Plata to open the doors of free trade imperialism, but it was rejected, if ever seriously considered, as a grand design for Europe. The obverse side of the Balance of

call for the reconstruction of the international economy and state system upon the principles of the Open Door and democratic elections. Although Wilson ultimately failed to sell his League of Nations to German or Irish-American voters within his own party, and although the majority of his cabinet was adamantly opposed to various proposals, like Keynes's, for a multilateral *state-led* recycling of reparations and war-loan repayments, his encouragement of a *private* American capitalist offensive in Europe was considerably more successful.

This first crusade to mobilize Americanism as a countervailing world ideology to Bolshevism was sustained, after the signing of the Dawes Plan, through the brief but extraordinary Weimar boom of 1925–29, which prefigured many of the ideological and political relationships of the 1950s. As American loans put German workers back to work, there was a naïve and euphoric celebration of Henry Ford's Brave New World across the Atlantic. However, with the collapse of the American economy in 1929 — largely as a result of the all-too-successful anti-labor drive of 1919–23, which halved the AFL's membership and froze mass incomes — the temporary honeymoon of German social democracy and the export sector of German industry also broke down. In the wake of Americanism's failed promise, brutal homegrown idylls replaced the flirtation with jazz and the Model-T.

The American intervention in Western Europe after 1945 was of a qualitatively different character: it focused far more directly on the overriding structural problems of creating a mass electoral support for bourgeois hegemony that would contain radical labor without destroying the function of labor reformism *per se.* The old Gordian Knot of capitalism and democracy in continental Europe was finally cut by the creation of a new, US-sponsored political current: Christian Democracy.

The contribution of Christian Democracy to the consolidation of an Atlantic capitalist order cannot be exaggerated. Yet, ironically, it was the Vatican itself that in earlier periods had been the principal antagon-

---

Power — the most useful English invention next to the steam-engine — was the refusal to become the patron of Liberal Revolution on the Continent. The preservation of the four absolutist empires, and the fine-tuning of their rivalries with one another and Republican/ Imperial France, became the strategic fulcrum which allowed the British to dominate the world market for a hundred years with a great navy and toy army. Thus, British capitalism supervised the retardation of political and economic development in Europe, contributing to the fatal compounding of bourgeois pusillanimity and aristocratic persistence, militarized heavy industry and subsidized rural backwardness, that eventually resulted in world wars and revolutionary crises.

ist to the growth of mass Catholic politics. From Pius XI's forced dismantling of Don Sturzo's populist Catholic party in 1921 to make way for Mussolini's accession, to Pius XII's extensive collaboration in the construction of Hitler's European empire, the Papacy had demonstrated a consistent preference for top-down concordats with anti-Communist dictators. After Stalingrad, however, and under counsel from the American Cardinals and FDR's special envoy Myron Taylor (former head of US Steel), Pius XII adroitly switched sides. The informal but intimate alliance between the Holy See and the White House which ensued was crucial in managing the post-war political crisis of European capitalism and in creating a popular surrogate for discredited and collaborationist bourgeois parties.

The vertiginous rise of Christian Democracy to the status of the largest single political bloc in Western Europe, however, was more than the sum of its endorsements from the Pope, the President or frightened capitalists. Particularly in the early post-war years when it had to compete vigorously against popular Communist and Socialist movements, Christian Democracy, supported with massive US aid, undertook its own local programs of preemptive, anti-radical reform — with results that were particularly striking in Italian agriculture, but no less apparent in the corporatist mechanisms of industrial relations established in Germany and France. The famous Catholic troika of Schumann, Adenauer and De Gasperi could claim to represent a unique amalgam of economic modernization, rural populism, anti-communism and civic piety.

If Christian Democracy thus mobilized the previously absent mass electoral base for the insurance of capitalist dominance in the European parliamentary state, it was still a majority current only in the Catholic countrysides and among the traditional petty-bourgeoisie. The left still overwhelmingly commanded the West European working classes, and the wartime experience of common resistance to fascism had encouraged avid rank-and-file hopes of continued Socialist-Communist cooperation and the reunification of the ideologically divided trade-union movements. The second major prong of the US offensive to 'liberalize' postwar Europe was the campaign, not just against the Communists, but against all really broad and inclusive forms of working-class unity, whether on the political or trade-union plane. Throughout the Allied zones of occupation in Germany, for example, left Social Democrats, as well as Communists, were purged from elected positions, local 'united fronts' outlawed, and strikes forbidden. Armed with wads of money and official support, the AFL (and later the CIO after the expulsion of its own left-led unions) was the cynical agent of the White House in subverting trade-union solidarity and sponsoring right-wing splinter groups. In France and Italy, the trade-union movement was fragmented into competing Socialist, Communist, and Christian centers; while in Belgium and Germany, where Communist influence was more easily suppressed, there was a single divide between Socialist and Christian unions.

Only after thus splintering the base of European trade-unionism, could the Christian Democrats, Gaullists and Americans move to the next stage of outright exclusion of the Communists from power-sharing in government. The great confrontation of the Winter of 1947/48, culminating in the Marshall Plan, the first Berlin Crisis and the defeat of the French miners' strike, was the founding moment of the NATO state system. With the Communists and left Socialists ostracized from coalition politics, and with the trade-union movements ideologically divided, the framework was created for a relatively stable party competition and circulation of elites between the Christian Democrats, Gaullists, and right-wing Social Democrats with minor roles played by pre-war liberal parties. Although local electoral alignments ranged from the volatile French Fourth Republic to the factionalized amalgam of Italian Christian Democracy, there was now a sanitized pluralism within a framework of loyalty to NATO, the Cold War, and the atomic bomb.

Without equally far-reaching transformations in the accumulation process of European capitalism, however, this state system, even with its nuclear glacis, might have proven as short-lived and crisis-torn as its Versailles predecessor. The first five post-war years were characterized by the widespread persistence of absolute impoverishment and the failure of initial attempts to liberalize commercial and monetary policies. Historical myth has enshrined the image of a European recovery that resulted from the massive transfusion of investment provided by the Marshall Plan. Certainly Marshall aid was decisive in assuring the short-term resources that enabled governing Cold War coalitions to defeat local Communist challenges and to surmount immediate consumption crises. But much of this initial impact was quickly dissipated by currency speculation, just as the earlier British loan of 1946 (which marked the final economic disestablishment of the British Empire by the United States) had been immediately re-exported overseas in a vain attempt to defend sterling convertibility. What rendered the recovery of the Marshall period more profound and thorough than the ephemeral Weimar boom were the greater scale of capital imports and the radical changes in the very composition of European capital.

As Kees van der Pilj has carefully documented in an important study,[4] the American corporate and financial establishment, through both state agencies and private channels, exerted a massive and multiform pressure to redirect European economic development away from cartelism and colonialism to auto-centered growth based on consumer-durable consumption within an integrated European domestic market. This Americanization of the European economy ultimately enacted Keynes's 'euthanasia of the rentiers': that is, a recomposition of internal economic and political power within the European bourgeoisies, displacing the traditional rentier/colonial-cum-protectionist/heavy industry blocs. The economic preconditions for this restructuring of capitals (and capitalists) were achieved during the Korean War boom and the formation of the European Iron and Steel Community; its political precondition was the emergence of new 'growth coalitions' with intimate American ties, linking together the leading cliques of all the NATO parties.

The US interest in promoting and subsidizing European Fordism was, of course, hardly selfless: on the one hand, an enlarged, dynamic European market fuelled demand for US mass production technology (whether as export or investment); on the other, high-productivity, mass-consumption capitalism immensely strengthened Europe as a bulwark in the Cold War. The general congruence of American and West European interests within a hierarchical Fordist order, however, was only achieved through periodic conflict and crisis — especially over the shape of NATO military integration and the fate of European imperialism. Given the American masterplan for global neo-colonialism (the universal 'Open Door' sought by successive US administrations since Cleveland), resistance to decolonization, the loss of empire, and military subordinancy all became momentarily potent rally cries for the declining fractions of the old European financial and rentier/colonial groupings. In this sense, the definitive accession of the metropolitan Fordist era was only achieved with the French and Belgian withdrawals from Algeria and the Congo, following on the heels of general monetary convertibility (circa 1958–1962).

Summarizing, we may say that the temporary American economic and military *supremacy* at the end of the Second World War was transformed into a more durable US *hegemony* only because American power was simultaneously deployed for counter-revolutionary ends (to break up the threat of a unitary European labor movement) and for bourgeois

---

[4] *The Making of an Atlantic Ruling Class*, Verso, London 1985.

revolutionary purposes (to liberalize and restructure European political economy). As a result, the axis of the world market economy shifted from inter-imperialist rivalries among semi-autarkic monetary-colonial blocs to inter-metropolitan exchange based on the generalization of Fordism in Europe, America and Japan.

II. The Domestic Growth Machine

Atlantic Fordism, the economic trajectory of American hegemony, assumed the possibility of simultaneous, interdependent expansion of the major capitalist economies (although not necessarily the actual synchronization of their individual business cycles). It was, above all, the growth of the domestic US economy that provided sustained momentum in the international system as a whole, allowing the European and Japanese economies to reconstruct their productive forces on US mass-assembly principles and to achieve the recovery 'miracles' of the late 1950s. The American economy, however, was only able to fulfil this happy function because its insertion into the world economy was uniquely asymmetrical: on the one hand, its absolute contribution to world trade and investment was sufficiently large to produce dynamizing demand and supply effects; on the other, it was relatively autarkic compared to the rest of the OECD economies (until 1970 only 7 per cent of the US GNP circulated in the world market) and, therefore, could flexibly accommodate the increasing shares of Western Europe and Japan in world manufacturing trade. Unlike earlier mercantile-colonial eras, its hegemony was not founded on a rigid preeminence in world trade, but on the maintenance of robust conditions of accumulation within the domestic economy.[5] In a general sense there have been two primary mechanisms of postwar domestic growth: a 'wage-led' dynamic of mass consumption; and a 'tax-led' dynamic of sectoral/regional expansion.

The first pattern of accumulation — what Aglietta terms the 'intensive regime' — was based on the full-circuiting of rising productivity, profits and wages via multi-year collective bargaining and a super-liquid domestic credit system supported by federal home loans and tax relief for mortgages. Previously, during the first great consumer-durable boom of the 1920s, the majority of the semi-skilled industrial working class remained trapped in poverty-level incomes, unable to

---

[5] For an extensive comparison of British and American hegemonies, see Lars Mjøøset, 'Developments in the Postwar World Economy', *Working Paper*, International Peace Research Institute, Oslo 1983.

participate in the hoopla of car and house buying. (In this sense, incipient Fordism was defeated by the very success of the employers' 'American Plan' in uprooting trade unionism and blocking wage advances.) As we have seen it took the decade-long struggle of the new industrial CIO unions to force the way for union recognition and the codification, in the collective bargaining agreements of 1948–50, of a dynamic wage system that synchronized mass consumption with labor productivity. In this fashion, perhaps a quarter of the American population — especially white-ethnic semi-skilled workers and their families — were raised to previously middle-class or skilled-worker thresholds of home ownership and credit purchase during the 1950s. Another quarter to one-third of the population, however, including most Blacks and all agricultural laborers, remained outside the boom, constituting that 'other America' which rebelled in the 1960s.

The two most striking indices of the advance of the intensive regime of accumulation were suburbanization and the growth of higher education. The former signified not only the integration of the auto-house-electrical-appliance complex as the mainspring of economic growth, but also the vast social-spatial transformation that resulted from it. Between 1950 and 1960, suburbs grew *forty* times faster than central city areas, while automobile registrations increased by 22 million.[6] The stability of the wage-productivity trade-off between capital and organized labor allowed the US working class increasingly to reproduce itself as a collectivity of privatized consumers.

Yet the ability of the autoworker finally to purchase a car, or of the house carpenter to afford a mortgage, constituted only one side of the mass-consumption dialectic; the other aspect, no less important, was the visible horizon of educational mobility. The 1944 'G.I. Bill of Rights', which provided government grants for veterans wishing to attend college or undertake vocational training, was as epochal a legislative initiative as Lincoln's Homestead Act. Almost eight million World War Two veterans, half of the total who served, received free college educations as a result, with a consequent massive expansion of higher education facilities.[7] As Table 5.1 illustrates, this educational

---

[6] See Richard Polenberg, 'The Suburban Nation', chapter four of *One Nation Divisible*, New York 1980.

[7] A useful distinction, and periodization, may be made between the legislation which provided a *regulatory* framework for the emergence of an intensive regime of accumulation, and legislative *programs* which actually underwrote specific structures of mass consumption and workforce mobility. Most of the classic New Deal legislation, including the Wagner Act of 1935 and the various reforms of the national banking system, belongs to the former

revolution, while affecting all social strata, has had particularly dramatic consequences for the skilled and upper-income levels of the working class — forty per cent of whose children (in contrast to only one in twenty in the UK) had gained entry into higher education by 1979.

By the mid-1960s, higher education had, in some of the richer states like California, become virtually a universal entitlement, and over half of the high school graduates were continuing into colleges. In other words, the 'historical' standard of labor-power, as Marx defined it, had, for large sections of the *white* working class, come to encompass both home-ownership *and* a college education for their children. Moreover, until the crisis of the 1970s, higher education did provide effective entry into expanding white-collar, technical and educational sectors of employment: an inter-generational job-upgrading dynamic that was as fundamental to the intensive regime of accumulation as the turnover of new car models or the sale of suburban lots.

Table 5.1[8]
The Postwar Educational Revolution

		% of each social groups' college age cohort entering college				
		1920	*1940*	*1950*	*1960*	*1970*
I.	upper class/ upper middle	40	70	75	80	88
II.	lower middle	8	20	38	45	64
III.	upper working	2	5	12	25	40
IV.	lower working	0	0	2	6	15
% of total age group entering college		6	16	22	33	47

category. A second cycle of legislative entitlements and spending programs was initiated with the Servicemen's Readjustment Bill of 1944 and continued through Eisenhower's massive Federal Highway Aid Act of 1956 and the National Defence Education Act of 1958. These latter acts determined the concrete forms of state subvention of suburbanization and higher education. As such, they represent the systematic triumph of an extreme model of privatized mass consumption over the vaguely social-democratic concepts of public housing, mass transit and national planning espoused by wartime New Dealers.

[8] Table compiled from Robert Havighurst and Bernice Neugarter, *Society and Education*, Boston 1975, p. 93.

The Sunbelt

This continuous transformation of the conditions of life for a large section of the US working class, and the correlative expansion of the primary, high-wage labor market, were co-ordinated in complex ways with the second engine of post-war accumulation: the formation of the Sunbelt. Between the beginning of the Second World War and the end of the war in Vietnam, an astonishing revolution in the sectoral and regional structures of American capitalism was accomplished. To comprehend the scale of this transformation — roughly equivalent in European terms to a shift in the economic center of gravity from the Ruhr to the Mezzogiorno — it is useful to recall the regional polarization of the American economy a half-century ago, when the New Deal came to power. There were two traditional Americas: a Northeastern-Great Lakes industrial *metropole*, which contained slightly more than half the population on only 15 per cent of the national land area while producing four-fifths of the industrial output; and a vast Western and Southern *hinterland*, based on agriculture and primary production, including the twenty million Americans trapped in the fetters of debt-peonage and subsistence tenancy.[9] Since 1940, the rapid urbanization and industrialization of the Pacific Slope, Texas and the non-cotton South has eroded this traditional metropolitan/hinterland dichotomy — shifting investment, urban population, income and manufacturing employment (Table 5.2) in such a way that by the end of the Vietnam

Table 5.2[10]
The Industrialization of the Domestic Periphery
% of Total Manufacturing Employment

	1950	1978
Heartland	72.4	57.0
Sunbelt	27.6	43.0

[9] As Walter Dean Burnham points out, the metropole had conveniently exact boundaries 'defined by the outer limits of the railroads' "scheduled territories", i.e., those with preferential freight rates.' (See 'Into the 1980s with Ronald Reagan' in *The Current Crisis in American Politics*, New York and Oxford 1982.)

[10] The 'Heartland' includes Northeast, Mid-Atlantic, East North Central, and West North Central states, while the 'Sunbelt' is composed of South Atlantic, East South Central, West South Central, Mountain and Pacific states. See *Statistical Abstract* 799 T-1373.

War boom a 'Sunbelt' urban-industrial region had emerged roughly equal in income and output to the old metropole, but distinguished by very different conditions of capital accumulation.

For example, the Sunbelt tends to be energy-rich, land-extensive, relatively non-union, and with significantly lower social overheads on a local government level. Its economy is founded on the sectoral predominance of science-based industries (aerospace and electronics), primary products, and amenities (tourism, retirement and recreation); while the North still retains most of the older heavy and consumer-durable industries. Correlatively, mass production workers still constitute a crucial component of the 'frostbelt' social structure, while the South and West are characterized by more extreme segmentation of the labor force into concentrations of technical-scientific professionals on one side, and low-wage primary and tertiary sector workers on the other. As John Mollenkopf has suggested, these divergent social structures produce distinctive balances of class power on metropolitan levels. In most Northern urban areas, local capitalist 'growth coalitions' had to engage in conflictual bargaining with politically influential unions and inner-city populations. In the Sunbelt, by contrast, local power structures have enjoyed a virtually untrammelled hegemony supported by electoral gerrymandering and widespread disenfranchisment of non-Anglo working-class neighborhoods.[11]

I describe this industrial revolution in the old hinterland as 'tax-led' because federal fiscal transfers, secured by the historically disproportionate congressional power of the South and West,[12] were the prime movers in the creation of the Sunbelt. Thus in California, Washington, Texas and Florida, military spending sponsored the rise of aerospace and electronic-industry complexes, while oil depletion allowances and agricultural credits rationalized the regional primary sectors and encouraged downstream diversification in oil technology and agricultural processing/merchandising. Immense long-term expenditures on highways, water projects and natural gas pipelines laid the basis for profligate metropolitan development in the desert West. Meanwhile, in the ex-plantation South, where millions of tenants and sharecroppers were displaced during the 1950s by farm mechanization, the Black rural poor bore the brunt of enforced emigration to the Northern inner-city areas being evacuated by suburban-bound white workers. In

---

[11] See John H. Mollenkopf, *The Contested City*, Princeton 1983.

[12] In the South's rotten boroughs, in particular, twenty to thirty year congressional reigns were frequent. The seniority system translated this into a lock upon the chairmanships of key military and appropriations committees.

Table 5.3[13]
The Military Tax Transfer to the Sunbelt

(a) % of prime contracts

	1951	1976
Heartland	73%	44%
Sunbelt	27%	56%

(b) % change in prime military contracts per capita (allowing for population shifts)

	1951-76
Northeast	− 29.5
North Central	− 45.8
South	+109.0
West	+ 32.1

aggregate terms, the Sunbelt was able to export its poverty northwards while simultaneously shifting the margin of federal expenditure southwards and westwards: as a result, the downtowns of Cleveland and Newark withered while the suburbs of San Diego and Dallas bloomed.

III. The Fordist Climacteric

Very generally, then, it is possible to say that the economic macro-dynamics of US hegemony, as maintained for over thirty years by a unified imperial military and state system, came close to fulfilling the popular clichés of the 'Americanization' of Europe and the 'Californi-anization' of America. The creeping trends towards the equalization of income levels between the United States and the Euro-industrial heartland, as well as an analogous convergence between the major regions of the United States itself, were incipient realities by the crest of the long post-war boom in the early 1970s.

The great European labor offensive of 1968–73, which resulted in wage and welfare indexation in several countries, pushed up popular earnings despite inflation, and by 1975 Benelux and West German wage levels had surpassed the US average. French wages were not far

[13] From Maureen McBreen, 'Trends in Federal Defense Expenditures: 1950–70', Congressional Research Service, *Patterns of Regional Change*, Washington D.C. 1977, p. 513.

behind, and despite their much lower starting point, Italian wages were rapidly reducing the differential. Only British, and to some extent, Japanese wages remained relatively stagnant in this period.[14] (See Table 5.4).

Meanwhile, within the United States, as a result of the Vietnam War boom, capital formation and income growth in the Sunbelt accelerated to twice the rate of the Northeast. Between 1969 and 1974, per capita income in Southern metropolitan areas increased from 93 to 98 per cent of the national average, and by the 1980 Census had surpassed it. Whereas in 1960, the gross income ratio between the old metropole and hinterland was still 58.1/41.9, by 1980, the two regions were almost exactly equal (49.4/50.6). Using more disaggregated nine-region data, we find that the spectrum of income differentials, which in 1940 ranged from .65 for the South to 1.15 for the Pacific Coast, had shrunk by the end of the 1970s to a total variation of merely .15.[15]

Along with this tendential equalization of income (and productivity) levels within the Fordist core of the world economy, there has been a collateral trend towards the *relative saturation* of the consumer-durable markets which have been the primary engines of the coordinated expansion of metropolitan capitalism. Although the social boundaries

Table 5.4[14]
Estimated Hourly Wages of Manufacturing Production Workers in 1980
(USA = 100)

Belgium	133
Sweden	127
Holland	123
Federal Republic	120
USA	100
France	95
Italy/Canada	91
UK	71
Japan	59

[14] Data compiled from *Monthly Labor Review* hereafter, MLR — March 1981. Figures take account of insurance costs borne by employers (*Bureau of Labor Statistics*, March 1981 news release).

[15] *Business Week* (1.6.81); *Statistical Abstract of the United States: 1981*, Washington D.C., Table 714.

of mass consumption differ according to the relative strength and solidarity of national labor movements, it would seem generally the case that the upper levels of demand led by 'automobilization' and household mechanization were being reached in the late 1970s.[16] Thus in France, the percentage of workers owning consumer durables increased as follows in the 1959–74 period: cars, 21.3 per cent to 60 per cent; televisions, 8.6 per cent to 81 per cent; refrigerators, 19.4 per cent to 87 per cent; and washing machines, 21.2 per cent to 72.9 per cent (equivalent middle-class consumption ratios were all above 90 per cent).[17] Whereas in the 1960s, North American and European car markets grew at 12–13 per cent per annum, they have now subsided into a replacement rate of merely 2–3 per cent yearly. It is predicted that even the dynamic Japanese domestic car market will reach maturity in the next few years.[18]

The significance of this threshold within the history of world capitalism, and specifically for the system of accumulation organized under US hegemony, can best be grasped by comparing it with the coming to an end of the great age of international rail construction, under the aegis of British rentier capitalism, in the 1905–1912 period. Like this earlier watershed, which produced the deep economic malaise and 'stagflation' prefatory to the First World War, the Fordist climacteric of the 1970s has entrained a series of profound structural consequences.

First, it raised metropolitan energy consumption to a level incompatible with artificially low, even depreciating, international oil prices. The oil shocks which inevitably ensued challenged the entire structure of existing capitalization, based, as it was, on super-cheap energy, and led to the forced depreciation of vast quantities of existing plant and technology.[19] Apart from the quasi-fictional transfers of

---

[16] The provision of housing, even more than the share of welfare transfers, remains the most variable component of the Fordist economies. Despite the homogenization of the conditions of production and consumption of consumer durables, there is no comparable tendency in relation to the production of housing. The composition of the housing stock, and its relative price and quality, differ greatly among the OECD nations. In North America and Japan, especially, the tendential saturation of consumer-durable consumption has gone hand in hand, since 1970, with growing underconsumptionism relative to housing.

[17] P. Souyri, 'La Crise de 1974 et la Riposte du Capital', *Annales*, July–August 1983, p. 798.

[18] See Robert B. Cohen, 'Brave New World of the Global Car', *Challenge*, May–June 1981, p. 29. He also quotes (p. 34) an *Economist* study predicting world car production growth of only 8 per cent in 1978–85, compared with 43 per cent in 1970–78.

[19] The ensuing write-offs and balance-sheet manipulations, together with inflationary price transfers, may form an important part of the solution to the mystery of declining productivity in US manufacturing during the 1970s.

income to OPEC, insurgent oil prices also induced a restructuring of the distribution of profit within 'core' capital itself: American oil majors, for example, were suddenly awash with one-third of total corporate profits, 'crowding out', as it were, other manufacturing sectors. Although these shifts in the energy-price substructure of manufacturing costs probably had some positive spin-offs for certain high-tech capital-goods producers, their principal result was spectacularly to strengthen metropolitan *finance and rentier* interests at the expense of the productive economy as a whole (a trend which, of course, has continued after the 1981 decline in energy prices).

Secondly, the explosive growth of privatized consumption during the 1960s and early 1970s imposed unprecedented strains on the fiscal resources available for its collective infrastructure (roads, new schools, protective services, etc.). Public spending and taxes increasingly became a terrain of division between suburbanized workers and middle strata on the one hand, and inner-city workers and non-waged poor on the other. Runaway inflation, with its perverse distributional effects and illusions (for example, working-class homeowners are simultaneously victims of higher property taxes and beneficiaries of inflated equities), polarized further these consumption-defined positions, tempting the stronger or more advantaged sections of the working class to abandon traditional solidaristic political alliances to join new inter-class 'have' blocs arrayed against the collective 'have-nots'. As we saw in the previous chapter, secondary distributional struggles thus acquired, at times, a greater political salience than 'old' class-defined alignments.

Thirdly, the consumer-durable industries and some of their primary suppliers have reacted, in classic fashion, to market saturation and growing foreign competition by undertaking the rationalization of existing productive capacity. The historic originality, however, of the present rationalization movement is that it has created genuine 'world industries'. Allowing part of their domestic plant to rust away, multinationals have shifted amortization funds overseas to the strategic handful of export platforms whose authoritarian political regimes maintain a combination of literate, skilled labor with low wages and access to key regional markets. The result is not just further branch production for local markets or mere non-union 'out-sourcing', but the emergence of truly integrated international assembly-lines financed by burgeoning offshore capital markets. This quantum leap from national to world scales of production in a number of industries (computer, communications, pharmaceutical, auto, and, of course, finance itself) not only forebodes a drastic reduction in the number of capitalist competitors,[20] but, as we saw in chapter three, it also challenges the capacity of nationally parochial trade-union movements to defend wage standards and employment levels.

Fourthly, the relative diminution of the previously dynamic regional and national differences within the Fordist core — what Aglietta describes as the tendential 'convergence of industrial structure'[21] — galvanized the search in the 1970s for new capital-goods markets in the industrializing semi-periphery. Ironically, it was the staggering accumulation of 'stateless' dollars, arising from the US trade deficit and the OPEC price explosion, that provided the fuel for the debt-led industrial boom which swept the American, Mediterranean and East Asian borderlands from 1976 to 1980. This giddiest of post-war expansions was based on the export of metropolitan debts, magically recycled by the international banking system as credit money, to industrializing countries whose future export growth was, in turn, pledged as collateral. Built into this amazing chain of growth via metamorphosed indebtedness was the virtual certainty that a recession in the core would produce rampant, negative multiplier effects in the overinvesting semi-periphery.

The maturation of Fordism, under American hegemony, has thus produced a constellation of crisis that interlaces contradictions at the levels of the composition of capital, the composition of labor, the relation of class forces, the international division of labor, and the relative autonomy of the world financial system. Although each of these 'crises within the Crisis' has its special weight and demands a particular analysis, their overall configuration can be most clearly synthesized by asking the question: 'what are the possible "solutions" to the crisis?' Current debate, as well as the logic of the analytic categories already adduced, suggest two alternative or combined paths for the resumption of long-term capital accumulation on a world scale and in continuity with the structures of the preceding phase.

First is the project of extending the mass production/consumption dialectic characteristic of Fordism into the belt of urban societies along

---

[20] Cohen (pp. 29–30) argues that with the advent of the 'world car', only those companies producing more than two million units per annum would continue to remain profitable within the new economies of scale. Just eight car producers (GM, Ford, Toyota, Nissan, Fiat, Peugeot-Citroën, Renault and Volkswagen) meet this competitive standard within mass markets. Similarly, there will probably be competitive space only for two international airframe manufacturers and three or four general-purpose computer manufacturers.

[21] See M. Aglietta, 'World Capitalism in the Eighties', NLR 136, November–December 1982, esp. pp. 16–21.

the metropolitan borderlands. This strategy, which Lipietz has termed 'global Fordism',[22] addresses the contradictions involved in the restraint of world market expansion by mass underconsumption and unemployment in the newly industrialized nations. The minimal conditions for its realization would include the socialization of the wage relation of industrial labor in these countries to ensure mass consumption and the productive reabsorption of the vast underclasses of unemployed rural migrants.

Secondly, there is the potential for deepening the Fordist dynamic within the metropolitan societies themselves through revolutionary productivity and wage advances in the growing service and information sectors. This is what Aglietta terms the scenario of 'neo-Fordism',[23] and it addresses the contradictions lodged in the reproduction of the wage relationship in the most advanced capitalist centers. The minimal conditions for its realization would seem to include the reduction of the working day, a dynamized and expanded state sector, and the social valorization of new cultural and communal needs.

If our earlier hypothesis is valid — that American hegemony has provided the structural coherence for the diffusion of Fordism within Europe and America — then the question of the character and prospects of the current crisis of that hegemony must be related to the potential capacity of the American imperial role to ensure that transition to these new forms of global accumulation. In other words, is the United States capable of carrying out a second international capitalist revolution to make Mexico or the Philippines advanced consumer societies and/or to 'reindustrialize' itself around a new 'educational-medical complex' linked to a shorter working life?

These questions have echoes from the recent past. To visualize them

---

[22] Alain Lipietz, 'Towards Global Fordism?', NLR 132, March–April 1982, pp. 46–47.

[23] According to Aglietta, what is at stake is the industrialization of collective services through their conversion into commodities susceptible to mass reproduction: see, most recently, M. Aglietta and G. Oudiz, 'Configurations de l'Economie Mondiale et Régulations Nationales', Centre d'Etudes Prospectives et d'Informations Internationales, Paris 1983. My usage of 'neo-Fordism' is more algebraic: stressing the problem of wage and productivity upgrading in the non-manufacturing sectors of the economy, independently of general 'commodification'. Finally, both of these usages must be distinguished from the application of the term 'neo-Fordism' in some Anglo-American literature to describe more delimited trends in the industrial labor process. Charles Sabel, for instance, defines 'neo-Fordism' as flexible factory automation, based on computer-integrated assembly and enhanced work-group autonomy, in order to encompass a more differentiated product range within the boundaries of mass production. See *Work and Politics*, Cambridge 1982, esp. pp. 209–19.

as practical options within the ambit of imperial politics today, it is necessary to recall the legacy of the ambitious reform program of US capitalism during the 1960s. In assessing the current possibilities of either extending the geographical range of 'Fordism' or deepening its metropolitan roots, it may be well to consider the antecedent experiences of Kennedy's erstwhile Marshall Plan for the Western Hemisphere — the Alliance for Progress — and of Johnson's War on Poverty, which sought to incorporate the 'Other America' within the mainstream of the domestic high-wage economy. The fates of these interrelated experiments in 'global Fordism' and 'neo-Fordism' during the 1960s tell us much about the prospects for the future of American hegemony in the late 1980s.

IV. The Alliance That Failed

Until Ronald Reagan stole the Democrat's traditional clothes in 1980, there had been a discernible rotation in power between alternative concepts of US hegemony respectively espoused by the Republicans and the Democrats. Within the broad parameters of the Cold War Atlanticism embraced by a bipartisan congressional majority (a coalition first constructed in 1940–41 by Roosevelt and then decisively defended against the right wing of his own party by Eisenhower in 1953), Republican administrations tended to advocate a more 'custodial' concept of hegemony, while the Democrats typically urged sweepingly offensive strategies.

Thus, despite their changed circumstances and personnel, the Eisenhower and Nixon-Ford administrations shared neo-mercantilist and anti-reformist impulses arising from traditional Republican antipathies to extreme free-trade liberalism (the GOP being, of course, the ancient party of protectionism) and to the extension of New Deal rhetoric to foreign policy. Republican regimes tended to emphasize instead a reliance on strategic air-power (rather than US groundforce commitments), the reduction of imperial overheads (like foreign aid), and the utility of more traditional balances of power. The Democrats, on the other hand, urged aggressive, military Keynesianism, combining economic expansion and domestic reform with trade liberalization, preemptive counterinsurgency and accelerated spending on strategic weapons. In other words, whereas Republicanism — despite Dullesian slogans about 'roll-back' — was more concerned with cost-conscious management of the imperial status quo and the protection of home-market industry, the Democratic Party — allied with both organized labor and key internationalist factions of capital, as well as Southern exporters — offered ambitious schemes for dynamizing and expanding the economic and military supports of hegemony.

The period from the Bay of Pigs to the Tet Offensive witnessed the most spectacular postwar attempt to apply the Democratic maximum program of expansion, reform and repression. While the 'New Economics' supposedly fine-tuned the domestic economy along a soaring full-employment growth path, the 'Grand Design', led by the 1963 Trade Expansion Act and the Kennedy GATT Round, enticed European capitalism to accept junior partnership in a liberalized (and Americanized) world market. The Peace Corps and development assistance were sent out to win hearts and minds, while the Green Berets shot away less tractable obstacles to 'modernization' (the favorite buzzword of the Kennedy gang). McNamara, announcing the era of 'flexible response', kicked out the jams in the defense budget and launched the biggest arms race in history. Finally, the War on Poverty at home and the Alliance for Progress in the backyard were patterned after the model of Marshall aid to create millions of new, anti-Communist mass consumers.

It is sobering to recall how much of this over-arching program was summarily buried in the imperialist debacle in Southeast Asia; or, more strangely, how much of it has been recently exhumed and repackaged as the last word in contemporary Republicanism. Walter Heller and Robert McNamara have odd, but recognizable reincarnations in the misshapen forms of Donald Regan and Caspar Weinberger. Yet if military Keynesianism — once the bogey-man of Eisenhower's conservative budget balancers — has been reborn as Reaganomics, it is equally striking how complete has been the putrefaction of international New Dealism or domestic egalitarianism. It is not merely that the slogans are out-of-date or moldering with the presidential hopes of Ted Kennedy; it is, rather, more profoundly that the projects they imply are no longer imaginable pretensions or interests of late-imperial America.

To consider the Alliance for Progress first. Between 1945 and 1960, Europe had received $30 billion in American aid, while the entire Western Hemisphere, despite grandiose wartime promises by Roosevelt and Hull, was given only $2.5 billion.[24] Without an immediate

---

[24] For a broad sketch of US and Latin American economic relations during the first Cold War, see Manuel Espinoza Garcia, *La Política economica de los EEUU hacia América Latina entre 1945 y 1961*, Havana 1971.

socialist threat to demand US attention, the Latin American capitalist states — suffering brutally from declining terms of trade — were repeatedly turned away from the door of the Eisenhower administration. After the Cuban Revolution and the mobbing of Nixon in Caracas, however, the socio-economic crisis in Latin America suddenly moved into the foreground of American foreign policy priorities. Kennedy appointed a special Latin America task force composed of the country's leading experts in preemptive, anti-communist reformism: Governor Luis Muñoz Marin of Puerto Rico, Marshall Plan administrator Lincoln Gordon, Roosevelt veteran Adolf Berle, State Department Latin Americanist Thomas Mann, and itinerant Kennedy ideologue Richard Goodwin (who later wrote the actual Alliance for Progress speech). Arthur Schlesinger, Jr., the premier theoretician of Cold War liberalism, was also given plenipotentiary powers to help fashion a bold counter-response to the gauntlet thrown down by Cuban Foreign Minister Che Guevara's demand for $30 billion in developmental aid for the hemisphere.

Basing themselves on the twin precedents of Truman's 'revolution from above' in Western Europe and Puerto Rico's 'Operation Bootstrap', Goodwin, Berle and Schlesinger conceived a program for injecting $20 billion in US aid over the course of the 1960s. Latin America, in turn, was supposed to invest $80 billion more on fundamental socio-economic and infrastructural reforms. As the task force put it, the United States 'cannot stabilize the dying reactionary situation. It must, therefore, seek to bring about stability at a tolerable level of social organization without leaving the transformation to be organized by Communists.'[25] The prospective roles of Adenauer and De Gasperi were to be played by Rómulo Betancourt in Venezuela, whose Acción Democrática was patterned after Schlesinger's own beloved New Deal, and Eduardo Frei, the hemisphere's darling Christian Democrat reformer. Ideally, the Alianza, so ceremoniously launched at Punta del Este in 1961, would unite Latin America's reforming anti-communists in a grand coalition for growth and stabilized bourgeois democracy.

As Pablo González Casanova has emphasized, this was 'the most ambitious social project of imperialism' to date — the major attempt to

---

[25] Quoted in John Lewis Gaddis, *Strategies of Containment*, Oxford 1982, p. 224. A confidential memorandum from Rostow to Kennedy is also cited; it asserted the possibility of making Argentina, Brazil, Colombia, Venezuela, India, the Philippines, Taiwan, Turkey, Greece 'and possibly Egypt, Pakistan, Iran and Iraq' into autonomous industrial societies by *1970*!

implant Fordism in the Third World.[26] Yet, as Fidel Castro caustically observed at the time, 'you can put wings on a horse, but it won't fly'.[27] The conjuncture of class forces was fundamentally dissimilar to Europe in 1945–50, and within the first eighteen months of the Alianza, there were five coups against constitutional governments, while only two countries — Mexico and Venezuela — even bothered to propose credible agrarian reforms. Above all, American corporate capital, which had a developed historical interest in promoting mass consumption in Western Europe, approached Latin America via a series of special relations of domination and alliance with local oligarchies. The business press vehemently protested the subversive illusions cultivated by Alianza propaganda about 'middle-class revolution', and Washington was allowed to disburse only two-thirds of the initial aid instalment. The 'Vital Center' mythologized by Schlesinger scarcely seemed to exist South of the Rio Grande; and where it did, as in the Dominican Republic in 1965, with Juan Bosch's mildly social-democratic movement, the Marines were on occasion sent to crush it.

Meanwhile, one of the most eminent members of Goulart's moderately reformist Brazilian government (overthrown with US complicity in 1964) noted the changes in Schlesinger's pet statesman: 'The new Betancourt, elevated to the presidency, quickly dropped all disguises to drown in blood, to silence with censorship, and to check with jail and torture the national emancipation movements that he himself had helped mature and unleash'.[28] Far more drastically seven years later, the Chilean Christian Democrats, the largest and most esteemed centrist party in the hemisphere, joined in the assassination of Chilean democracy. Class relations and accumulation conditions in Latin America, combined with the almost congenital treason of the 'center', were hardly auspicious for the establishment of democratic, mass-consumption capitalism *à la* Belgium or Ohio. Only a decade after Schlesinger's memos to Kennedy, another well-known Yanqui ideologue, Milton Friedman, was busy mapping out a different and darker, free-enterprise future for the continent.

Without giving undue credence to its possibilities, it is nonetheless important to contemplate some of the implications of the Alianza's failure for the continuing the crisis of US hegemony. By blowing popu-

[26] Pablo Bonzalez Casanova, *Imperialismo y Liberación en América Latina*, Mexico 1978, p. 38.

[27] Quoted in Arthur M. Schlesinger, Jr., *Robert Kennedy and His Times*, New York 1978, p. 623.

[28] Darcy Ribeiro, *The Americas and Civilization*, New York 1971, p. 277.

lists and social democrats out of the water, the United States has perpetuated and reinforced a system of class relations that is incompatible with elementary reform or the mass exercise of democracy. As Atilio Borón has argued so cogently, democracy in present-day Latin America has become an essentially *revolutionary* goal which only a left steeled to the daunting but indispensable task of protracted struggle can realistically make a permanent popular acquisition.[29] In this sense, the cautious *aperturas* and guided elections being attempted by some of the more hard-pressed military regimes are misleading: the current debt bondage of the major Latin American industrial economies, and the draconian austerity with which this is enforced, point in the direction of a yet more explosive, and thus intolerably subversive, relationship between democratic rights and social demands. It is all too likely that the unfolding process of repoliticization in the Southern Cone (including Brazil) will produce a new cycle of militant mass mobilization, reactionary violence and Yanqui intervention — as is already the case in Central America. Even the exceptional cases of Mexico and Venezuela, now that their internal regulative mechanisms for growth and social co-optation have been upset by IMF-dictated recessions, may now see new class polarizations.

In a period when Eurocommunism has become practically defunct, the Arab left destroyed, and Asian capitalism (with the signal exception of that quasi-Latin American social formation, the Philippines) seems eerily stabilized — the massive, deep and continuing process of popular radicalization in Latin America and the Caribbean has truly become *the* specter haunting American imperialism. The situation, of course, is all the more significant in that the classical ideological relations of American hegemony are inverted: instead of the allure of capitalist 'democracy', here capitalism has cancelled democracy. As Lipietz and others have pointed out, the crisis-resolving option of 'global Fordism', to which the Alianza vainly pretended, has yielded to the crisis-maintaining reality of a 'bloody Fordism', based on the transfer of advanced technological conditions of labor exploitation *without* mass consumption or bourgeois democracy.[30] No *deus ex machina*, acting in the higher self-interest of the world capitalist system, is available to restructure the rigid barriers of class formation, congealed around *comprador* accumulation models that block further integration of the industrializing economies of Latin America (or, for that matter, of Turkey, Egypt,

---

[29] See Atilio Borón, 'Latin America: Between Hobbes and Friedman', *NLR* 130, November–December 1981.

[30] Lipietz, 'Towards Global Fordism'.

Indonesia or Thailand) into an OECD-type growth scenario.

Thus, at least under the specific form of American hegemony, the extension of democratic capitalism and the Fordist dynamic to the semi-periphery has become effectively unrealizable — especially in the region (the Western Hemisphere) where the threshold to such a transition has seemed in the past so near at hand. This is not to suggest, however, that, in the face of the defeat of capitalist reformism, relations between core economies and their borderlands have remained stagnant. Quite the contrary: dense new patterns of labor mobility and interdependent production have emerged — above all in North America, where the growth of the US Sunbelt has structurally interpenetrated Mexico and the Caribbean Basin (as well as Western Canada). Bereft of any higher political legitimation or vision (hemispheric 'common markets' and the like), this virtually geological process — thrusting upward unprecedented relations of transnational integration and dependency — is a major symptom not of the extension of core Fordism, but of a new and malign accumulation logic that is supplanting Fordism in the United States itself.

V. The Rise of Overconsumptionism

Unlike the ill-starred Alliance for Progress, the War on Poverty (conceived under Kennedy, launched by Johnson, and, surprisingly, continued by Nixon) has been generally adjudged — at least by liberals — a great historic success. By 1976, for instance, it was estimated that the ranks of the poor, a quarter of the nation in 1960, had been reduced to a residual twelve per cent: a diminution in relative poverty comparable to that achieved in the aftermath of the New Deal and the CIO. In the earlier period, as we have seen, the Fordist integration of the industrial working class gave a sustained impetus to the economy. The War on Poverty, in contrast, did not provide the same positive catalyst to accumulation as did the Wagner Act and the rise of the CIO. Official poverty statistics disguise some of the most important, and harrowing, facts about the tendential trends of the contemporary American political economy.

First, the 'victory' in the War on Poverty was largely an artefact of income transfers *within* the working class which left structural employment situations intact. With the removal of these federal income supports, as the Reagan cutbacks have shown, the original 1960-levels of designated poverty reappear. In fact, the *pre-transfer* inequality of market incomes has increased over the past generation. Whereas in

1965, the poorest forty per cent of the population earned eleven per cent of total market income, the corresponding figure for 1978 was only 8.5 per cent[31]. As the following statistics compiled by the Urban Institute (Table 5.5) reveal, both market income and post-transfer measures of poverty have risen rapidly since 1979. In other words, despite the long sixties boom, the private economy failed to generate 'decent' jobs — if any jobs at all — for the millions of ex-farm tenants and laborers displaced to the central cities in the 1950s and early 1960s, while their children are now being directly threatened with Reaganism's new immiseration.

The American economy has signally failed to re-integrate Black male workers, whose participation rate in the labor-force (a key index of structural unemployment) has fallen from eighty per cent in 1945 to barely sixty per cent today. The Civil Rights Revolution, propelled by hundreds of thousands of Black working people, succeeded in dismantling the more blatant apparatuses of *de jure* segregation in the South, as well as sponsoring the rise of an expanded Black professional and managerial stratum, but fundamentally failed in its ultimate goals of achieving the mass incorporation of Black labor into the high-wage

Table 5.5[32]
The Incidence of Poverty (household income)
% of households

	(1) market income	(2) plus all cash transfers
1965	21.3	15.6
1968	18.2	12.8
1972	19.2	11.9
1976	21.0	11.8
1979	20.5	11.7
1982	24.0	15.0
% change 1965-79	− 3.8	−25.0
% change 1979-82	+17.1	+28.2

[31] Sheldon Danziger and Robert Haveman, 'The Reagan Budget', *Challenge*, May–June 1981, p. 8. According to Robert Kuttner, the United States has the most inegalitarian income distribution of any advanced capitalist society, except possibly France. Thus the current differential between the incomes of the top 5 per cent and the lowest 5 per cent of the population in the United States is 13.3 to 1; in Britain the corresponding ratio is 5.9 to 1; in Sweden, 3 to 1. See Kuttner, *Revolt of the Haves*, New York 1980, p. 217.
[32] Cited in *Challenge*, September–October 1984, p. 27.

economy and of surmounting the barriers of *de facto* segregation in Northern schools and suburbs. A generation after the first March on Washington for Jobs and Freedom, Black unemployment remains more than double that of whites, while Black poverty is three times more common. Sixty per cent of employed Black males (and fifty per cent of Hispanics) are concentrated in the spectrum of the lowest-paid jobs.[33]

Secondly, official poverty figures, with their ludicrously low standards of subsistence, hide massive and rapidly increasing numbers of the *working poor* — the prime victims of Reaganomics. At least a third of the hundred-million-strong US labor-force consists of wage-earners trapped in a low-wage ghetto suspended precariously above the official poverty line.[34] Lest it be imagined that this 'semi-poverty' is primarily a by-product of the stagnation of employment during the last crisis-ridden decade, it should be emphasized that during the 1970s new jobs were created at *twice* the rate of the three previous decades: twenty million jobs in all. As Emma Rothschild has noted, 'this is as though the entire labor force of Canada had moved south and found employment in the United States'.[35] But even more astonishing than the scale of job creation was its composition: between 1972 and 1980 'women accounted for about 65 per cent of the employment rise — an amount disproportionate to their 38 per cent share of total employment in 1972.' As women's labor-force participation doubled between Eisenhower and Reagan, their relative earnings declined from 65 per cent of the male average to 59 per cent; in 1980, one-third of full-time women workers earned less than $7,000, while the white male median wage was $17,000.[36]

Thus relative poverty is being mass produced, not only through the exclusion of third-world men from the primary labor-market, but

[33] US Bureau of the Census, *Current Population Reports*, Series P-60, No. 136, Table 3; see also William H. Harris, 'Who Needs the Negro?', chapter eight of *The Harder We Run*, Oxford 1982.

[34] The evolution of analyses of the problem of the working poor can be charted by comparing: Laurie Cummings, 'The Employed Poor', MLR, July 1965; Barry Bluestone, William Murphy, and Mary Stevenson, *Low Wages and the Working Poor*, Ann Arbor 1973; and David Gordon, *The Working Poor: Toward a State Agenda*, Washington D.C. 1979.

[35] Emma Rothschild, 'Reagan and the Real America', *New York Review of Books*, 5 February 1981, p. 12. Between 1960 and 1980, the US economy added 32 million new jobs — the equivalent of the Brazilian work-force, while Western Europe actually shed a million jobs. See the discussion in Michel Albert, *Un Pari Pour l'Europe*, Paris 1983.

[36] *Statistical Abstract: 1981*, Table 681; US Department of Labor, *The Earnings Gap Between Women and Men*, Washington D.C. 1979; and Nancy Rytina, 'Earnings of Men and Women', MLR, April 1982.

especially through the dynamic incorporation of women into burgeoning low-wage sectors of the economy. Low-wage employment, far from being a mere 'periphery' to a high-wage core, has become the job growth-pole of the economy. This development, with its attenuation or reversal of the previously dominant Fordist wage/productivity nexus, is a resultant of different trends within what I will later argue is a unifying politico-economic context.

These interrelated trends include the decline of unionization (discussed in Chapter Three) and, since 1978, the stagnation of public employment, which, during the 1950s and 1960s, was the single largest provider of new high-wage jobs.[37] Instead, there has been a proliferation of a heteroclite 'tertiary' sector with its pervasive gender and/or racial typifications of particular occupations as less skilled, regardless of actual content or comparability. More specifically, the 'low-wage revolution' includes such discrete phenomena as the expansion of outsourcing and sub-contracting, the growth of personal services, a new rise in 'extra-economic' labor coercion (as in the denial of citizen rights to 'undocumented' workers), the startling advance of anti-union campaigns, as well as, ironically, the explosion of menialized jobs associated with the diffusion of the most advanced information technology. To understand how these various tendencies — some of them rampantly atavistic (like the resurgence of sweated industries), others almost futuristic (like the plight of computer operators) — coalesced unexpectedly during the 1970s to drive the US economy along a new course, it is useful first to consider, counter-factually, the alternative political economy whose possibility was suppressed in the ultimate buildup to Reaganomics.

The Turning Point

According to a consensus of economic analyses, the late sixties were the turning-point in the post-war boom, registering the full impact of Great Society and Vietnam War spending, together with the acceleration of inflation and, thereby, of compensatory wage pressure. As the original, post-war Fordist impetus of growth via suburbanization and automobilization began to reach a relative saturation point, a new structure of consumption, characterized by increasing demands for

---

[37] In a study of job creation from 1950–74, Eli Ginzberg claims that whereas only thirty per cent of new jobs in the private sector were 'good' jobs by virtue of income and security, two-thirds of public sector jobs were 'good'. See Ginzberg, *Good Jobs, Bad Jobs, No Jobs*, Harvard 1979, p. 30.

health-care, education, recreation and urban redevelopment, emerged. Simultaneously, there was acute political pressure, in lieu of private market job expansion, for new income and welfare entitlements to quell the wave of Northern ghetto revolts. The overall conjuncture abstractly contained the political opportunity for a general mobilization for a social-democratic and 'neo-Fordist' reorientation of public spending and taxation to encompass a general upgrading of skills and productivity in the provision of expanded public services and collective consumption (assuming, also, a continued relative decline in military spending). Such reforms, as part of an alternative economic strategy leading towards an American welfare state of a more Northern European standard, might have supported the high-wage job absorption of Blacks, Hispanics and women. Moreover, they would probably have assured externalities, such as cheaper medical care and more qualified labor-power, that would have raised productivity and profitability in the goods-making sector of the private economy (which, of course, is something quite different from the profits of capital as a whole). However, the minimal preconditions for such a hypothetical mobilization in the late sixties would have included a high degree of conscious trade-union solidarity, the creation of a broad labor/Black/poor-people's alliance (as envisioned by Martin Luther King in the year before his assassination), and the internal transformation of the Democratic Party.

In the next section I will briefly consider the reasons for the failure of the second precondition (as well as some symptoms of why the third is almost certainly an impossibility). As to the first, it must be noted that the drastic decline in trade-union membership during the 1970s, from 26 to some 16 per cent of the private-sector workforce, is probably more an effect than a cause of the sectionalism and egoism of the American union movement. The 1955 reunification of the AFL and CIO was something of a Gompersian restoration, with the dominant building-trades bloc on the AFL–CIO Executive (led, of course, by a plumber — George Meany) continuing to espouse traditional craft exclusivism and benign neglect, if not overt racism, towards the plight of Black and Hispanic workers. Despite occasional initiatives by more progressive unions like the Meatcutters or the Autoworkers (outside the AFL–CIO from 1967 to 1981), the Federation, as we have seen, has been more concerned to support the Cold War than to commit resources to organizing the unorganized.

Similarly, as stronger unions bargained for 'welfare states in single industries' via contractual health and retirement supplementals, the general thrust for national, inclusive welfare policies was diffused and weakened.[38] Moreover, at the height of the anti-war and Black-power movements in 1968–70, the old-line craft unions, along with their allies in the Mafia-controlled teamsters and maritime unions, wrecked any hope of a New Deal-type social alliance by viciously attacking anti-war protests, opposing schemes for Black control of local institutions (like the police or schools), rejecting demands for affirmative action in apprenticeship programs, and, in a majority of cases, aligning with the urban-Democratic *anciens régimes* against ghetto and campus demands, even frequently against newly unionized public-sector workers. Because the trade union movement was fundamentally disinclined to become a genuinely hegemonic reform force — or, still less, to accept the lead of the civil rights movement — a welfare-statist or 'neo-Fordist' outcome to the social and economic crises of the next decade was almost *a priori* excluded. Finally, as we have seen, while business unionism rested comfortably in the niche of the high-wage sector of the economy, it had little incentive in vulgar cost-benefit terms to organize low-wage workers, even when they were centralized in giant hospital or office complexes. The result of this abdication was that American trade unions surrendered their ability to influence the processes of class and occupational formation in the fastest-growing sectors of the economy, including the new science-based industries.

What then *did* occur in the 1970s — with the exclusion of any social-democratic alternative — was the emergence of a new, embryonic regime of accumulation that might be called *overconsumptionism*. This has little to do with the sumptuary habits of the very rich, whose wasteful profligacy with yachts, mansions and exotic drugs is an incomparably smaller social problem than their control over the global means of production. Rather, by overconsumptionism, I wish to indicate an increasing political subsidization of a sub-bourgeois, *mass* layer of managers, professionals, new entrepreneurs and rentiers who, faced with rapidly declining organization among the working poor and minorities during the 1970s, have been overwhelmingly successful in profiting from both inflation and expanded state expenditure.

Unusually large middle strata and a plethora of people in 'contradictory class locations' have been permanent features of the twentieth-century American social landscape; what is new is the way in which the 'tertiarization' of the economy has been harnessed to the

---

[38] Organized labor also opposed introduction of contributions from general income to fund social security (the usual arrangement in other countries); given the regressive character of the social security tax (same rate for all, with an upper limit on taxed income), this ensured that the burden was disproportionately concentrated at the lower income end.

distributive advantage of an expanded managerial-professional stratum, as well as opening new frontiers of accumulation for small and
medium-sized entrepreneurs. Correlatively, the Fordist circuitry of
patterned wage/productivity agreements, which used to assure the
channelling of part of the social surplus back into the expansion of real
wages and the upgrading of labor-power, is breaking down.[39] The
old charmed circle of the poor getting richer as the rich get richer
is being superseded by the trend of poorer poor and richer rich, as the
proliferation of low-wage jobs simultaneously enlarges an affluent
market of non-producers and new bosses.

This dialectical connection between middle-class overconsumptionism and the increasing degradation of new-job creation needs to be
viewed — successively — from the standpoints of comparative class
structure, specific, sectoral employment trends, and the prospective
shape of future occupational and wage structures.

To begin with an international comparison, it is clear that a major
difference between the class structures of the advanced capitalist
societies is the relative size and composition of their middle strata.
France, Italy and Japan, for example, are all characterized by an
unusual persistence of the *old middle strata* of peasants, independent
shopkeepers and artisans (i.e., those classes based on essentially pre-
capitalist relations of production). In 1976, for example, these
traditional groups constituted, respectively, 17.6 per cent, 26.2 per cent
and 22.7 per cent of the French, Italian and Japanese economically
active populations. Moreover, it is well known that the social weight of
these groups is artificially preserved by political subvention. Because
these strata were indispensable supports for ruling bourgeois parties
(Gaullists, Christian Democrats, and Liberal Democrats), their
economic positions have been stabilized by massive state intervention:
ranging from agricultural subsidies (including the Common Agricultural Policy of the EEC) to special tax relief and 'anti-monopoly'
legislation (like the Royer Law of 1973 in France protecting small
business from the competition of chain stores).[40]

---

[39] 'The growth of the real wage has for more than a decade ceased to be the principal
motor of private consumption, which has instead come to depend upon demographic
growth and, for each family, on indirect and secondary sources of income, including part-
time work and the black economy. In other words, a *regressive and extensive development* of
norms has come to regulate the employment of labor-power and the formation of income'.
R. Boyer and J. Mistral, 'Le Temps Présent: La Crise (II)', *Annales*, July–August 1978, p.
778. A similarly suggestive comment on the centrality of wage degradation in the current
crisis of American capitalism is contained in Aglietta and Oudiz, *op. cit.*, pp. 9–10.

[40] See Val Burris, 'Class Formation and Transformation in Advanced Capitalist Societies: A Comparative Analysis', *Social Praxis*, 7, 3/4, 1980, pp. 147–79.

In the United States, on the other hand, the *new middle class* of professionals, salaried managers and credentialled technicians comprised 23.8 per cent of the labor force in 1977 — a higher proportion than in any other OECD country except Sweden.[41] Since the US state sector is no larger than in other major capitalist countries, it is important to inquire into the special characteristics of the private economy that support such enlarged new middle strata, as well as looking for any evidence of the kinds of state intervention or social subsidy that might be tantamount to a political regulation of the class formation.

Of course, it is necessary to take into account that the special position of the United States in the world division of labor, attributable to its hegemonic status, involves such phenomena as the headquartering of so much transnational production in the United States or the unusually large scale of its research and higher educational establishments. Nevertheless, few comparative statistics are so striking as the apparent hypertrophy of occupational positions in the United States associated with the supervision of labor, the organization of capital and the implementation of the sales effort. In per capita terms, the United States is monumentally overstaffed with line managers and foremen (twice as many as Germany), salesmen (two-and-a-half times as many as France), and lawyers (twenty-five times as many as Japan).[42] Despite much publicized 'white-collar blues' and managerial retrenchments in certain industries, the relative size of supervisory labor has continued its spectacular advance. Thus, of the 3.6 million manufacturing jobs added to the American economy since 1948, 3 million were filled by non-production employees and at least half of those were managerial posts. Likewise, although blue-collar employment has fallen by 12 per cent since the onset of recession in 1980, by Christmas 1982 there were nearly 9 per cent *more* managers and administrators working in the US economy.[43] Meanwhile, the old middle class in the United States — at 8.5 per cent the smallest of the advanced industrial nations[44] — has suddenly started to grow again.

Sectoral Trends

To explore further the roots of this unprecedented parallel expansion of

---

[41] *Ibid.*

[42] See *The Economist*, March 6 and September 19, 1982 ('Business Brief').

[43] See Karen Arenson, 'Management's Ranks Grow', *New York Times*, April 14, 1983.

[44] Val Burris, *op. cit.*

the old and new middle-strata positions, it is necessary briefly to consider some of the more important sectoral trends in the US economy. Between 1966 and 1981, twenty-eight million new jobs were created: for each job added in goods-production (including research and transportation), *ten* jobs were added in the tertiary sector (minus state employment).[45] Private-sector tertiary employment growth, in turn, was disproportionately concentrated in three industries: health care, business services and fast food. An examination of each of these three cases reveals specific combinations of low-wage employment combined with middle-strata 'rents' or political subsidies.

The *private health-care industry*, including geriatrics, has become the largest industry in the American economy, surpassing the construction sector in employment. Moreover, its 5.5 million workforce exemplifies an extreme income/skill polarization: at the top, half a million doctors and dentists — the highest paid in the world; below them, a million-and-a-half nurses and technicians (the relatively *worst* paid of college-graduate professionals); and far below, at the bottom of the heap, more than three million blue-collar and clerical medical workers — the largest single segment of low-wage labor in the nation.[46] Although the United States now spends ten per cent of its GNP on health care and geriatrics, more than any other OECD nation, the quality of this care is far below the standards of the more efficient and egalitarian nationalized medicine of Northern Europe.[47] Its class-stratified health system, with its separate levels of provision for the poor/aged, the unionized working class, and the corporate salariat, extracts oligopolistic rents from both fiscal revenue and deferred wages. While the privileged, quasi-entrepeneurial position of doctors is protected by the political clout of the American Medical Association (which blocks the socially necessary para-medicalization of treatment and preserves a rigid division of medical labor), the minimally regulated private health industry is allowed to continue the inflation of hospital and laboratory charges which have raised its profit levels consistently higher than those of any other industry group, except perhaps the oil majors.[48]

The *business service, banking and real-estate sectors* have doubled since 1969, with the onset of the fantastic and interrelated increases in

---

[45] See Eli Ginzberg and George Vojta, 'The Service Sector of the US Economy', *Scientific America* ', 244, 3 March 1981.

[46] Cf. Bluestone *et. al.*, p. 136; MLR October 1981 and June 1981.

[47] See Robert Maxwell, *Health and Wealth*, New York 1981.

[48] *Financial Times*, December 1, 1982.

consumer debt, real estate inflation and the costs of business services. By the inauguration of Ronald Reagan, and for the first time since the Depression, corporate interest payments comprised a larger share of the GNP than corporate profits. In 1980 corporations spent over $10 billion suing each other (an amount almost equivalent to the entire federal foodstamp program); while, in the following year, $83 billion was expended on corporate take-overs, mergers, and demergers — paper transactions that involved $11 billion more than the total of new productive investment in basic plant and machinery.[49] This explosion of exchanges in fictional capital has, like the health-care sector, produced occupational income/status extremes unmediated by substantial middle ranges: senior corporate lawyers earning 'wages' of $250 per hour, alongside $4-an-hour tellers and secretaries. To ensure the continued superexploitation of their largely female workforce, and to escape the future threat of a '9–5' rebellion, the great banks and financial 'supermarkets' like Merrill Lynch, American Express, Citibank and Bank America Corp. are, in the words of the *Wall Street Journal*, 'targeting low-cost Sun Belt areas for future growth, such as industrial companies did decades age when they moved from the Northeast to the South. They seek places where labor, land, electricity and taxes are cheap.'[50]

The growth of the *fast-food sector* is a dramatic expression of what might be called industrialization via 'reproduction-substitution' in the wake of increased female proletarianization. The decline of real wages during the 1970s helped double the labor-force participation of married women, as working-class families sought the two pay packets necessary to sustain a Fordish level of mass consumption. Meanwhile, female-headed households increased in the face of rising 'male flight' from marriage (a phenomenon partially associated with the decline in male labor-force participation and, as we have seen, epidemic structural unemployment among Black males). In either case, the incorporation of women into the workforce has raised the demand for cheap meals outside the home. Thus, in the last decade, the percentage of meals eaten out has increased from a quarter to a third, with indications that mass-produced 'fast food' will provide half of all family meals by the end of the decade. The result is that McDonald's alone now employs more workers than the entire American basic steel industry. For myriad investors and new entrepreneurs, fast-food franchises (like condominiums or home-computer outlets) have become lucrative

---

[49] Harrington, p. 408.
[50] April 6, 1983, p. 22.

investments. For the million-plus fast-food workers (as well as another two million food-service employees in more traditional restaurants and institutions), the industry is employment of last resort, with average wages below those of farm labor.[51]

The Split-Level Economy

What of the future shape of the American occupational and class structures? Recent official projections of the US Bureau of Labor Statistics indicate the continuing incorporation of women into low-wage occupations as the predominant trend. Thus, the following estimates of the ten occupations expected to show the largest absolute increase during the 1980s:

Table 5.6
(Numbers in 1,000s)[52]

Occupation	total emp. 1981*	est. increase 1990	% female in 1981	average weekly wage in 1981
All	72,491	16,800	39.5	$289
1. Secretaries	3,199	700	99.3	$230
2. Nurses' Aids	832	508	84.3	$172
3. Janitors	993	501	14.6	$219
4. Clerks (Sales)	1,032	479	60.3	$178
5. Cashiers	712	452	85.1	$227
6. Nurses	1,168	438	95.8	$332
7. Truckdrivers	1,560	415	2.1	$314
8. Fastfood	1,000	400	50.9	$171
9. Clerks (Office)	2,082	378	76.2	$201
10. Waiters	532	360	85.1	$150

*Full-time employees only

[51] See Martin Carnoy, 'Los Cambios en la Estructura del Capitalismo Americano', *Zona Abierta*, 27, 1983, pp. 36–37.

[52] 1981 data from Nancy Rytina, MLR, April 1982; 1990 estimates from Valerie Personick, 'The Outlook for Industry Output and Employment Through 1990', MLR August 1981; and Bureau of Labor Statistics figure quoted in A.F. Ehrbar, 'The New Unemployment', *Fortune*, April 1981. The 'top ten' jobs of the 1970s included three high-wage classifications — engineers, accountants and computer specialists — significantly missing from the 1980s projections. See Carol Boyd Leon, 'Occupational Winners and Losers', MLR June 1982.

In sectoral terms, direct services are expected to grow by 53 per cent (or 7,202,000) by 1990; trade (wholesale and retail), by 28 per cent (or 6,184,000); and manufacturing by only 5 per cent (durable goods +1,014,000; non-durables −257,000). Public-sector employment — which in the previous quarter-century was responsible for 2 per cent of new job creation — will drastically decelerate (adding 100,000 fewer new jobs than banking and real-estate), while post-elementary teaching, once a powerful source of job-upgrading, will shed 251,000 positions in the wake of the new 'baby bust'.[53] Nonetheless, the supply of college graduates will increase by 12 or 13 million during the decade, probably a quarter of whom will be consigned to the burgeoning ranks of 'overeducated' clerical or service workers. (Between 1970 and 1982 the percentage of college graduates attaining entry to technical and professional occupations declined from 65 per cent to 54 per cent — despite the much-vaunted rise of new 'high-tech' industries.[54])

Meanwhile, the traditional unionized working class in manufacturing, construction and transportation will continue to be subjected to ferocious employer pressures. The most powerful unions in the durable-goods sector have been blackmailed by the threat of massive plant closures into yielding concessions on wages and, even more importantly, work rules that cumulatively presage the dissolution of national pattern bargaining. This creeping fragmentation of industrial unionism (which also menaces workers in the de-regulated transportation and communications industries) is less catastrophic, however, than the recent success of union-busting in construction and non-durable manufacturing. As we saw in Chapter Three, the meat packers have actually reversed fifty years of militant unionism and 'model' bargaining, to convert a high-wage industry back into a low-wage, non-union sector (wage slashes in pork packing have averaged 50 per cent or more) — a dire example that is being repeated in wood products and tire.

Within this emerging class structure of the 1990s, both the modal Fordist working class and the traditional mass market which it has sustained may well lose their structural centrality. As Richard Parker has emphasized, the economics of class will increasingly be amplified by the gender and demography of class: reshaping the traditional American income pyramid into a new income hourglass: 'Middle-class

[53] Personick, pp. 28–41. Two-thirds of the new jobs will be created in firms with twenty or fewer employees.

[54] MLR, February 1983, pp. 40–41. See also John T. Tucker, 'Government Employment in An Era of Slow Growth', MLR, October 1981.

218

families — truly in the middle — are disappearing, displaced by two-income, two-person households ... on the top of the hourglass, and single-earner blue-collar families, clerical singles, women in many jobs, the welfare poor, and the retired on the bottom.'[55] Statistics already released by the AFL-CIO purport to show the emergence of this new income hourglass by 1975 (see Table 5.7):

Table 5.7[56]
The Polarizing Income Structure

		Distribution of total private, non-extractive labor-force	
		1960	1975
Earning Classes (% of average national earning			
I.	20% and above	31.6	34.2
II.	80–119%	35.9	27.8
III.	79% and below	32.5	38.0

Correlatively, as *Business Week* notes, a more sharply bifurcated consumer market structure will emerge, with the masses of the working poor huddled around their K-Marts and Taiwanese imports at one end, while at the other there is a (relatively) 'vast market for luxury products and services, from travel and designer clothes, to posh restaurants, home computers and fancy sports cars.'[57] Already California, where nine per cent earn over $50,000 annually, prefigures this polarized market configuration; nationally, it is estimated that by 1990 some 23 million households earning more than $35,000 a year (in 1980 dollars) will provide the affluent market-sector capable of sustaining the projected trends in low-wage service and trade employment.[58]

It is essential to emphasize, however, that this emergent 'split-level'

[55] Richard Parker, 'Winning Through Inflation', *Mother Jones*, July 1981, p. 11. In 1981, the median income of dual wage-earner families was $31,600; of male-headed households, $25,000; and of female-headed households, $18,900. See *Economic Report of the President — 1983*.

[56] AFL-CIO, *Deindustrialization and the Two-Tiered Society*, Washington D.C. 1984.

[57] America's Restructured Economy', *Business Week*, June 1, 1981, pp. 64–66.

[58] *Ibid.*

economy is not the inexorable result of some abstract and unavoidable stage of 'tertiarization'. Rather, it stems from the coincidence of two *political* logics: on the one hand, the adaptation of American industry to new conditions of internationalized production (where world demand is ultimately constrained, as we have seen, by the class relations of the semi-periphery); and on the other, the fetter that middle-strata over-consumption has placed on the productive economy and the structure of the job market. Overconsumptionism is both heteroclite and coherent. It signifies both state-originated transfers to the middle class and the conditions of extra-economic coercion or menialization which now nurture the luxuriant growth of super-exploitative small businesses geared to the 'affluent' market. It also involves a politically constructed stratification of occupational categories in the tertiary sector that disqualifies and deskills the majority of workers to the advantage of a credentialed or managerial minority.

Overconsumptionism, in short, is a growing social subsidization of the new middle strata through ongoing degradation of job creation and erosion of mass Fordist consumer norms. But what establishes a congruence of interest and purpose between this trend and the position of corporate capital? Are there not powerful, latent contradictions between big capital and the expanded middle-strata, between the goods-producing and service-providing sectors, between financial and productive capital? To take one, not atypical, example: medical insurance now constitutes a larger cost element of auto-making than raw steel.[59] So why shouldn't General Motors have a direct interest in reducing the oligopolistic power of doctors that inflates the costs of health-care? I can present no simple or conclusive answer, except to suggest the obvious point that General Motors and other giant corporations, which often align with the awesome lobbying power of the AMA in joint campaigns in Congress (over tax expenditure, for instance), find it easier and far more direct simply to squeeze the unions on the financing of supplementals. More generally, and despite the inevitability of innumerable interest-group clashes of an ordinary kind, the political trends of the 1970s have tended to unify corporate capital and most of the new middle strata in a strategy of cost-displacement towards the working and unwaged poor. Their economic discordances have, at least until the second Reagan administration, been overridden by the mutual advantages of political alliance. Thus the struggle to maintain corporate profitability in a period of rising rentier incomes and profes-

---

[59] *Financial Times*, January 12, 1983.

sional salaries is transformed into further pressure on wages, unionization and welfare expenditure.[60]

The New Labor Market

Before examining the actual political incarnation of overconsumption-ism, however, it is necessary to add a few final notes about the future trends of high-technology manufacturing and trans-border industrializ-ation as they will probably affect the job market. There has been much ballyhoo about the potential of the 'high-tech' industries — including semi-conductors, computers, telecommunications, aircraft, pharma-ceuticals, and so on — to provide a compensatory source of high-wage employment. In fact, detailed projections prepared for the Bureau of Labour Statistics indicate that the high-tech sector of the economy (using the most inclusive and sweeping definition) will create less than half as many new jobs over the next decade as were wiped out in manufacturing alone during the 1980–82 recession (approximately two million). At present, high-tech comprises only three per cent of the work-force, and fewer than a third of the new jobs it will create will be for engineers, scientists or technicians: most will be for old-fashioned low-paid operators or for managers.[61] In a well-known analysis of the high-tech 'renaissance' of the New England economy during the 1970s, Bluestone and Harrison confirm the 'hourglass' image of current job market trends (the growth of a dual economy of some high-wage jobs, many low-wage jobs, and a 'missing middle') — emphasizing that inequalities were greatest in the high-tech firms at the core of the reindustrialization boom.[62]

As to the emerging border economy, it is a primary reason for the judgment that various 'overconsumptionist' trends are cohering into a

---

[60] Thus, to resume a comparative perspective, it may be more accurate to assert that in Europe the success of the solidarist trade-union offensive of the 1967–73 period, and, thereby, the dual expansion of wages and welfare, imposed a direct constraint on capital, especially in the absence of further expansion of the world market. In the United States, on the other hand — with no comparably generalized trade-union insurgency, with falling real wages over the last decade, and with small relative increases in state spending — it is probably more accurate to relate much of the problem of corporate profitability and of the fiscal crisis of the state to the success of the economic and political offensives of the new managerial, entrepreneurial and rentier strata. In this sense there has been a salary-and-rent 'squeeze' on profits.

[61] *Business Week*, March 28, 1983, pp. 50–60.

[62] Between 1958 and 1975, the number of traditional manufacturing jobs in New Eng-land's mills fell from 833,200 to 159,000. Of the 'compensatory' new jobs being created in

new social structure of accumulation. As the rapidly industrializing and urbanizing Sunbelt converts much of Mexico and the circum-Caribbean region into it own 'domestic' hinterland, the social crisis of Latin America is likely to become inextricably absorbed into the over-consumptionist transformation of the US economy. Unlike the *gastarbeiter* of Europe, who can be more or less repatriated at governmental will, the flow of *trabajadores sin papeles* across the Rio Grande (or Pacific) is part of an irreversible structural assimilation of adjacent economies and labor markets. With almost half of its workforce unemployed or underemployed, and with real wages plummeting under the current IMF austerity regime, Mexico alone provides an almost infinite reserve army of labor for the Sunbelt.

As immigration flows — both legal and illegal — exceed the 1901–1910 peak of trans-Atlantic migration, the long tracts of border zone have become an integrated economy of twin cities, one rich, one poor, from San Diego/Tijuana to Brownsville/Matamoros. The accelerated formation of this *borderlands economic system* since the late 1960s has become integral to the new accumulation patterns characterized by a co-ordinated expansion of low-wage employment and middle-strata affluence. The Department of Labor has speculated that the new immigrants may contribute as much as 45 per cent to the increase in the workforce during the 1980s.[63] Moreover, as labor markets are transnationalized, their segmentation grows more extreme, and wages become subject to determination by bantustan-like conditions of social reproduction. The neo-colonial logic of Sunbelt capitalism ensures that no fundamental challenge can be mounted against the domestic low-wage economy without a simultaneous change in the borderland structures of hyper-unemployment and domination.

VI. The Conservative Revolution

This epochal shift in the American economy during the 1970s from a

---

the region's restructured economy, 'the majority ... are hardly sufficient to provide an adequate standard of living for the normal-sized family. Most pay significantly less than the jobs replaced in the mill industries. A family is required to take two full-time jobs at a McDonald's fast food outlet or in a discount department store to make up for the loss of one job in a unionized woollen mill'. Barry Bluestone and Bennett Harrison, *The Deindustrialization of America*, New York 1982, p. 95.

[63] MLR, October 1980, p. 47; see also Kevin McCarthy, 'California: Ellis Island of the "80s"', *Challenge*, July–August 1983.

Fordist to an overconsumptionist dynamic was politically catalyzed by what might be called 'class struggles of a third kind', involving neither militant labor nor reactionary capital, but insurgent middle strata. Grassroots political mobilization during the 1970s was on the whole an inverse mirror-image of that of the 1960s. If the latter decade was dominated by the mass civil rights movement, followed by the new student left and various cognate liberation currents, then the 1970s were, without quite so much sound and fury, the decade of the revanchist middle strata. During the mid-1960s, thousands demonstrated in the South for school integration and educational opportunity; a decade later, hundreds of thousands of Northern whites counter-marched, even rioted, to prevent the school busing necessary to accomplish this integration. If the modal activist organizations of the 1960s were SNCC and SDS, those of the seventies were groups like BUSSTOP (Los Angeles) and the innumerable taxpayers' leagues.

Retrospectively, it can be argued that the space for the advent of Reaganomics in American politics was opened by two parallel displacements of class power. First was the demobilization of the popular constituencies of the 1960s to the advantage of the suburban-based middle-strata movements of the 1970s. Second was the closure of the electorate during the 1970s — via both alienated, popular self-disenfranchisement and a fundamental restructuring of electoral processes — which dramatically increased the effective weight of the corporations and the middle classes (see above, Chapter 4). In both respects, the conservative 'revolution' of the early 1980s was,when finally achieved, the result more of prior exclusion and disorganization of the majority than of its conversion to a new ideological agenda.

The demobilization of the movements of the 1960s was brutally sudden and is still, to many of their survivors, inexplicable. The mass civil rights movement, the dynamo of all post-war egalitarian currents, collapsed as a coherent force in the South after the climax of Selma in 1965; SNCC split up after 1966; while by 1969 over thirty Black Panthers had been slain by the police and more than a hundred imprisoned. SDS, with almost 100,000 campus followers, imploded at its 1969 convention, while the anti-war movement, mobilizing several millions during the Cambodian Spring of 1970, was virtually extinct by the time of Nixon's mining of Haiphong harbor two years later. Rank-and-file labor militancy, rekindled by the Vietnam boom, reached its crescendo in 1970, with a violent wildcat teamsters' strike, a postal walkout that prompted Nixon to use troops to deliver the mail, and the longest auto strike since 1946. Thereafter, the wildcats rapidly ebbed, and the rank-and-file insurgencies, with the exceptions of the miners and teamsters, disappeared.

While the 'Movement', in its many incarnations, was thus divided or disintegrating, the Democrats were engaged in a major attempt to recuperate the urban political power that was being eroded by the flight of white ethnics to the suburbs and by the decline of old-style Tammany political machines. The Johnson administration used federal poverty and employment programs to build a direct patronage nexus between Washington and community organizers in the riot-torn inner cities. This enlarged bureaucratic network enabled thousands of local neighborhood activists, and their welfare professional counterparts, to make the double shift into government-funded jobs and participation in Democratic politics. At the same time, in the wake of the devastating ghetto rebellions of 1967, the ruling corporate 'downtown interests' in many Northern cities were preparing to transfer their trust in the maintenance of law and order in the decayed, fiscally-looted central cities to a new generation of Black politicians — a development that further expanded and reinforced the new mechanisms of patronage and co-operation.

Theoretically, this absorption of grassroots cadres into the party, at the expense of the new left and Black power movements, should have reinvigorated the Democrats' sagging New Deal social base. Indeed, a small but influential circle of social democrats within the party had predicted that a major new social recruitment would unleash a partisan realignment guaranteeing liberal hegemony in the Democratic Party (see Chapter 7 below). The cruel irony, of course, was that the incorporation of youth and Blacks detonated a head-on clash with the party's traditional liberal power structure that virtually split the party down the middle. At the base, for example, the emergence of demands for power-sharing and positive discrimination for Blacks, Hispanics and women directly threatened the exclusivist operation of ethnic patronage politics and craft union apprenticeships. Within the national party, the tepidly anti-war, anti-imperialist orientation of the new liberals provoked hysterical counter-attacks from the keepers of the Achesonian Cold War tradition.

By 1968, the forces of the so-called 'New Politics' — emboldened by their local successes and consecrated by the martyrdom of Bobby Kennedy — were engaged in full-scale warfare with the AFL–CIO's Coalition for a Democratic Majority, led by rabidly anti-communist social democrats tied to Humphrey and 'Scoop' Jackson. The unexpected victory of the new liberals in securing McGovern's nomination in 1972 on an explicitly anti-war platform was immediately countered by the scorched-earth policy of the 'Democratic Majority', which, for the first time since 1924, withheld most trade-union support from the Democratic nominee, and thus virtually guaranteed Nixon's re-election and the prolongation of the war.

Falling Voter Participation

Although the aftermath of Watergate did give a second lease on life to the New Politics (which, after losing its brief influence over the Democratic National Committee, retrenched in municipal politics and local populism), none of the popular *élan* of the sixties was ever recovered. The notional 'left' pole of American bourgeois politics remained bitterly divided, while the once-vigorous community politics of the mid-sixties was converted into the passive, bureaucratized clientelism of the 1970s. At the same time, voter participation, which had been relatively stable for more than twenty years, suddenly underwent a sharp decline. Studies of voting behaviour during the 1970s uncovered the astonishing 'drop-out' of 18 million *former voters* (as distinguished from the never-voted segments of the potential electorate).[64] As Table 5.8 reveals, the most dramatic significance of this decline was its heavily skewed class bias:

Table 5.8[65]
Reported Voter Participation by Family Income (1976)

Income	Voters	Former voters	Never	1,000s
less than $5,000	46%	27%	27%	21,801
5–10,000	53%	21%	26%	30,096
10–15,000	60%	19%	21%	30,921
15–25,000	70%	15%	15%	31,748
25,000+	77%	12%	11%	14,153

Viewed from the standpoint of other popular categories, this voter fall-off appears equally calamitous. Despite the historic travail of the Southern voter rights campaign, national Black voter registration during the 1970s reached scarcely more than half its potential. Hispan-

---

[64] Thomas E. Cavanagh, 'Changes in American Voter Turnout, 1964–76', *Political Science Quarterly*, Spring 1981, p. 56.
[65] *Ibid.*

ics remained equally unmobilized, while only a quarter of the unemployed — of all races — bothered to vote. In spite of the new liberals' buoyant optimism that the 26th Amendment, enfranchising 25 million 18–20 year olds, would create a left-liberal electoral majority, only 23 per cent of potential voters under thirty participated in the 1970 mid-term election (the first under the broader franchise).[66] Overall, the effect of this increasing abstentionism was approximately the same as if a property-franchise limitation had been introduced to guarantee a middle- and upper-class electoral majority. Walter Dean Burnham invokes a telling example to make just this point: 'In 1978 ... turnout for the gubernatorial election in New York State reached a 150-year low, 38.5 per cent of the potential electorate, even lower than it had been in the gubernatorial election of 1810, when nearly three-fifths of the potentially eligible population was disenfranchised for failure to meet a property qualification.'[67]

Further, as Cavanagh has pointed out, 'the shrinking size of the electoral universe magnified the destabilizing impact of well-organized interest groups'.[68] 'Electoral reform', through encouraging the proliferation of private-interest political action committees (PACs) weakened the old intermediary role of the party machines in fund-raising and mobilization — as did also the doubling of the number of direct state presidential primaries (as opposed to party-controlled delegate caucuses). The trend was to encourage a California-style politics based on television, virtually permanent primary competitions, and the organizational and financial pre-eminence of the PACs (See Chapter 4 above).

Although in a few cases this new PAC/interest group configuration favoured candidates to the left of the local or national party apparatuses, the general trend in *both* parties after 1976 was the ascendent influence of business PACs and aroused middle-strata constituency groups in reshaping political agendas and determining nominations. Much attention has been focused on the particularly skilful and sophisticated inter-linking of various single-issue themes — deregulation, accelerated depreciation, anti-labor law reform, and so on — by the Business Roundtable and the National Chamber of Commerce as the

[66] For a comparative discussion of the relationship between the 'massive failures ... in the political incorporation of the lower classes' and 'in the political socialization of the young', see Burnham, 'The Appearance and Disappearance of the American Voter', in *The Current Crisis*, pp. 124–25.

[67] Burnham, 'Into the Eighties', p. 262.

[68] Cavanagh, p. 62.

main lobbyists for corporate interests.[69] But, as I have suggested, the revolutionary element in the politics of the late 1970s was the increased intensity of middle-strata political mobilization and interest representation. In a pattern that to some extent recalls the emergence of the Progressive movement at the turn of the century (which also, partially, was an insurgency of new professional and business cohorts), a whole generation of young professionals, middle managers and new entrepreneurs entered local and state politics at approximately mid-decade: i.e. just as the movements of the 1960s, with the single, important exception of feminism, were becoming almost totally disorganized.

This phenomenon was and is far broader than the nominal zealotry of the New Right. It might be better described as a larger, private-sector-oriented equivalent to the public-sector-based 'New Politics' of the McGovernites, encompassing as its respective poles, 'neo-liberalism' *and* 'neo-conservatism'. (In this sense, both Gary Hart and Jack Kemp merely articulate variations on the same meta-theme of over-consumptionism.) The coherence of this political spectrum is provided by three ever-present, if often implicit, themes: 1) The 'deregulation' of free enterprise and the belief that only private capital, endowed with ample profit margins and tax breaks, can 'reindustrialize' America; 2) the further remoulding of state expenditure and intervention to reinforce the subsidized position of the middle strata and new entrepreneurship; and 3) the curtailing of Great Society-type income and employment programs targeted at minorities, women and the poor.[70] (On the other hand, entitlement programs disproportionately favorable to the middle class, like social security, are politically untouchable.)

The organized expression of this socio-economic program was the rolling earthquake of suburban protests after 1976, including the anti-busing movements, campaigns for a return to educational 'basics', landlord and realtor mobilizations (truly massive, with hundreds of

---

[69] Cf. Kim McQuaid, 'The Roundtable: Getting Results in Washington', *Harvard Business Review*, May–June 1981; and Richard Kirkland, 'Fat Days for the Chamber of Commerce', *Fortune*, September 21 1981. The Roundtable is a recent creation, open only to the chief executive officers of the top 200 corporations; the Chamber of Commerce, traditionally the organizational core of the conservative coalition in Washington, has 165,000 member companies.

[70] In effect, the working poor are as excluded from the political discourse of neo-liberalism as from that of neo-conservatism. Thus Felix Rohatyn, fulminating against the unaffordable extravagance of the Great Society in the pages of *The Economist*, sounds indistinguishable from David Stockman pontificating on the same subject in the *New York Times*. Similarly, both groups of ideologues have become avid salesmen for the 'Puerto–Ricanization' of the inner cities via so-called 'urban enterprise zones.'

thousands of ardent members organized against rent control and public housing), and, most importantly, what the Los Angeles *Herald Tribune* once called the 'Watts Riot of the Middle Classes' — Proposition 13 and its spin-off revolts, which forced nineteen states to enact legislative or constitutional limits on property or income taxes. Although obviously besotted with law-and-order and racialist themes, these campaigns were in most cases organized on a different socio-economic plane — with a more hegemonic political project — than the earlier backlash outbreaks of the ethnic Northern working class or the national Wallace movement.

They tended to move from mere defense of existing socio-economic inequalities (as symbolized by the political integrity and fiscal autonomy of white suburban areas) to shrewd, assertive strategies for new upward redistributions of power and income through shifting tax burdens, privatizing collective consumption, and removing obstacles to the exploitation of cheap local labor. More than merely transient forms of protest against minority group demands, these mobilizations have been exploited to reinforce a now dense infrastructure of local interest representation and political influence which safeguards and perpetuates the position of the popular *nouveaux riches*. Overrepresentation at the electoral level has been creatively manipulated to consolidate over-consumptionism at an economic level.

Through the rise of the these new movements, a broadly embracing 'Have' politics was forged which gave a political interpretation to stagflationary trends in the economy, stressing the immanent themes of privatization, redirected state spending and the new inegalitarianism. A section of the traditional New Deal coalition, especially suburban white skilled workers, was conscripted to the 'Have' side. This was easily possible since, as we saw in the previous chapters, within the context of a weakly solidaristic and highly segmented workforce, inflation during the 1970s had tremendously disorganizing and centrifugal effects on the cohesion of working-class economic interests. On the one side, there were widening wage differentials within the working class; on the other, the increasing grievance of intra-class fiscal transfers — especially where this coalesced symbolically around property taxes.[71]

---

[71] Before the abrupt 1980 deceleration of union wages, workers in the more powerful unions were largely index-proofed against inflation by contractual cost-of-living-adjustments (COLAs). COLA-less groups, like clerical and service workers, on the other hand, suffered drastic wage attrition. As a result, union wage differentials, conventionally calibrated for the 1950s by H. Gregg Lewis's well-known study as 10–15 per cent, were reestimated for the 1970s by Daniel Mitchell as 20–30 per cent: see *Unions, Wages,*

228

Thus the *subordinate* logic of the 'Have Rebellion', exemplified in the innumerable property owners' and suburban residents' movements, was a defensive participation of skilled workers and the lower salariat in support of their threatened prerogatives of social mobility and consumption (home-ownership, superior suburban education, nepotistic apprentice systems, and so on). Faced with genuinely collapsing standards of living in many sectors of the traditional white working class,[72] these groups increasingly visualized themselves — even if their own concrete situation was one of appreciating property values and rising wages — as locked into a desperate zero-sum rivalry with equality-seeking minorities and women.

The *superordinate* logic of the Haves, on the other hand, was the *nouveau riche* drive to increase social inequality — indeed to harness it dynamically to expand low-wage labor supplies, reduce tax overheads and ensure a 'union-free environment'. Although the rhetoric of the various campaigns and tax rebellions that paved Reagan's road to power was vigorously anti-statist, the real programmatic intention was towards a restructuring, rather than diminution, of state spending and intervention in order to expand the frontiers of entrepreneurial and rentier opportunity. Typical explicit or underlying demands included: accelerated depreciation allowances, unfettered speculative real-estate markets and rampant condominiumization, sub-contracting of public services, transfer of tax resources from public to private education, lowering of minimum wages, abolition of health and safety standards for small businesses, and so on.

All these modalities of professional, entrepreneurial and rentier claims on society presume, of course, the high and sustained rate of economic expansion typified by Sunbelt urbanization over the past few decades. The bundle of interests which I have tried to tie together with the notion of 'overconsumptionism' is manifestly not compatible with

---

Inflation, Brookings Institute, Washington 1980, p. 214. Studying wage and income data, Burnham has discovered both a '1968–1981 decline of *one-fifth* in the real standard of living among "typical"factory workers with three dependents' *and* 'a quite substantial rise in PCDI (per capita disposable income) from 1970 to 1979: from $3,619 to $4,509 in constant dollars, a gain of 24.6 per cent'. (See 'Into the 1980s', pp. 274 and 315; his data sources were, respectively, the *Survey of Current Business* and the *Economic Report of the President*.) These 'remarkable' movements of the falling fifth and the rising quarter can only be interpreted. Burnham rightly suggests, as indices of the 'rapid escalation of *uneven development*' in income formation, i.e., the extensive inflationary transfers within the working class and between workers and the new middle strata (see p. 274).

[72] The percentage of the population able to afford private housing has declined from 50 per cent in 1970 to *20 per cent in 1980*. The current (August 1983) 'housing affordability

the kind of disciplinary recession which the *haute bourgeoisie* now and then finds necessary to impose on everyone else. Hence the significance, as Gar Alperovitz has noted, of the struggle between Reagan's key economic advisers which broke out the day after his election. On one side, two leading traditional-conservative economists, Arthur Burns and Herbert Stein, argued bluntly for a full-scale recession to punish wages and squeeze demand. On the other side, David Stockman and Jack Kemp, recognizing the costs of deflation to Reagan's crucial *nouveau riche* constituency, denounced Burns and Stein for 'Thatcherism', warning ominously against an 'economic Dunkirk'.[73]

In the event, the recession that Volcker had already unleashed in Carter's last days was one-sidedly confined to the Midwest and the manufacturing sector: the service sector and the Sunbelt continued to expand while the heartland became a 'rustbelt'. Moreover, within the Administration it is clearly 'reactionary Keynesians' — undaunted by twelve-digit deficts — who have repeatedly carried the day for reflationary Reaganomics. Despite the worried denunciations of fiscal irresponsibility in the financial pages of the *New York Times*, most members of the Business Roundtable are more obsessed with how best to take advantage of current governmental largesse in order to restructure their corporate empires around the overconsumptionist dynamic of the Sunbelt; and, having so successfully piggy-backed the middle-strata tax rebellion to the accomplishment of their own legislative agenda, the Washington lobbyists of big capital are generously sensitive to the continuing dependence of the corporate offensive upon the *nouveau riche* ascendancy in American politics and the socio-economic conditions that sustain it.

This is not to discount the fundamental paradox that the power of US finance capital, indissolubly linked to maintenance of the dollar's international sovereignty, must now learn to sleep in the same bed with the longings of a neo-bourgeoisie bloated by inflationary privateering.[74] It is a conjugal relationship which, ultimately, is only possible under the auspices of the Department of Defense. For it is Caspar Weinberger's ever-fattening military pork-barrel that provides the ongoing

---

index', measuring the gap between the income needed to purchase a typical resale home and the median income of US families, hovers around 80 (in 1972 it reached a high of 153). See Martin Giesbrecht, 'The Sad (Statistical) Reality', *National Review*, April 17, 1981; and the *International Herald Tribune*, December 1, 1983.

[73] See Gar Alperovitz, 'The New Inflation', *Annals*, July 1981.

[74] 'Millionaires', George Brockway observes, 'have multiplied like fruit flies'. There were about 180,000 in 1976, 500,000 in 1981, and (he estimates) perhaps a million in 1984. See his column in the *New Leader*, October 17, 1983, p. 11.

reconciliation between the voracious appetites of the *nouveaux riches* and the accumulation needs of a broad sector of core capital. Deficit-funded militarism may seem to be out of control, but for the present it supplies the necessary cohesion of overconsumptionism. That is to say, it is doing the right things for the right people: keeping General Dynamics rich, raising engineers' salaries, seeding new low-wage military subcontractors on the Mexican border, even inflating the portfolios of wealthy doctors who invest in Orange County shopping malls (and who, in turn, employ Salvadoreña house cleaners and send their kids to expensive psychotherapists). In the next chapter, we will see how this arms-led expansion is preparing the way for the first serious crisis of the new 'overconsumptionist' social formation.

6

Reaganomics' Magical Mystery Tour

The re-election of Ronald Reagan has unleashed new debate on the causes of the continuing conservative ascendancy in North America and Western Europe. Following in the well-worn grooves of discussions in 1980–1, some have stressed the renewed importance of a reactionary-populist social discourse centered on 'right to life', family traditionalism and religious obscurantism. Others, particularly sensitive to its impact on the vulnerable minds of the video-game generation, have emphasized the hallucinatory euphoria of the patriotic revival enacted in the Los Angeles Coliseum and on a small Caribbean island. Still others — conscious that the media remain, more than ever, their own message — have placed the greatest weight on the Holly-woodization of the presidency abetted by a sycophantic news establishment. Each of these optics focuses on an important set of factors. Yet, squatting awkwardly astride all refinements in the analysis of political discourse, has been the simple, massive fact of the Reagan 'boom' and its mobilization of economic self-interest. All the major pre-election polls' as well as the network 'exit' polls on November 6, revealed the paramount importance of the 'comfort/discomfort' index of family economic position in orienting voter affinity. Some sixty per cent of voters who thought the economy was better off than in 1980 landslided to Reagan by a margin of six to one, while, conversely, the forty per cent who thought the economy, or themselves, worse off swung to Mondale by four to one. The overriding role of the prosperity issue — especially in an election where the Democratic candidate so successfully obfuscated the war-and-peace dimension — was demonstrated by the fact that over a fifth of Reagan voters indicated that they had 'strong disagreements' with the incumbent over foreign policy or social issues, but gambled on his continued management of the recovery.[1] There is a vulgar irony in the fact that it was Reagan's lusty embrace of that false god of the Democrats — John Maynard Keynes — that guaranteed his re-election, while Mondale and the AFL-CIO once again looked like Republicans in their conservative insistence on fiscal probity and restrained growth.[2]

---

[1] *CBS/New York Times* Exit Poll, November 6, 1984.

[2] The *New York Times* (henceforth, NYT) characterized Mondale's economics as

But the boom did more than re-elect the prophet; it also confirmed his prophecy. The zealots of Reaganomics — from the original supply-side apostles like Jack Kemp and Paul Craig Roberts to the newer, 'high-tech' conservatives led by Rep. Newt Gingrich (Georgia) — are busy scouring the GOP of disbelievers and deflationists. In spring 1984, the White House officially projected a staggering, 28-quarter-long expansion, with cumulative 38 per cent GNP growth and diminishing deficits through the end of fiscal 1989. Embarrassed that Reagan had, so to speak, stolen their underwear, rueful traditional Keynesians like Walter Heller could only rationalize that the 'supply-side piano' was playing 'pure demand-side music'.[3]

Meanwhile, Reaganomics suddenly made enthusiastic conversions in heathen Europe, where, as *Business Week* gloated at the end of the summer, the French were now in 'awe', and erstwhile left-wing papers asked 'could Reagan be right?'[4]. Nowhere, of course, was the upswing welcomed with such sheer ideological ecstasy as in Tory Britain, although carefully filtered through a Thatcherite mind-set that censored the contribution of federal deficits in order to emphasize the wonders of America's de-unionizing labor markets. (At the October 1984 Tory conference, an ovation followed one speaker's evocation of the inspiring example of New York's entrepreneurial poor operating elevators and performing other servile duties for a dignified pittance.)

However, this adventitious economic upturn, which renewed the domestic mandate of the New Right, provided international cohesion to Cold War military escalation and, far more than expected, accelerated the breakup of welfarist political coalitions, is now tottering into recession, with warning signs of flagging demand and falling profits. As the historically high rates of real interest attest, business confidence has been made qualitatively more precarious and volatile by the experiences of the 1974–5 and 1980–2 recessions: any faltering in the self-proclaimed expansion threatens to trigger financial panic, the fall of the 'super-dollar', compensatory increases in interest rates, and a likely collapse of the global debt pyramid. At the same time, the Reaganites are well aware that the long-heralded 'partisan realignment' in their direction entirely depends upon the maintenance of a prosperity encompassing, at least, the suburban middle strata and the

---

'bluntly conservative ... no major jobs programs, no sizable anti-poverty measures, and no substantive housing and welfare measures'. September 11, 1984, p. A24.

[3] Walter Heller, 'President Reagan is a Keynesian Now', The *Wall Street Journal* (henceforth, WSJ), March 24, 1983.

[4] See *Business Week* (BW), September 24, 1984.

Sunbelt speculators. For all these reasons, it is obvious that the second Reagan administration will go to extraordinary and dangerous lengths to sustain the expansion and to prevent a precipitous unraveling of its triumphant electoral bloc.

To understand what a new crisis phase may entail, and what its political consequences might be, it is first necessary to consider how the Reagan boom has been reshaping the domestic and world market structures of capitalism. In contrast to Ernest Mandel, who has recently argued that debt-fed growth is only restraining a 'true' restructuring of the world economy and prolonging the basic tendencies of American decline,[5] I will show how the upturn dramatically accelerated the transformation of American hegemony away from a 'Fordist' or mass-consumption pattern. Three trends in the current expansion have particular theoretical interest and salience. First, the general shift that is occurring in the profit-distribution process towards interest incomes, with the resultant strengthening of a neo-rentier bloc reminiscent of the speculative capitalism of the 1920s. Secondly, the striking reorientation of mainline US industrial corporations away from consumer-durable mass markets and towards volatile high-profit sectors like military production and financial services — a trend that is reinforced by the recent merger mania. Thirdly, the virtually systematic dislocation of dominant trade relationships and capital-flows, as the locus of accumulation in new technologies has been displaced from Atlantic to Pacific circuits of capital.

I. USA: a Pathological Prosperity

The 1983–4 recovery was trumpeted as a break from 'the yoke of the 1970s' and a return to the growth levels of the 1960s. Indeed, the White House has long defended Reaganomics by alluding to the supposed role of the Kennedy/Johnston tax cuts in stimulating the 1960s boom. But the New Frontier's fiscal stimulus was minuscule in comparison with Reagan's 1981 tax revolution: even with the 1982 and 1984 tax increases, the Reagan cuts represent a fourfold larger percentage of the GNP.[6] Moreover, although the Kennedy/Johnson tax program was certainly regressive, it pales beside the upward income distribution effected by Reagan. The widely publicized evaluation of the Reagan

[5] New introduction to *La Crise, 1974–1984*, Paris 1984.

[6] Allen Sinai, chief economist at Shearson Lehman, quoted in NYT, September 18, 1984, p. D6.

record by the middle-of-the-road Urban Institute reveals the following shifts:[7]

Table 6.1
After-Tax Income Changes, per quintile ('average family incomes')

(1) dollars	I	II	III	IV	V
1980	6913	13,391	18,857	24,886	37,618
1984	6391	13,163	18,034	25,724	40,880
diff.	−7.6%	−1.7%	−4.4%	+3.4%	+8.7%
(2) % of GNP					
1980	6.8	13.2	18.5	24.5	37.0
1984	6.1	12.5	18.1	24.5	38.9

According to the Congressional Budget Office, low-income families have so far lost at least $23 billion in income and federal benefits, while high-income families have gained more than $35 billion.[8] (Expressed another way: 20.2 million poor households — earning under $10,000 — lost an average of $400 each in benefit cuts, while 1.4 million wealthy families — $80,000+ — received an average of $8,400 in tax cuts.[9]) Moreover, these figures only refer to fiscal transfer effects and budget cuts. If the differential rates of change in market income under Reagan are factored in, the increased share of the top quintile would be even greater. As collectively bargained wages were increasing at less than three per cent per annum, a leading firm of management consultants — Towers, Perrin, Forster and Crosby — was reporting that the average salary of corporate CEOS had skyrocketed forty per cent since 1980, from $552,000 to $775,000.[10] Similarly, David Gordon discovered that the share of management in the national income had increased from 16.5 per cent in 1979 to almost 20 per cent in 1983.[11] These trends are further indices of the change which I discussed in the previous chapter towards an 'overconsumptionist' model of accumulation based on the tendential substitution of upper-middle-strata for working-class consumption in the regulation of the economy. A related phenomenon is the dominant place of top-range products in the current pattern of consumer-durable sales: witness the highly profitable demand for luxury and big cars that has led Detroit's recovery.

[7] Urban Institute figures cited in *Challenge*, September–October 1984, p. 14.

[8] Ibid, p. 2.

[9] Ibid., p. 28.

[10] *International Herald Tribune*, October 10, 1984, p. 1.

[11] Cited in NYT, July 11, 1984, p. A25.

Normally, it would be assumed that a relative decline in the leading role of wage-goods in the recovery — to the benefit of a notional 'department three' of luxury and military production — would rapidly fuel inflation. Superficially, the most unusual aspect of the present upswing is the supposedly incompatible coexistence of large deficits with dampened inflation. This is the highly precarious result of an artificially low domestic price-level created by the fifty per cent trade-weighted appreciation of the dollar against other OECD currencies since 1980, and a flood of ensuing cheap imports. The maintenance of the 'super-dollar', sustained by unprecedented real interest rates of eight per cent or more, has allowed the Administration to internationalize the financing of its $500 billion in cumulative new debt. The Bank of International Settlements estimates that over one-third of the aggregate US credit demand (government plus private sector) is now supplied by foreign capital inflow.[12]

For the first time since 1914, the foreign liabilities of the United States exceed its assets (approximately $800 billion), and if present trends were to continue, it would become by 1990, a net debtor to the extent of an unbelievable sixteen per cent of GNP.[13] But the United States is scarcely a debtor nation in the same sense as Brazil or Mexico. Wall Street money-center banks and the US Treasury remain sufficiently hegemonic to enforce interest-tribute from the Third World and an unwonted 'Marshall Plan in reverse' from Europe and Japan. Particularly important in the current expansion has been the ability of the rapidly deregulating American financial system to bring onshore euro-dollar deposits formerly held in Europe or on island money-havens. The rise of money market funds, and the removal of ceilings on interest rates, have blurred the distinction between savings and speculation, and enhanced the global role of the dollar. New York's claim to have eclipsed London as the world's banking capital is based on its success in attracting the kind of international liquidity that formerly sheltered in Curaçao or Grand Cayman.[14]

Financial deregulation, through dismantling many of the New Deal structures that subordinated money-capital to productive-capital (interest-rate ceilings, clear separations of commercial and investment banking, and so forth), has also stimulated the formation of a *nouveau*

---

[12] Max Wilkinson, 'Maintaining Balance on a Narrow Gauge', *Financial Times* (FT), September 17, 1984, 'World Economy Survey', pp. I–II.

[13] In 1967, at the height of its outward investments surge, the United States was a net creditor to the tune of 9 per cent of GNP. *Financial Times*, November 8, 1984, p. 19.

[14] See special section on New York City, BW, July 23, 1984.

rentier class. Between 1979 and 1983, *gross* interest increased from 26 per cent of GNP to 34 per cent — a growth rate twice that of other income categories.[15] The percentage of *personal* income derived from interest has similarly doubled in the last five years, rising 24 per cent in the first year of the Reagan presidency alone.[16] Since the December 1982 changes which allowed banks to offer market rates on deposit accounts, a broader middle-class segment has been able to take advantage of higher interest rates. Similarly, affluent investors have been attracted to lucrative 12 per cent Treasury bonds: a $20,000 three-month 'TB', reinvested quarterly for a year, earned interest in 1975 equivalent to an average wage for seven weeks; today it equals three months of a wage-earner's income.[17] As skyrocketing interest on the federal debt ($1.5 trillion principal) drives up Federal outlays faster than OMB can find ways to cut school lunches or reduce welfare payments, the net effect is simply to shift government expenditure from the class of the poor to the class of debt-holders. Thus in April of 1984, interest surpassed transfer payments, for the first time since the New Deal, as the third largest income category.[18]

In a slightly more collectivist fashion, the current role of institutional investors (pension funds, trust departments, mutual funds) demonstrates the extent to which an autonomous rentier interest has seized the high ground within the economy. With $1 trillion in investments, the institutions have almost displaced private individuals in the equity markets, engaging in 80–90 per cent of daily trades and owning 60 per cent of stocks and bonds.[19] Seeking the highest yield in the short-term, and with no incentive to prefer capital gains over dividends (since they pay no current tax), the institutions relentlessly restructure their portfolios, with ephemeral loyalty to any particular investment. Thus the average turnover of shares held by institutions has increased from 21 per cent per year in 1974 to 62 per cent today.[20] The result has been the erosion of long-term corporate investment horizons with 'fewer startup operations, less development of new products, ore bodies or oil fields, and more service businesses at the expense of capital-intensive manufacturing'.[21]

---

[15] BW, October 1, 1984, p. 9.
[16] Council of Economic Advisors, *Economic Indicators*, September 1984.
[17] David Morris, 'Marx's '84 Issue', NYT, September 3, 1984, p. 25.
[18] CEA, op. cit.; NYT, June 17, 1984, p. D14.
[19] 'Will the Money Managers Wreck the Economy?' BW, August 13, 1984, p. 74.
[20] Ibid; BW, September 24, 1984, p. 93; and July 9, 1984, p. 29.
[21] BW, August 16, 1984; see also, NYT, August 8, 1984, p. 4F.

Corporations have reacted to the pressures of institutional investors and the new rentier interest in several ways. First, a staggering amount of the liquidity generated by recent wage concessions, tax breaks and subsidiary sell-offs — estimated at over $20 billion in 1984 alone[22] — has been deployed, not for capital investment, but rather to enhance stock values through buy-backs and increased dividend payouts. Alternatively, corporate treasurers have ballooned short-term borrowings with the aim of preserving operating autonomy and of lessening the pressure to increase dividends. As the gearing ratio of long-term to short-term debt has fallen from 2.5 to parity,[23] heavily leveraged financial balance-sheets have become correspondingly vulnerable to rises in the interest rate. Like so many small third world countries, scores of *Fortune's* 500 corporations threaten to become financial basket-cases in a new recessionary period.

The obverse of the super-dollar's levy of international saving has been its depressive effect on traditional US manufacturing exports. The appreciation of the dollar has erased any competitive advantage that might have accrued from the ten per cent increase in industrial productivity over the past three years.[24] In scores of cases, local unions have made sweeping work-rule and wage concessions 'to stay competitive', only to find their plant closed or relocated at the end of the day. In 1980, according to a Chase Econometrics study, the United States still maintained a strong competitive advantage, with average manufacturing export prices ten per cent below the OECD average. Today, US manufacture export prices are twenty-five per cent above the OECD average, while, not surprisingly, the US volume share of world exports, steady from 1972 until 1983, has plummeted in the current 'boom'.[25] Viewed sectorally, the export share of 15 US industries has increased, but that of 26 others has sharply declined — an almost exactly inverse ratio of sectoral competitiveness to Japan's.[26]

We shall be looking below at the role of the $160 billion American trade deficit in promoting an unbalanced restructuring of the international division of labor. But first, it is important to consider the specific impact on the home industrial base. The current import invasion may be seen as the third wave in the gradual 'internationalization' of the American economy, as the proportion of US GNP committed

---

[22] See *Dun's*, July 1984, p. 46.
[23] BW, July 9, 1984, p. 29.
[24] BW, October 15, 1984.
[25] BW, September 10, 1984, p. 68.
[26] Ibid.

to world trade has grown from a near-autarkic one-twelfth in the early 1960s, to the present one-fifth. The first import boom during the 1960s was primarily composed of labor-intensive consumer goods and cheap electronics (although this era also saw Volkswagen's pioneering conquest of a significant auto market niche); the second ratchet move in the 1970s was primarily a result of rising energy imports. Today's third wave, however, is notable for the leading role of capital goods and high technology, whose import value has more than doubled since 1979 (to approx. $58 billion, or fourteen times the 1970 level).[27]

Table 6.2[28]
Import Shares of us Markets %

	1960	1984
Auto	4.1	22
Steel	4.2	25.4
Apparel	1.8	30
Machine Tools	3.2	42

In the most dramatic case, the American machine-tool industry is in semi-collapse after the sudden spurt of imports during 1984, from 32.5 per cent to 42 per cent of the market. General Motors' decision, in particular, to retool with $100 million of Italian imports symbolizes the growing breach in the complex of formerly oligopolistic domestic industries integrated by auto production.[29] Other hard-hit industries include tire (import share rising from eight per cent in the late 1970s to over twenty per cent today), farm equipment (formerly a US export monopoly, now being captured by the Japanese) and apparel (import share increasing at 25 per cent per year).[30] Ten years ago, giant American construction companies like Bechtel and Fluor controlled half of the international contract construction market, accounting for almost 20 per cent of the manufacturing, and 10 per cent of the service, exports of the United States. Today their world market share has shrunk below 30 per cent, while the entire US building industry is barely half of its former size.[31] Still, construction is undoubtedly

---

[27] BW, October 8, 1984, pp. 97–100; and NYT, June 3, 1984, p. 28F.
[28] From BW, June 30, 1980 and October 8, 1984; NYT, June 3, 1984, p. 28F; FT, November 5, 1984, p. 11; and *Forbes*, November 7, 1983.
[29] BW, October 8, 1984, pp. 97–100.
[30] See *Forbes*, November 7, 1983 and August 13, 1984.
[31] BW, September 24, 1984, pp. 72–75, and *Dun's*, September 1983, p. 38.

healthier than American steel-making which, barring last-minute protectionism, will continue its decline into a mere finishing operation for imported steel production.[32]

While imports were growing by 28 per cent over the course of 1983, foreign investment was also climbing by 17 per cent — a rather surprising statistic in view of the rising cost of American assets caused by the super-dollar.[33] The explanation is the relative stagnation in the European, and even Japanese, home markets, which has plunged profits below prevailing interest rates, and driven foreign multi-nationals to fight for larger permanent shares of the US domestic market. Faced with creeping US protectionism, but also attracted by relatively low-wage, non-union labor conditions in the American Sunbelt, foreign companies are continuing to acquire US-based production facilities, often by the preferred route of buying up undervalued American equity; hence the spate of recent foreign acquisitions, culminating in Nestlés' purchase of Carnation — the largest non-oil deal (at $3 billion) in business history. The Swiss food giant explained the move in terms of a strategy of raising US sales to 30 per cent of its world-wide revenue.[34]

This increasing dependence of foreign-based multinationals on the US market is reciprocated by American capital's attempts to out-source production to circumvent the competitive disadvantages of the strong dollar. In the most extreme cases, such as US Steel's plan to import British steel or Lonestar Cement's dumping of foreign cement, leading American manufacturers have simply become middlemen for the import invasion. Indeed, the possibility exists that formerly protected or oligopolistic US manufacturers may choose the option of 'leasing' part of their traditional market-share — especially at the downmarket end — to lower-cost foreign competitors. Thus General Motors, having publicly abandoned its much vaunted plan to introduce a new small car last year, is pursuing a so-called 'Asian strategy' of importing subcompacts from Suzuki and Isuzu, to be followed by even cheaper Korean Daewoos in 1987, and complemented with 250,000 Toyotas per year co-produced under Japanese management at GM's old Fremont, California plant.

These marketing and co-production agreements have been represented as temporary palliatives until GM's futuristic 'Saturn Project' can automate small car production in the United States at cost

---

[32] FT, 'World Steel', November 5, 1984, p. 14.

[33] BW, October 8, 1984, p. 93.

[34] BW, September 24, 1984, p. 27.

levels below the Japanese. As we observed in chapter three above, autoworkers made sweeping concessions in their new 1984 contract — including implicit abandonment of their traditional shorter work-year strategy and acceptance of mass redundancies — in return for vague GM promises to bring Saturn onstream. But Chrysler Chairman Lee Iacocca has questioned GM's real motives and insinuated that the largest US automaker is, in fact, consolidating a far-reaching condominium agreement with the Japanese that would rent them the small-car market, while allowing GM to concentrate on competitive supremacy in the lucrative medium and large-car markets.[35] Planning for this eventuality, Ford and Chrysler are rapidly moving ahead with their own Asian strategies, with deleterious consequences for domestic auto employment (already one-quarter below 1978 levels). Auto industry analysts generally agree that if the quotas on Japanese imports are removed, the Japanese share of the American market will probably double from its present 19 per cent with domestic job losses of more than 250,000.[36]

The New Corporate Order

A great ballyhoo has been made about the supposed role of capital spending in leading the recovery and assuring a decade-long prosperity. During his campaign Reagan repeatedly bandied figures about the 'greatest increase in investment in twenty-eight years', 'capital spending at three times the rate of consumption', and so on. In fact, the high rates of increase are first of all only an effect of the low starting point at the beginning of 1983, following the severe investment decline during the 1981–2 recession.[37] At the end of 1984 the investment share of GNP was still 6 per cent below the 1981 level, although consumption was one per cent higher — scarcely an unambiguous index of an investment-led expansion.[38] *Business Week* predicts that capital spending in 1985 will be only one-quarter of the 1984 figure.[39]

The celebrated role of fresh entrepreneurship in promoting the

---

[35] Iacocca interviewed by Jill Bettner in 'What's Good for GM Isn't Good for the Country', *Forbes*, November 7, 1984, pp. 43–44. Since Chrysler sold off its overseas production, it has become the leading voice of protectionism in Detroit, in uneasy union with the UAW.

[36] FT, October 16, 1984, 'Motor Industry Survey', p. 6.

[37] NYT, June 3, 1984, p. 28F.

[38] BW, July 9, 1984.

[39] BW, November 19, 1984.

upturn — an article of faith in French and British homages to Reaganomics — is belied by the current decline in the stock sales of small companies and in the net supply of venture capital, whose volume is no more than one-sixty-ninth of the capital involved in recent merger deals.[40] The real momentum of the expansion has come from 'services', which have been responsible for the lion's share of growth and investment, and 85 per cent of new job creation.[41] As to new manufacturing investment, the major trend is job-displacing rationalization rather than job-creating expansion of capacity. With new plant construction stagnating below pre-recession levels, most capital spending has either gone toward items like small computers, imported machinery and robots; or, more dramatically, toward a speculative expansion of corporate office space and prestige towers — shades of the skyscraper boom that preceded the Great Depression.[42]

Perhaps the most significant tendency of the last several years, however, has been the remarkable tropism of manufacturing and transportation capital towards high-profit sectors like energy reserves, financial services, real estate, emergent technology, and, above all, defense. In some cases, the metamorphosis is startling, as in the recent conversion of US Steel into a medium-sized oil company. When the corporation purchased Marathon Oil in 1982 for $6 billion, it produced an outcry among the tens of thousands of steelworkers who had accepted wage concessions in order to allow the company 'to re-vitalize basic steelmaking'. Now Chairman David Roderick, oblivious to the 100,000 jobless steelworkers in US Steel's home state of Pennsylvania alone, is hastening the pace of deindustrialization by diverting eighty per cent of the corporation's capital budget to oil development, following the purchase of a second oil company (Husky Oil) in April 1984 for $505 million.[43] In a similar, albeit less drastic, vein, the recently merged Santa Fe and Southern Pacific railroad system is retrenching in real estate, with plans to spend $3 billion or more on waterfront developments in San Francisco and San Diego.[44]

---

[40] BW, July 9, 1984.

[41] BW, October 29, 1984, p. 15. By September 1984 the industrial recovery appeared to have run out of steam, as manufacturing employment decreased by 124,000 jobs, with the promise of more layoffs to come. (See WSJ, October 26, 1984.) Stagnation in the goods-producing economy continues through 1985.

[42] See *Dun's*, July 1984, p. 46; and NYT, June 17, 1984.

[43] NYT, July 10, 1984, p. 26F; for unemployment in Pennsylvania, see WSJ, August 23, 1984.

[44] BW, August 27, 1984, p. 19. Only 16 per cent of SFSP earnings now come from railroad traffic.

These mutant oil rentiers or marina proprietors, however, are only extreme examples of the general movement toward corporate diversification. Thus American Can, Ashland Oil, Ethyl, Greyhound and St Regis have become major insurance sellers, while National Steel has gone into savings and loan, RCA into personal finance, Weyerhauser into mortgage banking, GE into aircraft leasing, and Xerox into investment banking.[45] Meanwhile, in the six years since Exxon squandered $500 million in its failed bid to capture the office automation market, large industrial corporations have gobbled up more than 500 new technology firms, usually with disastrous end results.[46] The major exception may be General Motors' $2.5 billion purchase of Electronic Data Systems from Ross Perot, the right-wing Dallas entrepreneur who once organized private commando raids on Laos and now sits on GM's board. Flush with over $9 billion in cash and securities, GM — which, as we have seen, is undertaking a radical restructuring of its global auto production — aims to make EDS the giant in computer services. According to some accounts, GM Chairman Roger Smith, a financial expert promoted out of GM's defense division, may be planning to raise the eventual share of upstream technologies and new non-auto acquisitions to as much as 45 per cent of total turnover.[47]

The single most important sectoral investment trend in the economy, however, is the rush to mine the motherlode at the Defense Department. Predictably, the new arms race has been the most important impetus in the recovery of key industrial sectors, supplying half the increased demand in aerospace and a fifth in primary and fabricated metals.[48] As Table 6.3 illustrates, military demand has also been the most dynamic sector of electronics growth in the upturn, and it is predicted that, as new military technologies go into production over the next decade, the electronics content of defense spending will increase thirty per cent.[49]

Overall, the projected $1 trillion military expenditure for 1985–87 is expected to have an economic impact comparable to that of the Vietnam War at its height, claiming an equal proportion of national

---

[45] The diversification of industrial corporations into financial services has been stimulated by Carter/Reagan tax laws that allow the financial subsidies to shelter in the tax 'shadow' of the parent company's write-offs and depreciation. Thus shielded, GE Credit Company — to take one example — has been able to become a major player in the leveraged buy-out game. See BW, September 13, 1984, p. 82; and NYT, June 3, 1984, p. 28F.

[46] 'Failed Marriages', WSJ, September 11, 1984.

[47] BW, July 16, 1984, pp. 70–75.

[48] Bruce Steinberg, 'The Military Boost to Industry', *Fortune*, April 30, 1984.

[49] *Electronic Business*, July 10, 1984, p. 97.

Table 6.3[50]
The US Electronics Market (billions $)

Sector	1983	1984	% change
computer/office	41	48	17%
military	**34**	**44**	**29%**
communications	23	26	13%
industrial	19	22	16%
consumer	11	12	9%
total	128	152	16%

durable goods output (13 per cent), even though the employment effect (1.2 million new defense-related jobs) will be less.[51]

For the old 'Fordist' industrial core of the American economy — that is, for the complex of mass production industries and their suppliers now threatened by import competition — the Pentagon has been the chief instrument of restructuring. Goodyear, for instance, is actively cannibalizing its tire production to shift into military aerospace (as well as oil and gas).[52] General Tire ($607 million in defense contracts) already forms a military conglomerate with Aerojet General, while the merged auto-component makers, Bendix/Autolite, are part of another (Allied Corporation), and both Ford and GM derive an important part of their cashflow from billion-dollar Pentagon contracts.[53] Meanwhile, traditional big-ten defense contractors like General Dynamics, Lockheed, Douglas and Raytheon are becoming *less* diversified and more strictly dependent on Pentagon fixes, as they move out of less profitable civilian product lines. Willard Rockwell, the legendary founder of Rockwell International — the manufacturer of the MX and B-1 systems — caused a minor storm when he resigned from the board, charging that the company's future had been irresponsibly mortgaged to the Reagan military program. (Not surprisingly, his successor, Robert Anderson, has cultivated special influence with the White House, twice being appointed by Reagan as chairman of National United Nations Day.[54])

If one cumulative result of these various trends is a centrifugal weak-

[50] Ibid.
[51] Steinberg, op. cit.
[52] *Fortune*, May 8, 1984.
[53] See the regular listings of defence contracts in *Aviation Weekly and Space Technology*.
[54] BW, June 25, 1984, and NYT, September 30, 1984.

ening of the coherence and economic centrality of older mass-production industries in the macro-economy, another is the considerable strengthening of the principle of financial conglomeration in corporate organization. The evolution of formerly integrated manu-facturing corporations into diversified, super-holding companies, dominated by speculative financial strategies (and abetted by new electronic technologies of centralized control), is undoing the famous 'Sloanian' revolution that rationalized the management of vertically integrated manufacturing oligopolies, after the model of Alfred Sloan's General Motors in the 1920s. Correlatively, it is also undermining, probably irretrievably, the system of industrial relations and union-company 'compromise' associated with the General Motors paradigm of corporate rationality. Arguably IBM — which now has a larger cash-flow than GM[55] — might be seen as the pioneer of a new, more advanced model of industrial integration with a corresponding (non-union) industrial relations practice. But IBM, like GM in the 1930s, is that unique instance of a self-financing giant, with super-profits capable of carrying its long-range investment programmes through periods of recession and soaring interest, while its diverse product markets grow and mature. Few of even the largest contemporary cor-porations possess the financial freedom of manoeuver of GM or IBM, or their planning horizons.

Instead, the hurried re-deployments of industrial capital towards primary, tertiary or military investments are paralleled by the preda-tory pursuit of other companies' assets. What Robert Reich calls 'paper entrepreneurialism' — 'the rearrangement of industrial assets in the hope of short-term gains' — has inexorably increased over the past decade, as 82 members of the Fortune 500 have been swallowed up, and $398 billion (the GNP of Italy) expended on mergers.[56] The Reagan recovery has brought this merger mania to a fever pitch reminiscent of the final days of the 1920s boom: by the end of the summer of 1984, 15 mergers in excess of one billion dollars had been made, and an aggre-gate dollar volume record had been set.[57] In the course of this convulsion, a new Wall Street language has been spawned to describe the strategems of takeover and resistance: 'two-tier tender offers, Pac-

---

[55] *Dun's*, July 1984, p. 49. IBM's revenues remain approximately 55 per cent of GM's but are expected to double over the next decade. IBM and GM, therefore, may well be of equiva-lent size in the 1990s.

[56] *Fortune*, April 30, 1984, p. 105; and Robert Reich, *The Next American Frontier*, New York 1983, p. 141.

[57] NYT, July 3, 1984, pp. D1 and D7.

Man and poison pill defences, crown jewel options, golden parachutes and self tenders'.[58]

Although the outbreak of this latest merger epidemic should probably be dated to the calamitous *ménage à trois* of Bendix, Martin Marietta and Allied in 1982, the leading actors have been the oil companies, pursuing the dictum that the cheapest place to find oil reserves is on Wall Street. Thus Texaco paid $10.1 billion for Getty, while Standard of California (now Chevron) forked out a cool $13.1 billion for Gulf. In most cases, the mergers have been shotgun marriages of a type, forced by alliances with institutional share-holders and financed by borrowed capital. Most of these so-called 'leveraged buy-outs' (LBOs) are 'overleveraged' by dint of the incentive given in the Carter and Reagan tax bills to the substitution of debt for equity capital. They are, in the words of *Forbes*, 'subsidized by the taxpayers'.[59]

The LBO phenomenon has allowed a flamboyant group of Sunbelt speculators — including independent oil leaseholders like T. Boone Pickens and the Bass Family, (now deceased) hotelier J. Willard Marriott Jr., and others — to become the latter-day buccaneers of Wall Street. Their strategy has been to intervene in impending takeover battles between major oil companies or other large firms, leveraging enough stock and stockholder proxies to demand lucrative 'greenmail'. Thus the Bass Brothers made $400 million in pre-tax profits from their takeover threat to Texaco (which ended up paying out a total of $1.29 billion to obtain the Basses' ten per cent share and their promise not to meddle for ten years), while Pickens creamed half-a-billion dollars one spring afternoon in 1984 when Chevron outbid him for Gulf. The Basses are now allied to Marriott, a notorious non-union employer, in pursuit of Conrail (in competition with a bid from the railroad's own employees); the redoubtable Pickens, whose own Mesa Petroleum has an annual turnover of only $422 million, built a $6 billion war chest in an attempted raid on $60 billion Mobil Oil.[60]

---

[58] Ibid., p. D7.

[59] *Forbes*, August 13, 1984.

[60] See Cathleen Stauder, 'How the Bass Brothers Do Their Deals', *Fortune*, September 17, 1984. A listing of the Bass Family's current assets is like a random compilation from a Chinese encyclopedia: a Minnesota underwear maker, the nation's largest pizza topping maker, a San Franciso shopping mall, a Jack Nicolaus golf course, 5 per cent of Walt Disney, 5 per cent of a fried chicken chain, nine industrial parks in Chicago, Baltimore, and Atlanta, a subsidized housing project in Puerto Rico, property in Florida, North Carolina, and California, $100 million cash for the recent sale of the Atlantic City Sands Casino, and, finally, the biggest chunk of downtown Fort Worth.

The possibility that a previously obscure Amarillo oilman could stalk the second largest American multinational exemplifies the way in which Reaganomics and the current boom are reshaping the map of corporate power and political influence. (Marriott was a leading Republican fundraiser; the Bass family, virtual rulers of Fort Worth, were prominent in organizing the Republican convention-cum-Nuremberg rally; and Pickens was widely tipped as Reagan's nominee for governor of Texas in 1986.) In *The New Politics of Inequality*, Thomas Edsall has described the crucial role of the dozen or so independent oil political action committees — dominated by Pickens, the Basses, the Murchisons, the Pewes, the Hunts, and so on — in engineering the end of Democratic control in the Senate and electing Reagan.

According to Edsall, the oil independents, flush with new billions from the 1970s energy price explosion and rapidly diversifying into real estate and leisure industries, have provided the 'financial glue' between the New Right and the Republican Party. Constituting an estimated one-third of the major joint contributors to Republican and conservative causes, the oil independents are the core of a new power-bloc which, thanks to the continuing shift of capital and tax revenues to the West and the South, is displacing Northeastern multinationals in the active control of the Republican apparatus.[61] In this sense, the recent near-extinction of 'moderate Republicanism' — i.e., the Dewey-Rockefeller wing dominant from 1940 to 1964 — is part of a larger pattern involving the supplantation of Fordism and the rise of new rentier and military contractor networks. Profiting so stupendously from the recent infusion of debt and defense spending, together with the perpetuation of the Sunbelt boom, the new powerbrokers of Republicanism, for all their anti-state rhetoric, are unlikely to act as anything other than the most avid supporters of the current, pathological prosperity.

II. The Wobbling Axes of World Trade

The burgeoning US trade deficit, projected to exceed $160 billion or three per cent, of GNP, has been the prime mover of the weak recovery of world trade. Exports to the United States are now calculated to comprise 25 to 40 per cent of GNP growth in Western Europe and capitalist East Asia.[62] But the celebrated Reagan 'locomotive' is hardly

---

[61] Thomas Edsall, *The New Politics of Inequality*, New York 1984, pp. 93–94, 100–02.

[62] *Fortune*, October 1, 1984, p. 31.

pulling trading nations in even tow. While Japan and the East Asian NICs have accelerated in pace with or ahead of the United States, the EEC has coasted along in low gear, and the larger economies of Latin America and Africa have remained derailed. The uneven, contradictory charcter of the 'upturn' is a surface expression of the structural disarticulation taking place in the world economy. Consider the following schema:

Circuits of World Trade

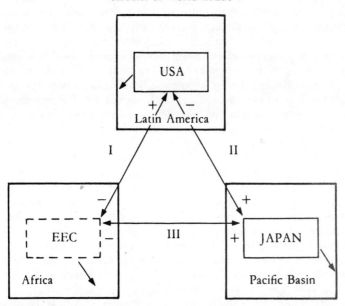

Abstracting from the redistributive role of energy trade balances in the organization of the world economy (and, therefore, from OPEC's role), we can say that a tendential coherence in world accumulation existed through the 1970s on the basis of the following interrelationships: (1) The United States' manufacturing deficit with East Asia (cars, electronics, apparel) was balanced by a more-or-less equivalent surplus (in 1980, $20 billion) with Europe (computers, aerospace). (2) Simultaneously, the net US trade surplus with Latin America was offset by an outflow of US direct investment, especially to Brazil and Mexico. (3) The European manufacturing deficits with the United States and Japan were compensated by capital-goods surpluses with the Third

World, especially Africa. 4) Finally, Japan's surpluses with Europe and North America enabled it to pay its energy and raw material bills, while exporting capital to the East Asian NICs and Australasia.

Where US military hegemony and monetary sovereignty once provided coherence for this system of interrelationships, it now has become the principal disorganizing force. First, the shift in internal American demand from mass consumption towards surrogate affluent and military markets has generated, as we have seen, the spiralling budget and trade deficits that have further unbalanced the 'great triangle' of intermetropolitan trade, while simultaneously siphoning off European and Japanese savings. Secondly, the collective trusteeship now operated by the Western banks over the economies of Latin America has confiscated whatever developmental gains they might have achieved in the current expansion of US trade. Indeed, the traditional relationship has been stood on its head, as Latin America runs a trade surplus *and* exports capital to the United States. The neo-classical burden of adjustment to this new trading order has been borne by the poorest inhabitants of the hemisphere, including the five millions of *flagelados* (or 'scourged ones') estimated to have starved to death in Northeastern Brazil in the course of the first Reagan administration.[63]

Thirdly, primary commodity prices have yet to recover from the ruinous collapse of 1981–2, when they fell to their lowest post-war level.[64] Mono-cultural producers are caught in a classic scissors crisis between the depressed prices of their exports and the high interest on their debts. Quite apart from the specter of sovereign default and the perils of a financial panic, the current depression in the third world, in Black Africa as well as Latin America, is an important restraint on any export-led strategy of European reflation, exacerbating the EEC's deficits with East Asia and increasing its dependence on American markets. Fourthly, while Japan — two-thirds of whose increased exports since 1983 have been absorbed by the United States — and the 'Four Tigers' — who shipped $8.5 billion to the United States in the first quarter of 1984 alone — are the primary beneficiaries of the Reagan boom, this has been achieved, as we shall see, at the price of postponed reform of their domestic market, and of increased vulnerability to an American recession.[65]

---

[63] Information publicized by Don Ivo Lorsheiter, President of the National Council of Brazilian Bishops.

[64] Primary commodities declined 15 per cent in 1981; 12 per cent in 1982. See Ke-Young Chu and Thomas K. Morrison, 'The 1981–82 Recession and Non-Oil Primary Commodity Prices', IMF *Staff Papers*, 31, I, (March 1984).

[65] See FT, 'World Economic Survey', September 1, 1984.

The obvious pattern is therefore one of growing incoherence and imbalance at each strategic trade juncture. But — to play devil's advocate on behalf of the neo-liberals — what if all this disorder in the world economy is only the confusion of a transition from an old smokestack capitalism to a new silicon-chip entrepreneurialism? Is not the Reagan boom shifting the center of gravity of world capitalism from the Atlantic to the brave new world on California's shore? Let us briefly consider the impact of the upturn on the Old World's competitiveness, as well as the evidence for the emergence of a new geo-economic axis in the Pacific.

European Sunset ...

One of the ironies of the present expansion is that the new European merchandise surplus with the United States — $14 billion in 1984[66] — far from signalling a renewal of European capitalist vigor, is merely a symptom of the stagnation of European internal demand that is reorienting the larger multinationals toward North America. European capital is caught in a structural scissors crisis of its own. On the one hand, the project of European capitalist unity is seriously, if not fatally, compromised by the competitive adaptations of the different national economies to a new international division of labor.[67] On the other hand, the class stalemate in Europe, which prevents labor from taking the offensive against unemployment, has also prevented the right from engaging in any experiment in American-style growth based on polarized immiseration and affluence within a reduced welfare state. In effect, European capitalism has been unable to achieve either the economies of scale associated with an integrated continental market, or the management of social demand associated with a more unilateral class power of the right or left.

As a result, Europe has virtually lost superpower status in the current technological-scientific revolution. Back in 1970, the 'Colonna Memorandum' of the European Community posed the urgency of confronting the American challenge in advanced technology, and out-

---

[66] German exports to the United States have increased by over 50 per cent during the last year. See BW, September 24, 1984, p. 27.

[67] Of the voluminous literature on the 'crisis of Europe', see particularly, Gilbert Ziebura, 'Internationalization of Capital, International Division of Labor, and the Role of the European Community', *Journal of Common Market Studies*, XXI, 1/2, September 1984; and M. Albert and R.J. Ball, *Towards European Economic Recovery in the 1980s*, working paper, European Parliament, July 1983.

lined bold moves to encourage cross-border mergers and hasten the integration of a common market in electronics. Now, fifteen years later, the leading European manufacturer of integrated circuits, Philips, ranks barely twelfth in the world, while Europe's premier computer-maker, Olivetti, has an annual turnover only $1/17$th that of IBM.[68] European-made computers supply only 17 per cent of the European market (US share, 81 per cent), while less than 6 per cent of the world's integrated circuits — the 'steam engines' of current technology — are produced in Europe.[69] In an investigation of competition in the world electronics industry, the Joint Economic Committee of the US Congress concluded in 1982 that 'the battle for preeminence [in integrated circuits] is today a fight between American (67 per cent of world markets) and Japanese (26 per cent) manufacturers, to be fought in American and European markets'.[70]

Cross-national co-operation and horizontal centralization have both proven quixotic goals for European electronics and information-processing industries, starting with the collapse of the first 'European' computer consortium, Unidata, in 1974. Of fifty major international information technology mergers or joint ventures between 1980 and 1983, only two were intra-European; of the rest, half were joint American and Japanese projects, and half were European and American.[71] Although the EEC finally initiated a common R&D program ESPRIT, in 1981, its fruits will probably only come on stream to industry in the 1990s. Meanwhile, the EEC's share of world information technology systems could fall over the next decade from 20 to 15 per cent, while its trading deficit in information technology, already $3.2 billion in 1982, could increase to $16 billion by 1992.[72]

With 70 per cent of the European mainframe market in its hands, IBM is poised to take commanding positions in all sectors of the evolving electronics and information complex.[73] The 'amicable' settlement of the EEC anti-trust suit last summer paved the way for its expansion into factory automation (a $30 billion market by 1990) and telecommunications. At stake are not merely market shares, but IBM's ability to impose its 'systems standards' over whole industries. The Thatcher

---

[68] Michel Richonnier, 'Europe's Decline Is Not Irreversible', *Journal of Common Market Studies*, XXII, 3, March 1984, p. 236.

[69] Stephen Woolcock, 'Information Technology: the Challenge to Europe', *Journal of Common Market Studies*, XXII, 4, June 1984, p. 318.

[70] Ibid.

[71] Ibid.

[72] Ibid.

[73] Cf. BW, June 16, August 13 and August 20, 1984.

government's 1984 veto of a proposed IBM-Telecom venture was explicitly justified in terms of preventing IBM from making its Systems Network Architecture the standard for British telecommunications. In the long run, however, it is unlikely that isolated rearguard actions by single European states can protect their postal and telecommunications systems — any more than their already marginalized computer industries — from being colonized by vertically integrated world giants like IBM and ATT (recently married to Olivetti). Indeed, the current expansion only seems to be accelerating the erosion of Europe's technological sovereignty, as local companies, even state monopolies, are forced into the grid of interdependency centered on the dominant foreign technology vendors.

... Pacific Sunrise?

One of Marx's more inadvertent exercises in futurology was his prediction, at the time of the California gold rush, that the nineteenth century would oversee the shift of commercial hegemony from the old lands of the Atlantic to the new lands of the Pacific.[74] In the event, the westward perambulation of the world spirit has been slower than prophesied. Indeed, it has only been since the inauguration of Ronald Reagan that the idea of a huge geopolitical displacement in the regulation of the world economy has gained more than superficial plausibility.

Several kinds of recent data can now be submitted on behalf of this thesis. First is the leading, almost one-sided, role of Pacific trade which distinguishes this expansion from other post-war upturns. Since 1980, the Pacific Basin has eclipsed the North Atlantic as the United States' principal trading zone, and, indicatively, Taiwan has now surpassed Great Britain as an American trading partner.[75] Moreover, as Table 6.4 illustrates, there has been a particularly dramatic reversal during the last decade in the relative importance of 'Atlantic' and 'Pacific' manufacturing imports to the United States.

---

[74] 'The centre of gravity of world commerce, Italy in the Middle Ages, England in modern times, is now the southern half of the North American peninsula ... Thanks to California gold and the tireless energy of the Yankees, both coasts of the Pacific Ocean will soon be as populous, as open to trade and as industrialized as the coast from Boston to New Orleans is now. And then the Pacific Ocean will have the same role as the Atlantic has now and the Mediterranean had in antiquity and in the Middle Ages — that of the great water highway of world commerce; and the Atlantic will decline to the status of an inland sea ...' Marx and Engels, 'Review', January–February 1850, in *Collected Works*, volume 10, London 1978, pp. 265–66.

[75] *Fortune*, May 28, 1984, p. 30.

Table 6.4[76]
Manufacturing Import Shares of US Market

	1973	1980	1983
I. 'Atlantic' (Europe + Canada)	61%	50%	43%
II. 'Pacific' (Asia + Latin America)	35%	48%	54%
II. Other	4%	2%	2%

Secondly, Pacific capitalism, including California (considered independently, the sixth largest capitalist economy), has continued to grow at twice the rate of Europe. During the 1970s, the ten countries that now comprise the EEC had a GNP equal to that of the United States, and twice that of the ten leading Pacific Basin economies. By 1984, the EEC's GNP had shrunk to 93 per cent of the United States', while the Pacific grew to two-thirds the size of the EEC.[77] Finally, the majority of the capitalist world's science-based industry and research and development is now probably located along the Pacific Rim, in California and Japan. Microelectronics is the first technological-scientific revolution not to be pioneered in Europe or primarily developed within the ambit of Atlantic trade.

These trends encourage the image of a 'Pacific sunrise', so soothing in the hot-tubs of California, so unsettling in the corridors of the Bourse or the City. But it is manifestly unrealistic to expect that the present patterns of Pacific exchange can substitute for the broken circuitry of Fordism in the United States, for the stagnation of demand in Europe, or for the strangulation of consumer production and cereal agriculture in the Third World. Quite the contrary: the present export boom to the United States is itself, in some sense, an unstable substitute for the failure of East Asian capitalism to raise domestic demand or to achieve a more balanced regional economic order.

In Japan, the Nakasone regime, to the disquiet of some factions of the ruling party, has continued to privilege the development of a high-tech arms industry, synchronized to Pentagon procurement needs, over the long overdue upgrading of the social infrastructure. Meanwhile, the spring 1984 *shunto* (or wage offensive) under the leadership of the

---

[76] Adapted from *Le Monde*, June 5, 1984.
[77] Brien Reading, 'Demise of Western Europe', *The Sunday Times*, February 5, 1984, p. 6.

right-wing enterprise unions produced the smallest wage increase since 1955. As the wage share of the GNP is held down, and the export offensive more than ever bears the burden of sustaining employment, the threat of European and American protectionism casts clouds over a risen sun.

The position of the four smaller Northeast Asian capitalist states is still more precarious, as their traditional export advantages in labor-intensive manufacture are being erased by the competition of poorer ASEAN neighbours, factory automation in the United States, and a significant relocation of sweated industry from Asia to the Caribbean. In the rush to win new niches in capital-intensive or high-tech exports, the virtuous product cycle that allowed them to take over Japan's cast-off industries (usually with the help of Japanese investment) has broken down. They have become more directly competitive with mainline Japanese export sectors and with advanced Japanese technology. South Korea's multi-billion-dollar gamble that it can create a national auto industry *ex nihilo* has been particularly questioned. In a major survey of the Northeast Asian division of labor, Bruce Cummings has argued that under the new conditions of international competition created during the 1970s, there remained room for only one 'new Japan'. In his estimation, 'Taiwan was chosen but the ROK was not', with grave implications for the latter's authoritarian stability.[78]

A Crisis of Tigers and Cowboys

In contrast to the Pacific sunrise scenario, I suggest the possibility that the present unstable expansion is creating the basis for a downturn that may deepen into crisis precisely along the current axis of growth, from the American Sunbelt to industrial East Asia. The hothouse economic conditions that have prevailed in these areas almost uninterruptedly since the beginning of the Vietnam War have created vast new productive complexes and working classes, but they have also nurtured unprecedented accumulations of fictitious capital. If at one shore of the Pacific the relative underconsumption of the East Asian proletariats sets an inescapable constraint on growth, so, on the other shore, the rampant mega-consumption of the California middle classes poses a threat to financial stability.

Since the 1970s, a disproportionate share of American wealth has

---

[78] Bruce Cummings, 'The Origins and Development of the Northeast Asian Political Economy', *International Organization*, Winter 1984, p. 35.

been absorbed in the capitalization of soaring real-estate values, commercial building booms, inflated mineral equities, and overdeveloped service industries in the Western and Southern states. Now, having battened off the decline of the old industrial heartland, this great superstructure of non-productive income claims is feeding off the savings of the entire capitalist world. In the meantime, financial analysts, still stunned by the Continental Illinois collapse, are nervously eyeing the health of a large group of Sunbelt banks (especially the behemoth Bank of America) that have recklessly validated local real-estate and energy-asset speculation while simultaneously over-extending themselves in Latin America.[79] One potential vector of such a financial crisis is the recent slump in Western states' energy industries, which has reduced employment and jeopardized the collateral value of reserves.[80]

In the short-run, of course, it may be possible for the Reagan administration to continue to avoid a deep recession by simply conscripting more liquidity into global lending circuits. One strategy is to internationalize the yen and recycle the Japanese trade surplus to the credit-hungry and unstable sectors of the world economy. Already the Americans have won a significant deregulation of the Japanese banking system and increased the volume of syndicated yen-loans available to international borrowers. But a full-fledged 'euro-yen' remains merely a theoretical possibility, with hotly disputed implications for the growth of world credit. As the boom stalls and threatens to expire, the most readily available and potent instrument of expansion remains the Federal Reserve's power to sanction monetary inflation. Thus, almost within hours of Reagan's re-election, supply-side scalping parties were once again after Paul Volcker, whose supposed refusal to increase the money supply was blamed for the sharp third-quarter 1984 slowdown. On the defensive, Volcker has tacitly abandoned any pretense of monetarist management; his decision to 'rebase' money supply targets in the summer of 1985 opened the way for the Fed's accommodation to whatever level of stimulus is necessary to sustain expansion.

The second wave of Reaganomics will undoubtedly lean even

---

[79] 'The Federal Deposit Insurance Corporation recently told Congress that classified assets — loans whose quality is questionable at best — rose to 58 per cent of capital for all insured banks last year, up from 30 per cent in 1979. And the bulk of the problem loans remains overwhelmingly domestic.' Most of the examples cited are located in California or Texas. ('Behind the Banking Turmoil', BW, October 29, 1984, p. 7.)

[80] It is little appreciated that the current oil slump has cost as many jobs (over 100,000) in metropolitan Houston as the steel slump has in Pittsburgh. On the structural crisis of the Texas economy, see NYT, September 16, 1984, p. F9.

further than the first toward a purely political regulation of the business cycle such as the Democrats never dared nor ever even dreamed. Indeed, one French observer has called the current recovery 'the greatest example of state voluntarism in the post-war epoch'[81] — a perverse Keynesianism that unexpectedly reinsured the unity of the 'Haves' coalition that first elected Reagan in 1980. This great conjuring act has created an illusion of Yuppie mobility and self-confidence — 'the conservative opportunity society' — that has besotted a large part of the white working class as well. Despite Mondale's desperate promotion of the deficit as *the* issue of the campaign, the contradictions between the economic interests of different sectors of capital, and between the corporate economy and the diverse middle strata, were once again repressed in the larger plebiscite on the new prosperity. But, as I have tried to indicate, there is an impending point at which the costs of assuring expansion cannot be entirely displaced onto the domestic poor.

---

[81] Philippe Norel, 'Comment l'Europe et le Japon sont mobilisés au secours de l'économie américaine', *Le Monde Diplomatique*, August 1984, pp. 20–21.

7

The Lesser Evil? The Left, The Democrats and 1984

In the summer before the 1984 presidential elections, Michael Harrington and Irving Howe, in a widely noted interview in the *New York Times Magazine*, boasted that 'by now practically everyone on the Left agrees that the Democratic Party, with all its faults, must be our main political arena'.[1] In recent historical context there was a peculiar irony in this assertion, with its smug self-limitation of the 'Left'. During the 1960s, American social democracy had been debilitated, almost discredited, by its advocacy of reform through the Democratic Party. The right wing of the old Thomasite Socialist Party, 'Social Democrats, USA', had broken away to become courtiers of Scoop Jackson and lobbyists for military victory in Vietnam. Meanwhile, a centrist current led by Harrington and Howe formed a small circle around *Dissent* with negligible influence on a burgeoning New Left which spurned their faith in the transformability of the Democratic Party. Indeed, the key radical organizations of the 1960s, SNCC and SDS, understandably regarded the Cold War liberalism incarnated by the Humphrey/Jackson wing of the Democratic Party (to which both camps of social democrats oriented) as *the* enemy, primarily responsible for genocidal imperialism in Southeast Asia as well as for the repression of the Black liberation movement at home.

From the McGovern candidacy of 1972, however, sections of the former New Left, together with a younger cohort of 1970s activists, began to slip back into Democratic politics, initially on a local level.[2] At first there was no sharp ideological break with the sixties' legacy. The 'New Politics', as it was typed, seemed just another front of the anti-war movement or another tactical extension of the urban populism

---

[1] *New York Times Sunday Magazine*, June 17, 1981, p. 24.
[2] The first major trial run for new left electoralism, however, was Robert Scheer's unsuccessful anti-war congressional campaign in Berkeley in 1966. This experience rehearsed in miniature all the problems and contradictions of trying to build a movement from inside the Democratic Party and under the constraints of a campaign schedule.

espoused by SDS's community organizing faction. By 1975, with the sudden end of the Vietnam War, a strategic divergence had become more conspicuous. On the one hand, an array of self-proclaimed 'cadre' groups, inspired by the heroic mold of 1930s radicalism, were sending their ex-student members into the factories in the hope of capturing and radicalizing the widespread rank-and-file discontent that characterized the end of the postwar boom. On the other hand, another network of ex-SDSers and antiwar activists — of whom Tom Hayden was merely a belated and media-hyped example — were building local influence within the Democratic 'reform movement': the loose collocation of consumer, environmental and public-sector groups, supported by a few progressive unions, that had survived the McGovern debacle.

Although its significance was only vaguely grasped at the time, this increasing polarization between workerism and electoralism coincided with, and was immediately conditioned by, the decline of the Black liberation movement that had been the chief social motor of postwar radicalism. A dismaying, inverse law seemed to prevail between the collapse of grassroots mobilization in the ghettoes and the rise of the first wave of Black political patronage in the inner cities. While Black revolutionaries and nationalists were being decimated by J. Edgar Hoover's COINTELPRO program of preemptive repression and infiltration, Black community organization was being reshaped into a passive clientelism manipulated by the human-services bureaucracy and the Democratic Party. Although, as we have seen, the civil rights movement remained an unfinished revolution with an urgent agenda of economic and political demands, its centrality to the project of a popular American left was tragically, and irresponsibly, obscured in the late 1970s. The ranks of the white, ex-student left, preoccupied with academic outposts and intellectual celebrities, showed a profound inability to understand the strategic implications of the halting of the civil rights movement. For all the theoretical white smoke of the 1970s, including the endless debates on crisis theory and the nature of the state, the decisive problem of the fate of the Second Reconstruction was displaced beyond the field of vision. With minimal challenge or debate, leading journals like *Socialist Review* and *Dissent* tacitly demoted Black liberation — *the critical democratic issue in American history* — to the status of another progressive 'interest', coeval with sexual freedom or ecology.

The crisis of Black radicalism, and its attendant white incomprehension, was soon followed by the disintegration of the workerist left. With the important but solitary exception of the International Social-

258

ists, who continue to play a vital role in Teamsters for a Democratic Union (the *only* surviving rank-and-file caucus from the 1970s), none of the workplace-oriented offshoots of the New Left proved to have the stamina or internal stability to weather the decline in union militancy that followed the 1974/75 recession. The bizarre implosion of the 'new communist movement', as the Maoist left moved from the factory floor to frenzied party building and street confrontations, reinforced, if only by harrowing negative example, the growing claim of the electoralists to represent the sole rational hope for a mass American left.

But it is unlikely that the transition towards the orbit of the Democratic Party could have occurred so rapidly without the intervention and coordination undertaken by the Harrington–Howe group, now reorganized as the Democratic Socialist Organizing Committee (DSOC). The charter concept of DSOC, according to a Harrington editorial written in the wake of the McGovern defeat, was the belief that 'the left wing of realism is found today in the Democratic Party. It is there that the mass forces for social change are assembled; it is there that the possibility exists for creating a new first party in America'.[3] To pursue this realignment, Harrington and Howe proposed a two-story organizational strategy, the DSOC conceived as a 'party within a party within a party'. It was intended to provide a kind of social-democratic inner sanctum within a larger liberal coalition, built from the top down through the selective recruitment of 'influentials': trade-union fulltimers, local Democratic luminaries and well-known academics. These 'influentials', in turn, helped sponsor the Democratic Agenda, the 'party within the party', that aimed to coalesce progressive forces within the national Democratic Party. In this fashion, the Harrington-Howe group contrived to obtain a political leverage disproportionate to DSOC's modest membership or its meager contributions to day-to-day struggles.

The Democratic Agenda enjoyed a brief heyday during the first half of the Carter Administration. It exerted influence at national and regional party conferences, as well as providing one of the main rallying points for supporters of the labor law reform campaign of the AFL–CIO. However, after the 1978 rightward turn of the administration (i.e., the rejection of détente, the firing of Andrew Young, the savaging of the domestic budget, the abandonment of health reform, the curtailment of urban jobs programs, and the defeat of labor law reform), the progressive pole notionally represented by the Democratic Agenda

---

[3] *Newsletter of the Democratic Left*, March 1973, p. 5.

steadily lost ground in the face of the rise of 'neo-liberalism'. Traditional liberals, influenced, as we have seen, by business PACs and insurgent middle-class constituents, deserted the labor and civil rights organizations in droves, recanting previous commitments to the legacy of the Great Society and Keynesian reformism. Ironically, it was precisely at this moment of crisis for the 'left wing of realism', as the old liberal coalition began to break up, that significant additional sectors of the ex-New Left began to gravitate towards DSOC's centrist and electoralist positions. This convergence was abetted by the shift in editorial and theoretical perspectives within the group of periodicals, mutually descended from the seminal *Studies on the Left* of the 1960s, that bore most of the intellectual mantle of the US New Left: *Socialist Review* (ex-*Socialist Revolution*), *Kapitalstate*, and *In These Times*. All three had originally proclaimed the advocacy of 'explicit socialist politics' and the building of a 'new American Socialist Party'; on the eve of Reaganism, each had retreated to pragmatic endorsements of reform Democrats and to the embrace of a pseudo–phenomenal 'New Populism'.[4]

Social Democracy's surprising conquest of the New Left in the teeth of the old liberalism's demise culminated in 1982 with the merger of the majority of the 2,500 member New American Movement with DSOC to form the Democratic Socialists of America (DSA), largely on the basis of political conditions (support for Israel, centrality of the Democratic Party, etc.) dictated by the DSOC leadership. Any serious, detailed analysis of the rightward transformation of the Democratic Party and the new internal power balances that it entailed was completely obscured by the rhetorical intoxication that became a hallmark of the new organization. 'Unity against Reagan' and unqualified support for the AFL-CIO Executive became the twin motivating slogans for DSA's headlong rush, first to Edward Kennedy, and then to Walter Mondale.

Although the invocation of 'practically everyone on the Left' was a sectarian exaggeration, Harrington and Howe could certainly savor their success in having brought a considerable fraction of the extant socialist left 'home' to the Democrats. Moreover, as other left groups, including significant numbers of repentant Maoists, became increasingly involved in Democratic politics from the 1982 midterm elections onward, a new orthodoxy arose. The principal object–lesson of the

---

[4] For a debate on the class–political trajectory of neighborhood movements — whether a rebirth of Populism or an insurgency of right-leaning middle classes — see Harry Boyte's essay in *Socialist Review*, 40–41, July–October, 1978, and my reply in the same issue.

militant 1960s, reliance on independent mass politics outside of and against the national Democratic Party, was stood on its head, Participation in bourgeois electoral politics was redefined as the admission ticket to serious popular politics *tout court.* Not since the meridian of the Popular Front during World War Two, when the Browderite Communist Party attempted to dissolve itself into the left wing of the New Deal, had the majority of the American left been so fully submerged in the Democratic Party.

In 1984, the spectrum of progressive groups who ultimately rallied behind the Mondale banner included CISPES and the Nuclear Freeze, as well as DSA and its 'influentials'. All calculated that entry into the campaign would strengthen their grassroots base as well as their influence over liberal Democrats. All believed the specter of Reagan's second term was most effectively combated through support of the national Democratic candidate. All assumed that four years of cutbacks and takebacks had jolted the Democratic electorate to the left, creating a new receptivity to progressive ideas and providing an incentive for millions of anti-Reagan non-voters to enter the rolls. The 1984 elections, therefore, provide a decisive test of the political realism of the strategic shift to electoralism. At the same time, the election results also offer important, if not completely unambiguous, evidence about the changing sociology of the electorate and the future of the party system in the post-New Deal era.

The Crisis of the Reformist Leaderships

The most original phenomenon of 1984 was the unexpected and dramatic demonstration of Black voters and their allies in favor of Jesse Jackson and the program of the Rainbow Coalition. The emergence of the Jackson campaign posed the electoralist left with the unexpected dilemma of choosing between insurgent Black politics or the traditional trade-union leadership. In the event, a majority of DSA, including the ex-DSOC leadership and most of the 'influentials', remained meekly aligned behind the AFL-CIO Executive in its pre-packaged support for Mondale. On the other hand, almost all the Black and Hispanic left, together with white 'Marxist–Leninists', dissident members of DSA, and, discreetly, the CPUSA, supported the Rainbow candidacy, some with the avowed intention of building a left-wing 'party within the party'. The old social–democratic goal of a 'progressive realignment' under institutional labor–liberal auspices was suddenly confronted with the fait accompli of a progressive electoral groundswell outside the franchised limits of official liberalism. To understand how this came about it is necessary to retrace, in their respective turns, the different reactions of the trade-union bureaucracy and the Black political establishment to the general crisis of reformism provoked by the domestic right turns after 1978.

A Counterfeit Labor Party?

To consider the plight of the trade–union bureaucracy first, the 'unified labor' strategy was born directly out of the failure of the AFL-CIO Executive in Meany's last years to find political or juridical redress for the organizational decline of union membership. The stunning defeats of labor law reform and *situs* picketing in the overwhelmingly Democratic 95th and 96th Congresses were interpreted by the Federation's leadership, not as failures of rank-and-file mobilization or grassroots alliances, but rather as deficits of rightful influence within the Democratic Party apparatus. The rise of neo-liberalism in the suburban outlands of Democracy was taken as tantamount to a disinheritance of Labor's accumulated good work for the Party cause. So, upon succeeding Meany in 1979, Lane Kirkland defined his principal brief as the concentration of labor's resources to recapture a dominating position within the Democratic power structure. In the chain of substitutions by which the AFL–CIO leadership had successively bargained away the role of shopfloor mobilizations for the sake of a variety of 'insider' positions within the industrial relations and legislative systems, its clout within the Democratic National Committee was reckoned to be the most precious asset of all. As Harold Meyerson put it, for the trade-union bureaucracy 'the DNC was to be the Archimedean point from which it would begin once more to move the world its way'.[5]

It is helpful to recall once again the peculiar form of labor's subordination within the New Deal coalition. From 1936 onward, the trade unions achieved an interest-group (non-class) representation as junior partners alongside the big urban patronage machines with their captive ethnic constituencies, and the Solid South of courthouse cliques and local ruling classes. This last component, of course, was guaranteed by Jim Crow and sweeping disfranchisement of Blacks, Hispanics and

---

[5] Meyerson, 'Labor's Risky Plunge into Politics', *Dissent*, Summer 1984, p. 286.

poor whites: national Democratic power was purchased by the addition of the working-class votes in the North and their substantial subtraction in the South. Although the national Democratic Party was also criss-crossed by ideological alignments, they were relatively ephemeral compared to the triad of socio-political blocs. Labor and liberal forces were frequently distempered by machine and Southern outrages — especially the latter's role in the informal conservative bipartism coalition that blocked social reform from 1938 to 1964 — but neither moved decisively against their erstwhile partners in the Cold War Democratic 'consensus'. To take the most famous apparent case to the contrary, Truman's brief struggle with the Dixiecrats in 1948 over civil rights planks in the party platform was immediately followed by appeasement, culminating in Adlai Stevenson's ignominious contrition to the citadels of segregation in 1953.[6] Similarly, the AFL under Green and then Meany paid respect to civil rights on ritual occasions, only to wheel and deal with the bosses and kingfishes on a day-to-day legislative basis.

During the 1960s, however, this unholy configuration of Rooseveltian unity began to collapse of its own weight in face of the social recomposition of the big cities, the challenge of the civil rights movement in the South, and the mass opposition to the Johnson administration's escalations in Vietnam. The national Democrats fractured along three axes. First, the declining big city machines, personified by Daley in Chicago, fought delaying actions alongside their white craft union allies against the federalized welfare and clientage networks constructed by LBJ, which attempted to incorporate public-sector professionals and a section of the Black leadership as a new pillar of the national Democratic Party. Secondly, the Solid South crumbled, as Blacks and conservative Republicans assaulted the Democratic *ancien régime* from opposite sides amid great radical polarization. Finally, Vietnam splintered first the liberal wing of the party, then the AFL-CIO itself as the Reuther–Meany feud became a schism. All three sets of contradictions condensed into the fractious infighting of 1968–72, as anti-war liberals refused to support Humphrey, Cold War liberals repudiated McGovern, and Wallace bolted with the white backlash.

With the collapse of the machines and the Solid South, the trade-

[6] For an unsparing discussion of Stevenson's assuasive cultivation of the Dixiecrats, see Herbert Parmet, *The Democrats: The Years After FDR*, New York 1976. Stevenson's 'Southern strategy' was a major impetus behind Reuther's attempts to reconstruct a new liberal–labor alliance committed to serious civil rights enforcement.

union bureaucracy, hitherto the minor actor of the trio, increasingly became the main institutional support for the continuity of party leadership and the maintenance of Cold War liberalism (with its implicit relegation of social reforms behind anti-Communism). Simultaneously, however, the fight over the recomposition of the Democratic Party became complexly entangled with the power struggles within the AFL–CIO Executive itself. In particular, the Reutherites and their allies in the ex-CIO and public-sector unions seized upon the new social forces of civil rights, anti-poverty and peace as potential levers to challenge the ascendency of the ex-AFL craft unions in the merged federation. Reuther's UAW, key proponent of a new liberal-labor alliance from the late 1950s, was in the forefront of efforts to reorient the AFL–CIO towards the reform forces in the Democratic Party who were pressing for a retreat from Vietnam and a greater sharing-out of power to minority and 'new-middle-class' constituencies. Through its generous financial support to SNCC and SDS community projects, the UAW attempt to coax the most serious organizers of the new left into the radius of liberal democracy. At the opposite extreme, of course, were the locals of the old AFL construction crafts. These last-ditch defenders of white job trusts in urban employment remained the foot soldiers of bossdom and the mindless supporters of whatever regime in Washington was currently bombing Southeast Asia.

Meany's role in this turbulent period was often more devious than the public image of cigar-chomping truculence suggested. In the chain of events leading to Reuther's exit in 1969 (partially as a result of deep disagreements over the Federation's political orientation) and then to the Executive's boycott of the McGovern campaign in 1972, Meany attempted to play the role of a conservative reformer. On the one hand, he unwaveringly defended the Gompersian labor-patriotism that wedded the AFL–CIO to the militarism of the Scoop Jackson faction of the party hierarchy.[7] The protection of precious union jobs in the military–industrial complex demanded no less. On the other hand, Meany was a cautious renovator who saw as clearly as Reuther, and perhaps more forcefully, that the disintegration of the Democratic ruling bloc might be labor's historic opportunity to claim a dominating

---

[7] According to John Herling, during the 1972 primaries the AFL–CIO provided a staff man as speechwriter for Jackson, who compiled a fifty-page 'white paper' that 'so distorted McGovern's record (nearly perfect COPE voting score) that it was distributed by Nixon's Committee to Reelect the President'. (See 'Change and Conflict in the AFL–CIO', *Dissent*, February 1974, p. 480.) Jackson led an anti-détente fraction of the Democratic Party that included, besides Meany and COPE, leading defense firms, major Jewish organizations and much of the party officialdom.

position within the councils of the national party. The old Albany lobbyist grasped from the beginning the significance of the Johnson Administration's attempt to use the Great Society to regenerate the social base of the Democratic Party, and repeatedly overrode the sectional interests of his own craft union supporters to ensure the AFL–CIO's influence across the breadth of emerging civil rights and urban legislation. Under the generalship of Meany and COPE director Barkin, the AFL–CIO's operatives on the hill claimed a central role in funneling and moderating the demands of Black, welfare and old-age groups through the Johnson Congress.[8] By making the new social movements dependent on the Federation's financial resources and legislative skills, Meany hoped to amplify the role of the trade-union bureaucracy in national politics. Although Reuther was willing, where Meany was not, directly to patronize the 1960s protest movements, their strategic aims were not dissimilar. Both thought the AFL–CIO's institutional political role could be powerfully expanded through skilful brokerage between the civil rights movement and national bourgeois politics.

But where Reuther and his successors were capable of conceding that the logic of incorporation of the new social forces required some opening up and reform of the party's nomination process, Meany remained obdurate in his opposition to the post-1968 Democratic reform movement. Again his response was that of a grizzled old politico. In the first place, he foresaw that Blacks, anti-war liberals and women were all too likely to be natural allies of the 'progressive' wing of the AFL–CIO, tilting the balance against his business union base. Secondly, Meany perceived that party reform was decentralizing and fragmenting an already weak and tenuous national party apparatus, dispersing power to increasing numbers of middle-class Democrats who were unbeholden to COPE and insensitive to the union's traditional

---

[8] Thus the AFL–CIO quietly bankrolled the National Council of Senior Citizens and helped it shepherd the Medicare plan through Congress in 1965. At the same time, it pressed for civil rights legislation through the Leadership Conference on Civil Rights headed by Andrew Biemiller, the Federation's chief lobbyist, Joseph Rauh of Americans for Democratic Action, and Charles Mitchell of the NAACP. The LCCR was designed as an alternative to the mass civil rights movements led by SNCC, CORE and the SCLC — the AFL–CIO refusing to endorse the great 1963 March on Washington. In pressing for the inclusion of a fair employment practices provision (Title VII) in the 1964 Civil Rights Act, Meany hoped to obtain 'an umbrella of law' to enforce the compliance of his own craft unions with job integration without having to confront them head-on. Yet at the same time by opposing the inclusion of affirmative action or super-seniority in Title VII, Meany aimed to ensure that integration of the workplace was basically token, leaving intact seniority structures and nepotistic apprenticeship practices. (See Joseph Goulden, *Meany*, New York 1972, p. 310 passim.)

economic demands. Finally, Meany was appalled by the prospect that a bureaucratized Black municipal power might succeed to the role of the old white urban machines. His tolerance of middle-class civil rights leadership was always conditional on its deference to the trade-union hierarchy. As civil rights forces entered politics and gained influence within the national Democratic Party, they threatened to undermine the AFL-CIO's claim to represent and hegemonize all popular constituencies. Under Meany, and continuing under Kirkland, the Federation became the major, implacable opponent of the reform process, fighting against open primaries and delegate quotas, then, after their adoption by the reform commissions of 1968–72, lobbying vigorously to repeal their implementation. Throughout this period, as William Crotty has emphasized in his study of the reform process, the AFL-CIO's overriding goal was 'to mute the effects of the quotas' that increased Black and female representation within the party.[9]

The rollback of Democratic reform, initiated in 1976 by the AFL-CIO influenced Winograd Commission, was consummated in 1981 by the work of the Hunt Commission. The Hunt Commission was a temporary alliance between the Federation, the Kennedy and the Mondale camps to shore up simultaneously the roles of Democratic officeholders and the union bureaucracy, minimizing the chance that an 'outside' candidate, like McGovern or Carter, could again use the primary path to win nomination. Originally Kirkland had wanted a third of convention delegates to be selected *ex officio*, a move that would have automatically returned the nomination process to the smoke-filled rooms of yore (as in 1968, when Humphrey won two-thirds of delegates with 2% of the primary vote). Unnerved at the prospect of such a flagrant anti-democratic restoration, the Kennedy representatives secured a compromise: 14 per cent of the convention or 568 'super-delegates' would be ennobled from among Democratic officeholders. Then, after reducing the required number of primaries (returning Michigan, for example, to the party caucus system), the commission restored the 'winner take all' rule in congressional district primaries and 'frontloaded' the now shortened primary season so that the 'official' candidate — presumably Kennedy or Mondale — would be guaranteed early success. Last but not least, the commissioners stripped the mid-term Democratic convention of the policy-making power it had briefly exercised during the 1970s, and substantially relaxed the quota requirements for sexual and racial balance.

---

[9] William Crotty, *Party Reform*, New York 1983, p. 132.

Although labor's leading role in the Hunt Commission has been retrospectively justified by some DSA writers as a 'social democratization' of the Democratic Party, increasing the role of 'responsible' elected officials representing lower-class groups as against increasing numbers of 'new class' interlopers, this is, most charitably, a convoluted rationalization.[10] In rolling back most of the ostensible new democracy within the party (as well as opposing reform of the seniority system in Congress), the AFL-CIO under Meany and Barkin struck directly at the representation of Black and minority Democrats. One aim was to blunt the emergence of a Black Democratic establishment as a power in its own right (the UAW, by contrast, welcomed the rise of Black electoral power). Another was to prepare the way for the nomination of an AFL-CIO backed presidential candidate. It was Kirkland's personal gambit to secure the pre-nomination of Mondale as a 'labor candidate', calculating that the early and massive concentration of AFL-CIO resources behind the winning nominee would maximize the Federation's influence over appointments and legislation in the next Democratic administration.

This scheme to counterfeit a surrogate labor party out of the Mondale candidacy depended — apart from the candidate's own, unlikely complaisance — upon the unity of the trade-union bureaucracy. In the face of relentless pressure from employers' concessionary demands, and with George Meany conveniently gone, the rebel unions that had been sporadically operating outside COPE since the McGovern schism now rejoined the majority. Although this reunion behind Kirkland's electoral strategy was celebrated as the triumph of 'labor unity', it in fact implied a recantation of the 'progressive alliance' with civil rights and feminist leaderships that the UAW under Fraser had explored in the late 1970s. Previously dissident voices on the Executive, like Wimpinsinger of the Machinists, were now more effectively

---

[10] 'Many of the more progressive unions, particularly the UAW, whose president, then Douglas Fraser, co-chaired the Hunt Commission on rules, entertained a more Europeanized model of party structure. Their goal was to restrict the prenomination franchise to party members, a transformation that could be accomplished *de jure* by having 30 state legislatures rewrite the laws or *de facto* by switching from primaries to caucuses. ... The UAW also had a longstanding concern over the lack of accountability of the Democratic Congressional Delegation to the party platform. What better way to promote their accountability than make them automatic convention delegates?' Meyerson, 'Labor's Risky Plunge', pp. 286–87. In this account of the UAW's move, after Reuther's death, to an anti-reform position kindred to Meany's and Kirkland's, Meyerson elides the fact that without formal constituency organization and/or official trade-union bloc votes, an unreformed Democratic Party would be most likely accountable only to officeholders, *apparatchiks* and business interests.

muzzled than would have ever been possible in Meany's day, while Kirkland licensed a mind-numbing cant that turned election day into 'Solidarity Day II', and Mondale into a working-class hero. Although crusty old piecards knew that Kirkland (whom A.H. Raskin apotheosized as 'a leader of supreme intelligence')[11] was really an emperor without clothes, a discreet, bureaucratic silence froze the doubts and suspicions about how an unconsulted rank and file might actually vote in the 1984 primaries.

The Dilemma of Black Democrats

An even more profound crisis has reshaped Black politics since 1978. The incorporation of Blacks into the Democratic Party, and the deradicalization of the civil rights movement, have depended on the precarious material infrastructure of expanding federal employment programs and urban grants-in-aid. The new Black professional-managerial strata of the 1970s have been disproportionately employed in the management of the social services and educational complexes of the inner city, as well as in administering the network of Great Society programs that provided temporary employment and minimal welfare to the ghetto poor. Similarly, the ability of Black Democratic city halls to pacify the cities and ameliorate their decay on behalf of their corporate landlords has been in direct proportion to the federal funding of urban budgets.

When in the spring of 1977, the Carter Administration announced a virtual moratorium on further social spending, it marked not only a betrayal of its own Black loyalists, but also a watershed in the historical evolution of the party. Since that date, the majority of the Democratic national leadership has retreated, as we have seen, from the politics of full employment and hegemonic reformism that characterized the Kennedy–Johnson revival of the New Deal. Democratic opposition to Reagan's dismantling of the remaining Great Society programs has been desultory at best. As Kirkland's right-wing advisor, Richard Scammon, put it, the Congressional Democrats' strategy has been to 'keep their mouths shut. Developing an alternative program is asking for defeat'.[12]

Underlying this apparent collapse of political will has been the insurgent power of middle-class voters, who, in collusion with corporate lobbyists and an avaricious Pentagon, have created a new, implicit

[11] Raskin, 'Labor Enters a New Century', *The New Leader*, November 30, 1981, p. 13.
[12] Quoted in *In These Times*, February 2, 1982, p. 7.

268

consensus in US politics. Choosing between the vast income transfer programs that disproportionately subsidize the middle class (Social Security, federal aid to education, mortgage interest deductions, and so on), the new arms race, and the much smaller sector of means-tested assistance to the poor, the neo-conservatives and the neo-liberals have banded together to slash the last. For its part, as Kim Moody has shown, the AFL–CIO has also retreated, since the emasculation of the Humphrey–Hawkins employment bill in 1978, from any energetic advocacy of full employment measures, emphasizing instead the protection of its own organized sectors.[13] Left without allies or partisans, Black America has been savaged by a new immiseration. Nearly half of all Black children are growing up in poverty, and in the upswing of the Reagan 'recovery', the Black unemployment rate, which historically has been double the white rate, is now three times higher (at 16 per cent).[14]

Meanwhile, the Reagan administration has been using its cutbacks in social spending to do far more than simply redistribute income upward. Just as Thatcher has launched a frontal assault on the institutional integrity of the Labour Party (the attack on trade-union political funds, the dis-establishment of Labor-led metropolitan governments, etc.) the Republican Administration has pursued a strategy of disorganizing the Democratic Party. Washington's blows have fallen with particular fury upon Black reformist leaderships. First, the Department of Justice and the Burger Court, in tandem with the similar rollback in NLRB practice, have grievously undercut the juridical supports of school integration and fair employment, foreclosing the kind of legal reformism that was the core of the 'moderate' civil rights activity exemplified by the NAACP's Legal Fund. This has occurred with the complicity of most Southern Democrats and the indifference of many Northern neo-liberals. Secondly, in the words of the American Enterprise Institute's budget expert, Allen Schick, the Administration has attempted to 'blow up the political infrastructure of the urban Democratic Party' by killing programs like Urban Development Action Grants or the Small Business Administration that 'buy power for people who walk around with a capital D'.[15] Again, the impact has been most devastating on the patronage powers of Black Democratic apparatuses. Thirdly, by permanently shrinking the federal social budget, the Republicans hope to deepen the schism between inner-city and

[13] Moody, 'Not Just Four More Years', *Labor Notes*, November 20, 1984, pp. 8–9.
[14] *Economist*, January 26, 1985.
[15] Quoted in the *Wall Street Journal*, February 4, 1985, p. 4.

suburban Democrats by increasing the competiton for scarce revenue sharing. Without control of federal spending, the national Democratic Party has always tended to become a political centrifuge, splintering along economic interest lines, as for example during the Stevenson years in the 1950s. Today, the cutbacks are aggravating the racial polarization within the party and sharpening the conflicts between Black Democratic mayors and white Democratic governors and legislatures.

With the unending economic depression in the Black inner cities fueling demands for relief that far exceed the diminishing material resources of the Black political establishment, and with Black influence in the national Democratic Party reduced by the AFL–CIO sponsored anti-reforms, it was inevitable that some elements of Black reform leadership would contemplate alternative courses of action. One option was a return to a civil rights movement format of protest mobilization — an idea favored by Black leftists and nationalists, but predictably unpopular with most Black elected officials. Another was the periodically canvassed proposal of forming an independent Black political party, possibly around the seceding nucleus of the Black Congressional Caucus.[16] Finally, there was the notion of somehow kindling a protest movement *within* the Democratic Party to force it to reaffirm its commitment to a Second Reconstruction.

In the event, the strategy that emerged through the Jackson campaign was to invoke the threat of the second option as a means to realize the third; that is to say, Jackson built upon an ethos of Black self-organization while limiting its aims to a renegotiation of the 'contract' between Black Democrats and their national party. The ambivalence and tensions of this strategy were reflected in the elusive slogan of 'empowerment', which meant voter registration while simultaneously connoting more transcendent and militant images of self-activity. The dual impetus and model for this rebellion against the party from within the party was, of course, provided by the 1983 Washington campaign in Chicago. The failure of both Kennedy and Mondale to support this long-overdue uprising on the Daley Plantation radicalized the frustration of key sectors of the Black political family with the official liberal leadership of the Democratic Party. At the same time, the spectacular success of Harold Washington's electoral united front in mobilizing 150,000 new Black and Hispanic voters awakened a new sense of Black political potential. The narrowly defeated

---

[16] For a history of modern attempts from the Gary Convention of 1972 onward to found an independent black politics, see Manning Marable, *Black American Politics*, London 1985.

candidacy of Black socialist Mel King in Boston a few months later was an added inspiration, showing in this case the practicality of a 'Rainbow coalition' of minority communities, white progressives, and elements of the trade-union movement.

The precipitous launching of the Jackson candidacy provoked an important symptomatic split within the Black political establishment. His earliest and most important institutional support came from the Black churches — indeed his campaign carried overtones of a rebellion of the old ministerial leadership of the civil rights movement against the newer hierarchy of Black politicians.[17] Moreover, his initial political sponsors, including Congresspersons Dellums and Conyers (the two-man left wing of the Black Congressional Caucus), Mayor Hatcher of Gary, California Assemblywoman Maxine Waters, and pioneer Black presidential candidate and feminist Shirley Chisholm, were most closely tied to Black working-class social bases. Their constituencies were devastated by Reaganomics, and their electoral credibility was most dependent on a willingness to strike a militant pose. Mondale's Black loyalists, on the other hand, tended to include figurehead crisis managers with substantial white and business support, like Bradley (Los Angeles), Goode (Philadelphia) or Arrington (Birmingham), as well as representatives of the Black bourgeoisie like the National Black Leadership Roundtable and Andrew Young (Atlanta having the most politically significant Black middle class in the country). Given the widely recognized and growing socio-economic wedge between the Black poor and the new Black middle classes, the original polarization over the Jackson candidacy could not help but have certain class overtones as well.[18] Where the loyalist camp followed the line of defeating Reagan at any price, the insurgent current represented by the Jackson campaign responded that a Democratic victory might be meaningless unless the party returned to supporting full employment and the welfare state.

---

[17] See Frances Beal, 'US Politics Will Never Be the Same', *Black Scholar*, September–October 1984.

[18] See the *Black Economist*, January 1985. It is important, however, not to overstate the new class contradictions within the Black community. Unlike the white social structure, the Black middle strata are predominantly based in the public sector, far more dependent upon two wage earners (the wife in a black middle-income household contributes about 60 per cent more than her white equivalent — see Ibid., p. 49), and generally more vulnerable to downward mobility. It is essential to distinguish between the small, but expanded, Black middle class of private-sector managers and entrepreneurs on one side, and on the other, the new 'state middle class' of public sector managers and professionals. This latter group, including Black teachers, welfare workers and lawyers, comprised some of the most vociferous supporters of the Jackson campaign.

Class Struggles on the Primary Trail

The Democratic primary battles turned out to be the most surprising events of the election year. After all the careful finagling of the nomination process by Kirkland and the Hunt Commission, the unbeatable Mondale machine collapsed in the first heat, as a majority of AFL–CIO members in New Hampshire bolted to Hart. Then the focus of issues in the primary competition, assumed to run along the center-right divide between Mondale and Glenn, abruptly shifted with Jackson's entrance and Glenn's disappearance in the oblivion of the Iowa caucuses. Although meaningless image manipulations frequently obscured the real substance and basis for division, the bitter three-person battle among Mondale, Hart and Jackson inevitably revealed the deep ideological divisions within the Democratic Party. The programmatic differences between the candidates were, in turn, indices of underlying social realignments taking place in the Balkanized constituencies of the national party. The following table summarizes the most salient divergences in the politics of the three camps.

Table 7.1

	Mondale	*Hart*	*Jackson*
1. politico-economic strategy	Corporatism	Neo-liberalism	Social democracy
2. growth motor	federal support for Northeast reindustrialization	tax and manpower subsidies to high tech private sector	expansion of public employment; rebuild cities
3. arms spending	+ 5%	+3–5%	−20%
4. welfare state	accept ½ Reagan cuts	ditto	restore, enlarge
5. Central America	'liberal-interventionist'	'neo-realist'	anti-imperialist
6. Grenada invasion	supported	supported	opposed
7. missiles in Europe	supported	opposed	opposed

The general economic strategies endorsed by the candidates, despite predictable vagueness and elision, were particularly revealing. Mondale, for instance, initially supported an eclectic industrial policy coupled with selective protectionism. The primary phase of his campaign was heavily influenced by the Industrial Policy Study Group set up in 1983 by the triumvirate of Kirkland, Felix Rohatyn (ex-financial overlord of New York City), and Irving Shapiro (former CEO of Dupont, the second largest non-union employer in the United States).

The Study Group was essentially a continuation of the Carter Administration's ill-fated efforts to sponsor a feeble American version of corporatism, and its membership, unsurprisingly, overlapped with the Labor-Management Conference as well as the Carter Cabinet, including Lee Iacocca (Chrysler), ex-Secretary of Treasury Blumenthal (Burroughs), ex-Secretary of State Vance (IBM), and Robert McNamara. Shorn of its more grandiose pretensions, the Study Group plan was an attempt by leading Democratic capitalists and their trade-union counterparts to find common ground for a federal rescue of the declining industrial base of the Northeast. Modelling themselves on the precedents of Rohaytn's austerity regime in New York from 1975 (the Municipal Assistance Corporation or 'Big MAC') and the Chrysler bail-out of 1979, the Study Group proposed a reindustrialization strategy based on tripartite consensus, a federal investment bank, incomes policies, and industry-specific protectionism.

In attempting to nail the Study Group's recommendations to the masthead of the Mondale campaign, Kirkland was implicitly committing the AFL–CIO to two extraordinary precedents. First, he was virtually promising to institutionalize concessionary bargaining when he accepted that the unions would trade off wage freezes or ceilings in return for federal loans to industry, in spite of the absence of any proposed reciprocal pledges by employers to ensure the maintenance of employment levels. Secondly, the Kirkland–Rohatyn–Shapiro plan was specifically targeted to preserve the unionized industrial base with scant concern for the plight of workers in low-wage industries, the public sector, the rapidly growing Sunbelt regions, or, most of all, for the inner-city unemployed. In fact, the Study Group proposals assumed continued fiscal austerity and cost containment in the public sector: in fiscal 1989, Mondale projected only a $30 billion increase over 1984 levels of funding for social programs, with most of the increase to be offset by savings elsewhere in the domestic budget.[19] In this sense as well, Kirkland was ready to codify the AFL–CIO's retreat from serious full-employment politics.

Hart's economic proposals shared in this benign neglect of the unemployed and the working poor. The Senator from Colorado had been one of the principal gravediggers of the Great Society during the Carter congresses, rising in 1978 to propose sweeping reductions in social spending, tax cuts, an expanded arms budget, tax-based incomes policy, and the deregulation of natural gas. Like Mondale's corporate-

---

[19] See Timothy Clark, 'New Ideas Versus Old', *National Journal*, March 17, 1984.

labor supporters, Hart also advocated an 'industrial policy', but his version had opposite regional and sectoral orientations: utilizing market-based mechanisms, like fiscal and manpower training incentives, to favor sunrise industries and the Sunbelt. (Where Mondale had sponsored the Chrysler bailout, Hart had sponsored legislation to rescue Johns Manville, a Denver corporation, from the costs of its asbestos litigation.) Vowing that he 'would not guarantee people something unless they are really down and out',[20] Hart fetishisized capital formation over welfare in almost identical formulae to Kemp and the supply-side Republicans. His core vision seemed to be the belief that if state spending were rigorously restructured to subsidize the occupational and entrepreneurial mobility of the professional and scientific middle classes, the ensuing boom would take care of the rest of society.

In contrast to Mondale's warmed-over corporatism or Hart's yuppie conservatism, Jackson's domestic program was arguably the first social-democratic alternative seriously offered to the American electorate in a presidential campaign (Debs's campaigns of 1912 and 1920 had been run on a revolutionary program). Whereas Mondale and Hart insisted that significant social spending had to be sacrificed to an expanding arms buildup (Mondale would have preserved most of Reagan's baroque arsenal with his projected $418 billion arms budget in 1989), Jackson straightforwardly proposed to shift massive resources from defense to human services, emphasizing the central role of public employment growth in the economy. He promised the restoration and expansion of Great Society levels of welfare expenditure together with aggressive enforcement of voting rights and affirmative action in employment. Moreover, he was the only candidate who actually fought for the full agenda of traditional labor movement demands (as distinct from Kirkland's Study Group concessions). It was Jackson, not Mondale, who insistently denounced plant closures, supported labor law reform, attacked the open shop and stood up for the organizational rights of undocumented workers.

In foreign policy, the divergence among the three campaigns was equally profound. The positions of Mondale and Hart descended in large part from the foreign policy split within the Carter administrations. Hart's views were closest to, if never completely identical with, the 'neo-realist' policies advocated within the Carter ranks by Cyrus

[20] Ibid.

Vance, George Ball and Andrew Young. The gist of neo-realism was the belief that it was in the best interest of the United States to 'de-link' the socio-economic crisis in the South from the Cold War, and that revolutionary challenges in the Third World could be managed by US diplomatic and economic power alone. The 'liberal interventionists', on the other hand, whose views suffused Mondale's campaign statements, clung to the Truman Doctrine paradigm that had guided the Democratic Party for forty years: military counter-insurgency combined with cosmetic reform. Within the Carter Administration, Brzezinski and Brown, from their respective power-bases in the National Security Council and the Pentagon, had crusaded against the Vance–Young 'human rights' approach, and, after the fall of the Shah, forced the neo-realists out of office. Mondale, of course, had presided over this purge, just as he had played a crucial role in determining the rightward shift in the administration's domestic policy.

During the 1984 primary campaign, these splits in the Democratic foreign policy establishment reverberated in the respective attitudes of Mondale and Hart towards Reagan's creeping military intervention in Central America. Mondale, sharing the New Right's preoccupation with the Cuban threat, dissented only from Kirkpatrick and Helms's *abrazo* of such fascists as D'Aubuisson and the Somoza palace guard. He did, however, hail the quiet US invasion of Honduras and gave discrete, but influential support to the bipartisanization of aid to El Salvador. (Duarte was given a hero's welcome by the Democratic Congressional leadership in May, and effective opposition to Reagan's intervention in El Salvador collapsed). Hart, in contrast, categorically rejected the US military presence in Central America, urged negotiations with the Sandinistas and closer coordination with Mexico and Venezuela. His stance seemed principled and courageous, a continuation of his original dedication to the antiwar purpose of the McGovern campaign. Unfortunately, Hart's neo-realism became indistinguishable from Mondale's interventionism in other sectors of the Cold War. In their embarrassing efforts to outbid one another for the support of Begin's American admirers in the New York primary, they embraced positions on the Middle East more bellicose and extravagantly pro-Israeli than those of Reagan.

Meanwhile, the Jackson campaign first befuddled, then enraged its erstwhile liberal critics (who, like the *New Republic*, had *a priori* dismissed it as a demagogic exercise in Black sectionalism) by unveiling a co-herent, alternative foreign policy — more comparable to a Nonaligned Movement manifesto than to any hitherto imagined Democratic platform. This foreign policy, with its central emphases on 'support for liberation struggles', US non-intervention, and nuclear disarmament, was elaborated through an extensive dialogue that involved the Hispanic community, the peace movement, the Catholic left, and the oppositional foreign policy establishment (notably the Institute for Policy Studies), as well as Black pan-Africanists and nationalists. Jackson personally underwrote the priority of these planks in his campaign by audacious meetings with Ortega and Castro, as well as by his visible participation in left-led demonstrations against the invasion of Grenada and intervention in Central America. These initiatives far exceeded the functional requirements of the primary campaign as a simple Black protest against Democratic neglect. As Maulana Karenga has pointed out, Jackson's defiance of the rules of the Cold War courted repudiation by the 'new Black patriotism' that had been ostentatiously endorsed by various Black sports and entertainment celebrities. Instead he won an overwhelming voter support, seconded by significant sections of the Hispanic electorate, that can only be interpreted as a popular mandate for the Rainbow coalition's strategic linkage of full employment, disarmament and anti-imperialism.[21] Given the generally dismal historical record of international social democracy on imperialism (from the capitulation of the *Reichstag* deputies to Prussian militarism in 1914, to the supine support of the British Labour government for US genocide in Southeast Asia), the combination of Jackson's economic and social with his foreign policy positions was extraordinary indeed.

In sum, there was a political chasm between the radical positions of the Jackson campaign and the varieties of 'Reaganism with a human face' offered by Mondale and Hart. Whereas the crisis of the trade-union leadership had propelled it rightward, away from its traditional commitment to full employment and into the dead-end embrace of concessionary corporatism, the crisis of the Black reformist leadership produced the leftward, populist schism of the Jackson campaign. In an electoral marketplace overstocked with conservatives, it offered the only reformist agenda that encompassed the actual immediate needs of every section of the US working class. Faced with this fortuitous emergence of a ready-made social-democratic program and mass constituency during the 1984 elections counterposed against the Cold

[21] Karenga, 'Jesse Jackson and the Presidential Campaign', *Black Scholar*, September–October 1984, p. 59. Karenga also emphasized the exemplary role of Jackson's campaign in combating the trivialization of Black culture, 'the focus on sports, vulgar careerism, music and music idols ...'.

War liberalism of the Democratic establishment candidates, what was the response of the electoralist left? The US affiliate of the Socialist International spurned its own destiny. Instead of recognizing the Rainbow as the harbinger of progressive realignment, DSA clung to Mondale and the labor bureaucracy — except in California where the local DSA initially supported the Senator from B-1, Alan Cranston. Despite some rank-and-file and local chapter sympathy for Jackson, the DSA leadership deflected any serious consideration of his campaign. Reading Harrington, Howe and Denitch, one would have scarcely known that the Rainbow Coalition even existed.[22] But where they merely ignored Jackson, a swarm of other white social democrats and liberal pundits were rushing to calumniate him. One of the most hysterical attacks was Paul Berman's article in the *Nation*, in which Jackson was compared to George Wallace and accused of running a 'rightwing populist' campaign that was 'antilabor' and 'a threat to progressive politics'.[23] Later, Jack O'Dell, a key Rainbow staffer and former Martin Luther King aide, incisively criticized the underlying attitudes of the Jackson-baiters: their implicit self-identification of the Left as 'white'; their minimalization of the Black social base;

---

[22] For one of the finest polemics of the election year, see Alexander Cockburn's and Andrew Kopkind's fiery denunciation of the white left's flight from the Jackson campaign, 'The Left, The Democrats and The Future', *The Nation*, July 21–28, 1984.

[23] 'The Other Side of the Rainbow', *The Nation*, July 4, 1984, pp. 408–09. For Berman, the 'real Rainbow Coalition is Blacks and liberal Jews' which Jackson has 'done most to disrupt'. Since anti-Semitism was the invariable pretext of left Jackson-baiters in the period following his unfortunate ethnic slur in a private conversation, it is useful to consider briefly what the Black–Jewish coalition has actually entailed. Although typically presented as selfless political altruism by which liberal Jewish organizations have sustained the civil rights movement with money and legislative support, Black electoral support has in fact been a principal means by which Jewish Democratic politicians have magnified their representation and power out of any proportion to the size of their ethnic base, as well as a means to reinforce the veto of the pro-Israel lobby on US foreign policy. As the following table demonstrates, Jewish representation in the House is almost equal to that of Blacks and Hispanics combined.

Table 7.2 (*National Journal* Figures)

	percentage of population	percentage of 1982 House
Blacks	11.7%+	4.6%
Hispanics	6.4%+	2.8%
Jewish Americans	2.6%	7.0%

and their refusal to accept that the progressive movement's 'majority leadership, not exclusive leadership, will be coming from the Afro-American community'.[24]

The Democratic Theater of the Absurd

Having lost the New England and California centers of academia and science-based industry to Hart, and menaced across the South by the strength of the Jackson vote, Mondale finally scraped by with the help of the AFL–CIO in Illinois, New Jersey and Michigan (where the return to the caucus system diminished the influence of the Black vote). The supposedly 'signed and sealed' labor vote in the event delivered Mondale only 45 per cent of union voters: 20 per cent supported Jackson, and 30 per cent Hart. As the following table shows, however, the Hunt Commission's system of delegate selection was brilliantly effective in disenfranchising the Rainbow electorate and inflating the Mondale delegation.

Table 7.3[25]

	% of primary vote	*% of delegates*
Mondale	38.7	51.6
Hart	36.1	31.7
Jackson	18.4	9.6

If the Jackson campaign was scandalously under-represented at the convention, it still preserved the ultimate weapon of an independent presidential effort that would take most of the Black vote from Mondale. In early meetings with the Mondale camp, Jackson had summarily warned that there would be a 'walk-out point' if important Rainbow demands were not incorporated into the platform. In the lengthy pre-convention negotiations between Jackson and Democratic National Committee head Charles Manatt, the party oligarchy offered a menu of procedural concessions and small adjustments (ranging

---

Small wonder that Jewish Democratic politicos, in this identical to labor chieftains, are loathe to see the emergence of an independent Black electoral pole with its own alliances and radical foreign-policy positions.

[24] Interview in *Black Scholar*, September–October 1984, pp. 55–56.
[25] Calculated from figures in the *National Journal*, May 26, 1984, p. 1234.

from affirmative action in convention catering to guarantees of representation on convention committees), while sidestepping the substantive policy issues. This struck a majority of Rainbow activists as small recompense for the campaign's avowed aims and its historic responsibilities. Considerable rank-and-file pressure thus arose within the Jackson delegation to walk out if serious concessions were not forthcoming.

But the transition from the primary battles to the convention saw a reassertion of the leadership of the moderate Black politicos among the Jackson leadership, like Hatcher, Pinckney, and Sutton, who were determined to rein in the secessionist impulses of the grassroots Jackson delegates and achieve some face-saving compromise with the Democratic National Committee. The contradictory impulses behind Jackson's candidacy came to a head as independent political action on behalf of the coalition's radical program was discounted in favor of the Black political establishment's strategy of levering more influence from the Democratic power structure. In the event, the failure of the campaign to invest the Rainbow Coalition with a formally organized constituency structure or mechanisms of democratic consultation by its activists ensured that the key decisions would be made by the inner circle of Black officeholders. Under their incessant pressure, Jackson finally agreed to play by the loaded rules of the convention, offering Manatt a no-walkout pledge and agreeing to submit only four minority planks to the convention in order to avoid a protracted platform fight. These planks, however, were a distillation of key sections of the Rainbow program: 1) abolition of Southern dual primaries; 2) substantial reduction of the defense budget and an end to the current arms race; 3) declaration of no US nuclear first use; and 4) strong enforcement of affirmative action.

The tightly disciplined Mondale delegation, fully half of whom were union members or officials, overwhelmingly voted down the first three planks with the collusion of most of the Hart contingent. The defeat of the no-first-use plank was particularly illustrative of the sordid spirit that infused the convention. Theoretically, the combined Jackson, Hart and pro-freeze forces should have easily commanded a majority on this issue, but Hart had already contracted with Mondale to oppose this plank in return for the latter's endorsement of a diffusely platitudinous resolution 'limiting American use of force'. Cranston, who had hinged his entire primary campaign on advocacy of the nuclear freeze, dragooned his unhappy supporters to vote against the Jackson position as well.

In planning to meet the Jackson challenge at the Convention,

Mondale had given many of his at-large delegate positions to his Black supporters (less than half of the 717 Black delegates at the convention were Jackson supporters). In the fight over the fourth plank, Mondale's managers made humiliating use of these Black loyalists. Andrew Young was sent down to the convention floor to be jeered by the Jackson delegation as he half-heartedly tried to defend Mondale's retreat from racial quotas (the AFL–CIO had always opposed them in principle). When Coretta Scott King then attempted to intervene on Young's behalf, she too was booed, an act of *lèse majesté* to the martyr's wife that previously would have been unthinkable. In the end, however, it was Jackson himself who flouted the expressed will of the majority of his delegation and allowed his platform manager, Walter Fauntroy, to accept a 'compromise' with the Mondale forces that substituted the meaningless expression 'verifiable measurements' for quotas.

The ignominious experience of voting against one's formerly most cherished principles — as exemplified by freeze activists voting against no-first-use or the Mondale Blacks rationalizing the betrayal of affirmative action — was raised to the level of surreal mass ritual as the Mondale and Hart delegations approved what the *Congressional Quarterly* characterized as 'economically the most conservative Democratic platform in fifty years'.[26] Ratifying the rightward evolution of the Democrats since 1977, the platform abandoned perennial commitments to full employment and national health care, and, for the first time in a modern Democratic convention, refrained from calling for substantial new social spending. Last minute entreaties from Jackson and other Black leaders to include a federal jobs program to ameliorate the depression in the inner cities were summarily rebuffed. The Hart forces, on the other hand, succeeded in incorporating language exalting the central role of the private sector, while de-emphasizing the traditional Democratic focus on economic assistance to the cities.

This damage to traditional liberalism was entirely self-inflicted, since the forces of old-fashioned Democratic conservatism were scarcely represented at the convention — just a handful of 'boll weevils' and Glenn delegates. Harold Meyerson, a leading DSA trade unionist and Mondale supporter, was struck by the 'equanimity' with which the

---

[26] *Weekly Report*, 1984, p. 1739. California Lieutenant Governor Leo McCarthy described the San Francisco platform, on a scale of one to ten, with ten most liberal, as a 'five': more less equivalent to the Republicanism of Henry Cabot Lodge or Nelson Rockefeller in the 1960s: 'It was only liberal compared the Republicans'. (Quoted by Dick Kirschten, *National Journal*, July 14, 1984, p. 1341) See also *The New York Times*, September 11, 1984.

hundreds of AFL-CIO and NEA delegates voted to retreat from the causes they had championed for their entire lives.[27] (Earlier in the primary season he had written evocatively of Kirkland's attempt to transform the Democratic Party into 'a labor party without ideology, without a distinct labor program ... without an activated rank and file — a spectral vision that came proximately true during the convention).[28]

White progressives found solace in the convention's social liberalism, as well as in its sentimental invocation of the New Deal ethos (without, of course, the 'beef' of New Deal policies). They were gratified by the historic recognition of gay rights and electrified by the selection of Geraldine Ferraro as Mondale's running mate. To most Blacks, however, the nomination of Ferraro was a bitter pill: a white backlash candidate from the most segregated neighborhood of New York (an area of Queens with barely 3 per cent Black population), she had extolled the death penalty and built her reputation as a fierce law-and-order district attorney. One of the most implacable foes of busing for school integration, she had crusaded in 1979 for a constitutional amendment outlawing it, and in 1982, defected from the New York Democratic delegation to support a New Right resolution barring the Justice Department from funding busing.[29] Symptomatically, this was a background that the social-democratic and liberal press ignored in its uncritical celebration of Ferraro.

Mondale's Corporate Strategy

Having grandfathered Mondale's nomination through the obstacles of political principle, Kirkland and his COPE chieftains were forced to watch haplessly as their 'labor strategy' was sex-changed into a 'corporate strategy'. As Robert Kuttner put it, 'the great industrial policy debate ended with a whimper' with the AFL-CIO's pet planks on reindustrialization and protectionism supplanted by Mondale's monomaniacal emphasis on deficit reduction.[30] This redesign of the Mondale candidacy was effected by a confluence of factors: political consultant Richard Leone's erroneous belief that the deficit was the soft

---

[27] Meyerson, 'Labor rebuilds for grassroots clout', *In These Times*, August 8–21, 1984, p. 2.

[28] Meyerson, 'Labor's Risky Plunge', p. 287.

[29] *New York Times*, September 23, 1984, B-9.

[30] Kuttner, 'Revenge of the Democratic Nerds', *New Republic*, October 22, 1984, p. 17.

underbelly of Reaganism; the opposition of leading Brookings economists to any form of industrial policy; and the conservative fiscal
instincts of the ex-Carter staff. Most decisive, perhaps, was the inability
of the unions to meet their original financial pledges to the Democratic
National Committee, leaving a huge shortfall — in the most expensive
campaign in history — that DNC chairman Charles Manatt proposed to
rectify by appealing to big business (his 'Lexington Club' had a minimum admission fee of $25,000). Robert Kuttner has recounted how, in
late August, Mondale was called to book by seventy of his principal
backers, aggravated by his rhetorical support for the Study Group
proposals: 'As Irv Kipnes, the California industrialist who was then
head of the Democratic Party's "Business Council", recall[ed] the ses-
sion: "Several of us said 'Fritz, quit knocking the rich; they're financing
your campaign.' Mondale replied, 'Oh my goodness, I'm so sorry.
There's nothing wrong with wanting to be rich. I want to be rich."'[31]

The last months of the labor-backed Mondale campaign were spent
in a quixotic crusade to win big business to the Democrats. Mondale's
appeal to the corporations and financial markets was based on twin
proposals to raise taxes by $70 billion and to place the new revenue in a
special 'deficit reduction fund' to ensure that it would not be used for
anything other than balancing the budget. In deference to Wall Street's
general qualms about industrial policy, he refused to endorse the
LaFalce Bill (HR 4360), the crucial industrial policy legislation
sponsored by House Democrats to establish a latter-day RFC or 'bank
for industrial competition'. Since his proposed budget provided for
only marginally slower growth in military spending (approximately five
per cent per annum) than Reagan's, he planned to restore only about
half of the 1981 cuts in social spending, emphasizing those programs
most beneficial to the white middle class. Lest there remained any
doubt about which party stood for anti-Keynesian fiscal restraint,
Stuart Eizenstat, Mondale adviser and architect of the Carter budget
retrenchment, urged businessmen to 'look at the platform Mondale
insisted upon: There are no specific spending commitments for the first
times; its central focus is on deficit reduction rather than stimulus of
the economy'.[32] Other Mondale advisers broadly hinted to the business
press that a Democratic Administration would be ready to undertake
even more drastic pruning as it became necessary. Ex-Secretary of
Treasury Blumenthal told *Business Week* he was convinced that
Mondale would trim entitlement programs and get social security

---

[31] Kuttner, 'Ass Backward', *New Republic*, April 22, 1985, p. 18.
[32] Quoted in *Business Week*, July 30, 1984, p. 35.

under control.[33] A plan to impose a general spending freeze, championed by Bert Lance and Felix Rohatyn, only failed to become a major Mondale plank because of the fear of alienating Jackson and the Black vote.[34]

By pandering to the Business Roundtable in the illusory hope that business might rally behind his campaign, Mondale repeated Carter's gigantic blunder of 1980: clothing the Democrats in the mantle of Hooverian fiscal conservatism while the GOP, invoking Roosevelt and Kennedy, crusaded as the party of economic growth. This relentless domestic right turn — largely unopposed by trade unionists and social democrats trapped in the logic of their 'lesser evilism' — was further complemented by a parallel attempt to outflank Reagan as the champion of Cold War toughness. 'Firmness' and 'resolution' became the key Mondale virtues, as his managers, advised by a coterie of ex-Kissinger and Brzezinski aides, (Robert Hunter, Barry Carter, Madeleine Albright, etc.) tried to project a new set of campaign themes: a 'quarantine' of Nicaragua, retaliation against terrorism, increased military support for Israel, funding for 'Midgetman' and Stealth bombers, and so on. In September, two leading hawks, James Schlesinger, Ford's Secretary of Defense, and Max Kampelman, sometime Reagan envoy, were brought into the campaign with remarkable ostentation in an apparent attempt to counter the roles of the ex-(Scoop) Jackson Democrats, like Kirkpatrick, on the Republican side.[35] Just as industrial policy had been summarily killed off as a campaign theme, so too were the nuclear freeze and Central America clouded over with ambiguous rhetoric and pushed into the background of foreign policy debate. As a result, peace and Central America activists were increasingly disorganized and muted where they had chosen to make support of Mondale their focus.

While the Democratic campaign was being reshaped for the benefit of the bankers and the hawks, the Blacks, whether Mondale loyalists or Jackson supporters, were being frozen out of the campaign leadership and the media spotlight. The treatment was so contemptuous that even Andy Young exploded at the 'smartassed white boys' on the Mondale staff who treated all Black Democrats as campaign liabilities. Again, it was only the conciliatory intervention of Jesse Jackson that headed off a rupture. A meeting of Jackson supporters in Chicago,

---

[33] Quoted in ibid.

[34] See Felix Rohatyn, 'The Debtor Economy: a Proposal', *The New York Review of Books*, November 8, 1984.

[35] See Mondale interview, *New York Times*, September 23, 1984, B-9.

debating the potential for Rainbow candidates at the congressional and local levels, had urged Jackson to run as an independent in the South Carolina senatorial race. Precisely because such an initiative might have had incalculable consequences — creating a third party precedent as well as radically challenging the political submission of the Black Southern electorate to lesser-evil conservative white Democrats — it was successfully squelched by Jackson's moderate advisers and the Democratic National Committee. This effectively marked the end of the nascent Rainbow Coalition's independent role in the 1984 elections.

As the last liberal vestiges of the Mondale platform disappeared in white smoke, his left supporters sought refuge in a wonderland of ever more fantastic scenarios. While noting the rightward deflection of their candidate, DSA argued that this was all the more reason to 'transform the election from an ordinary campaign into a bold progressive crusade' — as if grassroots mobilization could somehow compensate for right-wing policies. Mondale was officially invested with 'exceptional left-liberal credentials' and crowned as the next 'peoples' president'.[36] An extraordinary tableau was unveiled to show how the 'party within the party' might be activated to defeat Reagan and reshape the Democratic Party leftward. Hopefully christened after Truman's famous come-from-behind effort of 1948 (despite the fact that Mondale's economics were now to the right of Dewey's), this fantasy of the 'people's campaign' presumed the dramatic activation of a 'silent majority' of anti-Reagan voters. A Mondale victory — it was imagined — would be delivered by the coincident of five strategic factors: 1) the AFL-CIO's capacity to deliver at least 65 per cent of the vote of union households (compared to 48 per cent in 1980); 2) a continuation of Black voter registration at the unprecedented levels of 1983 and early 1984, with an equally high Black turnout to assure Democratic victory in at least some of the seven Southern states that Carter lost by less than 3 per cent of the vote; 3) a widening gender gap — at least 15 per cent — and increased female voter turnout; 4) the inability of the Republicans to exploit comparable reserves of conservative 'hidden voters'; 5) a dramatic leap in voter participation, reversing the twenty-year decline and assuring an overall turnout of at least 100 million out of a voting-age population of 174 million.

---

[36] Timothy Sears, *Democratic Left*, September–October 1984, pp. 4–6.

The Deluge

Every one of these hopes was drowned in the Reagan tide of November 8. Although the Black vote contributed a historic share of the total Democratic presidential vote — over half in the South and nearly a quarter nationally (compared to 7 per cent in 1960) — it shrunk by one point as a percentage of the total popular vote (from 9 per cent to 8 per cent) as did the womens' vote (from 50 per cent to 49 per cent).[37] At the same time, the 'labor strategy' central to Mondale's campaign debouched in an uneven union effort, ranging from enthusiastic to dispirited depending on union, region and degree of previous rank-and-file electoral organization. The unions delivered only a slim majority of union households to Mondale (53 per cent), instead of the 65 per cent that had been vouchsafed to the Democratic National Committee, and the NBC exit polls in Michigan actually showed UAW households sliding to Reagan, 52 per cent to 48 per cent. Although the AFL–CIO would later claim posthumous victory by referring to the percentage of union members, rather than households, voting for Mondale (60-65 per cent, exclusive of the pro-Reagan Teamsters and the unaffiliated NEA), the Federation's own polls indicated a decisive Reagan majority among their younger white male members.[38] The really catastrophic statistic, however, was the Gallup Poll's discovery one month after the elections that a plurality of skilled workers indicated allegiance to the Republicans for the first time since the 1920s.

Table 7.4[39]
Partisan Identification of Skilled Workers
(according to Gallup)

	November 1981	December 1984
Democrat	51%	39%
Republican	21%	41%
Independent	28%	20%

[37] For Black vote, *National Journal*, October 11, 1984 p.2132; 1960 figure from Richard Rubin, *Party Dynamics*, New York, 1976, pp. 92–93; decline of relative vote, Thomas Edsall, 'Politics and the Power of Money', *Dissent*, Fall 1985, p. 150.

[38] See *AFL–CIO News*, December 1, 1985, p. 6; and discussion of union vote by David Moberg in *In These Times*, November 21–December 4, 1984, p. 7. COPE was also battered by deindustrialization and the loss of 2.5 million manufacturing jobs between 1980 and 1984. In West Virginia, traditionally the most tightly organized state in the nation, union membership has declined from half to a third of the labor force since Reagan's inauguration, with devastating results for the state COPE and Democratic Party.

[39] Cited in the *National Journal*, September 2, 1985, p. 346.

It is difficult to resist comparing this tendential Reaganization of the white craft working class in the United States with the similarly massive defection of skilled English workers from the British Labour Party over the past four years. It would seem that in political terms, if not also in socio-economic status, the working class in both countries is becoming increasingly disunited in a way that repeals the solidaristic achievements of earlier decades of labor struggle and drastically reduces the claims of either the Democratic Party or the Labour Party to represent most of the industrial proletariat — never mind the growing numbers of effectively disenfranchised low-wage service workers.

In the larger working-class electorate, non-union and unorganized as well as union, the AFL–CIO labor strategy was clearly and unambiguously defeated. From the beginning of the campaign, Mondale's pollsters and strategists had been aware that the crucial battle of the election would be the competition for the hearts and minds of the third income quintile: the fifth of the population midway up the income ladder with average annual earnings of $19,000. This quintile includes both organized semi-skilled and many skilled workers; it was the least affected, positively or negatively, by the 1981 tax redistribution, but is highly sensitive to changes in the employment level or to threats of tax increases. In December 1983, Mondale seemed to enjoy a comfortable margin among this fifth of the population, as various polls showed him with a majority of votes from families earning $20,000 or less per annum (Hart also won this group from Reagan). Less than a year later, following the Democrats' move to fiscal conservatism and the acceleration of the Reagan recovery, the Mondale threshold dropped below $10,000 (compared to $15,000 for Carter in 1980). Reagan's support in the crucial $12,500 to $24,999 income range rose 13 per cent and in November he won a clear majority of the overall blue-collar vote (even increasing his union vote by 2 per cent over 1980).[40]

There still might have remained some comfort for the Democrats if the gender gap had widened or held to its 1980 level. Instead, it unexpectedly narrowed, as 10 per cent more women voted for Reagan and the global male/female differential (vis-à-vis the Democratic vote) declined by half. In the South, the only region in the country to give Carter a majority of the female vote in 1980, the gender gap simply disappeared, as women shifted sides by a massive 16 per cent.[41]

[40] *Washington Post*/ABC Poll, December 1983 and November 1984; also data from Everett Carll Ladd, 'On Mandates, Realignments and the 1984 Presidential Election', *Political Science Quarterly*, 100, 1, Spring 1985.

[41] CBS, ABC and NBC exit polls; Seymour Martin Lipset, 'The Elections, the Economy and Public Opinion,' *PS*, Winter 1985, p. 36.

Similarly, in key Western and Northern industrial states where the Democrats had hoped for a powerful confirmation of 1980 trends, they were stunned to see their advantage amongst women voters tumbling, with only New York remaining an exception.

Table 7.5[42]
The Shrinking Democratic Gender Advantage
% female Democratic/Republican vote

	1980	1984
California	+ 7%	+ 2%
Connecticut	+ 9%	+ 5%
Illinois	+15%	+ 5%
Michigan	+14%	+ 3%
New Jersey	+16%	0
New York	+16%	+15%
Pennsylvania	+16%	+ 3%
Texas	+25%	+ 6%
USA	− 5%	−12%

This national reversal of political gender differentiation is undoubtedly linked, particularly in the South, but also elsewhere, with the increasing racial polarization among women voters. Indeed, a racial disaggregation of the female vote reveals one of the most glaring gaps in the electorate: the 65 per cent of white women (compared to 68 per cent of white men) who voted for Reagan versus a bare 6 per cent of Black women.[43] Without slighting the long-term political implications of the continuing incorporation of white women into the economy as low-wage workers, it would appear incontestable that much of what remained of the gender gap in 1984 (approximately 7 per cent differential) was an epiphenomenon of the remarkably Democratic vote of Black and minority women. To this fact must be counterposed the refusal of the National Organization of Women (presigned by the AFL-CIO for Mondale) and most feminist groups to give a serious hearing to the Rainbow Coalition.[44]

---

[42] Compiled from Laurily Epstein, 'The Changing Structure of Party Identification', *PS*, Winter 1985.

[43] Ibid.

[44] Jackson was the only candidate who campaigned for the restoration of social service programs for women and children, linked the passage of the ERA to the defense of the Voting Rights Act, pledged a female running mate, and, despite his personal beliefs, advocated the legal right to abortion.

As with workers and women, the sun again failed to rise for the Democrats with new voters. The broadly shared expectation on the left that opposition to Reaganism was drawing millions of new Democratic voters into polling booths was cruelly disappointed. In the first place, Democratic registration drives became ensnared in a tangle of rivalries between candidates and constituencies. During the primaries, for example, when Black voter interest was most intense, the national Democratic apparatus refused to finance registration efforts for fear that they would enhance the Jackson vote. Later in the campaign, Black voter groups retaliated, refusing to share names with some white-led registration campaigns.[45] Meanwhile, the trade-union voter drives which had been expected to be the backbone of the surge of new voters frequently failed to meet minimal quotas. One major campaign in Los Angeles, crucial to Democratic chances in California, registered barely 10,000 new voters despite large expenditures over many months. After its New Hampshire debacle, the AFL–CIO had made a last-minute attempt to launch 'one-on-one' canvassing and registration on the shopfloor. Successful in a few progressive unions, this theoretically plausible approach more typically ran afoul, as Harold Myerson has chronicled, of the atrophied, depoliticized state of shop-steward organization across the country.[46] In unhappy contrast, the National Republican Committee, which since 1974 has functioned as a kind of a super-consulting firm, coordinated a streamlined registration drive that drew awe-inspired accolades from jealous Democratic operatives. With a $30 million budget, as well as the corroborative efforts of the Moral Majority's separate registration crusade among born-again Christians, the Republicans were able to match the Democratic registrars voter by voter, and better.[47] Where the 'Human Serve' campaign — inspired by radical social scientists Piven and Cloward's idea of 'movement-building' through aggressive assertion of voter rights — sought to use social service employees as registrars of the poor, the Republicans countered by deputizing members of the Rotary and the Chamber of Commerce.[48] Where the AFL–CIO attempted to mobilize union households and public employees, the Republicans, with their unassailable mastery of direct mail techniques, successfully targeted millions of

---

[45] For a detailed account of these rivalries, see Joan Walsh in *In These Times*, September 26, 1984, p. 9.

[46] See Meyerson, 'Labor's Risky Plunge'.

[47] See *National Journal*, September 29, 1984, p. 1812; *Guardian*, December 5, 1984.

[48] See Richard Cloward and Frances Fox Piven, 'Towards a Class-Based Realignment of American Politics: a Movement Strategy', *Social Policy*, Winter 1983.

288

employees of non-union businesses and military personnel. Using high-tech survey methods pioneered by GOP poll-master Richard Wirthlin and his cadre of Mormon computer hackers, the Republicans were able to identify and register only pro-Reagan voters, avoiding duplication or the registration of Democrats. It was in the South, where Reagan's 1980 margins had been thinnest, that this logistical disparity between the two campaigns became truly decisive. The almost non-chalant attitude of the DNC toward Black voter registration was parried by the Republicans' vigorous enlistment of fundamentalists, military families and anti-Castro Cubans, who helped tilt the South one-sidedly to Reagan by unexpected margins of 18 per cent and more.[49]

Just as the 1964 Goldwater debacle had dashed belief in a 'hidden conservative majority'; so 1984 destroyed the analogous left-wing hope of reshaping the electoral balance of power with millions of progressive new voters. In the event, Reagan's margin among first-time voters was identical to his majority amongst previous voters. Although the 'people's campaign' may have registered as many as two million new Democrats, the combined total of the Republican National Committee and the Moral Majority was probably twice as great.[50] Even more importantly, the Republicans were able to motivate their new voters to turn out on election day. Although the Jackson primary campaign had inspired Southern Black voters to register in historic numbers, almost closing the gap with Southern whites (71% versus 77%), 62% of the whites actually voted (overwhelmingly for Reagan) as against only 41% of eligible Blacks (7% less than in 1980) — a vivid indication of their disenchantment with Mondale.[51] Nationally, the overall turnout was only 0.7 per cent higher than the postwar low point of 1980; although 12 million new voters had been registered since 1980, only 4 million bothered to vote. The final total of 92 million voters fell disastrously short of the 100 million minimum targeted by the Democrats and their allies, and most of the increase over 1980 seems to have consisted of new Republican voters.[52] Despite the 'labor candidacy' and four years of Reaganomics, almost as many workers occupied barstools instead of polling booths in 1984 as in 1980.

Finally, rampant crossover voting ensured that the relationship between the Reagan landslide and the national congressional vote was

[49] Lipset, 'The Elections, The Economy and Public Opinion'.
[50] Edsall, 'Politics and the Power of Money', p. 149; Lipset, ibid.
[51] From a study by William Kimmelman, University of Alabama at Birmingham, quoted in *Seattle Times*, February 8, 1985.
[52] *Washington Post*, January 8, 1985, p. A5.

the most disarticulated in history. Despite a near tie in the aggregate congressional popular vote, the House remained Democratic by a three to two margin thanks to an all-powerful incumbency effect (95 per cent of incumbents were reelected) and the partisan reapportionment of congressional districts carried out by majority Democratic statehouses since 1980. Although House minority leader Michels complained about the selfish fit of Reagan's coattails, he might more fairly have blamed the business PACs which, by and large, refused to subsidize Republican congressional challengers. The election was a pyrrhic victory for Mondale's corporate strategy in so far as Tony Coelho and his Democratic Congressional Campaign Committee had attracted business contributions to Democratic incumbents.[53] To an increasing extent, opposite trends are operating within what James MacGregor Burns once characterized as the American 'four party system' of autonomous Democratic and Republican congressional and presidential coalitions.[54] In the case of the Democrats, while the presidential coalition has become more dependent upon the contribution of Blacks, minorities and labor, the congressional wing, as Thomas Edsall has emphasized, is increasingly reliant upon business PACs and middle-class interest groups.[55]

Revenge of the Neo-Liberals

Well before Mondale's November doomsday, his impending defeat was being celebrated by leading neo-liberals. At the end of July, Senator Tsongas of Massachusetts, a pioneer neo-liberal and Hart confidant, was already boasting that 'the next crop of candidates will all come out of our wing of the party. For that reason, several of us would be just as comfortable if Mondale loses as if he wins'.[56] An even more brazen advocate of sending Mondale and old-style liberals to hell in a handbasket was Mayor Koch of New York. He had been barnstorming since the fall of 1983 to turn the Democratic Party away from the 'left-wing special interests' (read 'Blacks') and toward the middle class: 'The Party's left wing doesn't give a rap about the middle class'. (Koch's alternative was a clone of Kemp's and Gingrich's prescription to the

[53] Cf. Kuttner, 'Ass Backwards'; Edsall, 'Politics and the Power of Money'; and Maxwell Glen, 'Corporate PAC Pie', *National Journal*, January 19, 1985.
[54] *The Deadlock of Democracy*, Englewood Cliffs 1963.
[55] Edsall, 'Politics and the Power of Money'.
[56] Tsongas, quoted in *Business Week*, July 30, 1984, p. 71.

Republicans: flat rate tax reform, victim's rights, the curbing of entitle-ments, urban enterprise zones, and so on.)[57]

On the morning after the election, Tsongas's and Koch's views were echoed by a vast chorus of depressed Democratic office-holders. At a meeting of the AFL–CIO-backed Coalition for a Democratic Majority, LBJ's son-in-law, Governor Charles Robb of Virginia, 'minced no words about the need to return the party to the middle class, against the "special interests."' He articulated the consensus of Western and Southern Democratic leaders that the Democrats must be the 'party of business leaders, doctors, pharmacists, stockbrokers, and profession-als.' Robb was immediately seconded by strikebreaking Democratic Governor of Arizona, Bruce Babbitt, who had shown his indepen-dence of special interests by twice sending in the National Guard to terrorize locked-out copper miners.[58] As a programmatic contribution towards such a middle-class reorientation, the *New Republic* urged the Democrats immediately to dump the nuclear freeze, election campaign reform, comparable worth, affirmative action, and bilingual education.[59]

Meanwhile, Black Democrats, far from reaping new influence because of their stalwart loyalty to the party ticket, were scapegoated by virtually the entire white Democratic establishment for losing the elec-tion. Former Johnson aide Harry McPherson, testifying before the Center for National Policy, warned that 'Protestant male Democrats are becoming an endangered species ... (since) Blacks now own the Democratic Party.'[60] Robert Strauss, the former DNC chairman, talked darkly to *Time* magazine about the 'hunger' of 'women, Blacks, teach-ers, Hispanics' and Jesse Jackson's grip on the party.[61] He was upstaged, however, by Morton Kondracke's shrill warning that 'Jackson could ... use this black base, the largest single bloc in the party, to push his agenda of drastic cuts in defense spending, large new social expenditures and identification with third world liberation causes ... This is a script for making the Democrats into an American version of the British Labour Party, with Mr. Jackson playing the role of Tony Benn.'[62] Kondracke's *New Republic*, the site of a particu-larly virulent strain of Democratic neo-liberalism, underlined the threat to Western Civilization posed by the Black electorate with a

[57] *New York Times*, August 7, 1983, p. 1.
[58] *International Herald Tribune*, November 30, 1984, p. 3.
[59] 'Now What'? *New Republic*, November 26, 1985, pp. 7–9.
[60] McPherson, quoted in *Washington Post*, December 17, 1984, A-6.
[61] Quoted in *Time*, November 19, 1984, p. 29.
[62] Quoted in *Wall Street Journal*, November 15, 1984, p. 33.

raving editorial in near *Goebbelssprache*. Submerged in 'pathologies of crime, violence, arson and drugs', Blacks 'were more stunted politically than at any other point in a generation'. This collective criminal class — 'exceptional' in its political immaturity and irresponsibility — would no longer be indulged by white liberals or other Democratic constituencies. 'In another time and under another ethos, perhaps we would all feel morally burdened by these humiliating pathologies of so many of our fellow citizens; but we would have to live a more spacious conception of citizenship than the one we now live by'.[63]

The chic racism that had invested liberal critiques of the Jackson campaign in the spring came flooding down the spillways after November in even more strident forms. Nor was the putatively left press immune to such fulminations. In January, *In These Times* published a retrospect of the Rainbow Coalition's role in the election by James Sleeper that sounded, even if more gently and paternalistically, many of the same themes of the *New Republic*: Jackson's rallies 'were group exercises in therapeutic self-assertion, bonfires that failed to illuminate the larger political landscape because they generated few constructive programs for American society as a whole ... Jackson's up-front appeals for racial solidarity in the election arena violate(d) traditional American political culture ...'.[64] *Dissent*, for its part, brought an ex-Black revolutionary turned born-again Jew, Julius Lester, to denounce Jackson as a racist and anti-Semite, of 'questionable morality', who had tried to pretend that he was a Black 'Wizard of Oz'. Lester blamed the Rainbow for attempting to build a futile coalition of 'rejected groups' instead of looking towards the broad middle classes, the true source of 'empowerment'.[65] Meanwhile, for Social Democrats USA, Bayard Rustin was on hand at Norman Podhoretz's birthday to denounce Black extremism and to praise the great man for 'refusing to pander to minority groups' in his fight against quotas and Black studies.[66]

Black Democrats and Jackson supporters were stunned by the vitriolic intensity of these attacks on themselves as an anarchic special interest. Jackson lashed back at what he described as a 'cultural conspiracy against Blacks', and criticized the Democratic leadership for its failure to provide 'a rational analysis of why it lost.'[67] He also specif-

---

[63] 'How Not to Overcome', *New Republic*, January 21, 1985, pp. 7–9.

[64] January 16–22, 1985, p. 8.

[65] Julius Lester, 'You Can't Go Home Again', *Dissent*, Fall 1984.

[66] See the account in *New York Times*, February 1, 1985, p. 13.

[67] *Washington Post*, February 11, 1984, A13.

ically condemned the AFL–CIO Executive for their role in scapegoating his campaign. Yet at the same time, the *New York Times* reported that he 'was chastened by the reaction of party regulars' and once again made conciliatory moves towards the DNC. A friend was quoted as saying, 'Jesse doesn't want to leave the party. He's afraid the party's leaving him'.[68]

Jackson's apprehension is probably correct. Mondale's incontestable defeat has dramatically accelerated the succession process through which younger neo-liberals, with scant loyalty to labor or minorities, are replacing the leadership of older New Dealers and Southern conservatives at all levels of the Democratic Party. During 1984, two new power poles emerged to contest the party's future. First, Kennedy liberals and Mondale regulars lost the leadership of the House Democratic Caucus to an aggressive group of young neo-liberals, sportingly known as the 'Wednesday night bridge club', led by Richard Gephardt, who succeeded Gillis Long as Caucus chair, and Tony Coelho, the corporate fundraiser extraordinaire of the Democratic Congressional Campaign Committee.[69] Frontrunner to become the next Democratic whip, Coelho has tended to supply the tactical skills, while Gephardt has provided the ideological direction. Indeed, this latter congressman from the white, segregated and heavily Catholic suburban fringe of St. Louis, who earned his seniority opposing programs for the poor, school busing, and women's rights, has become something like the Doctor Faustus of congressional neo-liberals. In 1982, he drafted the Democratic Caucus's economic blueprint that shoved aside traditional Democratic welfare priorities to argue for a high-tech industrial policy along lines that anticipated Hart's platform in 1984. Since then he has been a passionate lobbyist for a Democratic realignment away from Blacks and labor, and towards the upwardly mobile middle classes.[70] He and Coelho have several times succeeded in defeating older New Dealers and Kennedy liberals, notably in their sabotage of a proposed American Defense Education Act that would have forced Reagan to provide $9 billion in aid to local schools. Long before November, his 'bridge club' was discussing how to turn a Mondale defeat to its advantage and impose 'a major overhaul of both the party's ideological image and the way its leaders communicate

---

[68] *New York Times*, February 15, 1984, p. 11.

[69] Richard Cohen, 'House Democratic Leadership', *National Journal*, July 2, 1984, and 'Damaged House Democrats', *National Journal*, December 1, 1984.

[70] Profile in *Washington Post*, December 5, 1984, A4.

with the public.'[71] This 'new Democratic agenda' has been spear-headed by the 'tax simplification' bill which Gephardt has co-sponsored with neo-liberal Senator Bill Bradley, in an obvious attempt to head the Reaganites off at the pass with a tax reform that offers even more to high-tech industries and to the professional middle classes.

Confronted with the onslaught of the Gephardt–Coelho current and their Senate allies, Kennedy liberals have given ground or changed their strips altogether. In the House, lame-duck Tip O'Neill has agreed to devolve power to the thirty to forty younger Democratic subcommittee chairs and caucus leaders. At the same time, O'Neill has virtually conceded that effective Democratic congressional opposition to Reaganomics is now impossible, given the overlapping of ideological perspectives between the neo-liberals and the administration. In what the *Washington Post* characterized as an 'extraordinarily conciliatory statement' about not blocking Reagan's budget proposals,[72] O'Neill sounded many of the neo-lib themes himself, saying he was 'willing to slash billions from revenue sharing and grants to local governments for community development and urban projects. He has told fellow Democrats they must shed the image of being "knee-jerk defenders of spending and weak on defense".'[73] No one has shed faster, however, than the 'West Side' machine of Congressmen Howard Berman and Henry Waxman in Los Angeles. This predominantly Jewish political network, which is the coming power in the California Democratic Party, has made a hard turn to neo-liberalism in the wake of the Mondale defeat, jettisoning its historic alliance with Los Angeles's Black Mayor, Tom Bradley, whose political aspirations and social base are now seen as a hindrance.[74]

A second center of neo-liberal succession has emerged among Democratic officeholders in the Sunbelt, particularly the Democratic governors. It is one of the ironies of recent American history that the middle-class tax 'revolt' of the late 1970s has been responsible for a great reinvigoration of the power of governors, as fiscally crippled cities have been forced to throw themselves on the mercy of statehouses and legislatures. In the Democratic Party, this has taken the specific form of strengthening the intra-party influence of governors against big city

[71] Cohen, 'Damaged House Democrats', p. 2288.
[72] January 23, 1985.
[73] Quoted in *New York Times*, January 10, 1985, IV, p. 1.
[74] See Bill Boyearsky, 'Democrats Divided by an Old Idea', *Los Angeles Times*, February 17, 1985, IV 1, 2.

mayors. Since early 1983, when they scrapped the Democratic Governors Conference — a subordinate arm of the DNC — to form the independent Democratic Governors Association, Southern and Western Democratic governors have been in the forefront of demands for a 'return' to the white middle class. As Texas Governor Mark White confessed to the *Wall Street Journal*: 'The national party has to get aligned with mainstream America and the group who can do that is the Democratic governors'.[75] *Business Week* was probably prophetic when it observed that the fundamental political direction of the governors is 'moving further right from neo-liberalism'.[76] Although Robb and hawkish Georgia Senator Sam Nunn are prominent spokesmen, the real ideologue of the Sunbelt governors, and functional counterpart to Gephardt in Congress, may be Babbitt. An exponent of 'radical centrism' (as well as scab-herding) he has connived to combine Gary Hart themes with consistent support for major Reagan programs like tax simplification ('a superb proposal'), merit pay, and anti-urban federalism. At San Francisco he was the leading proponent of Iacocca for vice-president.[77]

In the immediate aftermath of the election, Babbitt and Robb led their confederates from the Sunbelt in a blocking action against any diminution of the power of white-dominated state party machines in the South or any increase in the influence of Black Democrats. In San Francisco, the Jackson delegation had demanded the reform of the nomination process towards a proportional representation system that would prevent the kind of disfranchisement which occurred in 1984. Similarly, Hart wanted a reduction of the power of elected officials in the selection process. Mondale had purchased Jackson's pledge not to bolt the convention and Hart's support of most of his program by agreeing to establish a 'fairness commission' to review the nomination process. But under ferocious counter-attack by COPE and labor delegates, Mondale postponed the appointment until after the convention, when Hart and

[75] December 3, 1984, p. A5. 'Digging in or Digging Out?', see also Ronald Braunstein, *National Journal*, December 29, 1984. The Sunbelt Democrats soon sent their message to the nation in the form of a TV extravaganza organized by Tony Coelho and called the 'Selling of the Democrats 1985'. In an embarrassingly baldfaced effort to disassociate the local and state parties from the national Democratic defeat, and to win the hearts of Yuppies and Reaganites, the scene opens with people praising Reagan and criticising Mondale while a voice intoned 'a party that knows it has to change'. Later, in the setting of an affluent Philadelphia suburb, ten 'average' Democrats, including several lawyers, insurance managers, a PR executive and a marketing expert, are joined by Robb and Sam Nunn. Needless to say there is no mention either of Ferraro or Jackson.

[76] January 21, 1985, p. 86.

[77] Ibid.

Jackson would have reduced leverage. In November, the Association of State Democratic Chairpersons, meeting in the Virgin Islands, unanimously voted to pack the membership of the commission with party regulars.

The liaison with Gephardt that was crucial to pulling off this Virgin Islands coup soon led Babbitt and Robb into a full-scale alliance with the House neo-liberals. In February 1985 they defied the Democratic National Committee by establishing, under Gephardt's chairmanship, their own dual-power Democratic executive, the Democratic Leadership Council. The initial membership of the DLC included ten governors, led by Babbitt and Robb, fourteen senators, led by Sam Nunn, and seventeen representatives, led by Jim Jones, the powerful chair from Oklahoma of the House Budget Committee. Only four of the founders were from the Northeast, there were no women, and only two Blacks (one of whom, however, is the potential spoiler of the Black Caucus: William Gray III of Philadelphia, highest ranking Black committee chair).

This concert of the House neo-libs with the Sunbelt statehouses has thrown the former followers of Ted Kennedy on the defensive, spoiling whatever hopes the younger dynast might have had of turning the Mondale defeat to his own advantage. Not only was new DNC chair and ex-Kennedy aide Richard Kirk forced to acquiesce in the Democratic Leadership Council's *coup de main*, but within days of his difficult election, he was signalling his own distance from the labor movement ('I am not a captive') and his Great Society past ('The Democrats must return to traditional values'; they must 'earn anew the political respect of mainstream America', etc.).[78] Concurrently the AFL–CIO virtually went to ground, fighting rear-guard actions over tax policy, and generally avoiding any sharp confrontation with the ascendent neo-lib Sunbelt alliance. The most energetic exercise of labor's lobbying power in the six months following the election was its combination with these same forces to attack minority caucuses. With the AFL–CIO leading the charge, the DNC voted to revoke the seats that the convention had allotted to caucuses on all standing committees, allowing only Blacks, women, and Hispanics to maintain a residual presence on the Executive, while disestablishing the gay, liberal and Asian–American caucuses. Then, according to the *New York Times*, labor 'helped punish one of its political enemies' by mobilizing to defeat Mayor Richard Hatcher, Jackson's campaign manager, as a vice-chair of the DNC.[79]

---

[78] Quoted in *New York Times*, February 15, 1985, p. 6.
[79] February 15, 1985, p. 12.

Since Hatcher was the official nominee of the Black Caucus, his rejection was a signal that the Jackson forces and their allies could expect to ride in the back of the bus of the neo-liberalized Democratic Party. As Hatcher himself put it, this was a message to white, male America that Blacks, Hispanics and women aren't going to control the Democratic Party.'[80]

What's Left After the Democrats?

Although some left-liberals profess to find a silver lining in the ascendancy of the neo-liberals,[81] and a few social democrats even propose what amounts to a strategy of 'constructive engagement',[82] the post-election power struggles, following in the wake of the sociological verdicts of the election itself, do not offer much solace to advocates of the 'left wing of realism'. Given the considerable investment of hope and resources by most of the left during the election, if not also in the long-range strategy of realigning the Democratic Party, it seems particularly urgent to debate the lessons of 1984. For my own part, I think a provisional balance-sheet of the left and the Democrats would have to include the following points:

(1) The turn of the ex-New Left toward the Democratic Party coincided, almost to the exact moment, with the liberal retreat from the Great Society program and the beginning of the abandonment of a hegemonic reformism that included the Black poor. Almost every major theme of Reaganism was prefigured in the 1977-78 domestic

---

[80] *National Journal*, February 9, 1985, p. 325.

[81] *Mother Jones*'s political columnist David Osborne, ignoring the Rainbow Coalition and the fate of minorities, argued that New Deal liberals 'deserved their beating' and urged a marriage of 'Hart's new ideas and Mario Cuomo's soul'. (*Mother Jones*, January 1985, p. 60)

[82] Within DSA, Joseph Schwartz and National Political Director Jim Schoch appear to have gone furthest in suggesting that left politics must accept part of the terrain offered by Neo-liberalism. As Schwartz has put it, 'the neo-liberal ideologues are at least taking on some tough questions about the transformation of the American political economy. Our role will likely be limited to struggling to get into the public arena a more sensitive, feasible and democratic alternative to their romance with "high-tech" and "picking winners". (See 'The role of DSA in the coming period', *Socialist Forum* 6, p. 54). In a similar vein, political scientist David Plotke, a former editor of *Socialist Review*, criticized Mondale's supposed over-identification with the poor, and taking the perspective of the Democratic Party's practical needs to sustain an electoral majority, called for 'combining Hart's themes with Jackson's means'. ('Democratic Dilemmas', *The Year Left 1985*, London 1985, p. 125).

and foreign policy shifts of the Carter administration (thereby inviting one to reverse Ted Kennedy's description of Carter as 'Reagan's clone').

(2) The ascendency of electoralism on the left, far from being an expression of new popular energies or mobilizations, was, on the contrary, a symptom of the decline of the social movements of the 1960s, accompanied by the organic crisis of the trade-union and community-service bureaucracies. Rather than being a strategy for unifying mass struggles and grassroots organization on a higher, programmatic level, electoralism was either imagined as a substitute for quotidian mass organizing, or it was inflated as an all-powerful catalyst for movement renewal.

(3) Most of the pro-Democratic left generally misread the direction of the class and racial polarization taking place in the United States and its impact on traditional electoral alignments. Starting from the misconception that a 'left' politics (whether hyphenated with liberalism or socialism) could be re-established directly on the basis of anti-Reagan populism, it seriously underestimated the power of the petty-bourgeois insurgency which is sweeping both parties and recomposing their leaderships. By the same token, it wildly overestimated the attraction of the Democrats, who lack any serious alternative economic program, to a divided and socially dispirited working class.

(4) The naive belief in a hidden left majority indicated a deeper incomprehension of how the electoral arena is socially structured and technically manipulated. Refusing to recognize the implacable fact that the power of US capital is reinforced by a field of property interests *millions* strong, the electoralist left acted as if middle-class and corporate domination of the institutions and media of the political system could be equalized merely by mass voter registration — at times appearing to give credence to the parliamentary cretinism that believes the electoral system to be a level playing field between social classes. In fact, the American electoral system, historically the most *structurally* antagonistic to radical or independent politics, has virtually become an extension of the advertising and television industries (See above, chapter 4).

(5) The role of the trade-union movement in 1984 demonstrates all too clearly the contradictions of attempting to manipulate the system through its own elite apparatuses. The AFL–CIO Executive mobilized a great deal of organizational and financial clout, with only paltry political result. The logistics of power-brokerage within the DNC, and of packaging a candidacy for sale in the national TV marketplace, led labor successively to minimize and then contain its own objectives. As a result, the AFL–CIO failed to defend the Second Reconstruction or to

advance a serious jobs program. Its Gompersian option for an alliance with finance capital, founded upon an abortive reindustrialization policy, abandoned any pretence of acting in the name of the entire working class. In retrospect, it would have been better in 1984 for the unions to have remained politically divided along previous lines (as from 1972 to 1980). At least some of the more 'progressive' unions, including the public sector unions with large Black and third-world memberships, might have been freer to express the will of their memberships, particularly toward the Jackson primary campaign.

(6) The 'top down' strategy of DSA and its various influentials was guaranteed to keep them minor pawns in the political machinations of the trade-union bureaucracy. Behind the rhetoric of 'labor unity', the Kirkland policy represented not a progressive opening, but a recrudescence of the political right wing of the union movement. By binding themselves to Mondale *in advance* of any programmatic agreement, and generally without any consultation of their memberships, the unions lost crucial room for maneuver around their own demands (like plant closure legislation) as well as any leverage at the convention. The last act in this charade was Mondale's ability to forge his own corporate alliance and make a definitive right turn immediately after the convention.

(7) The decision of the Nuclear Freeze and sections of the anti-war movement to make the Democrats the main priority in 1984 was an unmitigated disaster. Far from creating a mass arena for anti-nuclear, anti-interventionist politics, participation in the Democratic camp seriously disorganized these movements, as they allowed themselves to be trapped in the process of accommodation and 'consensus management' that defeated the freeze at the convention and made Central America a non-issue in the fall. Ironically, the most effective electoral actions were carried out by local anti-war and peace groups on the West Coast who remained completely independent of the Mondale campaign and relied on traditional referenda.

(8) Because, as James Weinstein has pointed out, the historic social-democratic leadership has conceived itself playing an essentially 'courtier' role vis-à-vis the trade-union and Democratic leaderships,[83] it was unwilling to ally with the one mass left constituency in American politics: the Black electorate. Indeed, with its explicit anti-imperialism, the Jackson campaign probably invited an impossible leap from DSA leaders like Harrington or Howe who have given life-long dedication to liberal zionist and anti-Communist causes. Moreover, the absence of

---

[83] Editorial, *In These Times*, August 8–21, 1984, p. 14.

any serious debate about the election in DSA, except from a passionate group of Black members, leaves open (and unlikely of positive resolution) the question of whether even the 'Debsian' grassroots of that organization are capable of challenging its traditional mortgage to Israel and the Cold War, or of realigning the organization toward mass political currents that do not have the endorsement of liberalism.

(9) At its worst, the backlash among sections of the white left against the Jackson campaign exposed an ugly neo-racism. More generally, the patronizing reactions to the Rainbow Coalition revealed how profoundly 'white' the self-concept of many left-liberals had become, and how unwilling they remain to accept even a modicum of non-white leadership. The contrasting reactions to Ferraro and Jackson are sobering in that regard. Moreover, as the shrinkage of the gender gap in the election indirectly showed, no matter how important feminist consciousness must be in shaping a socialist culture in America, racism remains the divisive issue within class *and* gender. There can be no such thing as a serious reformist politics, much less an effective socialist practice, that does not frontally address the struggle against racism and defend the full program of a Second Reconstruction.

(10) The Jackson campaign had a complex, ambiguous significance. On the one hand, it tested the waters for a left politics of jobs and peace based on a multi-racial coalition of the most oppressed groups in American society. Among Black people especially, it revealed a profound yearning to revive the liberation struggles of the 1960s — a desire that flowed easily and self-confidently into channels of independent political action and protest against the Democratic establishment. On the other hand, the Jackson candidacy remained circumscribed by its self-defeating goal of renegotiating the terms of Black *subordinacy* in the Democratic Party. In this sense, Jesse Jackson acted as the Father Gapon of Black reformist politics, leading a supplication of inner-city office-holders to the 'little father', Walter Mondale.

(11) In the event, of course, the galvanization of the Black primary vote by the Jackson campaign cut directly across the path of the neo-liberal succession in the Democratic Party. The clearest aftermath of November 1984 is the bitter message that the white yuppie establishment-in-formation has sent to Black Democrats. Self-effacing loyalty to the party has only brought hypocritical charges that Blacks are a power-hungry 'special interest'; unprecedented contributions to the national Democratic vote have brought the accusation of causing the white backlash. Far from having won a new deal within the party, Black Democrats now face the prospect of becoming pariahs in the

post-New Deal party of Gephardt, Babbitt, Koch and Hart.

(12) Although this closure of the reformist space within the national and local Democratic parties opens new, long-range possibilities for independent political action, its immediate consequences will almost certainly be demoralization and disorganization. The Jackson campaign was too tied to the prospects of immediate victories and breakthroughs. In the face of a more corrosive neglect from a revamped neo-liberal party, Black politicians will have even fewer resources — real or symbolic — to offer their followers. A continuing high level of interest in electoral politics is thus unlikely without the prospect of material returns or, at the least, a visible line of march. The political crisis will probably provoke more divisions in the Black political family between party loyalists, willing and able to settle for local deals and a few prestige appointments, and a more militant leadership looking for a strategy to resurrect the civil rights movement.

Epilogue
Inventing the American Left

What will American politics be like after Reagan? I have argued in this book that the decisive political event of the 1978–85 period has been the emergence of a protean 'broad right' born of the mobilization of new middle strata in defense of the economic and social status gains which they won during the 1970s. Although the New Right has been the midwife to this historic transition, and remains the single most powerful ideological constituency in the country, it will probably not be its principal beneficiary. Rather, within both parties, a potential third party of the center–right, or 'conservative populism', is struggling to emerge from the shell of the old. Among the Democrats, as we have seen, a neo-liberal succession is reshaping the party's power structure, marginalizing labor and minorities. On the Republican side, the analogous development features the high-growth, pro-entrepreneurial platform of Kemp and Gingrich versus the traditional corporate Republicanism of Senate leaders like Dole.

Just as the Democratic neo-liberals have been consistently willing to displace the costs of middle-class mobility onto the backs of the working poor and unemployed, disregarding the price in party unity, so too has the 'Conservative Opportunity Society' startled some observers by the alacrity with which it upsets Republican solidarity to advance the 'broad interests' of the middle class and high-tech industry against older industrial 'special interests'. In both cases, the traditional shape of political discourse has been remodelled around a new, assertive definition of social hegemony. Neither 'the people', in the expansive Rooseveltian sense, nor 'General Motors', in the Republican Eastern establishment sense, any longer determines 'what's good for America'; the general social good is now equated with a middle-class 'mainstream' shorn of special interests, especially when these latter are poor or Black. The social demobilization of the lower classes and the narrowing of the electoral universe during the 1970s have made it easier for the baby-boom *nouveaux riches* to imagine themselves as the new heartland of a high-tech economy.

It is instructive to compare these simultaneous insurgencies and parallel discourses of neo-liberalism and supply-side Republicanism with the great bipartisan revolt of the 1898–1912 era. In spite of the universal romance of the younger generation of bourgeois politicians

301

with 'populism', it is the Progressive movement of Roosevelt and Wilson that provides the comparable precedents of right-wing reform, middle-class self-assertion, generational succession, the rise of frontier capital, a fetishism for efficiency and new technology, and a confident white supremacism. But just as the two wings of Progressivism left a complex, ramified heritage, while failing — despite Bull Moose and, later, Lafollette — to create a permanent petty-bourgeois third party or to supplant the McKinleyite configuration of class and ethno-religioius alliances, so too it is unlikely that the present ideological affinities between new Republicans and new Democrats augur permanent solutions to the dealignment crisis of the party political system that has been traded back and forth between the two parties like a hot potato for twenty years.

One can, of course, imagine some form of bipartisan coalition or further convergence between supply-siders and neo-liberals, but such a regroupment could only take root and produce a new 'critical realignment' if it were to possess a compelling economic logic conformable with the interests of the most powerful fractions of capital. Both New Deal Democracy and its satellite, Dewey Republicanism, were firmly anchored in the institutionalized class collaboration made possible by the political economy of Fordism. Reaganism, in contrast, has had the success of a transitional form, temporarily welding together, through military Keynesianism and financial hyper-accumulation, the interests of all propertied layers at the expense of a new immiseration for the poor and a broken social truce for the unions. It has been an attempt to preserve the entire structure of property values and capitalization accumulated by the bourgeoisie, the middle strata and the more privileged segments of the white working class over the past thirty years — a popular front against the depreciation of inefficient fixed capital or the deflation of speculative equities. But the very success of the first phase of Reaganomics, as I argued in chapter six above, has only prepared the way for the inevitable second phase of conflict and zero-sum competition within the Reaganite coalition itself.

My central point in the preceding chapters is that the common program of the new Progressivism is unlikely to charm a new golden age of high growth into existence. Its deployment of state spending, fiscal transfers and deregulation to fertilize the entrepreneurial and professional opportunities supposedly immanent in the new technologies and services can at best stave off the inevitable day of reckoning for the imperial hegemony of the US economy. A more likely scenario is that the middle strata and the *nouveaux riches* will have to confront in the next downturn what they feared (but avoided through Reaganomics) in the last: a closing frontier of income and status mobility. Only when broad sections of the middle classes have had to live for a time on diminished rations will the true politics of 'overconsumptionism' become visible in mature form.

Anticipating the effect of such a crisis cutting through the tinsel of Yuppie lifestyles, Arthur Schlesinger, Jr. has predicted the return of a chastened middle class to the fold of Keynesian liberalism (even though he is a bit hazy about where its remaining adherents may be hiding).[1] Others, including an apprehensive Kevin Phillips, have foreseen a rather different future: the further growth of the New Right and its potential metamorphosis into a home-grown fascism.[2] More likely than either, if difficult to visualize in any concrete detail, is the radicalization of the broad right spectrum represented by neo-liberalism. Unlike the 1929–33 period, when the chain reaction of crisis proceeded via virtually automatic economic mechanisms, the coming crisis of the Yuppie boom will at every crucial juncture pass through the political system, overloading the circuits of Congress with insistent, hysterical demands to abate any deterioration of the middle strata's socioeconomic position. As the experience of the last decade has made abundantly clear, middle-class and neo-entrepreneurial interest formation is now so well funded and powerfully embedded in the new 'post-party' electoral system, that it can override any attempts by labor or Black groups to lobby for preferential relief for their constituencies. As neo-liberals and their Republican compeers pull out all the stops to prevent the ruination of their social base, the political system will respond first, and most powerfully, to their demands.

Precisely because there is no 1990 Keynes nor any armory of alternative economic policy waiting to be wheeled in to save late capitalism, crisis management will proceed by the cult of political will, rather than by the invocation of any particular schema. After the collapse of the supply-side 'revolution', it is unlikely that purely economic ideology will again hold dominant sway; Hobbes, rather than Adam Smith or Milton Friedman, may be the business school deity of the next decade. Reagan's successors — be they of the stamp of regular Republican Robert Dole, or of corporate magician Lee Iaccoca — will almost certainly be compelled to continue down the path of voluntarist economic management, treading the well-worn tracks of Nixon and Reagan. While it would be imprudent to predict with any confidence

---

[1] In a symposium with Kevin Phillips, Walter Dean Burnham, and Jerry Brown in *The New York Review of Books*, August 16, 1984, pp. 33–38.

[2] Kevin Phillips, *Post-Conservative America*, New York 1981.

the precise outcome of these tendencies, one plausible scenario would have the neo-liberals, shorn of their adolescent panaceas and chastened by the rigors of crisis, re-emergent as pragmatic, hardheaded economic nationalists.

Domestically, the chief concern in a crisis period will be to launch crash programs to shore up high-tech industries and regional growth poles in the South and the West. 'Star Wars' — Reagan's version of industrial policy for the Sunbelt military-scientific complex — would be likely to assume strategic centrality in such a rescue operation. Similarly, neo-liberals, in league with like-minded Republicans, may adopt budgetary and fiscal policies that would further speed the net transfer from older industrial areas and inner cities. Constrained by the costs of such massive deficitary programs, they could scarcely avoid savaging the domestic budget to scare up the last pennies to support middle-class entitlements and defense spending. But the political and social repercussions of such a cynical strategy might be more than even the neo-liberals could safely bear. To contain an explosive general immiseration and deal with yet higher plateaux of unemployment, they would probably attempt to squeeze major productivity increases out of the public sector with further privatization and actual cutbacks in state employment.

What the Kerner Commission Report found to be 'two societies, separate and unequal', may by 1990 be three distinct societies, as segregated from one another as if apartheid were economic common law in the United States. At one pole will be the sumptuary suburbs and gentrified neighborhoods occupied by the middle classes, the rich and elements of the skilled white working class. Undoubtedly, neo-liberalism will seek to preserve the superstructures of social liberalism — sexual toleration, free and virtually unlimited choice among cultural commodities, and the general ethos of human potential — while building new parapets between this gilded paradise and the other social orders. Outside, in the first circle of the damned, will be the ghettoes and barrios, now joined by déclassé and deindustrialized layers of the white working class. Possessing 'citizen' rights to a minimal social safety net, this enlarged low-wage working class would remain politically divided and disenfranchised, as unions continue to be destroyed and the influence of labor and minorities within the political system declines. With fading hopes of entry into the norm of consumption defined by the boutique lifestyles of the middle strata or the 'secure' employment status of the shrunken core workforces of the great corporations, this sector of the nation will increasingly encounter social degradation and relative impoverishment in the next crisis cycle.

But by 1990 there will also be a large outer perimeter of US society composed of workers without citizen rights or access to the political system at all: an American West Bank of terrorized illegal laborers or, if the Simpson–Rodino legislation is successful, of officially third-class *Gastarbeiter*. In the next twenty years, this third tier could be a social layer of twenty to thirty million people, a poor Latin American society thrust into the domestic economy.

Policing the widening divisions in American society in a time of economic crisis and vanished hopes for the return of a full-employment economy may involve not only futuristic techniques of surveillance and pre-emptive repression (sanctified by the longevity of the Burger Supreme Court), but also the further dissemination of a culture that justifies the spiralling viciousness necessary to justify socio-economic apartheid. This ideology, already on the horizon in such night-time TV staples as *Miami Vice, Hunter,* and *Hill Street Blues,* and in the streets in the disgusting popular outcry in support of the New York City 'subway vigilante' Bernhard Goetz, reposes on a simultaneous sentimentalization of middle-class life and a demonizing of a putative 'underclass'. Insider the *laager* of Yuppie comfort and professional–managerial values, an enlightened psychological sensitivity informs the management of human relations, while outside, in the second and third tiers of US society, there exists a virtual free-fire zone. Girding themselves for the defense of their accumulated affluence, the new and old middle strata are taking on the armor of merciless resolution — celebrated in *New Republic* editorials and iconized in popular consciousness by films like *Rambo* and *Sudden Impact* — to exclude and repress the dangerous classes that prowl the circumference of their pleasure dome.

The same survivalist instincts will regulate neo-liberalism's approach to international affairs. Bereft of any grand design for restoring order to a world market rocked by financial defaults and huge trade disequilibria, a neo-liberal regime, after fruitless wrangling for multilateral coordination, would probably resort to bilateral diktats aimed at extracting drastic economic accommodations from unwilling 'allies'. As the protectionist tide bursts its dike, US trading partners will be faced with a broad range of retaliatory threats, from the restriction of their imports to the pullback of US troop deployments in Europe and Northeast Asia. Great as tensions between Japan and the United States may well become, the new economic nationalism is likely to reach even more acute pitch in the Western Hemisphere, as future administrations accelerate the trend towards the integration of North America into a single, complex economic system. The management of Mexico's unemployment and social unrest could eventually require militarization of the border zone (as opposed to the half-hearted militarization of the current INS regime), and, not impossibly during the 1990s, a return to the the intervention of the Wilsonian period.

I have earlier argued that the emergent system of post-Fordist American hegemony will increasingly depend upon the substitution of US military for economic power in an unstable international configuration. If there is a long interregnum of financial disorder and declining trade through the 1980s or early 1990s, a virtual social collapse of many of the already stricken societies of the Southern Hemisphere cannot be excluded. In that event, whatever the immediate outcome of US intervention in Central America, Washington would probably be confronted with a revolutionary crisis of much wider proportions in South America within the decade. Although the variety of forms this crisis will assume cannot be entirely foreseen, its dominant ideological colour, unlike in the Middle East or East Asia, is more likely to be an insurgent socialism than any other — perhaps on a new, Bolivarian scale.

The bunkered, economically insecure middle strata of the USA — the mass ruling class of the American world system — will not look with sympathy upon further revolutionary unrest in the Western Hemisphere. It is scarcely plausible that, having turned their backs on the new poverty of US cities, they will endorse the level of economic aid and co-development necessary to restore growth and absorb escalating social tensions in Latin America. More likely is the prospect that the current counter-revolutionary interventions in Central America are merely opening salvos in a generalized social war pitting the insurgent poor of the Hemisphere against not ony their local ruling classes but, increasingly, the rich classes in the North as well. For the 'broad right' in North America would, in these circumstances, see the revolutionary process in Latin America and the Caribbean (including the potential Yankee Ulster of Puerto Rico) as an immediate and overarching threat to a US economy that has become increasingly entrenched in its hemispheric fortress. Even with militarized borders, this war could soon spill over into the barrios and ghettoes of the US, with every sympathizer of Latin revolution, or perhaps simply brown-skinned worker, assimilated to the already demonized imagery of the Black unemployed as the internal 'enemy'.

The recent acclamation of the 'Reagan Doctrine' by the self-styled 'Rambo Democrats' in the House surely gives some indication of the character of neo-liberal reaction in the darker periods ahead. In a virtual declaration of war on the Third World, 'liberals' fused with Southern Democrats and Republicans in authorizing terrorism against anti-imperialist Third World regimes, while at the same time voting for a new chemical arms race and the stockpiling of nerve gas. Neo-liberals have occupied the front row in criticizing the Reagan administration for failing to live up to its promises of exemplary violence against 'terrorists' and revolutionaries. By the summer of 1985, a bipartisan consensus was being forged in support of an invasion of Nicaragua and a global offensive against all revolutionary regimes. The image of a trigger-happy vigilante stalking the world spoiling for a fight, which Democrats tried to hang on Reagan during the 1984 election, has come back to haunt them a year later, as they look into a mirror and see only the benign smile of the national patriarch masking the blend of viciousness, complacency, and potential for irrational violence that are now mainstream political ideology in 'the age of Reagan'.

A Popular Left for the 1990s?

If the details of this scenario — hastily sketched but not, for all that, empty exercises in imagining the future — strike the reader as unduly pessimistic, the reason why they are so drawn is that the political and economic supports for a more humane capitalism no longer seem to exist. The view expressed here is diametrically opposed to that of many recent left-liberal and social-democratic writers, who profess to see vistas of new liberations and reformist possibilities in late imperial America. A virtual cottage industry has come into existence since 1980, providing visionary recipes for workers' control, the restoration of craft production, expanded welfarism, economic democracy and social control of investment. Most of these heartening schemes, typically offered as brains trust advice to the left wing of the Democratic Party, have been characterized by a complete absence of strategic design: that is, they lack any specification of the means for their realization. They contain no hint of how, in a period of rampant deunionization and the self-immolation of traditional liberalism — when to stem the tide of either would suppose some massive shift in the balance of forces to the left — they could find a conceivable agency.

Rather than taking hope from make-believe social democracy, it seems better to prepare for the colder climate ahead by reflecting as carefully and critically as possible upon the fate of the US left in the 1970s and early 1980s. What would be a summary balance sheet? The left in these years, it might be argued, invariably came back to the revival of one of three alternative projects, each with classical precedent in the history of American radicalism: the Debsian, the Fosterite and, finally, the Browderite strategies. The first, advanced most energetically by NAM and the original editors of *Socialist Review* (when it was still called *Socialist Revolution*) as a counterweight to the 'new communist' movements, encompassed an attempt to create a small, explicitly socialist public sphere as a prelude to more active and broader based socialist politics. The second project — which probably could be typed as neo-syndicalist as well — grew out of the belief, exemplified by William Z. Foster's life and writings, that militant unionism matures almost naturally into political radicalism. This was the inspiration for the workerist groups of the 1970s, who believed that the rank-and-file revolt of the Nixon era would be a seedbed for a new labor left (if not for a new communist party). The third project, akin to Browder's attempted dissolution of the Communist Party during World War Two into the ranks of the New Deal, was based on the idea that the left should act as the most militant and consistent wing of the Democratic Party in the conviction that liberalism could be gradually meta-morphosed, via a program of economic democracy or populism, into a practical, Americanized version of socialism.

Each of these projects suffered major, arguably definitive, defeats during the 1970s and 1980s. As chapter seven explained, both neo-Browderism and its companion social-democratic strain (these representing the two principal lineages of DSA) were consumed on the pyre of the Mondale campaign and the anti-New Deal right turn of the Democratic Party. Fosterism foundered during the 1970s on the same reef it had struck in the 1930s: working-class economic militancy in the US is not in any sense automatically conducive to political radicalization — rather, the first is often a pragmatic limitation upon the second. Just as the 'consistent' liberal often remains a liberal, so too the consist-ent trade-union militant remains just that.

As Lenin pointed out three quarters of a century ago, with a perspicacity that has yet to be fully assimilated, 'political' consciousness comes from outside the immediate field of the economic class struggle — which is not to say that it is superimposed on the working class by intellectuals, but rather that it grows out of the overdetermination of the economic class struggle by other contradictions and forms of oppression. For instance, as I argued in my opening chapter, the 'Jacobin' path to political class consciousness in Europe arose because of the fusion of early demands for suffrage with struggles for elemental workplace organization, while in Britain and the Antipodes, 'laborism' emerged in response — among other things — to repression of trade-union organizational rights. One must not forget that in the USA too the hard core of Debsian socialism derived from the situation of an immigrant proletariat that endured economic exploitation along with cultural discrimination and, most often in factory towns, *de facto* political disenfranchisement.

The Fordist absorption of the new immigrant strata and their eventual 'Americanization' during the 1940s and 1950s destroyed the social and cultural base of the existing forms of American socialism and communism. Their project could not be revived, as NAM and others essayed, by personal witness and local activism, however cleverly blended with popular culture. Nor is it likely, given the record of such movements up to the present and the growing fractures among various economic strata described above, that a mass socialist politics could ever grow incrementally from molecular conversions or from single issue campaigns of a sporadically radical character. It is equally implausible that such a mass movement could take the form of an 'extension' of American laborism, as much of the traditional left has consistently imagined. For all its recurrent threats to form a third party, the trade-union bureaucracy remains firmly and closely, for this generation at least, tied to the Democratic Party. In turning from its original Debsian ideal toward entrism into the Democratic Party, most of NAM and the intellectual left aligned with it tacitly abandoned the hope of an explicit socialist politics, to become what Irving Howe has described as 'loyal allies and supporters' or 'friendly critics' of liberalism.[3]

In the wake of these failed projects and lost directions, it remains to be asked whether there is any visible social constituency in the United States for a popular left. Or, to frame the problem in Lenin's terms: are there any subaltern strata whose class position is fused with a special oppression that transcends the limits of bourgeois political reform, and whose struggle for daily survival, therefore, generates anti-systemic elements of protest and political solidarity?

The traditional, despairing Hartzian answer, of course, is 'no'; there has been no socialism in America precisely because of the absence of any great, unfinished democratic agenda. Constitutional guarantees of suffrage and individual rights have consistently defused the explosion of mass socialist movements on a European model. But this answer, which is the most frequent (if not always acknowledged) justification given for 'American exceptionalism', is both myopic and inaccurate. Early suffrage and a pioneering mass party system did help to deflect the thrust of early white working-class organization from independent political expression, but this has not altered the fact that the oppression of Blacks has remained a central contradiction at the

---

[3] Irving Howe, *New York Times Sunday Magazine*, June 17, 1984, p. 24.

heart of the American bourgeois democratic system. If after the founding of the Republic, the contradiction that shattered the Union was slavery, the demise of the 'peculiar institution' was followed by the defeat of the first Reconstruction, and the new servitude of debt peonage and Jim Crow. It was these that posed the sharpest democratic challenge to the nascent American left in the 20th century. It should be recalled that in 1933 there were two great oppressed social groups in North America: the first, we have observed, were the second-generation new immigrants who formed the bulk of semi-skilled labor in the mass-production economy; the second were the masses of Southern rural poor, a majority of whom were Black. While the New Deal reluctantly sponsored the successful reform struggle of the first through the new industrial unions, it was the agent of the social defeat of the second. The New Deal utterly failed to bring any liberation for Southern Blacks; instead, it strengthened the power of their masters by federalizing support for Southern landowners and big planters.

As I have argued at some length, the failure of the postwar labor movement to form an organic bloc with Black liberation, to organize the South or to defeat the power of Southern reaction in the Democratic Party, have determined, more than any other factors, the ultimate decline of American trade unionism and the rightward reconstruction of the political economy during the 1970s. The frustration of any second Reconstruction was the pivotal event marking the end of the Rooseveltian epoch of reform and its underlying economic base: the integrative capacities of a Fordist mass consumption economy. The minimal democratic program of the civil rights movement, involving the claims to equal housing, equal employment and equal political representation, has proved to be an impossible set of reforms for contemporary American capitalism to enact.

The struggle for substantive social equality for the Black and Hispanic working class is no longer simply part of the unfinished agenda of liberalism, currently on hold while those concerned wait patiently for it to be resumed in the next Democratic administration. Their struggle has evolved, rather, towards what might be called a 'revolutionary–democratic' platform that challenges the current political economy of capitalism. At this juncture in history, as the Jackson campaign demonstrated, the return toward even the unsatisfactory Great Society levels of welfare maintenance and job subsidization would require halting the new Cold War and entail a massive shift of resources from the military to the social budget. Any real movement towards an economic integration of the working poor into a new high-wage environment would involve a radical expansion of the public sector and a complete undoing of the 'overconsumptionist' logic that expresses the social power of the expanded middle strata. Substantive economic citizenship for Black and Hispanic America would require levels of change dangerously close to the threshold of socialist transformation.

Into the foreseeable future, the historic agenda of the civil rights movement will become increasingly incompatible with the tendencies of capital accumulation and distribution of political and social power now operative in the US. For the moment Black reformist politics have anyway reached a crisis — a macabre symptom of which was the police massacre in the spring 1985 of MOVE militants in Philadelphia, which burnt out whole blocks of a black neighbourhood under the administration of Black mayor Wilson Goode — which might issue in a new road toward radical, independent political action. Whether such radicalization could be realized along the lines of the mass left politics prefigured in the Jackson primary campaign will depend, above all, on the organizational unity and political strategy of Black and Third World socialists. The single most important organizational problem confronting the North American left today is the huge disjuncture between the progressive political consciousness of Black America and the weakness of any national Black socialist cadre (the same dilemma applies to Chicanos/Mexicanos·in the Southwest). Faced with the catastrophic social deterioration that has resulted from the crumbling of inner-city employment structures, there is an understandable urgency in the ghettoes and barrios for a resumption of the liberation movements. But precisely because reformist options have become so restricted, it will be very hard for collective action to generate the immediate concessions and victories that could provide momentum for a wider popular militancy.

The problems of political organization in working-class communities of the oppressed are in many ways perhaps greater today than they have ever been. But the crucial lesson to be learned from the political debacles of 1984 is two-fold. Democratic reformism has effectively and unceremoniously died. Yet in the face of hostile media and a concerted (if often unpublicized) effort against it from within the existing Democratic power structure (white and Black, conservative and 'progressive'), the Jackson campaign nonetheless succeeded in overcoming the barriers to mass reception of anti-imperialist ideas in the US. My thesis is that, if there is to be any popular left in the 1990s, it will develop in the first instance through the mobilization of the radical political propensities in the Black — and, perhaps, Hispanic — working classes. Reciprocally, the validity and popular appeal of any socialist program or strategy will depend on the degree to which it addresses the axial problem of the revolutionary–democratic struggle for equality. To do so, leftists must reject the 'majoritarian' fallacy, nurtured by fellow-traveling in the Democratic Party, that all socialist politics must be cut to fit the pattern of whatever modish liberalism is in fashion or to conform with the requirements for securing 'practical' Democratic pluralities. The horizon of the possible — and the necessary — is not the quixotic project of becoming a 'loyal' fringe of one or another of the capitalist parties, but the fight to build an independent left politics that has real and effective social anchorage. To the extent that sections of the Democratic Party or elements of the middle strata can brought to return to more traditional liberal positions, it will only be because independent forces to their left are militant and well organized, with demands unvetted by the 'realism' of consensus-building with establishment politics.

What, then, of the organized labor movement? To recognize that the Black working class is the potential cutting edge for socialism in North America does not diminish the urgency of defending the — still overwhelmingly, white — trade-union movement. Among the central tasks of the left throughout the remainder of this decade will be to support the construction of national networks of anti-concession locals and rank-and-file activists. The first effects of the next downturn will undoubtedly be a worsening of the conditions of struggle between labor and capital. As the trade-union movement is forced into ever more desperate defensive battles, the strategic task of greatest moment is unlikely to revolve around new 'qualitative' demands: it will be to defend, at all costs, the principles of egalitarianism and solidarism. Above all the left must oppose the trend, exemplified in the fateful auto settlement of 1984, to abandon the unemployed and the inner cities in exchange for precarious security for senior (white) workers.

Furthermore, an alternative strategy will need to develop new links and alliances, from the bottom up, between trade-union groups and community/political organizations in the inner cities. Only radical protest — on a scale comparable to and utilizing the direct-action tactics of the 1960s civil rights movement — has any realistic chance of winning battles over plant closures or abating the rampant deindustrialization that has devastated areas like Eastern Pennsylvania and West Virginia, and will certainly spread to other locales with the rapidity of a modern-day plague. The crucial question will be whether struggles of unionized industrial workers to save their jobs can be united with struggles by the young jobless, and whether local unions can become broader campaigning organizations. In this regard, the British miners' strike, which led to the creation of extraordinary networks of support between mining villages and inner-city ghettoes, is a premonitory example. But all these questions come back to the central, burning issue for the American working class as a whole: whether, through the agency of some form of activist Rainbow Coalition, a nascent trade-union left can form organic and sustained linkages with revived Black and Hispanic movements.

Another pivotal difficulty, of course, is the degree to which Blacks and Hispanics, poor citizen working class and undocumented immigrant working class, can find bases of common civic unity and action. The recent sabotage of a broad Black–Hispanic anti-Koch coalition in the New York mayoral contest by a clique of Black Democratic wardheelers typifies the kind of narrow ethnic maneuvering that will surely become more frequent in a period of declining resources and exacerbated inter-group competition for jobs and patronage. A true Rainbow Coalition would have to build largely from below, in opposition to the ethnic machines. It will have to confront the desperate competition in job markets that divides not only Blacks from Hispanics, but Hispanics from Asians, and, in the Southwest, Chicanos from Mexicanos. One of the most innovative experiments, however still provisional in scale, has been the emergence in California of political workers' organizations of a general kind that combine strike support, community organization, union building, and left political education.

But the ability of any resurgent social movement in the ghettoes, barrios or factories to challenge the present mass property bloc of capital and the middle classes in the United States is more closely linked today than ever before to the fate of US imperialism on a world scale. If one precondition for the future of a popular left in the United States is a revived struggle for equality based on independent socialist political action, the other and equally crucial condition will be increasing solidarity between the liberation movement in Southern Africa and Latin America and movements of the Black and Hispanic communities in the USA.

The possibility for organizing mass solidarity must be one of the principal hopes of international socialism. Just as the struggles in South Africa and Central America can provide models of commitment, creativity and organization to youth in the inner cities, so could the development of a broadly based solidarity movement in the United States act as a major constraint on America intervention abroad, and a common basis for political action that crosses the color barrier which has inhibited much of the left's political activity during the past decade. It is no disparagement of the existing anti-nuclear or anti-intervention movements to insist that the real weak link in the domestic base of American imperialism is a Black and Hispanic working class, fifty million strong. This is the nation within a nation, society within a society, that alone possesses the numerical and positional strength to undermine the American empire from within.

Ultimately, no doubt, the left in the United States will have to confront the fact that there is never likely to be an 'American revolution' as classically imagined by DeLeon, Debs or Cannon. If socialism is to arrive one day in North America, it is much more probable that it will be by virtue of a combined, hemispheric process of revolt that overlaps boundaries and interlaces movements. The long-term future of the US left will depend on its ability to become both more representative and self-organized among its own 'natural' mass constituencies, and more integrally a wing of a new internationalism. It is necessary to begin to imagine more audacious projects of coordinated action and political cooperation among the popular lefts in all the countries of the Americas. We are all, finally, prisoners of the same malign 'American dream'.

Index

Pius XII, 187
Piven, Frances Fox, 287
Podhoretz, Norman, 291
Powderley, Terence V., 32-3
Preis, Art, 86

Quill, Mike, 128

Rambo, 305-6
Randolph, A. Philip, 81
Raskin, A.H., 124, 267
Reagan, Ronald, ix, 3, 103-4, 121,
    139, 140-2, 145, 148, 151-2, 160,
    162, 167-8, 172, 174, 177, 179,
    181, 201-2, 206, 215, 228-9, 231-
    4, 236, 240, 244-6, 248, 251,
    254-5, 259, 260, 262, 267-8, 274,
    281-2, 283-6, 288, 292-3, 296,
    301, 303-4, 306-7
Regan, Donald, 202
Reich, Robert, 244
Reilly, Hugh, 139
Reuther, Walter, 76, 80-1, 86-7,
    93, 129, 263-4
Robb, Charles, 290, 294-5
Roberts, Paul Craig, 232
Robespierre, Maximilien, 13
Rockefeller, David, 176
Rockefeller, Nelson, 167, 174-5
Rockeller, family, 109, 173
Rockwell, Willard, 243
Roderick, David, 241
Rohatyn, Felix, 271-2, 282
Roosevelt — Trueman era, 9
Roosevelt, Franklin Delano, 5, 54,
    57, 62-3, 65, 67-8, 72-4, 76-8,
    81, 83-5, 89, 95-6, 110, 165, 187,
    282, 302
Ross, Arthur, 124
Rothschild, Emma, 208
Rustin, Bayard, 291

Saint-Just, Louis de, 13
Salvatori, Henry, 172
Scammon, Richard, 267
Schatz, Ronald, 120-1

Schick, Allen, 268
Schlafly, Phyllis, 170
Schlesinger Jr., Arthur, 203-4, 303
Schlesinger, James, 282
Schumann, Franz, 187
Schweiker, Richard, 174
Serrin, William, 121
Shapiro, Irving, 271-2
Simon, Norton, 172
Sinclair, Upton, 66, 159
Sleeper, James, 291
Sloan, Alfred, 244
Smith, Adam, 303
Smith, Roger, 242
Smith, William French, 172
Socialist Review, 257, 259, 308
Socialist Revolution, 259
Sombart, Werner, 7
Spies, 45
Stein, Herbert, 229
Stevenson, Adlai, 93, 262
Stevenson, Adlai Jr., 161
Stockman, David, 229
Strauss, Robert, 290
Sturzo, Don, 187
Sudden Impact, 305
Sutton, 278
Swope, Gerard, 109-10, 119-20

Taft, Robert A., 118, 166-7
Taylor, Myron, 187
Thatcher, Margaret, ix, 116, 250,
    268
Thomas, Norman, 87
Tobin, 59, 73
Tocqueville, Alexis de, 6, 26
Towers, Perrin, Forster and
    Crosby, Management
    Consultants, 234
Trotsky, Leon, 4, 7
Truman, Harry, 83, 85-7, 90-1,
    96-7, 125, 166, 203, 262, 283
Tsongas, Senator Paul, 289-90
Tuttle, Holmes, 172

Van Buren, Martin, 19